Intercultural Pragmatics

Intercultural Pragmatics

Istvan Kecskes

OXFORD
UNIVERSITY PRESS

Oxford University Press is a department of the University of Oxford.
It furthers the University's objective of excellence in research, scholarship,
and education by publishing worldwide.

Oxford   New York
Auckland   Cape Town   Dar es Salaam   Hong Kong   Karachi
Kuala Lumpur   Madrid   Melbourne   Mexico City   Nairobi
New Delhi   Shanghai   Taipei   Toronto

With offices in
Argentina   Austria   Brazil   Chile   Czech Republic   France   Greece
Guatemala   Hungary   Italy   Japan   Poland   Portugal   Singapore
South Korea   Switzerland   Thailand   Turkey   Ukraine   Vietnam

Oxford is a registered trademark of Oxford University Press
in the UK and certain other countries.

Published in the United States of America by
Oxford University Press
198 Madison Avenue, New York, NY 10016

Library of Congress Cataloging-in-Publication Data
Kecskes, Istvan
Intercultural pragmatics / Istvan Kecskes.
pages cm
Includes bibliographical references and index.
ISBN 978-0-19-989265-5 (hardcover : alk. paper)
1. Pragmatics.   2. Intercultural communication.   3. Language and culture.
I. Title.
P99.4.P72K46 2013
401'.45—dc23
2013013083

9 8 7 6 5 4 3 2
Printed in the United States of America
on acid-free paper

CONTENTS

ACKNOWLEDGMENTS

It would be very difficult to list all the people who have shaped my thinking, given me support and encouragement, advised me on hard issues, and helped me with this manuscript. I still need to mention some of them because they are "built" into the book in some way. I must start with my former professor, Ferenc Papp, who taught me the generative grammar of Russian, and with whom we used concordances at the beginning of the 1970s to analyze English and Russian texts on huge Odra mainframe computers. That work had not much to do with pragmatics but helped me get to know linguistics and learn analytic skills, in addition to teaching me discipline. Pragmatics came into my life through the works of Ferenc Kiefer and his personal support. His book on presuppositions and his paper on "situational utterances" were eye-opening for me and significantly contributed to my thinking about language and language use. More recently, Jacob Mey's work and personal mentorship helped me learn about the societal side of pragmatics. A couple of joint projects with Larry Horn brought me close to "hard core" linguistics pragmatics and helped me revise some of my ideas about speaker meaning. Reading her books and papers and having some conversations with Deirdre Wilson contributed to my understanding of Relevance Theory and hearer interpretation. I also have to mention the influence of Chinese pragmatics on my way of thinking about the cultural side of pragmatics. Frequent encounters with my Chinese colleagues, He Ziran, He Gang, Ran Yongping, and Wang Xiaolu, just to mention a few, as well as my position as Yunshan Chair Professor in the National Research Center for Linguistics and Applied Linguistics at the Guangdong University of Foreign Studies, Guangzhou, helped me experience a unique kind of thinking about pragmatics that is attached to the Chinese language. I owe a lot to my colleague Robert Sanders for reading a significant portion of this manuscript and giving me suggestions about some of the chapters in the book. Although we never agreed on anything, his advice was invaluable because it encouraged me to rethink what I was writing about. I owe many thanks and appreciation to all of these colleagues and friends. I would also like to thank my PhD student, Zhiqi Gong, for helping me with the proofs.

However, my most sincere gratitude goes to my wife, Dr. Tunde Papp, whose unconditional love and support for more than 43 years has helped me become who I am.

She is not only my wife in the traditional sense but also my soul mate and coauthor ("Foreign Language and Mother Tongue," 2000, Erlbaum). Whenever I came to a difficult point in writing this book, I could turn to her to discuss the issue and get some advice that helped me through the difficulties. Thank you, Tunde.

Istvan Kecskes

Intercultural Pragmatics

Introduction

1. Why is This Book Needed?

There are many excellent books out there on pragmatics, and it is not easy to justify why we need another one. To write a new book on pragmatics makes sense only if the new book has unique features that distinguish it from other books on the similar subject. In this book, the reader need not bother looking for usual chapter titles such as "implicatures," "indexicals," "presupposition," "speech acts," and so on, which can be found in most of the books about pragmatics. Instead, there are chapters, for instance, on "pragmatic competence," "formulaic language," and "salience," which are quite neglected topics in current pragmatics research but need to be addressed in a book that has an intercultural perspective.

What makes this book on intercultural pragmatics different from the other ones is *its multilingual, intercultural, socio-cognitive, and discourse-segment (rather than just utterance) perspective* as well as the view that considers intercultural communication a *normal "success-and-failure" process* rather than a collision of cultures, in which it is not only the cultural differences and misunderstandings that should be emphasized but also the role of prior and actual situational context and common ground building in achieving success. But if multilingualism is considered "normal," shouldn't this affect the ways linguists build their models of language and pragmaticians develop their models of meaning and language behavior? I argue that given the rapid growth in the number of people in the world who speak more than one language and the increasing importance of intercultural interactions in communicative encounters, the main linguistic and pragmatic models must also be evaluated on their capacity to explain multilingual competence as well as multilingual language use and its traces appropriately. However, this is not exactly what is happening. In the monolingual approach governing mainstream pragmatics today, anything that is "societal" (Mey 2001) and /or whatever pragmatic phenomenon has not reached "grammaticalized" status (as Levinson calls it; 1983:9) on principle is excluded from consideration in many versions of pragmatics. This is how Jacob Mey (2013:488) described the current situation: "it has been the custom for partisans of linguistics to fire away from their hideouts and shoot down pragmatics (of the "wrong" kind) as being "Continental" (Levinson 1983:2), as "not stringent enough" (as one colleague of mine once told her students), or simply as being outside the realm of scientific description (as many linguists and semanticists seem to believe; witness the fact that they, intentionally or unconsciously, omit any mention of the "other" kind of pragmatics in their writings)."

I think intercultural pragmatics may bring something to the fore that standard pragmatics misses, or at least seems to be missing. What standard pragmatics assumes about how things work in communication depends on there being commonalities and conventions between speakers and hearers that can hardly be counted on cross-culturally in the same way as in intracultural communication. Commonalities, conventions, common beliefs, shared knowledge, and the like all create a core common ground, a kind of collective salience on which intention and cooperation-based pragmatics is built. (Of course, there are plenty of varieties within those communalities.) However, when this core common ground appears to be missing or limited, as is the case in intercultural communication, interlocutors cannot take them for granted. Rather, they need to co-construct them, at least temporarily. So what seems to be happening here is a shift in emphasis from the communal to the individual. It is not that the individual becomes more important than the societal. Rather, since there is limited common ground, it should be created in the interactional context in which the interlocutors function as core common ground creators rather than just common ground seekers and activators, as is mostly the case in intracultural communication. So the nature of intersubjectivity seems to be undergoing change. There is more reliance on language created ad hoc by individuals in the course of interaction than on prefabricated language and pre-existing frames. In the case of communicators who use a common language and whose L1s differ (intercultural communication), the lack of full control over language skills (L2) and full knowledge of conventions, beliefs and norms in the target language (L2) used as the medium of communication may lead *to a more conscious approach to what is said, and how it is said.* Furthermore, in intercultural communication more conscious recipient design may be involved than in intracultural communication in which interlocutors do not have to deal with language skill issues and may rely on more spontaneous speech and much less monitoring.

Consequently, there seems to be reason to take up the question of how people go about formulating utterances and interpreting them when they can't count on, or have limited access to, those commonalities, conventions, standards and norms and in a sense, they are expected to create or co-construct them in the communicative process. What people depend on that makes pragmatic meaning reliable within a speech community—the focus of standard pragmatic theories—becomes more visible when we see the troubles, misunderstandings, and different routes to success that may arise when those commonalities and/or conventions are missing or limited cross-culturally. This means that while working on intercultural pragmatics and analyzing language use in intercultural communication, we may be able to see and notice things that standard theories of pragmatics may miss or just take for granted. For instance, in the Gricean paradigm, cooperation is considered rational behavior of human beings. It is essential that human beings are cooperative in the course of communication subconsciously and automatically. In intercultural communication, however, this rational and subconscious behavior is enhanced with a conscious, often monitored, endeavor of interlocutors to be cooperative and make deliberate efforts to comprehend others and produce language that is processable by others. It is therefore even more emphasized that the goal of coming to an understanding is "intersubjective mutuality...shared knowledge, mutual trust, and accord with one another (Habermas 1979:3)."

Another positive outcome of research in intercultural pragmatics can be the attempt to reconcile micro and macro perspectives on language, culture, and interaction. The micro perspective includes the study of interactions between individuals, and the cognition underlying those communicative encounters. The macro perspective deals with establishing norms, patterns, and expectations about language use in speech communities. The socio-cognitive approach to be discussed in Chapter 2, which is the underlying theory of intercultural pragmatics, calls for the integration of the micro and macro perspectives. "Intercultures," as discussed below, are good examples of this integration.

I do not want to say that intercultural communication is completely different from intracultural communication. In fact, there is more overlap than difference between the two. There are underlying principles that govern both. What I find important, however, is that there are differences between intracultural and intercultural communication in emphasis and tendencies that will be discussed in detail in different chapters of this book.

2. The Multilingual Perspective

There has been a long-standing problem in pragmatics-oriented research. Communication is becoming more and more intercultural because it involves interlocutors who have different first languages, communicate in a common language, and represent different cultures (Kecskes 2004a). Theoretical pragmatics, however, does not appear to pay much attention to this issue and remains predominantly monolingual. Major issues of pragmatics are researched and discussed in a monolingual framework lacking or excluding any explanation of or reference to the applicability of ideas, theories, and research findings to bi- and multilingual scenes. Why is this lack of interest in multilingual framework in theory development a problem? What is wrong with the monolingual view, if anything? Well, the problem is that the monolingual view seems to presuppose that rules of communication, ways of communication, communicative principles, and interpretation and production processes are basically universal—the same or very similar no matter what language we use and/or what language we are talking about.

Nobody denies that human communication contains several universal features. However, a close look at bi- and multilingual language production and comprehension as well as intercultural interaction demonstrates that not all features are universal. There are both similarities and differences between intracultural and intercultural communication, the same way as there are similarities and differences between the acquisition and use of L1 and that of L2. The language learner/user does not have to start everything from scratch. However, language use is governed not only by universal but also language- and culture-specific rules. A person who speaks two or more languages may share the universal features with a monolingual speaker, but s/he will have to consider and use two or more different sets of culture-specific, language-community-specific rules and features that will result in production and comprehension in both languages. This is not exactly the same as the language production and comprehension of a monolingual speaker of either language. *A bilingual is not two monolinguals in one body* (cf., Grosjean 1989). Bi- and multilingualism is characterized by a unique synergism of more than one language and culture, which significantly affects how bi- and multilinguals behave and use language. Consequently, there are, for instance, differences in how a bilingual English–German speaker uses his English and his German from how a monolingual English speaker and a monolingual German speaker use his/her language.

However, we should neither underestimate nor overestimate the fact that someone has two or more languages in his/her mind. According to Gumperz & Gumperz, *monolingual people and multilingual people do not differ in what they do with language, but in how they do what they do* (Gumperz & Gumperz 2005). Bi- and multilingual people's communication should not be conceived of as something distinct from everyday communicative interaction. People with more than one language are not abnormal communicators. They are normal human beings whose communicative actions are affected by the knowledge of more than one language and culture. According to Blommaert (1998:3), it is a mistake to consider intercultural communication only as a matter of colliding cultures and cultural gaps, something that is abnormal. He argued that the "abnormalization of intercultural communication is based on a gross hypostasis of 'culture' as the all-eclipsing contextual factor, and a massive overestimation of the degree and the nature of differences in speech styles. The way in which empirical answers can be found for patterns and problems in intercultural communication is a detailed and nuanced analysis of concrete communicative events." This is exactly what intercultural pragmatics attempts to do.

Culture in intercultural pragmatics is seen as a socially constituted set of various kinds of knowledge structures that individuals turn to as relevant situations permit, enable, and usually encourage. It is a system of shared beliefs, norms, values, customs, behaviors, and artifacts that the members of society use to cope with their world and with one another (Bates & Plog 1980:6). It is an important characteristic of culture that it is differentially distributed, and that not all the members of a given social and/or cultural group adopt, live, or reflect their relatively common culture in a similar way in every moment and every life circumstance, nor do all members of the same social and/or cultural group demonstrate the same feeling of identification (cf. Durkheim 1982; Benedict 1967). Culture has fuzzy boundaries and in this book it is considered neither relatively static nor ever-changing, but both. It has both a priori and emergent features. Culture changes both diachronically (slowly through decades) and synchronically (emerges on-the-spot, in the moment of speech). This is where my line of thinking may differ from the (current) mainstream, which insists on the contingent, situational, and emergent nature of cultural phenomena in speech and emphasizes that culture in no way imposes ethnic or cultural characteristics onto the communicative behavior a priori (e.g., Gumperz 1982, Gumperz & Roberts 1991; Blommaert 1991; Rampton 1995). I argue that this approach is just as one-sided as the one that considers culture relatively static and sees a linear connection between "culture" and "communication" (cf. Knapp & Knapp-Potthoff 1987:3). The nationality or ethnic membership of people may suggest the possibility of ethnic or cultural marking in communicative behavior. However, in the actual situational context, intercultures are co-constructed, which process may contain elements from the participants' existing cultural background and ad hoc created elements as well. This dialectical and dynamic approach to culture is what intercultural pragmatics is based on.

The interlocutors on whom intercultural pragmatics mainly focuses usually have two or more languages in their mind. Whichever language channel they use for expressing their thoughts, they experience both constraints and triggers originating in two or more languages. Language functions not only as a restrictive device but also as an initiator and supporter of idea/thought formulation. It channels thoughts into linguistic signs by formulating utterances, and at the same time helps the speaker shape his/her thoughts by "offering" several linguistic options. Slobin (1996) argued that language is a transmitter of real-world experiences, and that these experiences are filtered through language into verbalized events. A bi- or multilingual has two or more transmitters. Why is this important? Croft and Woods argued that "it is not the case that any time we think we must conceptualize our experience the way that our language requires us to. But it is the case that any time we express our thoughts in language, we must conceptualize our experience in the way that our language requires us to. Cognition may be linguistically neutral, but language is not semantically neutral (Croft and Wood 2000: 55)." Slobin (1991) also made a similar point when he described "thinking for speaking" as the appropriate domain for the influence of language on thought. This is where it is important to emphasize the difference between *what we do* and *how we do it*. *What we do* may have more universal features than *how we do it*. For instance, I can be polite both in English and Russian, but the linguistic means each language allows me to use differ to a great extent. If one language has fewer tools to express certain functions and features than another one, this does not mean that speakers of that language are less developed in any way. It is just that, for instance, Russians are polite in a different way than Americans are, and they have all the means they need to be polite the way their communalities require them to. If societal or communal needs change, their language will adjust to the new circumstances and develop new or different means to express politeness.

Cultural expectations and phenomena that members of a speech community attend to are the main variables that motivate the use of available linguistic means.

Roman Jakobson (1959:236) pointed out a crucial fact about differences between languages in a pithy maxim: "Languages differ essentially in what they must convey and not in what they may convey." This claim offers us the key to unlocking the real force of language. If different languages affect our minds in different ways, it is not because of what our language allows us to think but rather because of what that language habitually obliges us to think about. It is the "habitual" (or better to say, customary) that culture builds into language use.

Life and interaction with the world shapes our thoughts and language. What people of a language community find important to be expressed in their life will definitely be expressed in that language. However, this is a two-way street because the ever-changing code will also impose some requirements on us as speakers. Language is like a channel through which you must pull your ideas. Nobody denies that there is thinking without language. However, the developmental span through which an infant can get access to huge amount of knowledge is, to a great extent, facilitated by mechanisms through which language helps us construct the incredibly complex knowledge systems we have. Consequently, a weak version of Whorfianism is in place when we talk about intercultural interaction.

3. The Socio-cognitive Perspective

Pragmatics is a branch of linguistics that focuses on the use of language in social contexts and the ways in which people produce and comprehend meanings through language. There is no intention here to change this definition. What this book attempts to offer is an alternative way to think about pragmatics. It discusses how the new subfield "intercultural pragmatics" has emerged as one of the possible solutions to bring together the two seemingly antagonistic lines of pragmatics research: the "*individualistic*" intention-based cognitive-philosophical line and the "*societal*," context-based socio-cultural–interactional line. This is a necessary attempt because we human beings have a double nature: we are both individuals and social beings at the same time. This fact is reflected in our communicative behavior. Recent neurological experiments on mirror neurons can be interpreted as confirming human beings' double nature as well as the interaction of their abilities (Rizzolatti and Craighero 2004; Arbib et al. 2005).

One of the main differences between the cognitive-philosophical approach and the socio-cultural–interactional approach is that the former considers intention an *a priori* mental state of speakers that underpins communication, while the latter regards intention as a *post factum* construct that is achieved jointly through the dynamic emergence of meaning in conversation. In this process socio-cultural factors play the leading role. Since the two approaches represent two different perspectives, it would be difficult to reject either of them entirely. The complexity of the issue requires that we consider both the encoded and co-constructed, emergent sides of intention when analyzing communicative processes. The *socio-cognitive approach* (SCA) serving as the theoretical foundation for intercultural pragmatics attempts to do that. SCA was proposed by Kecskes (2008; 2010) and Kecskes and Zhang (2009) as an attempt to unite the two perspectives and emphasize that there is a dialectical relationship between a priori intention (based on individual prior experience) and emergent intention (based on actual social situational context). SCA emphasizes that language production and comprehension involve both prior experience and knowledge, and emergent, actual situation experience and knowledge co-constructed by interlocutors. It claims that the meaning values of linguistic expressions, encapsulating prior contexts of experience, play as important a role in meaning construction and comprehension as actual situational context.

When language is used, its unique property is activated in two ways. The individual and the social are intertwined in language use. When people speak or write, they craft what they need to express to fit the situation or context in which they are communicating. But, at the same time, the way people speak or write the words, expressions, and utterances they use creates that very situation, context, and socio-cultural frame in which the given communication occurs. Consequently, two things seem to be happening simultaneously: in communication individuals attempt to fit their language to a situation or context that their language, in turn, helped to create in the first place (e.g., Gee 1999). This dynamic behavior of human speech and reciprocal process between language and context basically eliminates the need to ask the ever-returning question, Which comes first: the situation that the speakers are in (e.g., faculty meeting, car renting, dinner ordering, etc.), or the particular language that is used in the given situation (expressions and utterances representing ways of talking and interacting)? Is this a "car rental" because participants are acting and speaking that way, or are they acting and speaking that way because this is a "car rental" situation? Acting and speaking in a particular way constitutes social situations and socio-cultural frames, and these frames require the use of a particular language. "Which comes first" does not seem to be a relevant question synchronically.

The main advantage of SCA is that it brings together the existing means and knowledge with emergent ones. The individual features such as prior experience (context), salience, egocentrism and prior intention are matched with actual situational experience (context), emergent intention, attention, situational relevance, and the two sides blend into interactional context and intercultures. Intersubjectivity in SCA refers to shared (or partially shared) divergences of meaning. The goal of intersubjective acts is to eliminate the difference between two or more subjective perceptions and/or definitions of reality as it will be explained in the upcoming chapters.

4. Discourse-segment (Rather than Just Utterance) Perspective

Pragmatics is an utterance-based inquiry. However, research in intercultural pragmatics (e.g., House 2002; Kecskes 2007a) demonstrated that in intercultural communication participants are creative on discourse level rather than on utterance level. This is mainly due to limited language proficiency that may result in, among others, not-very-well formulated utterances. Consequently, intercultural interactions may require not only a bottom-up, sequential utterance by utterance analysis but also a top-down, holistic discourse-segment analysis if we want to make sure to understand the message of interlocutors. Beyond utterance analysis is an issue not only in intercultural pragmatics but also in other subfields of pragmatics, since several papers have recently talked about "narrow pragmatics" and "wide pragmatics," discussing the relationship of pragmatics and discourse analysis (e.g., Puig 2003; Taboada and Mann 2006; De Saussure 2007). The issue of beyond utterances analysis has also been on the agenda of dialogue studies (e.g., Weigand 2000, 2010a, 2010b; Cooren 2010). The importance of these studies is that they consider language as action that is always shared. Whenever someone appears to act, others also proceed into action. They also emphasize that communicative function and communicative agenda are two separate things.

Because "utterance" is hard to define, and its meaning is both in the building elements of an utterance (lexical units) and in the subsequent utterances produced in response, pragmatics, which is also defined as a theory of meaning in context, has been looking for meaning "ingredients" both inside and outside the utterance. As a result, currently there seem to be three different approaches represented in the broader field of pragmatics. Firstly, there is a strong *pragma-semantics approach*, which is pursued by the followers of Grice and a number of scholars with a referential-logical background, and with various degrees of commitment to truth-conditionality (e.g., De Saussure 2007). This trend is mainly interested in the construction of meaning by the hearer, through cognitive or formal models. Secondly, there is *pragma-dialogue*, which calls attention to the dialogic nature of communication by emphasizing that interlocutors are actors who act and react (e.g., Weigand 2010a; Kecskes 2012). So the speaker-hearer not only interprets but also reacts to the other interlocutor's utterance. The basic dialogic principle is that human beings are dialogic (social) individuals who communicate in dialogic interaction not only by producing and understanding utterances but also by acting and reacting (e.g., Weigand 2010a, 2010b). The dialogic principle defines dialogue as a sequence of actions and reactions. Thirdly, there is a view that looks beyond the utterance and pays special attention to socially determined linguistic behavior. I have called this trend "*pragma-discourse*" (Kecskes 2012).

Before looking into these three lines of thinking, we should discuss why utterance interpretation is problematic and how we have come to the "separation" of pragma-semantics on the one hand and pragma-dialogue and pragma-discourse on the other.

4.1. SENTENCE AND UTTERANCE

It is difficult to give a precise linguistic definition of what utterance is. Phonetically it is considered a unit of speech bounded by silence. In conversation each turn by a speaker is usually considered an utterance. Sometimes linguists use the term "utterance" to refer to a unit of speech they study. Pragmatics rests on the difference between the meaning of a linguistic unit, and the meaning of *uttering* that same unit (usually a sentence). So a crucial issue in pragmatics is the difference between "sentence" and "utterance." As defined in linguistics, a "sentence" is an abstract entity—a string of words divorced from nonlinguistic context—as opposed to an "utterance," which is a concrete instantiation of a speech act in a specific situational context. According to the traditional approach, sentences do not have meaning intrinsically. As it will be discussed later, the socio-cognitive approach does not accept this line of thinking. This view (Myers and Myers 1998; Evans 2009) claims that there is no meaning associated with a sentence or word—they can only symbolically represent an idea. *The duck is ready to eat* is a sentence of English that can mean different things depending on the context of use. If your mother says, holding a tray with a fried duck on it, "The duck is ready to eat," this is an example of an utterance. However, if the sentence "The duck is ready to eat" is uttered in another situation, the meaning of the uttered sentence can change. For instance, I show my pet duck to my friend and say, "The duck is ready to eat. Let's give her some food." Thus, according to the traditional view, there is no such thing as a sentence, expression, or word symbolically representing a single true meaning. A sentence is underspecified (see the examples above) and potentially ambiguous. The meaning of an utterance, on the other hand, is inferred based on linguistic knowledge and knowledge of the nonlinguistic context of the utterance. This rather simplistic approach to the sentence–utterance dichotomy is, of course, not satisfying for pragmaticians. We will return to this issue when the "propositional meaning–explicature–implicature" relations are going to be discussed. At this point, what is important for us is the fact that disambiguation is expected to be resolved by the context that may or may not be sufficient to resolve ambiguity. Actually, one of the problems of present pragmatics research is that the immediate context does not always give enough information for proper interpretation of a given utterance. Consider the following example:

(1)

> SAM: Coming for a drink?
> ANDY: Sorry, I can't. My doctor won't let me.
> SAM: *What's wrong with you?*

We need to look at the whole discourse segment to give a proper interpretation of the utterance "*What's wrong with you?*". In this case, Sam's utterance is ambiguous. The utterance could be asking for what's wrong with him medically that the doctor won't let him drink, or what's wrong with him psychologically that he's listening to the doctor and refusing the social opportunity and the drink. Utterance-level interpretation will not always help. We will need further information to solve the problem at discourse–segment level.

Utterance-level interpretation is especially problematic in intercultural communication in which given the significant difference in belief systems, conventions, and socio-cultural background knowledge of participants, the traditional bottom-up pragmatics analysis based on the Gricean modular view may not result in correct interpretation. The following conversation illustrates this problem.

(2)

>PAK: You said you live with your son. So your wife is not here.
>CH: Yes, I am alone, I am with my son.
>COL: Will your wife come to visit?
>CH: Yes, she came yesterday.
>PAK: Did she come from China?
>CH: Yes, she arrived from Nanjing.

In this conversation between a Pakistani, a Colombian, and a Chinese speaker, an utterance-by-utterance analysis will not necessarily lead to a clear interpretation of what the Chinese speaker wants to say, because the utterances taken one by one are ambiguous and clumsy, containing contradicting pieces of information. For instance, the first and second part of the utterance "Yes, I am alone, I am with my son" contradict each other. However, if we look at the whole dialogue sequence or discourse segment, the meaning that the Chinese speaker tries to convey (he lives alone with his son and gets visits from his wife from Nanjing) becomes clear. It is not surprising, therefore, that intercultural pragmatics seems to require not only an utterance-by-utterance interpretation but also going beyond the utterance and analyzing the whole dialogue or discourse segment.

4.2. PRAGMA-SEMANTICS, PRAGMA-DIALOGUE, AND PRAGMA-DISCOURSE

Analyzing trends in pragmatics, De Saussure (2007) argued that "pragma-semantics" focuses on the theory of human language understanding, assuming a "bottom-up" view where global–discursive–issues are explainable by local semantic and pragmatic phenomena. The top-down, holistic view of pragmatics is represented both in pragma-dialogue and pragma-discourse (Kecskes 2012). They focus on a theory of speaker's productions of utterances within structural patterns of dialogue and discourse, assuming a "top-down" view where issues concerning single utterances are explained by global discursive or social constraints.

Pragma-dialogue

Pragmatics analyzes individual utterances (organized set of words) in context. A dialogue is a sequence of utterances, a reciprocal conversation between two or more entities. It is an effective means of ongoing communication. Buber believed that genuine dialogue can be obtained between two people "no matter whether spoken or silent" (Buber 1955). Buber further claimed that "each of the participants really [must have] in mind the other or others in their present and particular being and turn to them with the intention of establishing a living mutual relation between himself and them (Buber 1955:22)." More simply, genuine dialogue can be understood as a momentary experience in which participants are consciously aware of the other/s. Preserving the original Buberian idea of dialogue being a reciprocal conversation in which interlocutors are consciously aware of the partners, current researchers of dialogue studies (e.g., Weingand 2010a, 2010b; Cooren 2010, Tracy and Craig 2010) go one step forward and emphasize that dialogue is constituted by the interactive purpose of coming to an understanding that is based on the sequence of actions and reactions, as the following conversation demonstrates.

(3)

Action-directive	BILL: Can I get a cup of coffee?
Info-request	SARA: Milk?
Signal-nonunderstanding	BILL: Hm?
Info-request	SARA: Do you want your coffee black?
Agreement	BILL: Oh yes, thanks.

Weingand (2010b) argued that action and reaction are not two actions of the same type that are arbitrarily connected and only formally distinguished by their position in the sequence. Action and reaction are functionally different types of actions: action is initiative while reaction is responsive. According to Weingand, orthodox speech act theory that is exclusively based on illocution should be adjusted. She continues arguing that Searle's theory of conversation is based on single illocutionary acts that are put together by what Searle (1995:26) calls "collective intentionality" and ignores the interdependence between action and reaction. Although Searle's collective action aims at a communal goal, it is not a dialogic act yet. Weigand claims that individual actions and reactions are organized into a dialogic sequence by their interdependence. Searle's speech act theory focuses on the communicative functions of speech acts (assertives, directives, commissives, expressives, declaratives) and says less about the communicative agenda of interlocutors. To interpret an utterance properly, the interlocutor has to arrive at an understanding not only of its communicative function of utterances but also of the communicative agenda of his/her dialogue partner, i.e., what s/he really wants to achieve in the dialogue. The underlying interests of the dialogue partners become evident through dialogic sequences. This is in line with what the socio-cognitive approach claims: occasionally, we should go beyond single utterance to understand the communicative agenda of interlocutors. Intercultural communication serves with several examples that prove this point. In the following excerpt, the Korean speaker is trying to explain the *sandy wind* they experience in Seoul in the spring. (Transcript by Robert Sanders)

(4)

10 NS: In Korea? =
11 NNS: =Yeah::. In (0.2) in ↑spring?
12 NS: Hm mm

13 NNS: There is a (0.5) um (0.7) how- how can I 'spl- ah:: how can I say::?
(0.5) **Send wind?**

14 (1.7) ((NS displaying mental effort))

15 NS: Uh:::m

16 NNS: **Sen::d (0.2) the wind?**   0:30

17 NS: ((now nodding)) Yeah::, it would blow around [the pollen?

18 NNS: [Yes.

19 NNS: Yeah yeah [yeah (0.2) yeah.

20 NS: [(from) the trees?

21 NNS: Ye[ah

22 NS: [Yeah::

23 NNS: Ah, the:: (0.7) **the wind came from China?**

24 NS: (0.7)

25 NNS: Do you know that wind?

26 (0.2)

27 NS: ↑No::.

28 NNS: The the:: (0.7) the- **many sand?** (("sand" sounds like "send"))

29 NS: (0.5) ((flashes little smile))

30 NNS: **Sen:d in a: (0.5) desert?**

31 NS: Oh, (.) **sa:nd.**

32 NNS: **Yeah, [sand** ((shift in pronunciation to match NS))

33 NS: **[Oh:::, [god, yeah**

34 NNS: [in deser::t. We've had- (0.2)wi:nd (0.2) go to- uh lan- (0.5)
come- (0.2) over

35 TO KOREA: also. (0.5) So in spri:ng, it's very difficult to (0.5) little bit difficult to (0.7) (?)hhh um::

In this dialogue the Korean speaker has a communicative agenda to explain to her American partner what the Koreans call "morae baram" [sandy wind]. However, her pronunciation is not correct and the American partner does not understand what kind of wind the Korean speaker refers to. Not until the Korean connected "sand" with "desert" in line 30 did the American understand what her Korean partner really meant. The action-reaction sequence shows that they could work out the misunderstanding after all. The segment as a whole makes perfect sense and directs our attention to how hard the Korean speaker has worked on making her partner understand what exactly she wanted to say.

Pragma-discourse

The basic difference between pragmatics and discourse is that while pragmatics analyzes individual utterances (organized set of words) in context, discourse focuses on an organized set of utterances. The relationship between the constituents of utterances (organized set of words) and the constituents of discourses (organized set of utterances) is quite similar. Analysts assume that utterances have properties of their own (which are not the properties of single lexical items) and discourses also have their own properties (which are not the properties of single utterances). Consequently, an utterance is not the sum of lexical items that compose it, and discourse is not the sum of utterances that compose it, either. Both utterance and discourse represent "third space" (cf. Evanoff 2000), which is not the sum of components but a qualitatively different entity. Intercultural communication represents a transactional model of communication (cf. Barnlund 1970) that moves beyond merely understanding or "respecting" cultural differences toward creating a "third culture" that combines elements of each of the participants' original cultures in novel ways.

The "third culture" perspective fits intercultural pragmatics as example (2) demonstrates. An utterance in itself in intercultural communication may make a different sense when analyzed separately than when it is analyzed within a whole discourse segment. As mentioned above, research (e.g., House 2002; Philip 2005; Kecskes 2007a) has demonstrated that in intercultural communication participants are creative on a discourse level rather than on an utterance level. I do not mean to suggest that we should reject the "discourse as a process" view (represented by Sperber and Wilson, Recanati, Carston, Moeaschler and others) in its entirety. In the socio-cognitive paradigm, I argue for the hypothesis that there exists a higher level of information besides the structural and propositional ones that are attached to single utterances in context (cf. De Saussure 2007; Moeschler 2010, van Dijk 2008). However, this does not mean that we should ignore the *contextual single sentence interpretation* that gives the basis for pragmatics research. In intercultural pragmatics, we need both the single utterances and span of utterances (dialogic sequence, discourse-segment) approach if we want to give a fair analysis of what is communicated by interlocutors. *Single utterances are reflections of individual human cognition while span of utterances in the discourse-segment reflect socio-cultural, environmental, background factors.* It is important to note that we need the discourse-segment analysis (discourse as a structured entity) because a sequential utterance-by-utterance analysis (discourse as a process) may not result in the right interpretation, as utterances can be attached to utterances other than the directly preceding ones. This is especially common in multi-party conversation, as is demonstrated in example (2) above.

An important claim in this book is that utterances in pragmatics research need to be analyzed both from the perspective of the hearer and the speaker. I have argued in some of my papers that current pragmatics theories are hearer- rather than speaker-centered (Kecskes 2010a, 2011). One of the main reasons of this hearer-centeredness is the Gricean modular view that requires splitting the interpretation process into two phases: what is said and what is communicated. Dialogue studies, however, eliminate this division and talk about action and reaction (e.g., Weingand 2010, Cooren 2010). So the concept of the hearer and speaker turns into the concept of the interlocutor who plays both roles. Human beings are speakers and hearers at the same time. They not only try to understand the utterance of the speaker but also react to it in their own utterance. There does not seem to be separate production and comprehension. Rather, human beings always evaluate and react verbally or mentally to what has been said. However, in pragmatics, in some sense, we analyze the two sides separately (production and interpretation). There is nothing wrong with that. But if we focus on the speaker and want to figure out *why the speaker said what he said the way he said it*, we need to use not only an utterance analysis but also a holistic, top-down approach (see above), and have to analyze the discourse segment (pragma-discourse) rather than just the utterance (pragma-semantics) in order to find cues that help us identify the real intention of the speaker. This means that the key to speaker meaning may be found not only in the given utterance itself but in utterances, utterance-chunks, or cues in the dialogue sequence or discourse-segment.

5. What is Intercultural Pragmatics?

Intercultural Pragmatics is concerned with the way the language system is put to use in social encounters between human beings who have different first languages, communicate in a common language, and, usually, represent different cultures (Kecskes 2004a; Kecskes 2010a). The communicative process in these encounters is synergistic in the sense that in them, existing pragmatic norms and emerging, co-constructed features are present to a varying degree. Intercultural Pragmatics represents a socio-cognitive perspective in which individual prior experience and actual social situational experience are equally important in meaning construction and comprehension. Focusing on both oral and written language processing research in intercultural pragmatics has four main foci: (1) interaction between native speakers and nonnative speakers of a language,[1] (2) lingua franca communication in which none of the interlocutors has the same L1, (3) multilingual discourse, and (4) language use and development of individuals who speak more than one language. The main focus of intercultural pragmatics is language use rather than pragmatic competence, which is considered a language socialization issue within this paradigm. Pragmatic competence is researched to the extent to which it affects interaction in intercultural communication, as will be discussed in Chapter 3.

The socio-cognitive approach (Kecskes 2008; Kecskes and Zhang 2009; Kecskes 2010a) to be explained in Chapter 2 defines interculturality as a phenomenon that is not only interactionally and socially constructed in the course of communication but also relies on relatively definable cultural models and norms that represent the speech communities to which the interlocutors belong. Consequently, interculturality can be considered an interim rule system that has both relatively normative and emergent components. In order for us to understand the dynamism and

---

[1] I am fully aware of the fact that the terms "native speaker" and "nonnative speaker" are not the best way to describe language proficiency. However, it is still these terms that make the distinction clearer than any other terms.

ever-changing nature of intercultural encounters, we need to approach interculturality dialectically. Cultural constructs and models change diachronically while cultural representation and speech production by individuals change synchronically. Kecskes (2011) defined *intercultures as situationally emergent and co-constructed phenomena that rely both on relatively definable cultural norms and models as well as situationally evolving features*. Intercultures are usually ad hoc creations. Koole and ten Thije (1994:69) referred to them as "culture constructed in cultural contact." They are created in a communicative process in which cultural norms and models brought into the interaction from prior experience of interlocutors blend with features created ad hoc in the interaction in a synergetic way. The result is intercultural discourse in which there is mutual transformation of knowledge and communicative behavior rather than transmission. The emphasis is on transformation rather than on transmission.

As said above, interculturality is an emergent and co-constructed phenomenon. It has both an a priori side and an emergent side that occur and act simultaneously in the communicative process. Consequently, intercultures are not fixed phenomena, but rather are created in the course of communication in which participants belong to different L1 speech communities, speak a common language, and represent different cultural norms and models that are defined by their respective L1 speech community. The following conversation (source Albany English Lingua Franca Dataset collected by PhD students) between a Brazilian girl and a Polish woman illustrates this point well.

(5)

> BRAZILIAN: And what do you do?
> POLE: I work at the university as a cleaner.
> B: As a janitor?
> P: No, not yet. Janitor is after the cleaner.
> B: You want to be a janitor?
> P: Of course.

In this conversation interlocutors represent two different languages and cultures (Brazilian and Polish), and use English as a lingua franca. This is the prior knowledge that participants bring into the interaction. They create an interculture, which belongs to none of them but emerges in the course of conversation. Within this interculture the two speakers have a smooth conversation about the job of the Polish woman. Neither of them is sure what the right term is for the job the Polish woman has. There are no misunderstandings in the interaction because each participant is careful to use semantically transparent language in order to be as clear as possible. When the Brazilian initiates repair to the term "cleaner," she is corrected. The Polish woman sets up a "hierarchy" that does not quite exist in the target language culture ("cleaner versus janitor") but is an emergent element of the interculture the interlocutors have been constructing.

6. Related Fields

6.1. SOCIOPRAGMATICS

Intercultural Pragmatics has to be distinguished from the socio-culture–centered lines in pragmatics research, which have developed from sociopragmatics created as an influential line of inquiry within pragmatics after Leech (1983) and Thomas (1983) divided pragmatics into two components: pragmalinguistics and sociopragmatics. Pragmalinguistics refers to the resources for conveying communicative acts and relational or interpersonal meanings. These resources include pragmatic strategies such as directness and indirectness, routines, and a great variety of linguistic forms that can intensify or soften communicative acts. For an example, compare these two versions of request:

(6)

POLICE OFFICER TO A DRIVER:

- Can I see your driver's license?

ALESSANDRO TO HIS AMERICAN FRIEND, BILL:

- Hey, dude, show me your driver's license?

In both cases, the speaker chooses from among a great variety of available pragmalinguistic resources of the English language that can function as a request.

However, each of these two expressions indexes a very different attitude and social relationship. This is why sociopragmatics is important in speech analysis. Leech (1983:10) defined sociopragmatics as "the sociological interface of pragmatics." He referred to the social perceptions underlying participants' interpretation and performance of their communicative action. Speech communities differ in their assessment of speakers' and hearers' social distance and social power, their rights and obligations, and the degree of imposition involved in particular communicative acts (Kasper and Rose 2001). According to Thomas (1983), while pragmalinguistics is, in a sense, akin to grammatical studies in that it examines linguistic forms and their respective functions, sociopragmatics is about the social appropriateness of communicative behavior. Speakers must be aware of the consequences of making pragmatic choices as the following example demonstrates.

(7)

BILL: Well, I have to go now. Why don't we have lunch some time?
DMITRIJ: When? Do you have time tomorrow at noon?
BILL: I am afraid not. I'll talk to you later.

It is clear that Dmitrij committed a socipragmatic error here. His American friend used the expression "why don't we have lunch some time?" as a politeness marker rather than a real lunch invitation.

Sociopragmatics was further developed in Gumperz's, Tannen's, and Scollon and Scollon's works, among others. Gumperz (1982) founded interactional sociolinguistics with his work, which demonstrated that systematically different ways of using language to create and interpret meaning contributed to employment discrimination against London residents who were from Pakistan, India, and the West Indies. Tannen's focus (1985; 2005) is not just on language, but on how communication styles either facilitate or hinder personal interactions. For instance, according to her, men and women are products of different cultures. They possess different, but equally valid, communicative styles. Scollon and Scollon (2001; 2003) located meaning in the richness and complexity of the lived world rather than just in the language itself. They consider communicative action as a form of selection that positions the interlocutor as a particular kind of person who chooses among different meaning potentials a subset of pathway (Scollon and Scollon 2003:205).

6.2. INTERLANGUAGE PRAGMATICS AND CROSS-CULTURAL PRAGMATICS

The socio-cultural–interactional line and developments in sociopragmatics have served as a basis for the development of several subfields including cross-cultural pragmatics and interlanguage pragmatics. An important reason for the emergence of intercultural pragmatics as a new field of inquiry at the beginning of the 2000s was to distinguish research on intercultural interaction and discourse from interlanguage pragmatics and cross-cultural pragmatics. Cross-cultural pragmatics represents the positivist research endeavors of the '80s and '90s with a motto of "when you are in Rome, do as the Romans do." In order for one to do that, one has to be familiar with the differences and similarities of language behavior in different cultures. This is why the major goal of the discipline has been to investigate and highlight aspects of language behavior in which speakers from various cultures have differences and similarities. According to Kasper and Schmidt (1996), the cross-cultural pragmatics approach is comparative, focusing on the cross-cultural similarity and difference in the linguistic realization and the sociopragmatic judgment in contexts.

"*Interlanguage pragmatics*" focuses on the acquisition and use of pragmatic norms in L2: how L2 learners produce and comprehend speech acts, and how their pragmatic competence develops over time (e.g., Kasper and Blum-Kulka 1993; Kasper 1998). According to Kasper & Dahl (Kasper and Dahl 1991:216), the focus of interlanguage pragmatics is on acquisition. It explores "nonnative speakers' comprehension and production of speech acts, and how their L2-related speech act knowledge is acquired," and also "examines child or adult NNS speech act behavior and knowledge, to the exclusion of L1 child and adult pragmatics." To date, many cross-sectional, longitudinal, and theoretical studies have been conducted mainly with a focus on L2 classroom interactions, which has resulted in a special tie between interlanguage pragmatics and second language acquisition research.

In a way, interlanguage pragmatics incorporates cross-cultural pragmatics (e.g., Wierzbicka 1991; 2003), although there is some difference between the two. The fundamental tenet of cross-cultural pragmatics was defined by Wierzbicka in the following way: "In different societies and different communities, people speak differently; these differences in ways of speaking are profound and systematic, they reflect different cultural values, or at least different hierarchies of values; different ways of speaking, different communicative styles, can be explained and made sense of in terms of independently established different cultural values and cultural priorities (Wierzbicka 1991:69)." Cross-cultural pragmatics "takes the view that individuals from two societies or communities carry out their interactions (whether spoken or written) according to their own rules or norms, often resulting in a clash in expectations and, ultimately, misperceptions about the other group" (Boxer 2002:151). Cross-cultural studies focus mainly on speech act realizations in different cultures, cultural breakdowns, and pragmatic failures, such as the way some linguistic behaviors considered polite in one language may not be polite in another language. A significant number of these studies use a comparative approach to different cultural norms reflected in language use (e.g., Wierzbicka 1991, 2003; House 2000; Spencer-Oatey 2000; Thomas 1983).

Interlanguage pragmatics and cross-cultural pragmatics are based on primarily three theoretical constructs: Gricean pragmatics, Brown and Levinson's politeness theory, and the so-called "interlanguage hypothesis" (Selinker 1972). (The latter claims that interlanguage is an emerging linguistic system being developed by a learner of a second language who is approximating the target language: preserving some features of their first language, or overgeneralizing target language rules in speaking or writing the target language and creating innovations). Recently, attempts have been made to integrate Relevance Theory (e.g., Escandell-Vidal 1996; Jary 1998) and Conversation Analysis (e.g., Markee 2000; Kasper 2004) into interlanguage pragmatics, although the main foci of research have remained pragmatic competence, speech acts, politeness, and pragmatic transfer.

7. What makes Intercultural Pragmatics Different?

The concerns of intercultural pragmatics significantly differ from those of both interlanguage pragmatics and cross-cultural pragmatics. The focus of intercultural pragmatics is intercultural communication that involves interactions among people from different cultures using a common language. The main features of intercultural pragmatics can be summarized as follows. First, the theoretical foundation of intercultural pragmatics is a socio-cognitive framework that will be discussed in detail in Chapter 2. Second, focus in this paradigm is on intercultures rather than just cultures as represented in the language use of interlocutors. Interculturality in that framework has both relatively normative and emergent components. As discussed above, it is not only interactionally and socially constructed in the course of communication but also relies on relatively definable cultural models and norms that represent the speech communities to which the interlocutors belong. These L1 cultural models and norms are never fully represented in intercultural interactions. In fact, sometimes they are not represented at all. The extent to which the speakers rely on them is affected by several variables, including the dynamism of conversation, emergent individual intentions, situational factors, process of common ground building, emergent situational salience, and so on. Third, the focus of intercultural pragmatics research is on the nature and characteristics of *actual language use* rather than on pragmatic transfer, language acquisition, or speech act realizations in different cultures.

What research in intercultural pragmatics tries to highlight is the unique features of intercultural communication that may differentiate it, to some extent, from intracultural communication, and that may lead to revision of some basic concepts in pragmatics such as cooperation, common ground, context-sensitivity, salience, and others. In this respect, in the following chapters special attention will be paid to the following issues:

(1) *Limited role of target language cultural norms, conventions, and beliefs.* More importance may be given to co-constructed and emergent elements. A group of nonnative speakers representing different L1s and using English (or any other language) as the medium of communication between them rely on the norms, conventions, and beliefs of English (or any other language) in a different degree.

(2) *Cooperation gains a new meaning in intercultural communication.* Interlocutors cooperate not simply because this is what human beings are expected to do in communication. Rather, they do so consciously and eagerly, to create understanding, common ground, and community.

(3) *Growing role of individual factors* since a somewhat new social frame has to be co-constructed in the course of interaction. Social frames do not affect interlocutors top-down as it happens in intracultural communication. Intercultural interactants will need to build up most of those frames bottom-up in the interaction. Thus, intersubjectivity is less a matter of common sense, and more one of intensive common ground–building.

(4) *Context-sensitivity* works differently in intercultural communication than in intracultural communication. Sometimes there is more reliance on prior context than on actual situational context in interaction.

(5) *Role of preferred ways of saying things* (formulaic language) and preferred ways of organizing thoughts in the target language is not as important and dominant as in intracultural communication.

(6) *More emphasis is put on certain communicative strategies* such as explicit negotiation of meaning and development and use of trouble anticipating and avoidance strategies.

In sum, this book aims to present and discuss current knowledge of intercultural pragmatics, analyze its relations to other subfields of pragmatics, and revisit some of the main tenets of pragmatics from an intercultural perspective. It is not an intention of this book to offer a radically different view from what has been known as the Gricean pragmatics. Rather, the purpose of the book is to call attention to factors that (1) may have been included in the Gricean thought but have been misrepresented or neglected in what has followed, or (2) that may not have been discussed because no attention was paid to intercultural communication in the Gricean paradigm. So the goal is not to change the Gricean approach, but rather supplement it from a multilingual and intercultural perspective. The first two chapters of the book focus on the theoretical foundation of intercultural pragmatics and its relationship to other subfields of pragmatics. Although most of the topics are expected to be familiar to pragmaticians, the book aims to raise, highlight, and elaborate on those issues that constitute intercultural pragmatics. Chapters 3 and 4 discuss pragmatic competence, encyclopedic knowledge, and cultural models that are basically responsible for the communicative behavior of interlocutors. Chapter 5 focuses on formulaic language that is quite neglected an issue in pragmatics but plays a unique role in intercultural communication. The next four chapters on salience, context, common ground, and politeness/impoliteness form a cohesive unit by explaining how formulaic language may serve as the basis for linguistic salience, how salience interacts with prior and actual situational contexts, how core common ground is attached to prior context, how emergent common ground is tied to actual situational context, and what role the above-mentioned factors play in discursive politeness and impoliteness. The book ends with a chapter on research methodology.

1

Current Pragmatic Theories

Intercultural pragmatics has grown out of current pragmatic theories. In the 1990s there started to develop a need to test the applicability of the major tenets of the Gricean approaches, which were mostly monolingual-centered in nature, to intercultural interactions because of the growing interest in cross-cultural pragmatics, interlanguage pragmatics, and intercultural communication. As a result, some of the major tenets of Gricean pragmatics have received different interpretations, and the others have needed to be modified, as we will see later. Although intercultural pragmatics after 2000 has emerged as an independent interdisciplinary inquiry with its own biannual conferences and journal, informed by not only pragmatics theory but also by anthropology, communication, linguistics, discourse, and dialogue studies, and second language acquisition, its major source of development has always been Gricean pragmatics. It is essential, therefore, to give an overview of present research in pragmatics from the perspective of intercultural pragmatics.

1. Definition of Pragmatics

Pragmatics is about meaning; it is about language use and the users. It is about how the language system is employed in social encounters by human beings. In this process, which is one of the most creative human enterprises, communicators (who are speaker-producers and hearer-interpreters at the same time) manipulate language to shape and infer meaning in a socio-cultural context. The main research questions for pragmatists are as follows: why do we choose to say what we say? (production), and why do we understand things the way we do? (comprehension). Before we begin to deal with these questions, it is necessary to give a background to the enterprise.

In the 1930s philosophers such as Morris, Carnap, and Peirce developed a semiotic trichotomy in which syntax was responsible for the formal relations of signs to one another, semantics addressed the relation of signs to what they denote, and pragmatics focused on the relation of signs to their users and interpreters. Morris defined pragmatics as "the study of the relation of signs to interpreters" (Morris 1938:6). Ever since, to some extent, all definitions of pragmatics have derived from his. What pragmatists have tried to do was to make the Morris definition more specific. Stalnaker argued that pragmatics is "the study of linguistic acts and the contexts in which they are performed." He added that pragmatics seeks to "characterize the features of the speech context which help determine which proposition is expressed by a given sentence" (Stalnaker 1972:383). Kasher (1998) considered pragmatics "the study of the competence of language use." For Wilson (2003), pragmatics is the study of how linguistic properties and contextual factors interact in the interpretation of utterances, enabling hearers to bridge the gap between sentence meaning and speaker's meaning. Horn and Ward (2004) claimed that pragmatics is the study of the context-dependent aspects of meaning that are systematically abstracted away from in the construction of logical form. As we see, the main elements are the same in all definitions:

> the linguistic code that is the means of interaction,
> the producer-interpreters of the code and
> the socio-cultural context (frame) in which interaction takes place.

Communication is the result of the interplay of these three elements, so *pragmatics should focus on how meaning is shaped and inferred during social interaction between human beings.* However, the matter is not that simple because the study of language is usually divided into a description of its structure and the description of its use. Thus, there is grammar-research and usage-research, and linguists are quite reluctant to combine the two, though they have never denied that there is strong link between structure and usage. As a result, pragmaticians are also divided. Despite the fact that they all emphasize language use as their main focus, there are linguistic pragmatists who are interested in the study of only those relations between language and context that are grammaticalized, or encoded in the structure of a language (Levinson 1983:9). On the other side are pragmaticians who are interested not only in the code but also in its interpreters and the socio-cultural context. They argue that inferential communication is possible only because of the dynamic and relatively harmonious interplay of all three participating elements (speaker, code, context), and an inquiry into the grammaticalized pragmatic features only fails to give an adequate picture of meaning construction and comprehension.

The endeavor to restrict pragmatics to purely linguistic matters has resulted in the *component view*, which considers pragmatics one of the components of grammar, together with phonology, morphology, semantics, and syntax. It is argued that there is a pragmatic module within the general theory of speaker/hearer competence. This view derives from the modular conception of the human mind, which is quite popular among cognitive and computer scientists as well as psychologists. The approach has been criticized by many. For instance, Sperber & Wilson (1986) argued that like scientific reasoning—the paradigm case of a nonmodular, "horizontal" system—pragmatics cannot be a module, given the indeterminacy of the predictions it offers and the global knowledge it invokes.

The *perspective view* was described by Verschueren (1999), who argued that pragmatics does not constitute an additional component of a theory of language, but offers a perspective. He considers pragmatics "a general cognitive, social and cultural perspective on linguistic phenomenon in relation to their usage in forms of behavior" (Verschueren 1999:7). The component view is exclusive while the perspective view is inclusive. The former focuses on particular segments of language such as sounds (phonology), words (morphology), and sentences (syntax), while the latter looks at language as a whole from a functional, operational perspective.

Mey (2001) following Östman (1988) argued that it would make sense to have the component view and the perspective view existing side by side, so as to expand, rather than narrow, our epistemological horizon. The pragmatic component is understood as the set of pragmatic functions that can be assigned to language while the pragmatic perspective refers to the way these functions operate. The first focuses on the question of how humans say what they mean, and the second refers to how humans mean what they say. Some recent views on pragmatics put meaning in the center of inquiry. Horn and Ward (2004) argued that pragmatics is the study of the context-dependent aspects of meaning that are systematically abstracted away from in the construction of logical form. According to them a regimented account of language use facilitates a simpler, more elegant description of language structure. Those context-dependent yet rule-governed aspects of meaning include deixis, speech acts, presupposition, reference, implicature, and information structure. Pragmatics seeks to "characterize the features of the speech context which help determine which proposition is expressed by a given sentence" (Stalnaker 1972:383). The meaning of an utterance can be regarded as a function from a context (including time, place, and possible world) into a proposition, where a proposition is a function from a possible world into a truth value. Pragmatic aspects of meaning involve the interaction between an expression's context of utterance and the interpretation of elements within that expression.

Intercultural pragmatics is based on the socio-cognitive approach that will be presented in the next chapter. According to this approach, our mind exists simultaneously both in the head and in the world. Pragmatics is about meaning construction and comprehension that is the result of interaction between two sides of world knowledge: individual world knowledge encapsulated in lexical items/concepts in the producer-interpreter's mind and societal world knowledge present in the actual situational context in which the interaction takes place and is internalized by the producer-interpreter in the process of communication. Meaning construction is a two-way street that takes place inductively and deductively. In the course of communication, these two processes run parallel. Inductive meaning construction refers to the speaker perspective and implies that preverbal thought is prompted in producer-interpreter "A" by internalizing utterance/s produced by producer-interpreter "B." Preverbal thought in producer-interpreter "A" triggers the selection and merging of lexical units to express that particular thought. The selected lexical items are merged in a particular structure that appears on the surface in the form of an utterance. This utterance triggers the deductive meaning construction in the mind of producer-interpreter "B," who internalizes the utterance by matching it to his/her existing conventionalized models, patterns, blends, and knowledge in his/her mind, and constructs the meaning of the utterance accordingly. Then the cycle continues with the preverbal thought generated by the constructed meaning. This preverbal thought again will trigger the selection and merging of lexical items, and so on, and so forth. I think pragmatic research has to come up with *a dualistic model* that is capable of doing two things. First, it would explain the production-interpretation process in the mind, and second, it would shed light on the actual communicative process from the perspective of both the producer and interpreter because each interactant participating in this process is a producer-interpreter in one body. This view will continue to be discussed in the following chapters.

2. Lines of Research

Recent pragmatic theories have been following two main lines of research: the linguistic-philosophical line and the socio-cultural–interactional line, which are based on the component view and perspective view as described above. In pragmatic interpretation the linguistic-philosophical line of research appears to put more emphasis on the proposition expressed (e.g., Horn 2005; Levinson 2000; Jaszczolt 2005), while the socio-cultural interactional line (e.g., Verschueren 1999; Mey 2001) emphasizes the importance of allowing socio-cultural context into linguistic analysis. Linguistic-philosophical pragmatics seeks to investigate speaker meaning within an utterance-based framework focusing mainly on linguistic constraints on language use. Socio-cultural interactional pragmatics maintains that pragmatics should include research into social and cultural constraints on language use as well.

Linguistic-philosophical pragmatics, often called Anglo-American pragmatics (such as represented by neo-Gricean Pragmatics, Relevance Theory, and Speech Act Theory), is based on the centrality of intentions and the principle of coop-eration in communication. According to this approach, communication is consti-tuted by recipient design and intention recognition (e.g., Arundale 2008; Haugh 2008b). The speaker's task is to construct a model of the hearer's knowledge rel-evant to the actual situational context. Conversely, the hearer is expected to con-struct a model of the speaker's knowledge relevant to the actual situational context. Communication usually goes smoothly if the speaker's intentions are recognized by the hearer through pragmatic inferences. Consequently, the main task of prag-matics is to explain how exactly the hearer makes these inferences, and determine what is considered the speaker's meaning. In a recent study, Levinson (2006a) con-firmed that (Gricean) intention lies at the heart of communication, and proposes an "interaction engine" that underlies human interaction. Neo-Gricean/formal-ist scholars base their analysis on the Cooperative Principle and Conversational Maxims of Grice (e.g., Carston 2002a, 2004b; Horn 2006, 2007; Levinson 2000a). They pay particular attention to generalized implicatures. The followers of the relevance-theoretic approach argue that the formalist approach has little to say about "particularized implicatures" (Sperber and Wilson 2004:358).

While Gricean, neo-Gricean, and post-Gricean theories consider intention as central to communication (cf. Sperber and Wilson 2004; Levinson 2006a), other pragmatists emphasized the decisive function of society in communication and rejected the central role of intention (cf. Verschueren 1999; Mey 2001), or challenged Gricean intention from cognitive perspectives (cf. Jaszczolt 2005, 2006; Keysar 2007). Conflicting views on intention were formed, "ranging from 'believers' through to 'skeptics' (with perhaps not a few 'agnostics' in-between)" (Haugh 2008b:106). Recent studies (e.g., Verschueren 1999; Gibbs 2001; Arundale 2008; Haugh 2008a) have pointed out that the role intention plays in communication may be more complex than proponents of current pragmatic theories have claimed. Although there is substantial recent evidence that works against the continued placement of Gricean intentions at the center of pragmatic theories, the linguistic-philosophical line (represented by neo-Gricean Pragmatics, Relevance Theory, and Speech Act Theory) still maintains the centrality of intentions in communication.

In contrast, the socio-cultural–interactional paradigm does not consider intention as central to communication, but rather underlines its equivocality. According to this view, communication is not always dependent on speaker intentions in the Gricean sense (e.g., Verschueren 1999; Nuyts 2000; Mey 2001; Haugh 2008b). Haugh proposed that the notion of intention need only be invoked in particular instances where it emerges as a postfactum construct, salient to the interactional achievement of implicatures. The field of Conversational Analysis (CA) is also very critical about intention. According to conversation analysts, the role of intention (or goal/plan), together with other mental resources such as awareness and mutual knowledge (e.g., Schiffer 1972), is considered equivocal and peripheral to the study of communication. What really matters is the situated action observable in the objective physical and social world and accountable by the inferred mental world of participants (e.g., Suchman 1987). CA analysts resist addressing mental representations of the participants and keep agnostic about how intention is inferred, how the state/level of awareness and mutual knowledge are involved in and affect social interaction, and how distinct facets of the mental world converge to make an influence on communication (e.g., Mandelbaum and Pomerantz 1990). Rather, communication is action-oriented, and intention is not central or indispensable to communication as preexisting artifact but only invoked as a possible account for social actions (e.g., Edwards 2006; Haugh 2008a). The socio-cognitive approach (see next chapter) proposed by Kecskes (2008; 2010a) and Kecskes and Zhang (2009) argued that the complexity of the communicative process requires that we consider intention both as an a priori and a co-constructed phenomenon. This view emphasizes that there is a dialectical relationship between a priori intention and emergent intention, both of which are motivated by attention. Some similar view was formulated about emergent intention by Taillard (2002), who said that communication creates an "interface" between the speaker's intention structure and the addressee's intention structure that enables the coordinating role of intentions. It is this coordinating role and the commitment inherent to intentions that make it possible for the interface to reshape both of the participants' intentions.

In fact, one of the main differences between the linguistic-philosophical approach and the sociocultural interactional approach is that the former considers intention an a priori mental state of speakers that underpins communication, while the latter regards intention as a postfactum construct that is achieved jointly through the dynamic emergence of meaning in conversation. Since the two approaches represent two different perspectives, it would be difficult to reject either of them altogether. The complexity of the issue requires that we consider both the encoded and co-constructed sides of intention when analyzing the communicative process. Haugh (2008a) proposed that the notion of intention need only be invoked in particular instances where it emerges as a postfactum construct, salient to the interactional achievement of implicatures.

The link between classical philosophically-oriented pragmatics and research in intercultural and interlanguage communication has led to the development of intercultural pragmatics, focusing on the roles and functions of language and communication within a worldwide communication network. Intercultural pragmatics attempts to combine the two traditions into one explanatory system that focuses special attention on characteristics of intercultural interaction.

3. Characteristics of Current Research

Recent research in pragmatics in both lines discussed above (linguistic-philosophical line and the socio-cultural–interactional line) shows two dominant tendencies: a somewhat idealistic approach to communication and context-centeredness. In current theories it is widely accepted that meaning is socially constructed, context-dependent, and the result of cooperation in the course of communication. Focus in this research is on the positive and social features of communication: *cooperation, rapport, common ground,* and *politeness.* The emphasis on the decisive role of *context, socio-cultural factors,* and *cooperation* is overwhelming, while the role of the individual's prior experience, existing knowledge, egocentrism, salience, and linguistic aggression is almost completely ignored—although these two sides are not mutually exclusive, as we will see later. Similarly, dependency on actual situational context is only one side of processing meaning. Individuals' prior experience of recurring contexts expressed as content in the interlocutors' utterances likewise play an important role in meaning construction and comprehension.

I would like to note here that there is nothing wrong with the focus on positive features of communication except that it is only one side of the matter. I am sure that none of the researchers has set out with the goal of focusing only on the positive features of human communication. The fact of the matter is that human beings are inordinately cooperative (e.g., Tomasello 2006), tend to be polite, and often seek common ground. Just as Chomsky did in formulating generative grammar, researchers in pragmatics had to "create" the "ideal speaker and hearer" in order to investigate and understand basic features of human communication. However, what we have in real communicative encounters is the actual "performance," which may not always be positive and idealistic at all. In fact, some of the confusion and debate in present-day pragmatics is caused by the fact that various authors do not take Gricean pragmatics for what it is—an "idealized picture of communication" (e.g., Dynel 2009; Watts 1992; Kecskes 2010) in which the Cooperative Principle is a guiding mechanism based on rationality and not efficiency of communication. The principle always holds unchanged among rational communicators (while it is the maxims that may be, and frequently are, flouted to generate implied meanings). So cooperation is always there in the communicative process, as Grice (1989) argued: "it is the rationality or irrationality of conversational conduct which I have been concerned to track down rather than any more general characterization of conversational adequacy. (Grice 1989:369)"

We need to make a distinction between *communicatively cooperative* and *socially cooperative* (personal communication with Robert Sanders). The "Cooperative Principle" is not about being positive and socially "smooth," or agreeable. It is a presumption that when people speak, they intend and expect that they will communicate by doing so, and that the hearer will work at helping make this happen. When two people quarrel or have a disagreement, the Cooperative Principle still holds, even though the speakers may not be doing anything positive or cooperative. So when I say that the individualistic aspect in communication has been ignored and that the focus has been mainly on communal resources, I do not mean to conflate social cooperativeness, agreeableness, or effort to get along with the Cooperative Principle and Gricean theory. What I want to emphasize here is that this is *just one side of the coin*. Even if individuals are aggressive, self-serving, egotistic, and so on, and not quite focusing on the other participants of the interaction, they can't have spoken at all to someone else without expecting that something would come out of it, that there would be some result, and that the other person/s was/were engaged with them. That is what the Cooperative Principle is all about, and it certainly does have to continue being considered as the main driving force in communication. As I mentioned in the Introduction, intercultural pragmatics adds a new aspect to understanding cooperation. Interlocutors in intercultural interactions cooperate not just because this is what human beings are expected to do in communication (as the Gricean rationality requires) but they also do so consciously and eagerly to create understanding, common ground, and community. Again, not that this is something that does not exist in intracultural communication. Of course it does. The question only is in what degree and how it is expressed linguistically.

4. Issues with Current Theories

The intercultural perspective has directed attention to four major issues in current pragmatic theorizing: intention, speaker meaning, cooperation versus egocentrism, and context-dependency.

4.1. RECONCEPTUALIZING INTENTION

Haugh (2009) argued that in socio-cultural–interactional pragmatics the study of communication is not exhausted by the expression and recognition/attribution of intentions, and pragmatics should include research into social and cultural constraints on language use as well (e.g., Marmaridou 2000:219; Verschueren 1999:164). While this is fully supported in intercultural pragmatics, speaker intention to some extent still remains (and should remain) in the center of conceptualizations of communication underlying such research (e.g., Haugh 2009; Mey 2001:85). It is not that we must stop considering intention the main driving force of communication, but rather it is that we need to reconceptualize it.

The Intercultural Pragmatics special issue on intention in pragmatics (Haugh 2008b) was motivated in response to Levinson's (2006b) call to elevate Gricean intentions to the center of cognition in interaction, given that Levinson's call seemed, in Haugh's view, a "somewhat reactionary move." The aim of this special issue was to stimulate discussion about both the characterization and scope of intention in pragmatics. Haugh (2008) and Arundale (2008) argued that one problem facing current models of inference that privilege the speaker's intention in determining whether communication has occurred (whether in moving from speaker intentions to communicative acts or vice-versa) is the failure to "address how the participants themselves could come to know whether the recipient's inference and attribution regarding that intention is to any extent consistent with it" (Arundale 2008:241). This means that there is no account in current intention-based models given as to how speakers and hearers determine something has indeed been communicated.

Interactional pragmatics also attests to the difficulty of locating intentions relative to meanings in discourse (rather than simply relative to utterances). Haugh & Jaszczolt (2012) argued that in tracing intentions in conversational interaction it becomes apparent that intentions can also be characterized as being "emergent," as both the speaker and the hearer jointly co-construct understandings of what is meant (Haugh 2008b; Kecskes 2010a:60–61). To demonstrate this, Haugh & Jaszczolt (2012) used Kecskes's example (2010a:60), arguing that John's initial intention to give Peter a chance to talk about his trip is not realized in the excerpt in (1).
(1)

> JOHN: Want to talk about your trip?
> PETER: I don't know. If you have questions...
> JOHN: OK, but you should tell me...
> PETER: Wait, you want to hear about Irene?
> JOHN: Well, what about her?
> PETER: She is fine. She has...well...put on some weight, though.

Kecskes suggested that John's original intention is sidelined by Peter talking about Irene, perhaps because he thinks John might want to know about her (being that she is his former girlfriend). He argued that "it was the conversational flow that led to this point, at which there appears a kind of emergent, co-constructed intention" (Kecskes 2010:61).

Haugh & Jaszczolt (2012) pointed out that there is growing evidence that we need to make clearer distinctions between speaker (intended) meaning, which pertains to the subjective processing domain and the utterance level, and "joint meaning," which pertains to the interpersonal domain at the discourse level (Carassa and Colombetti 2009; Kecskes 2008, 2010). Different types of intentions arguably have different roles to play relative to these different types of meaning.

The role of emergent intention in intercultural communication is very significant. Interlocutors will start a conversation expressing particular intention. Then one of them may suddenly and unexpectedly change the topic based on an emergent intention that may have been triggered by any of the following factors: loss of interest, language difficulty, inconvenient topic, and so on. (e.g., Toyoda and Harrison 2002; Li et al. 2005). The following conversation between a Japanese and Korean student illustrates this point properly (source: Albany Lingua Franca Database):
(2)

> J: I play baseball with Japanese and Korean men.
> K: Ah there must be a lot of competitions no?
> J: Hm?
> K: You know like.... You know like…you are going…things are bad in Korea because of history. So maybe competitions?
> J: Competi…
> K: Ok maybe you guys feel like ok we have to win. Japan has to win…no no?
> J: No.
> K: Ok that's good nice nice…do you like American food?
> J: Yes I like. I like steak I like hamburger.
> K: Do you miss Japanese food though?
> J: Hm?
> K: Do you miss Japanese food?
> J: I like cooking.

When the Japanese student started to talk about his playing baseball with Japanese and Korean students, the Korean student referred to the historically bad relations between Japanese and Koreans. He said that the Japanese probably felt the need to win. When he saw that it might be inconvenient for the Japanese to continue this topic, the Korean suddenly changed the course of conversation: "Ok that's good nice nice…do you like American food?"

4.2. SPEAKER MEANING: HEARER-CENTERED PRAGMATICS

Kecskes (2008:404) argued that in order to give an adequate explanation of communicative processes, we need a dialectical model of pragmatics that combines the

perspective of both the speaker and hearer. This change is warranted because current pragmatic theories—both those that have grown out of Grice's theory, such
as the various neo-Gricean approaches, and the approach proposed by Relevance
Theory—appear to be hearer-centered. They derive from the Gricean modular view
that divides the interpretation process into two stages: *what is said* and *what is implicated.* Although the Gricean theory, with its cooperative principle and maxims, was
supposed to embrace conversation as a whole, basically its further development has
remained hearer-centered, with less emphasis on interest in the speaker's position—
a rather paradoxical turn, as Grice himself always emphasized speaker's meaning.
Even so, the Gricean divide of truth-conditional semantics and pragmatics has led
to a somewhat impoverished speaker's meaning, without regard for the *pragmatic*
features embedded in the utterance.

The division between *what is said* and *what is implicated* was made for the sake
of utterance interpretation and for distinguishing the semantic meaning from the
pragmatic meaning of an utterance. However, a theory that is concerned about
the speaker's [or speakers'] meaning should focus not only on the truth values of
the speaker's utterance, but also on its pragmatic elements and on the speaker's
commitment and egocentrism (in the cognitive sense, as will be explained later)
deriving from prior experience and dominated by salience. I think the dominance
of the hearer's perspective in current pragmatic theories can be explained by three
facts: (1) the focus on what is said, and the truth values of the speaker's utterance without due regard for its pragmatics features in the neo-Gricean approaches,
(2) emergence of the powerful Relevance Theory, and (3) the partial misinterpretation of the Gricean approach. Let's discuss them one after the other.

Although the neo-Griceans' main concern is the speaker's meaning, they still
view communication as designed with a view toward the recipient and his/her recognition of speaker's intention. In this view, the speaker designs his/her utterance
for the hearer and the hearer's task is to recognize the speaker's intention. But what
is recovered is not always what was intended, because of the interlocutors' differences in private cognitive contexts and prior experience. So an adequate account
of interaction should consider interlocutors not only as common-ground seekers,
but as individuals with their own agendas, their own prior experience, their specific
mechanisms of saliency (based on prior experiences), and their individual language
production systems. This issue is especially important in intercultural communication where interlocutors representing different L1s and cultures cannot be certain
how much they have in common with each other. They *may have to* create common
ground almost from scratch. Consequently, the balance between the individual and
societal factors in intercultural interaction is rather lopsided toward the individual
factors. Individuals in these cases also work under the constraints of societal factors, but those happen to be different for each participant depending on their L1
and cultural background. This may lead to too much emphasis on individual factors like personality, experience, egocentrism, and so on in intercultural interaction.
So we may have an intercultural exchange that is affected by societal factors that

are different on each side about how much self-promotion you should do during a job interview (these aren't individual factors), but it may be further affected by individual differences, such as condescension or defensiveness by one party because of those societal differences (and these are entirely individual factors).

The second reason is the Relevance Theory. Unlike the neo-Griceans, who attempt to give an account of the speaker's meaning, relevance theorists focus on developing a cognitive psychological model of utterance interpretation, which does not address the question of how and why the speaker, given what s/he wants to communicate, utters what s/he utters. Saul (2002a) suggested that the main difference between the neo-Gricean theory and Relevance Theory lies in "whose meaning" they model. While the neo-Griceans follow the original perspective and consider utterance meaning, including implicature, to be the speaker's intended meaning, relevance theorists discuss intentional communication from the perspective of the addressee's reconstruction of the speaker's assumptions.

There is a third reason that we also have to deal with: Grice's implicature is often misinterpreted by pragmaticians. The Gricean implicature is one possible aspect of speaker meaning; what is said and what is implicated by the speaker. Although Horn (2004) and Bach (2001) called attention to the difference between implicating and inferring, not everybody has listened. Horn said: "Speakers implicate, hearers infer (Horn 2004:6)."

Bach (2001) argued that "People sometimes confuse infer with imply....When we say that a speaker or sentence implies something, we mean that information is conveyed or suggested without being stated outright....Inference, on the other hand, is the activity performed by a reader or interpreter in drawing conclusions that are not explicit in what is said."

Grice may (unwillingly) also have contributed to this misunderstanding by bringing the "audience" into the explanation of implicature. According to Grice, a speaker's intending to convey that *P* by saying that *Q*, is not enough for the speaker to implicate that *P*. The audience must also need to believe that the speaker believes that *P* in order to preserve the assumption of the speaker's cooperativeness. With this claim Grice attempted to give some degree of intersubjectivity to the notion of conversational implicature. However, speakers have authority over what they implicate as an utterer but can't fully control what they conversationally implicate (Saul 2002a). The following short conversation (3) demonstrates this very well.

(3)

> ROY: Is there something wrong, Susie?
> SUSIE: *I am fine, Roy.*
> ROY: I would have believed you if you hadn't said "Roy."
> SUSIE: OK, OK, just stop......

Susie's utterance "I am fine, Roy" gives way to different possible interpretations. What really matters is what the audience is required by the speaker to believe, not what the audience does believe. Davis argued that Grice was wrong to include audience-oriented criteria in his characterization of conversational implicature (Davis 1998:122). The speaker's intentions do not depend on what anyone else presumes. "To mean or imply something is to have certain intentions." Saul (2002a) found it important to distinguish between "utterer-implicatures" and "audience-implicatures." Utterer-implicatures are claims that the speaker attempts to conversationally implicate (intended by the speaker, but not necessarily recognized by the addressee). Audience-implicatures are claims that the audience takes to be conversationally implicated (recognized by the addressee but not necessarily intended by the speaker).

Most attempts to revise/correct the problems of the modular view and recognize pragmatic features of the speaker's meaning (e.g., Sperber and Wilson, 1986; Carston 2002a; Moeschler 2004: explicature/implicature; Burton-Roberts 2006: what-is-A-said/what-is-B-said; Bach 2001: what is said/ impliciture/ implicature) have not gone far enough because they still were interested primarily in utterance interpretation, without paying due attention to private/individual knowledge, prior experience, and the emergent, rather than the *a priori* only intentions of the speaker.

The main problem with the hearer-centered views is that they want to recover *speaker* meaning from a *hearer* perspective. As a result, what is actually "recovered" is hearer meaning, in the sense of how the hearer interprets what the speaker said. The proposition the speaker produces will not be exactly the same as that which will be recovered by the hearer, because, as we said above, interlocutors are individuals with different cognitive predispositions, different commitments, different prior experiences, and different histories of use of the same words and expressions.

4.3. COOPERATION versus EGOCENTRISM

As discussed above, current pragmatic theories attach great importance to cooperation in the process of communication. Communication is considered an intention-directed practice, during which the interlocutors mutually recognize their intentions and goals, and make joint efforts to achieve them (Clark 1996). Grice's (1975) four maxims formulate the guidelines for speaker's production of an utterance, and it is on the basis of a mutual agreement on these maxims that cooperation is recognized and comprehension is warranted.

Cooperation was questioned by Relevance Theory (RT) when it referred to counter-cases of cooperation, with interlocutors being unwilling to build relevance because of their preferences for certain interests, as opposed to cases when they are unable to be relevant because of lack of the needed information or mental resources. In RT, the interlocutors are free to be cooperative or uncooperative, and their preferences for cooperation or the reverse are driven by their own interests. However, we have to be careful here and refer back to what was discussed above about being communicatively cooperative or socially cooperative. What RT speaks about is being socially cooperative versus uncooperative so the communicatively cooperative aspect of the Gricean Cooperative Principle still holds.

The most robust evidence against cooperation and common ground as an a priori mental state derives from empirical cognitive research, which reported the egocentrism of speaker-hearers in mental processing of communication and postulated the *emergent property* of common ground. Barr and Keysar (2005a) claimed that speakers and hearers commonly ignore their mutual knowledge when they produce and understand language. Their behavior is called "egocentric" because it is rooted in the speakers' or hearers' own knowledge instead of in their mutual knowledge. Other studies in cognitive psychology (e.g., Keysar and Bly 1995; Giora 2003; Keysar 2007) have shown that speakers and hearers are egocentric to a surprising degree, and that individual, egocentric endeavors of interlocutors play a much more decisive role, especially in the initial stages of production and comprehension, than is envisioned by current pragmatic theories. Here, however, we must be very careful not to misunderstand what "egocentrism" refers to both in cognitive psychology and intercultural pragmatics. In everyday language, when somebody is called "egocentric," we mean that that person regards himself and his own opinion or interest as being the most important or valid. Self-relevant information is seen to be more important in shaping one's judgments than do thoughts about others and other relevant information (Windschitl, Rose, Stalkfleet and Smith 2008). I think in these cases we should use the label "egotistic" rather than "egocentric." Egocentric or egotistic people do not try to fully understand or cope with other people's opinions and the fact that reality can be different from what they are ready to accept. This kind of egocentrism is usually conscious, and often premeditated. This is *not*, however, what cognitive research and intercultural pragmatics understand by "egocentrism." The egocentric behavior they speak about is rooted in speakers' and hearers' relying more on their own knowledge and prior experience than on mutual knowledge and shared experience. This egocentrism is the result of extensive prior experience, frequent exposure to certain events, actions, feelings, as well as acquisition of conventions and norms, and so on. All this leads to a subconscious, automatic, instinctive behavior and salience that usually characterizes the first phase of language production and comprehension in communicative encounters. This is why people turn out to be poor estimators of what others know. They usually start with their own knowledge and interpret things accordingly, and either act as if that is the only, and the self-evident, way, or they have a hard time setting that aside and entertaining an alternate understanding even when they know the other person has a different perspective and different knowledge. Speakers usually underestimate the ambiguity and overestimate the effectiveness of their utterances (Keysar and Henly 2002). Language processing is anchored in the assumption that what is salient or accessible to oneself will also be accessible to one's interlocutors (Giora 2003; Barr and Keysar 2005; Colston and Katz 2005; Kecskes 2007a). Interlocutors look at everything through their prior experience, relying on what is on their mind. This is the way the mind operates. It is just that once one way of understanding is formed, it is difficult to set one's own understanding aside and see any other possibility, even when you know there might be one. In this respect a good example is Florida Sen. Marco Rubio's behavior during the 2012 elections. He insisted that even if Mitt Romney offered him a spot as the GOP's No. 2 in November, he would decline. "I don't want to be the vice president right now, or maybe ever. I really want to do a good job in the Senate," Rubio said. But in an interview with the *National Journal*, it seemed like the possibility of running for vice president was still on his mind: "If in four to five years, if I do a good job as vice president—I'm sorry, as senator— I'll have the chance to do all sorts of things," he said. Was this a Freudian slip-of-the-tongue? What we call "slip-of-the-tongue" occasionally appears to be strong salience that is on one's mind and comes out automatically if not controlled.

There is an important difference between RT researchers and cognitive psychologists about understanding cooperation and egocentrism. In the Relevance Theory, interlocutors may not be cooperative because of lack of information or mental resources, or unwillingness to cooperate because of a preference for certain interests (usually personal). In this case, egocentrism of the interlocutor involves a certain kind of consciousness, which may be negative as was explained above. Egocentrism is, however, different for cognitive psychologists and also for intercultural pragmatics. It is not a negative notion because it involves a subconscious processing bias based on individual salience and prior experience. Interlocutors just cannot help saying something or comprehending something from their own perspective, or expressing something that is on their mind subconsciously. Of course, if what is said or comprehended does not match the actual situational context, repair and adjustment may happen right away. (This issue will be discussed in the chapter about salience.)

These findings about the egocentric approach of interlocutors to communication are congruent with Giora's (1997, 2003) graded salience hypothesis and Kecskes's (2003, 2008) dynamic model of meaning. They posit that interlocutors consider their past conversational experience a more important basis for producing and understanding language than what would conform in this moment to norms of informativeness. Giora's (2003) main argument is that knowledge of salient meanings plays a primary role in the process of using and comprehending language. She claims that "privileged meanings, meanings foremost on our mind, affect comprehension and production primarily, regardless of context or literality" (Giora 2003:103). Kecskes's dynamic model of meaning (2008) (to be discussed in Chapter 6) also emphasizes that *what* the speaker says relies, to some extent, on prior conversational experience, as reflected in lexical choices in production. And similarly, *how* the hearer understands what is said in the actual situational context depends partly on his/her prior conversational experience with the lexical items used in the speaker's utterances. Smooth communication depends primarily on the extent of the match between the two. This is a key issue especially in intercultural communication, where the difference between prior individual experiences of the interlocutors gets more emphasis, and speakers' egocentrism and salience become more articulated. As a consequence, common ground building may become more difficult and the likelihood of conflict and misunderstanding may grow. But this does not at all mean that intercultural interaction is full of failure and misunderstandings, as we will see later.

4.4. CONTEXT-DEPENDENCY

The next issue I am raising about the main characteristics of current pragmatics is context-dependency. According to the dominant view, context-sensitivity (in various forms) is a pervasive feature of natural language. Nowadays, everybody seems to be a contextualist. Literalism according to which (many or most) sentences express propositions independent of context (actual situational context) has been extinct for some time. Carston claimed that "linguistically encoded meaning never fully determines the intended proposition expressed" (Carston 2002a:49). Consequently, linguistic data must be supplemented by nonlinguistic, contextual interpretation processes. This contextualism requires a discussion of what is understood by "context" in pragmatics research.

In linguistics, context usually refers to any factor—linguistic, epistemic, physical, social—that affects the actual interpretation of signs and expressions. The notion that meanings are context-dependent has informed some of the most powerful views in current linguistic and philosophical theory, all the way from Frege to Wittgenstein and beyond. Frege's Context Principle (1884) asserts that a word has meaning only in the context of a sentence. Wittgenstein (1921) basically formulated the same idea, saying that an expression has meaning only in a proposition; every variable can be conceived as a propositional variable. Such *external* perspectives on context hold that context modifies and/or specifies word meanings in one way or another. Context is seen as a selector of lexical features because it activates some of those features while leaving others in the background. Some versions of this "externalist" contextualism take this line of thinking to the extreme and claim that meanings are specified entirely by their contexts, and that there is no semantic systematicity underlying them at all (e.g., Barsalou 1993, 1999; Evans, 2006). According to this view, the mind works primarily by storing experiences and finding patterns in those experiences. These patterns shape how people engage with their subsequent experiences, and store these in their minds.

In Sperber & Wilson's original formulation of Relevance Theory, relevance is something that is not determined by context, but constrained by context. A context-driven pragmatic process is generally top-down. It is usually not triggered by an expression in the sentence but emerges for purely pragmatic reasons: in order to make sense of what the speaker says. Such processes are also referred to as "free" pragmatic processes. They are considered "free" because they are not mandated by the linguistic expressions but respond to pragmatic considerations only. For example, the pragmatic process through which an expression is given a nonliteral (e.g., a metaphorical or figurative) interpretation is context-driven: we interpret the expression nonliterally in order to make sense of the given speech act, not because this is required by linguistic expressions. We should, however, use caution here because nonliteral interpretation may not necessarily be initiated by the context but by the semantics of the sentence. For example, "there is a razor thin opportunity here" leads us to context because "razor thin" and "opportunity" don't cohere semantically. "That woman is his father" requires attention first to the referent in that context, and then to the real-world circumstances that make it possible because of an internal contradiction in the semantics. Metaphoric understandings can hardly be formed without starting with the sentence.

Opposite to the externalist view on context is the *internalist* perspective. It considers lexical units as creators of context (e.g., Gee 1999; Violi 2000). Violi (2000) claimed that our experience is developed through a regularity of recurrent and similar situations that we tend to identify with given contexts. Standard (prior recurring) context can be defined as a regular situation that we have repeatedly experienced, about which we have expectations as to what will or will not happen, and on which we rely to understand and predict how the world around us works. It is exactly these standard contexts that linguistic meanings tied to lexical units refer to in utterances like: "License and registration, please."; "Let me tell you something."; "What can I do for you?"; "How is it going?", and so on. These "situation-bound utterances" (Kecskes 2003) are tied to standard recurring contexts, which they are able to (re)create. Gumperz (1982) argued that utterances somehow carry with them their own context or project that context. Similarly, Levinson (2003), referring to Gumperz's work, claimed that the message-versus-context opposition is misleading, because the message can carry with it, or forecast, its context. In the socio-cognitive approach this is referred to as the "double-sidedness" of context.

In the semantics–pragmatics interface debate, contextualists are committed to deriving rich pragmatic effects from what is said by a sentence, from the proposition expressed, or from the semantic content. Contextualism has its origin in speech act theories of meaning, as I have argued above. Moderate contextualists will claim that only some expressions outside the basic set are context-sensitive and/or semantically incomplete, while radical contextualists claim that every expression or construction outside the basic set is context-sensitive. Radical contextualists include Searle and Recanati as well as relevance theorists such as Carlston, Sperber, and Wilson; among the moderate contextualists, we find those who argue for the context sensitivity of quantified phrases (e.g., Stanley and Szabo), of belief statements (e.g., Richard and Perry), and of epistemic claims (e.g., DeRose).

From the perspective of intercultural pragmatics, the main problem with both the externalist and internalist views of context is that they are one-sided inasmuch as they emphasize either the selective (externalist) or the constitutive role (internalist) of context. However, the dynamic nature of human speech communication requires a model that recognizes both regularity and variability in meaning construction and comprehension, and takes into account both the selective and constitutive roles of context at the same time. Millikan (1998) claimed that the conventional sign (the lexical unit) is reproduced (or "copied," as she said), not discovered or invented anew by each producer–processor pair. This can only happen if the linguistic unit has some kind of regular reference to certain contexts in which it has been used. Leibniz (1976 [1679]) said: *"si nihil per se concipitur, nihil omnino concipietur"* ("if nothing is understood by itself, nothing at all will ever be understood"). Words of a particular language can create context because they encapsulate prior situational contexts in which a speaker has used them (e.g., Violi 2000; Kecskes 2008). Violi argued that "it is not the existence of a given context that makes the use of the word possible, but the use of the word that initiates a mental process in the listener which seeks to construct a context in which its present use could be most appropriate." (Violi 2000:117). When *"get out of here"* or *"license and registration, please"* are uttered without any actual situational context, these expressions will create a situational context in the mind of hearers because of their prior experience with the lexical units. This relative regularity attached to lexical units of a language changes diachronically, while variability (variety) changes synchronically. That is to say, standardized lexical meanings change diachronically while variations in the context of their utterance change synchronically. What we need is an approach to communication that recognizes both the selective and constitutive role of context. It is necessary to make a difference between *actual situational context*, which pragmatics theories mean when they use the term "context," and *prior experience-based context that we carry in our memory*. Both are equally important in meaning construction and comprehension, as we will see in Chapter 6, where we discuss the different effect of context-sensitivity in intracultural and intercultural communication. What intercultural pragmatics analysis has found is that the constitutive role of context is much more important in intercultural communication than in intracultural interactions that are dominated by the selective role of context as described above.

There is some difference in the understanding of context-dependency between the cognitive-philosophical line and socio-cultural–interactional line. In pragmatic interpretation the cognitive-philosophical line of research appears to put more emphasis on the proposition expressed (e.g., Horn 2005; Levinson 2000) while the socio-cultural– interactional line (e.g., Verschueren 1999; Mey 2001) highlights the importance of allowing socio-cultural context into linguistic analysis. This means that the former focuses on the semantics of an utterance, and how that connects with the context (actual situational context) so as to shape its situated meaning. The other view starts with the context and focuses on how the semantics of the utterance are shaped by that. In short, the former takes the semantics as given and considers how that connects with and shapes the context. The latter takes the context as given and considers how the semantics is contingent on and shaped by that. There seems to be a *from-the-inside-out approach* (analytic) in the cognitive-philosophical paradigm while in the socio-cultural–interactional line the interpretation goes *from-the-outside-in* (holistic).

The main reason behind contextualism is hearer centeredness. Of course, the linguistic sign is underdetermined from the perspective of the hearer but not necessarily from the perspective of the speaker, as I will argue later.

5. Societal- Rather than Individual-centered Theory

The socio-cultural-interactional line of research has resulted in societal-centered theories where interpretation goes *from-the-outside-in* (holistic) and less attention is paid to the proposition expressed. In this paradigm it is especially interesting for us to look at Mey's and van Dijk's work.

Mey's (2001) Pragmatic Act Theory originates in the socio-cultural–interactional view emphasizing the priority of socio-cultural and societal factors in meaning construction and comprehension. He argued that the problem with the Speech Act Theory is that it lacks a theory of action, and even if it does have such a theory it is individual- rather than society-centered (Mey 2001:214). His main criticism against the Speech Act Theory is that in order for speech acts to be effective, they have to be situated: "they both rely on, and actively create, the situation in which they are realized" (Mey 2001:218). In short, "there are no speech acts, but only situated speech acts, or instantiated pragmatic acts." Sanders (personal communication) does not think that Searle would disagree with the spirit of this approach. The refined version would be that there are generalized speech acts (e.g., a promise) but what counts as a promise is entirely situated. As a consequence, the emphasis is not on conditions and rules for an individual speech act, but on characterizing a general situational prototype (what Mey calls a "pragmeme") that can be executed in the situation. Going back to Searle, we would expect him to take the position that his conditions and rules specify what Mey calls the prototype. So there seems to be no contradiction here between Searle's speech acts and May's pragmemes. A particular pragmeme can be substantiated and realized through individual pragmatic acts. In other words, a pragmatic act is an instance of adapting oneself to a context, as well as adapting the context to oneself. For instance:

(4)

> - There is soccer on the telly.
> - *Not interested.*

"Not interested" is a pragmatic act (refusal) that expresses the pragmeme [I do not care], which can also be substantiated by several other concrete pragmatic acts such as "*I do not care,*" "*I do not mind,*" "*whatever . . . ,*" and so forth. All these expressions perform the same pragmatic act, giving rise to a common illocutionary point. But this seriously underspecifies what is actually going on here, and does not identify the speech acts themselves. We first have to identify the speech act performed by uttering the report of "there is soccer on the telly," which (depending on context) could count as the speech act of invitation or offer to join in watching the game. In that case, "not interested" is a response to that speech act, and is the act of "refusing" or "declining." While it may be uninteresting that there are paraphrases of the semantics of the "refusal" that say the same thing, more interesting is that there are completely different semantic objects that also decline (e.g., "I'm just going to a meeting."). And those different objects can only be shown to be the same act by reference to Searle's rules and conditions (what Mey calls "the prototype").

According to Mey, pragmatic acts are situation-derived and situation-constrained. There is no one-to-one relationship between speech acts and pragmatic acts because the latter do not necessarily include specific acts of speech. For instance:

(5)

> MOTHER: Joshua, what are you doing?
> JOSHUA: Nothing.
> MOTHER: Will you stop it immediately. (Mey 2001:216)

The pragmeme represented by the pragmatic act "Nothing" can be described as "trying to get out (opt out) of a conversation." Again, the pragmeme here is the prototype. It can be considered a speech act of rejection realized by different semantic units. Thus, there does not seem to be any contradiction here between Searle's approach and what May intends to offer.

Mey's pragmatic act approach is correct in many respects. It is definitely true that speech acts never come in isolation, always carrying with them several other acts that also contribute to their success in conversation. Some of these other acts are strictly speech-oriented, while others are more general in nature, and may include, besides speech, extralinguistic aspects of communication such as gestures, intonation, facial expression, body posture, head movements, laughter, and so on. The role of context is also inevitable. "No conversational contribution at all can be understood properly unless it is situated within the environment in which it was meant to be understood" (Mey 2001:217). In Mey's opinion, human activity is not the privilege of the individual. Rather, the individual is situated in a social context, which means that s/he is empowered, as well as limited, by the conditions of her/his social life. This looks like quite a deterministic view that leaves limited space for individual initiatives. It is true that in any social context we are not at all free to do just anything we want, but neither is what we do fully determined. I do not have to hit the ball when I am a batter at the plate, I don't have to steal a base as a runner, I have choices about where to throw the ball when I catch it...(example by Sanders). So we can say conduct is "constrained," not determined.

For Mey it is the situation and extralinguistic factors such as gestures and intonation rather than "wording" that define pragmatic acts. He argued that "*a fortiori*, there are, strictly speaking, no such 'things' as speech acts *per se*, only acts of speech in a situation" (Mey 2006:24). Further, he claimed that "indirect speech acts derive their force, not from their lexico-semantic build-up, but instead, from the *situation* in which they are appropriately uttered." Mey is right in emphasizing the importance of situation, environment, and extralinguistic factors in meaning construction and comprehension. However, Kecskes (2010) argued that the "wording" of linguistic expressions is as important in shaping meaning as the situation in which they are used and supplemented by extralinguistic factors. Both sides are equally important contributors in meaning construction and comprehension. Words, expressions, and speech acts are tied to prior experience of the individual with these linguistic elements in social situations (Kecskes 2008). The question is not whether it is the actual situational context or the prior context tied to linguistic expressions that have priority in meaning production and comprehension. Rather, the real questions are (1) *to what extent* the linguistic (encoding prior experience) contextual factors and the actual contextual factors contribute to meaning construction and comprehension and (2) *at what stages* of the communicative process they do so.

Van Dijk pays special attention to participants' co-constructing context in his socio-cognitive view of language use. In his theory, it is not the social situation that influences (or is influenced by) discourse, but the way the participants define the situation (2008:x). He goes further and claims that "contexts are not some kind of objective conditions or direct cause, but rather (inter)subjective constructs designed and ongoingly updated in interaction by participants as members of groups and communities (van Dijk 2008:x)." Van Dijk is right when he talks about the fact that actual situational context is co-constructed by participants in the process of communication. However, he speaks about actual situational context only and seems to forget about prior context with which participants enter into the actual communicative situation, and which they combine with their present situational experience in co-constructing actual situational context.

Both Mey and van Dijk seem to overemphasize the importance of co-constructing of the actual situational context by the participants and give less attention to the prior context and experience that interlocutors bring into the communicative process. The main difference between their view and the view represented in intercultural pragmatics is that intercultural pragmatics emphasizes that both normative and emergent elements are present in the co-construction process. Interlocutors do not start from scratch but enter the communicative process with a "baggage" that is the cumulative result of their prior experience. So there seems to be some kind of "clash" or "interplay" between prior experience and actual situational experience, which produces the dynamism of meaning construction.

6. The Explanatory Movement in Pragmatics

As discussed so far, communication appears to be a trial-and-error, try-and-try-again, process that is co-constructed by the participants. It relies on both a priori and emergent factors. The process seems to be only partly summative and emergent interactional achievement (cf. Arundale 1999, 2008; Mey 2001). Rather, it is both an individual and social achievement in which both prior and actual situational experiences are involved (Kecskes and Mey 2008; Kecskes 2010a). Consequently, due attention should be paid to the less positive aspects of communication, including breakdowns, misunderstandings, struggles, and language-based aggression— features that are not unique but seem to be almost as common in communication as are cooperation and politeness. Similarly, dependency on actual situational context is only one side of the matter, while individuals' prior experience of recurring contexts expressed as content in the interlocutors' utterances likewise plays an important role in meaning construction and comprehension.

This is what Mey says about pragmatic acts: "The theory of pragmatic acts does not explain human language use starting from the words uttered by a single, idealized speaker. Instead, it focuses on the interactional *situation* in which both speakers and hearers realize their aims. The explanatory movement is from the outside in, one could say, rather than from the inside out: instead of starting with what is said, and looking for what the words could mean, the situation where the words fit is invoked to explain what can be (and is actually being) said" (Mey 2006a:542).

The problem with this definition is that it emphasizes only that the explanatory movement should go from the outside in. I argue that *the explanatory movement in any pragmatic theory should go in both directions: from the outside in (actual situational context → prior context encapsulated in utterances used) and from the inside out (prior context encapsulated in utterances used → actual situational context).* This view is based on the socio-cognitive approach, which serves as a theoretical framework for intercultural pragmatics and will be discussed in the next chapter.

2

The Socio-cognitive Approach

Intercultural pragmatics adopts a socio-cognitive approach (SCA) to pragmatics that takes into account both the societal and individual factors including cooperation and egocentrism that, as being claimed here, are not antagonistic phenomena in interaction (see Kecskes 2008; 2010a). In this approach interlocutors are considered social beings searching for meaning with individual minds embedded in a socio-cultural collectivity.

SCA argues that Grice was right when he tied cooperation to the speaker-hearer's rationality. However, egocentrism must be added to speaker-hearer's rationality. We human beings are just as egocentric (as individuals) as we are cooperative (as social beings).

"Egocentrism" in the SCA refers to attention-bias that is the result of prior experience of individuals. It means that interlocutors activate and bring up the most salient information to the needed attentional level in the construction (by the speaker) and comprehension (by the hearer) of the communication. So there is nothing negative about egocentrism if the word is used in this sense, as will be explained below.

1. Background

There are several socio-cognitive approaches out there in different disciplines. The important thing is that there is a core thinking applied by most socio-cognitive approaches, and then specific elements are added to the core depending on the given paradigm. The use of the term *"socio-cognitive" describes integrated cognitive and social properties of systems, processes, functions, and models.* In the socio-cognitive paradigm, human functioning is viewed as the product of a dynamic interplay of personal, behavioral, and environmental influences. For example, how people interpret the results of their own behavior informs and alters their environments and the personal factors they possess, which, in turn, inform and alter subsequent behavior (Bandura 1986).

Figure 2.1 models the Social Cognitive Theory (Bandura 1986): B represents behavior, P represents personal factors in the form of cognitive, affective, and biological events, and E represents the external environment.

In Bandura's approach individuals are viewed both as products and as producers of their own environments and of their social systems. It is important to

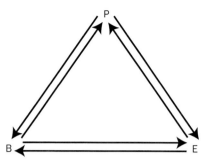

FIGURE 2.1 "The model of the Socio-Cognitive Theory of Badura"

note that Bandura expanded the conception of human agency to include collective agency. People work together on shared beliefs about their capabilities and common aspirations to better their lives. Collective agency is especially important from the perspective of common ground and collective salience in communication as we will see later in Chapters 7 and 8. The interplay of the individual and the environment can be interpreted as follows: "the fact that behavior varies from situation to situation may not necessarily mean that behavior is controlled by situations but rather that the person is construing the situations differently and thus the same set of stimuli may provoke different responses from different people or from the same person at different times (Jones 1989:26)."

In pragmatics and communication, the dialogically based socio-cognitive approach has gained significant influence, deriving from the Bakhtin Circle with M. M. Bakhtin and V. N. Voloshinov as the main representatives, and also promoted by, among others, Rommetveit (1992) and Linell (1996). In the introduction to his edited book, Wold (1992:1-2) described the approach in the following way:

> The dialogically based, social-cognitive approach reflects an insistence on the necessity to study language use, a conception of the world as multidimensional and always only partially understood, and Man as a social being in search of meaning with individual minds embedded in a cultural collectivity. Linguistic meaning is conceived as open and dynamic, and constituted in the dialogic process of communication. It is not to be seen as formal and static representations. Concepts like dialogue, intersubjectivity, intentionality, perspective taking, 'attunement to the attunement of the other,' temporarily shared social realities, fixation of perspectives and meaning potentials are all frequently used...The tension between language as a conventionalized system and specific acts of real communication is a recurrent topic.

The socio-cognitive approach serving as a theoretical framework for intercultural pragmatics has its origin in the view presented above by Wold. However, at certain points there are differences. Before turning to them we need to review the development of previous socio-cognitive approaches, which will help us understand the major tenets of SCA being presented here.

1.1. THE SYNTHESIS OF THE POSITIVIST AND SOCIAL CONSTRUCTIVIST VIEWS

The socio-cognitive theory makes a dialectical synthesis of positivism and social constructivism. According to the positivist epistemology, knowledge is about objective facts that can be measured independently of the inquiring, interpreting, and creative mind. As Bernstein (1983:8) argued, "there is some permanent, ahistorical matrix or framework to which we can ultimately appeal in determining the nature of rationality, knowledge, truth, reality, goodness, or rightness." In the positivist paradigm, research focuses on procedural measures rather than interpretive perspectives. It is usually assumed that stored knowledge provides templates for thinking as well as acting (e.g., Alvesson and Kärreman 2001). Meaning is embedded in words and symbols rather than in the mind that perceives them. In contrast to the positivist approach, the social constructivist perspective holds that knowledge and meaning are socially constructed. They are constituted and transferred through practices and activities (e.g., Wittgenstein 1953; Garfinkel 1967; Gherardi 2000, 2001; Brown and Duguid 2001). According to Vygotsky (1978), social reality and meaning only exist as we create them. Social constructivists see language use as socio-cultural construction. They put an emphasis on usage, and value the ways people currently use the language. Instead of looking for one self-professed authority to pronounce correct usage, constructivists would take a consensus of expert users. In sum, positivists consider words and texts as carriers of objectified meaning, while for social constructivists practices (action, doing) play that role. The difference is between words and texts whose meaning lies in the objective things they refer to, versus words and texts whose meaning lies in the practices they are used in. Berger and Luckmann (1966) argued that all knowledge, including the most basic, taken-for-granted commonsense knowledge of everyday reality, is derived from and maintained by social interactions. When people interact, they do so with the understanding that their respective perceptions of reality are related, and as they act upon this understanding their common knowledge of reality becomes reinforced. The socio-constructivists' agenda includes showing that what we deal with as objective, is socially constructed.

The socio-cognitive approach goes one step further than the constructivist approach and argues that to equate practice with knowledge is to ignore the huge amount of preexisting knowledge that both speakers and hearers must have in common for the hearer to infer and categorize the intended meaning of a practice. We need both preexisting knowledge and practice. What is especially important for the SCA, I propose here, are the three types of knowledge that interplay in meaning construction and comprehension: *collective prior knowledge, individual prior knowledge, and actual situationally created knowledge* (Kecskes 2008; 2010a). What is co-constructed in practice contains prior social and material experience of the individual and the given speech community as well as situationally, socially constructed knowledge. Both sides are equally important. Practice can hardly work without the presence of relevant cultural mental models with which people process the observed practice, or which they use to actually create practice. Even when we pass along simple routines by sharing them in practice (e.g., how to make a dish) we rely on the presence of a large amount of preexisting knowledge. Social practices are conventionalized routines. They are about shared/conventional ways of doing social things in talk, such as the way phone calls are closed, or servers take an order in a restaurant.

However, practice does not provide semantic codes for its own decoding (i.e., sense making). The blueprints of those codes must already exist in the mind of the interpreter (Ringberg and Reihlen 2008). Without taking into account that meaning is mediated by people's mental predisposed socio-cultural models, practice-based research is unable to explain creativity, innovation, and the transfer of meaning among interlocutors. The social character of communication and knowledge transfer should not put community-of-practice theory at odds with individualistic approaches to knowledge. After all, social practices pass "through the heads of people, and it is such heads that do the feeling, perceiving, thinking, and the like" (Bunge 1996:303). While communities of practice exist, members of those communities may still interpret shared practices differently. This is a key issue in communication. Collective knowledge exists but it is interpreted, "privatized" (subjectivized) differently by each individual (Kecskes 2008). Collective cultural models are distributed to individuals in a privatized way. In order for members to share the meaning of a particular practice, a huge amount of shared knowledge must already be present to assure common ground. Levinthal & Rerup (2006) argued that practice is similar to sentences in a text. Its grammar or structure is not meaningful apart from the meaning that is assigned by the receiver.

Both the positivists and the social constructivists are aware of the individual and the collective and their interplay. But, while the positivists put more emphasis on the individual, social constructivists focus on the collective. How does all that individuation get integrated and leveled out in the collective? And how is the collective acquired, preserved, and passed on by individuals? The synthesis of the positivist and social constructivist views in a socio-cognitive approach acknowledges the equal importance of both societal and individual factors in meaning creation and comprehension as well as knowledge transfer. Shared cultural models privatized through individuals' private experience and prior practices interact with the actual situational context in social interaction and practices (Kecskes 2008).

1.2. CALL FOR THE REVISION OF THE SOMEWHAT IDEALIZED VIEW OF COMMUNICATION

A call for revision of the idealized view of communication (summarized in the previous chapter) from the socio-cognitive perspective does not imply its denial. If we compare the pragmatic idealized version (originating in the Gricean view) and the cognitive coordination approach (e.g., Barr and Keysar 2005; Keysar and Bly

1995; Giora 2003; Keysar 2007), we can see that the two approaches are not contradictory, but rather complement each other. The ideal abstraction view of communication adopts a top-down approach. It works well for a theoretical construct of pragmatics that warrants successful communication in most cases. In contrast, the cognitive coordination view adopts a bottom-up approach. It provides empirical evidence supporting a possible explanation of miscommunication originated in egocentrism in most cases; it can be applied in general as well. From a dialectical perspective, cooperation and egocentrism are not conflicting, such that the *a priori* mental state supporting intention and common ground versus the *post factum* emergence of intention and common ground may converge to a body of integrated background knowledge for the interlocutors to rely on in pursuit of a relatively smooth communication. However, so far no attempt has been made to combine the two approaches (at least to my knowledge). Therefore, the aim of the socio-cognitive approach proposed here is to eliminate the ostensible conflicts between the two views, and propose an approach that integrates their considerations into a *holistic concept of communication*.

2. Communication in the Socio-cognitive Approach

The socio-cognitive approach (Kecskes 2008, 2010a; 2012; Kecskes and Zhang 2009) emphasizes the complex role of cultural and private mental models, how these are applied categorically and/or reflectively by individuals in response to socio-cultural environmental feedback mechanisms, and how this leads to and explains different meaning outcomes and knowledge transfer. In meaning construction and comprehension, individuals rely both on preexisting encyclopedic knowledge and knowledge created (emergent) in the process of interaction. It is important that we realize that there are social conditions and constraints (contexts) that have some objectivity from the perspective of individuals. Of course, there can always be differences in how individuals process those relatively objective societal factors based on their prior experience. But it would be a mistake to deny the presence of any objectivity in social contexts.

The socio-cognitive approach to pragmatics as a theoretical framework for intercultural pragmatics is based on two important claims. First, speaker and hearer are equal participants in the communicative process. They both produce and comprehend, while relying on their most accessible and salient knowledge as expressed in their private contexts in production and comprehension. They are not different people when they produce language and when they interpret language. They are the same person with the same mindset, knowledge, and skills. However, their goals and functions are different when acting as a speaker and as a hearer. Consequently, only a holistic interpretation of the utterance, both from the perspective of the speaker and the perspective of the hearer, can give us an adequate account of language communication. Interlocutors should be considered as "complete" individuals with various cognitive states, with different commitments, and with possible different interpretations of the same core common-ground information and actual communicative situation—all of which has a profound effect on what the same linguistic structure may mean for any of them. *One of the main differences between current pragmatic theories and SCA is that there is no "impoverished" speaker meaning in SCA. The speaker utterance is a full proposition with pragmatic features reflecting the speaker's intention and preferences and expressing the speaker's commitment and egocentrism (in the cognitive sense). The proposition expressed is "underspecified" only from the hearer's perspective but not from the speaker's perspective.*

Second, communication is a dynamic process, in which individuals are not only constrained by societal conditions but also shape them at the same time. As a consequence, communication is characterized by the interplay of two sets of traits that are inseparable, mutually supportive, and interactive:

Individual traits	Social traits
prior experience	actual situational experience
salience	relevance
egocentrism	cooperation
attention	intention

Intercultural pragmatics is rooted in the socio-cognitive approach (SCA) that combines the intention-based, pragmatic view of cooperation with the cognitive view of egocentrism to incorporate emerging features of communication (Kecskes 2010a, 2012). In this approach, as stated earlier, interlocutors are considered as social beings searching for meaning with individual minds embedded in a socio-cultural collectivity. Individual traits (prior experience → salience → egocentrism → attention) interact with societal traits (actual situational experience emerging features of communication relevance → cooperation → intention). Each trait is the consequence of the other. Prior experience results in salience, which leads to egocentrism that drives attention. Intention is a cooperation-directed practice that is governed by relevance that (partly) depends on actual situational experience. SCA integrates the pragmatic view of cooperation and the cognitive view of egocentrism and emphasizes that both cooperation and egocentrism are manifested in all phases of communication, albeit in varying degree. Communication is the result of the interplay of intention and attention motivated by socio-cultural background that is privatized individually by interlocutors. The socio-cultural background is composed of environment (actual situational context in which the communication occurs), the encyclopedic knowledge of interlocutors deriving from their "prior experience," tied to the linguistic expressions they use, and their "current experience," in which those expressions create and convey meaning. In communication we show our two sides. We cooperate by generating and formulating intention that is relevant to the given actual situational context. At the same time, our egocentrism means that we activate the most salient information to our attention in the construction (speaker) and comprehension (hearer) of utterances.

A crucial element of SCA is *privatalization (making something private, subjectivizing something)*, a process through which the individual blends his prior experience with the actual situational (current) experience, and makes an individual understanding of collective experience. The following example from the film *Angel Eyes* illustrates this process. Mother and son are talking while the mother is examining the groceries the son brought. She knows that the son had a fight with a man that morning.

(1)

SON:	I met someone today.
MOTHER:	Good. Oh, you got the broccolini? Thank you.
SON:	She is a woman.
MOTHER:	You did not have to tackle her too, did you?
SON:	She is a police officer.
MOTHER:	Are you in trouble?
SON:	I don't think so.

The utterance "I met someone today" sets the scene; it partly creates the actual situational context. The son wants to talk about his current experience. However, the mother's attention focuses on the groceries. She starts to get interested when the son says that the person he met was a woman. However, even then she does not pay full attention, but rather jokes about a previous event the son talked about. When the mother finds out that the woman her son met was a police officer, the son gets her full attention. She wants to know if he was in trouble. They have a different understanding of "police officer," which usually has a highly conventionalized negative context attached to it (collective salience). The actual situational context cannot override this stigmatism for the mother, as her question "are you in trouble?" demonstrates. However, her son's public context (collective salience) is changed (privatized) as a consequence of his positive experience with a police officer. As a result of this private experience, the term "police officer" loses its negative connotation for the son.

Privatalization is the process through which the interlocutor "individualizes" the collective. This process is prompted by the actual situational context, and results in a dynamic process of meaning construction in which nothing is static. The two sides (prior and current) constantly change and affect each other. Meaning construction relies both on relatively definable cultural models and norms as well as situationally evolving features. Prior experience is represented in relatively definable cultural models and norms that are related to and/or blended with actual situational experience. This approach is supported by the Durkheimian thought mentioned in the "Introduction" (Durkheim 1982), according to which cultural norms and models gain individual interpretation in concrete social actions and events.

Before describing the main tenets of SCA, we have to make a clear distinction between the socio-cognitive approach I am proposing here and van Dijk's understanding of the socio-cognitive view in language use. In van Dijk's (2008:X) theory, it is not the social situation that influences (or is influenced by) discourse, but the way the participants define the situation. He goes further to claim that "contexts are not some kind of objective conditions or direct cause, but rather (inter) subjective constructs designed and ongoingly updated in interaction by participants as members of groups and communities (van Dijk 2008:X)." SCA adopts a more dialectical perspective by considering communication a dynamic process in which individuals are not only constrained by societal conditions but also shape them at the same time. Speakers and hearers are equal participants of the communicative process. They both produce and comprehend speech relying on their most accessible and salient knowledge expressed in production and comprehension. As I said earlier, when referring to Leibniz, it is very important that we realize there are social conditions and constraints (contexts) which have some objectivity from the perspective of individuals. Of course, there can always be slight differences in how individuals process those relatively objective societal factors based on their prior experience. In intercultural pragmatics, blending is considered the main driving force of intercultural interactions, which is more than just a process of co-constructing. It is combining the interlocutors' prior experience with the actual situational experience, which creates a blend that is more than just a merger. In blending, the constituent parts are both distinguishable and indistinguishable from one another when needed. Blending incorporates the dynamic interplay of crossing (parts are distinguishable) and merging (parts are indistinguishable). Depending on the dynamic moves in the communicative process, either crossing or merging becomes dominant to some extent. Blending will be discussed further in the next chapters.

3. The Interplay of Intention and Attention in SCA

In the SCA the interplay of the cooperation-directed intention and the egocentrism-governed attention is the main driving force in meaning production and comprehension. Cooperation means that attention is paid to others' intention. Successful communication requires communicators to recognize that others' perspectives may differ from their own and that others may not always know what they mean (Keysar and Henly 2002). SCA posits a dialectical relationship between intention and attention. As previously argued, the pragmatic view and the cognitive view are concerned about intention and attention in an isolated way. There is no explicit explanation of the relations between the two. Relevance Theory defines relevance by effects of both attention and intention, but does not distinguish the two effects and never clarifies their relations explicitly, as revealed by their claim that "an input (a sight, a sound, an utterance, a memory) is relevant to an individual when it connects with background information he has available to yield conclusions that matter to him" (Sperber and Wilson 2004:3).

3.1. INTENTION

With regard to intention, the socio-cognitive view on the one hand incorporates the Searlean understanding of the term (Searle 1983), and on the other, it extends the notion to emphasize the dynamism of intention and its emergent nature. SCA not only considers the centrality of intention in conversation, just as the cognitive-philosophical approach has done, but also takes into account the dynamic process in which the intention can be an emergent effect of the conversation. In SCA, intention is considered a dynamically changing phenomenon that is the main organizing force with attention in the communicative process. Intention is not only private, individual, preplanned, and a precursor to action; it is also emergent and social. Here, it should be underlined that we are not talking about a dichotomy: rather, *a priori intention* and *emergent intention* are two sides of the same phenomenon that may receive different emphasis at different points in the communicative process. When a conversation is started, the private and preplanned nature of intention may be dominant. However, in the course of conversation the emergent and social nature of the phenomenon may come to the fore. These two sides of intention are always present; the question is only *to what extent* they are present at any given moment of the communicative process. This view does not contradict Searle's claim that intentionality is directedness; intending to do something is just one kind of intentionality among others (Searle 1983:3); it is also in line with Joas's claim that intentionality consists in a self-reflective control that we exercise over our current behavior (Joas 1996:158).

The basic property that renders intention a central element of communication is its functionality (see in Kecskes and Zhang 2009). There is always a reason and/or a goal behind a conversation; without intention, there would be no need to initiate communication, and we could hardly make any sense of this social action. Searle (1983; 2007) considered intention, along with other mental acts such as perception, desire, and belief, as prerequisites to communication.

Communication is a process in which intention is formed, expressed, and interpreted. From the speaker's perspective, intention is something that s/he bears in mind prior to the utterance; alternatively, it is generated in the course of conversation and expressed in the form of utterances. From the hearer's or analyst's perspective, intention is something that is processed by the hearer simultaneously with the utterance, or after it has been completed. The primary intention expressed in a particular situation serves the function of guiding the conversation. Knowledge or information explicated in linguistic forms, implied connotation, along with inferable background, all unite to achieve comprehension and communication under the driving force of intention.

However, this is just one side of intention. The emergent side is co-constructed by the participants in the dynamic flow of conversation. This means that intention is not necessarily an a priori phenomenon; it can also be generated and changed during the communicative process. This dynamism is reflected in emerging utterances: they may be interrupted and started again. It is not only the context, but also the dynamism of the conversational flow and the process of formulating an utterance that likewise affect and change the intention. Emergent intention was demonstrated and explained in Chapter 1 in examples (1) and (2), where it was also mentioned that emergent intention is very common in intercultural interaction. In the following excerpts between an African French and a Korean speaker the interlocutors appear to jump from one topic to another, seemingly changing their intention and interrupting the flow of communication. However, a closer look shows that communicators think along topic-comment lines, and co-create a coherent narrative in which emergent intention plays an important role. The topic-comment lines are as follows: living in Albany—likes/dislikes—likes: quiet, nice neighbors—dislikes: offices and forms.

(2)

> K: I like living in Albany. Because the Albany is the...especially I [word] almost two months...it's quiet...nice people...neighbor...
>
> AF: Yeah you have nice neighbors.
>
> K: Yeah, yeah.
>
> AF: The manager in the apartment is good?
>
> K: Yeah good.
>
> AF: ah...so you have good neighbors...it's quiet...good...so everybody has difficulties where they live so since you came from Korea what kind of difficulties you...what are the problems that you have to live in Albany?
>
> K: Ah I came...when I came here...the first time about...I applied the driver's license and you go to there
>
> AF: Yeah.
>
> K: DMV...yeah yeah...driver station
>
> AF: Yeah.
>
> K: And then they require so many documents
>
> AF: I see.
>
> K: So I had to go another office.
>
> AF: To apply to school.
>
> K: Yeah social number or...officer...anybody...anyway I had to go there and then...receive the document I gave them...so long time I ...take a long time

3.2. ATTENTION

Attention refers to those cognitive resources available to interlocutors that make communication a conscious action (see in Kecskes and Zhang 2009). When intention is formed, expressed, and interpreted in the process of communication, attention contributes to the various stages of the process with different strength. Three factors will affect salience of knowledge and ease of attentional processing in all stages: (a) interlocutors' knowledge based on prior experience; (b) frequency, familiarity, or conventionality of knowledge tied to the situation; and (c) the interlocutors' mental state and/or the availability of attentional resources. Based on these three factors, the knowledge most salient to the interlocutors in a particular situation is the information that is included in their knowledge base, is pertinent to the current situation, and is processed by the necessary attentional resources. No matter what mental state the interlocutors are in, and at which stage of the communication they are operating, the most salient knowledge will be available as a result of the interplay of these three factors.

All stages in the communicative process require the commitment of attention in order for successful communication to occur. As stated above, cognitive research (e.g., Giora 2003; Barr and Keysar 2005; Colston and Katz 2005) has documented the interlocutors' egocentric behavior in the process of communication. However, as explained in the previous chapter, "egocentrism" is not a negative term in intercultural pragmatics. It refers to the state of mind of the interlocutor, who can hardly control this phenomenon because it is the result of the individual's prior experience. *Egocentrism means that interlocutors act under the influence of the most salient information that comes to their mind in the given actual situational context both in production and comprehension.* Consequently, the speaker will use the linguistic resources (e.g., the lexical units) that s/he thinks are most salient for expressing his/her communicative intentions and/or goals; similarly, the hearer will cooperate by capturing those salient units and assigning them a proper place in the communicational process. Because of their different knowledge bases, the frequency/rituality of their knowledge in the situation, and the attendant attentional resources available to them for processing the salient items, the interlocutors' knowledge has different levels of salience. As a result, they conduct the attentional processing of communication in an egocentric manner.

There are specific ways in which attention contributes to different stages of communication as characterized by the processes of intention. When intention is formed, attention plays a crucial role. Consider the following (construed) example:

(3) Sally is speaking to Bill.
SALLY: Don't move! There is a snake over there!

Without Sally noticing the existence of a snake nearby, her intention of warning Bill wouldn't come into being. When expressing intention in an utterance, the speaker also needs the necessary attention, so as to formulate the utterance in a comprehensible way. The frequency or familiarity of the intention and especially of the linguistic expression in question determines the extent of attentional processing. Greetings require less attentional resources and appear more automatic than doing snake warnings, the latter being less frequent and also harder to process. When intention is interpreted by the hearer, the amount of attentional resources needed is similarly proportional to the resources required in the formulation of intention. The person being greeted can easily comprehend the speaker's intention and respond to it in an effortless way. However, in example (3), Bill, when warned of the snake, may need to undertake some effort in order to read the intention and deploy the relevant reaction. Intention directs attention to relevant information resources so that the intention can be realized, and communication be conducted in a coherent and comprehensible way. By selecting those resources, intention becomes central to the processing of communication.

The socio-cultural background has an overall influence on the interplay of intention and attention (Kecskes and Zhang 2009). The interlocutors' prior knowledge directs their attention to becoming aware of different features, or different parts, of the same phenomenon. For example, an architect, an engineer, and a janitor may form different views when looking at the same building. Also as a consequence of this, different intentions may be formed, and the effect of interplay is also affected by the accessibility of the knowledge. As a result, *communication is achieved with intentional action guaranteed by attentional processing; both are motivated by the common socio-cultural background (environment).* In this process, interlocutors are both cooperative (in terms of intention) and egocentric (in terms of attention). The part of knowledge that is relevant to intention, salient to attention, and available in the socio-cultural background will contribute to successful communication.

4. Focus Both on the Speaker and the Hearer

The speaker-hearer perspective of the socio-cognitive approach requires a revision of the recipient design and intention recognition views espoused by current pragmatics theories. In SCA, the *speaker's utterance* is the result of a commitment that is a private reaction to a communicative situation, as it is expressed in lexical items that are affected by the mechanism of salience and speaker intention. This view is different from *explicature*, the latter being a proposition explicitly expressed by the speaker (cf. Sperber and Wilson 1986; Carston 2002; 2004). Explicature is distinguished from "what is said," in that it involves a considerable component of pragmatically derived meaning, which is added to linguistically encoded meaning. In SCA, the *speaker's utterance* is more than that. It is a full proposition with pragmatic features added by the speaker.

According to Carston (2004), the derivation of an explicature may require "free" enrichment, that is, the incorporation of conceptual material that is wholly pragmatically inferred, on the basis of considerations of rational communicative behavior. In SCA, this enrichment of the uttered sentence is the result of the speaker's private and subjective treatment of the utterance in an actual situational context. How the hearer will infer this speaker-subjectivized/privatized commitment is another issue. Consider the following example:

(4) Chris's friend Peter arrived by plane and Chris met him at the airport.
CHRIS: Are you hungry?

PETER: I had something to eat on the plane. I am OK.
CHRIS: All right. Let's go to a Wendy's.

In this conversation, Peter's utterance, "I had something to eat on the plane" can be interpreted by the hearer in three different ways: kind of hungry, not hungry, and don't really know. However, his adding, "I am OK," points to implying "not hungry." Chris either misses this interpretation or thinks that his friend needs encouragement. Or, maybe, he is hungry himself. In any case, his suggestion to go to a Wendy's does not quite match Peter's intention.

While admitting that an *explicature* is defined as committed and endorsed by the speaker, SCA stresses that the enriched proposition is actually owned by the *speaker*. It is not something recovered by the *hearer* as a result of the latter's inference, as it is the case in the Relevance Theory. The *speaker's utterance* is the speaker's product, his private reaction to an actual communicative situation, and it is based on the speaker's prior and emergent knowledge and intention. In current pragmatic theories, the main issue is to figure out how the hearer recognizes and recovers what the speaker said. Less attention is paid to the question of *why exactly the speaker said what s/he said in the way s/he said it.* SCA differs from current theoretical approaches in its attempt to give equal attention to speaker production and hearer interpretation. In SCA, *speaker's utterance is a full proposition constructed by the speaker; in contrast, explicature is a full proposition of the hearer's reconstruction.* Speaker's utterance is underdetermined from the hearer's perspective. There is nothing like underdetermined speaker's utterance from the speaker's perspective unless the speaker deliberately wants to leave the utterance open for interpretation. *Speaker's utterance makes the context, the hearer's interpretation is made by the context.*

In the Gricean paradigm, speakers are committed to offer linguistic forms, while the rest is left to the hearers: what is said is an inference trigger. The neo-Griceans have gone further, by saying that speaker's commitment includes not only the truth-value in the Gricean sense but also some automatic pragmatic enrichment. Thus, *what is said* is revised from being limited to sentence meaning to comprise utterance meaning. Since the neo-Griceans' main concern is *speaker's meaning*, the familiar divide between speaker's meaning and utterance interpretation is still in existence, and intention is restricted to the hearer's recovering process. In SCA, *speaker's utterance* is a full proposition in its own right, operating with speaker-centered pragmatic enhancement and speaker's intention in order to satisfy primarily the speaker's agenda (See example 4). The full proposition the speaker puts out in this scenario will not necessarily mean the same as that which is recovered by the hearer. Interlocutors have different privatized background knowledge and experience, they may perceive the actual situational contexts differently, use lexical items in different sense, and in general, differ greatly as to what is salient for them and to what extent. So the speaker's production is not only recipient design. It is more than that. *Speaker's utterance also contains the speaker's pragmatic considerations that constitute "the puzzle" that hearer's interpretation focuses on.* What is recovered by the hearer cannot replace what the speaker produces on his/her own. This is especially important in intercultural communication where the knowledge of the interlocutors about each other's background and common ground is usually very restricted. Within a community, a workplace, a relationship…recipient design is done and usually succeeds because both parties have shared knowledge and experience. And speakers and hearers do the same things when they are culturally and linguistically not that different, but in intercultural communication those things don't necessarily work the same way because the parties don't have the shared knowledge and experience they generally presume of the other. So there is a process for composing and interpreting utterances that does work on home turf despite there being psychological and other differences between the parties. However, those things work differently when there are significant cultural and linguistic differences between international interlocutors.

The Relevance Theory concept of *"explicature,"* as we have seen, includes not only the truth-conditional semantic meaning, but also some contextual pragmatic enrichment. There have been attempts to enlarge the pragmatic scope of explicature toward "full propositions" (e.g., Carston 2002a; Burton-Roberts 2005; Jaszczolt 2005), but the RT approach remains hearer-oriented. Explicature is something that is recovered by the hearer, and as such it is not necessarily equal to what the speaker has explicated. In fact, in the hearer's perspective of RT, what the hearer can recover by automatic and default pragmatic inference is what the speaker was supposed to have explicitly offered; any additional inference goes to implicatures. In SCA, on the other hand, *speaker's utterance* is a "pragmatized" full proposition that involves speaker intention, personal attitude, and privatized actual contextual elements. This approach shares some features with what Jaszczolt has called *"merger representation"* (Jaszczolt 2005); her notion of representation is comprehensive and integrative. But unlike Jaszczolt's proposal, the scope of speaker's utterance in SCA is wider because it contains not only the automatic pragmatic inference part recovered by the hearer, but also the part new to the hearer, which comes from the speaker's private knowledge and privatized actual situational context. The main concern of SCA is how the speaker's public knowledge (collective knowledge) and private knowledge are integrated into a speaker's utterance.

Kecskes (2008) made a distinction between private context and actual situational context (see details in Chapter 6). Private contexts develop through individuals' situational experience. Some of these experiences get tied to lexical items in the minds of speakers of a particular speech community. These private contexts incorporate core knowledge (tied to prior experience), which is the public part of the private context, and individual-specific knowledge that may not be shared by other members of the speech community, because it is the individualized reflection of prior socio-cultural contexts. The public context, that is to say, the public part of the private context, however, is available to each speaker of that speech community because it refers to relatively similar, conventionalized conceptual content. We saw an example of this in (1) above. Consider another example from intercultural communication where the conceptual public load attached to a lexical item may be entirely different for speakers with different L1 background.

> (5) A Chinese and an American student are talking:
> XIAOJING: Did you read the paper of Norton on social identity?
> SARAH: Yes, I did.
> XIAOJING: Do you know in what *magazine* it was published?
> SARAH: Magazine? Do you mean journal?
> XIAOJING: Oh, yes.
> SARAH: It was in TESOL Quarterly.

For some reason Chinese students very often use the word "magazine" when refer-ring to an academic journal. That word, however, means an entirely different thing for an American. The public knowledge associated with that word in Chinese English and American English differs to a great extent. The mismatch between the two may result in misunderstanding.

5. Salience as Guiding Mechanism in SCA

Since salience plays a crucial role in SCA, I will briefly introduce it here, although there will be an entire chapter (Chapter 8) on it later. As a semiotic notion, salience refers to the relative importance or prominence of signs. The relative salience of a particular sign when considered in the context of others helps an individual to quickly rank large amounts of information by importance and thus give attention to that which is the most vital. In SCA, prior experience results in salience, which leads to egocentrism, which in turn drives attention. This has a profound impact on intercultural communi-cation because communality and conventions within a speech community create what I call "collective salience" (see Chapter 8 on salience) that is almost nonexistent for interlocutors (with the exception of universal elements) who speak different L1s and represent different cultures. One of the main things that should be consolidated in the process of intercultural communication is the wide difference in saliency of lexical items in the lingua franca and interpretation of actual situational context.

SCA differs from previous and current approaches to salience in three features:

A) It emphasizes that since interlocutors both produce and interpret lan-guage, their linguistic behavior is affected by salience both in production and comprehension.
B) It is not just linguistic salience that affects production and interpretation but also perceptual salience. In fact, the interplay of linguistic salience and perceptual salience is what influences both processes.
C) Salience is language and culture specific. Since it is about the dominance of signs, entities, and phenomena in relation to other signs, entities, and

phenomena, much depends on what experience and encounters, in what environment, and through which language an individual has had with those signs, entities and phenomena. These three features will be discussed in detail in Chapter 8.

5.1. SALIENCE IN INTERCULTURAL INTERACTIONS

The following conversation between a Korean student and an American student demonstrates very well what an important role salience plays in intercultural interaction. Both students study linguistics and are required to write an essay. (this example can also be found in Kecskes 2010a).

(6)

> KOREAN: Jill, do you want me to help you with your essay?
> AMERICAN: Don't patronize me, please.
> KOREAN: You say, you don't want support?
> AMERICAN: Please just don't...Okay?

Although both speakers work with lexical units from the same language, their private meaning construction system may give different interpretations to the same items. Differences can be significant, depending on the speakers' prior experience (frequency, familiarity, motivation, etc.) with the same words, expressions, and utterances. This is especially so in intercultural communication where, because of cultural differences, not only can the speakers' private contexts differ significantly but also their collective salience (public contexts) tied to the same lexical item.

    There is a difference in how the American student uses the word "patronize" and how the South Korean student understands it. The main sense of "patronize" in American English can be described as follows: [to act as a patron to someone or something]. This is the sense both interlocutors are supposed to have because in conversation, it is usually the coresense of a lexical unit that constitutes the minimum set of features that we can assume to be shared by interlocutors. However, especially in intercultural communication, when interlocutors represent different languages and cultures the same word may have different culture-specific conceptual property for a native speaker and a nonnative speaker. This is what may have happened in example (6). In American culture the word "patronize" usually has quite a negative culture-specific conceptual property if the subject of the verb is animate referring to a person or persons ("patronize someone"). In South Korean culture the closest equivalent of the English word "patronize" is "huwonhada," which has a positive culture-specific conceptual property attached to it. For Koreans, if they are patronized, it means that they receive a favor. This positive cultural load from Korean may be transferred to the English word when used by a Korean speaker. This may be the reason why the South Korean student does not seem to have understood the negative attitude of the American speaker.

5.2. RECIPIENT DESIGN AND SALIENCE

In the previous chapter we characterized current pragmatics theories as recipient design from the perspective of the speaker and intention recognition from the perspective of the hearer. According to the socio-cognitive approach, recipient design is paired with salience in language production. Recipient design is the result of cooperation while salience is the driving force behind egocentrism. In order to succeed in recipient design, speakers must correctly express intended illocutionary acts by using appropriate words, and make their attempt in an adequate context. Speakers relate propositional contents to the world (actual situational context; audience) with the intention of establishing a correspondence between words and things from a certain direction of fit. While fitting words into actual situational contexts, speakers are driven by not only the intent that the hearer recognizes what is meant as intended by the speaker (social), but also by salience that affects production subconsciously (individual egocentrism). The following conversation from the movie *Angel Eyes* demonstrates how salience can affect the process of word selection.

(7)

> Situation: A policewoman in uniform is driving the car, and the man sitting beside her is staring at her.
>
> PW: What.. ?
>
> M: I was trying to picture you *without your clothes on*.
>
> PW: Excuse me?
>
> M: Oh no, I did not mean like that. I am trying to picture you *without your uniform*.
>
> PW: Okaay?
>
> M: I mean, on your day off, you know, *in regular clothes*.

The man makes three attempts to find the appropriate description of why he was looking at the policewoman the way he did. There is a strong effect of perceptual salience on the selection of words (linguistic salience). As a result, the man has difficulties finding the acceptable words. There is an intuitive possibility of a distinction between what a speaker says and what s/he actually implicates. Salience (motivated by prior experience), or what is on our mind (Giora 2003), which operates subconsciously and automatically, may affect word selection and utterance formation. So on the one hand we have the speaker with an intention to tell the woman why he was looking at her the way he did, and on the other hand there is the subconscious salience that affected how he formulated his intention.

I could compare this phenomenon to what has been happening nowadays with language use in general. People may get into trouble because what is on their mind subconsciously may result in selecting semantically too powerful, socio-culturally loaded words, expressions, or utterances that create their own context, and the actual situational context cannot cancel them. Mitt Romney's case during the 2012 presidential elections can demonstrate this issue very well. While speaking to a group of investors during his presidential campaign, Romney uttered the following sentence: "I am not concerned about the very poor." In that actual situation context he wanted to say that the poor are usually taken care of in the US because there are a great variety of programs helping them. However, the utterance was so powerful semantically with a strong socio-cultural load that it made its own context. What happened was that prior context, or collective salience, overrode the effect of actual situational context. The wording of the utterance reflected what was on Romney's mind subconsciously while he was talking to the investors.

6. Intercultural Communication is not a Deviation from Intracultural Communication

The socio-cognitive approach with its principles and tenets helps to identify inter-cultural communication as just as normal as intracultural communication but different in certain features, emphases, and strategies as discussed earlier. This is especially important to note because intercultural communication as a field of inquiry was basically constituted as an analysis of misunderstandings (e.g., ten Thije 2003; Gumperz 1982; Gudykunst and Kim 1992). What is unfortunate is that when misunderstanding occurs in intercultural interactions, people usually start to search cultural differences for a cause without considering other factors. Recently, however, the focus of attention in the field of intercultural communication has shifted to beyond misunderstanding (Clyne 1994; Koole and ten Thije 2001; ten Thije 2003). Several studies have attempted to answer the question of how people with different cultural and linguistic backgrounds act and react in intercultural discourse, how common-ground or intercultural understanding is established, and what new discourse structures result from intercultural communication. The following conversation between a Korean student and Thai student illustrates well how common ground is developed and what strategies interlocutors use.
(8)

- So what did you have...what did you eat in that American restaurant?
- I have salad.
-Salad.
-Yeah.
-Yeah...was it good? Which do you prefer like a rice...I mean the Thai or Chinese restaurant or...American restaurant?
-I have a lot of rice and soup.
-Same here (laughing).
-I eat American I feel so exhausted.
-Right...even for me after eating pizza I really want to have rice.
-Yeah.

-Really? I'm really happy we have the same opinion about that...and...so
  you like rice the most.
-Yeah.

The two nonnative speakers had a smooth conversation without misunderstand-ings, although there were a couple of places where there was the possibility of mis-interpretation. Such was when the Korean started with, "Which do you prefer like a rice..." and continued with "I mean the Thai or Chinese restaurant or...American restaurant?". The Thai student let the second question go and answered the first one about what food she likes to eat. Another potential for misunderstanding was when the Thai student said, "I eat American I feel so exhausted." Although she used the word "exhausted," the Korean understood perfectly what the Thai had referred to. If the conversation partner had been a native speaker of English, that choice of word may have led to some confusion, but not here.

The issue of success and misunderstanding will be discussed and analyzed in the upcoming chapters from different perspectives. Now, however, we should turn to an issue that is quite neglected in several branches of pragmatics, with the excep-tion of interlanguage pragmatics: the question of pragmatic competence that will help us understand why interlocutors in intercultural interactions behave the way they do.

3

Pragmatic Competence

1. What is Pragmatic Competence?

It was argued in the introduction that the analysis and research of pragmatic competence is not a primary goal of intercultural pragmatics because it is mainly a developmental issue and intercultural pragmatics primarily focuses on language use. However, it would be a mistake to avoid discussing it, since pragmatic competence of nonnative interactants plays a significant role in second and foreign language use and intercultural communication. It is important for us to understand the complexity of this side of language knowledge if we want to be able to analyze the language use of participants in intercultural communication. However, it should be emphasized that the description of pragmatic competence in this book has a relatively limited scope. It focuses mainly on discussing how the developing new language, with its own emerging socio-cultural foundation, affects the existing L1-governed knowledge and pragmatic competence of adult sequential bi- and multilinguals that operates language use. It is assumed that these bi- and multilinguals already have an L1-governed pragmatic competence in place, which will be adjusted to accommodate the socio-cultural requirements of the new language(s).

I am not in favor of the kind of complex competence taxonomies that talk about different elements of pragmatic competence or communicative competence and separate it from intercultural communicative competence (e.g., Byram 1997; Wiseman 2003). The reason I do not support the distinction between pragmatic competence and intercultural communicative competence is that it is almost impossible to draw a dividing line between them. In intercultural communication the existing L1-based pragmatic competence of interlocutors is adjusted as required by the actual situational context and allowed by the preferences of the individual speaker/hearer. This adjustment usually is only temporary and does not have a significant effect on the existing pragmatic competence of language users. Of course, the more a person is engaged in intercultural encounters, the more likely it is that his/her pragmatic competence will change more significantly.

There is no doubt about the fact that besides grammatical competence there exists pragmatic competence attached to the L1, which keeps being modified with the exposure and/or addition of other languages and cultures. Because of the monolingual focus, pragmatic competence has never been a primary item in the agenda of linguistic/philosophical pragmatics or in other subfields of pragmatics, with the exception of interlanguage pragmatics. This lack of attention may also be explained by the fact that linguistics proper has never really focused on pragmatics competence. Chomsky (1978:224) introduced a distinction between "grammatical competence," which is related to form and meaning, and "pragmatic competence," which involves "knowledge of conditions and manner of appropriate use, in conformity with various purposes." Appropriateness of use is expressed in terms of the relations between intentions and purposes and between linguistic means, of certain forms and meanings, within linguistic institutional settings (Kasher 1991). Chomsky, however, did not take any interest in this pragmatic competence and considered the separation of linguistic competence from pragmatic competence to be indispensable, for practical reasons, for the ability to explore and discover the pure, formal properties of the genetically preprogrammed linguistic system.

As far as the second/foreign language user is concerned researchers focusing on L2 pragmatics have had to pay attention to the different nature of grammatical competence and pragmatic competence. Grammatical competence is about correctness, while pragmatic competence is more about appropriateness. Grammar contains facts and rules about the given language system that must be followed (at least loosely), otherwise the language is unrecognizable. This is something that can systematically be acquired by the language learner. Pragmatic rules (language use rules), however, are different: not following them may cause misinterpretation of linguistic behavior. If grammar is bad, the utterance may not convey the right message or any message while if pragmatics is bad, the utterance will usually convey the wrong message. Yorio's (1980) example of a North American shop-attendant's saying "What can I do for you?" versus "What do you want?"—the former being a routine formula while the latter is a grammatically and semantically accurate question—highlights how the latter could be inappropriate and even impolite at the pragmatic and sociolinguistic levels due to the preferences of the situational context or speech community. Rules of language use are like suggestions, recommendations by the members of a speech community, which are based on norms, conventions, and standards. So the language user has more leverage here. It is common knowledge that people can learn second/foreign languages studying/developing mainly grammatical competence only, and being able to put together correct sentences of that language. Of course, that language use may sound unnatural and somewhat inefficient in conveying information, but it is still a recognizable version of the use of that language, as example (1) demonstrates:

(1) Sign in a Hotel in Zurich:

Because of the impropriety of entertaining guests of opposite sex in the bedroom, it is suggested that the lobby be used for this purpose. (Source: The Octopus. (October, 1995)

Pragmatic competence in the L1 is the result of language socialization. Language and social development in the L1 go hand in hand, and are inseparable. However, this is not the case in L2 or subsequent languages, as we will see later. The sociopragmatic norms concerning appropriateness developed through L1 are very influential and difficult to change. L2 learners see things in L2 through their L1 socio-cultural mindset. Thomas (1983) indicated that if we try to force nonnative speakers (NNS) to conform to a native speaker (NS) norm, it would be nearly the same as NS's ideological control over NNSs or cultural imposition on NNSs by NSs' socially hegemonic strata. Some recent studies have pointed out that NNSs may have some kind of resistance toward the use of NS norms and speech conventions to maintain their own identity, and so they may commit pragmatic negative transfer "on purpose" (e.g., Al-Issa 2003; Fujiwara 2004; Siegal 1996). Siegal (1996) discussed the case of a Western female learner of Japanese who felt affective resistance to a Japanese norm because Japanese female language appeared too humble to her. According to Siegal (1996), these findings mean real difficulty for researchers because frequently it is impossible to establish whether some inappropriate or misleading language use results from the NNS affective resistance to the NS practice or whether it is just a lack of native-like pragmatic competence.

Willingness, motivation, and ability of individual learners to assume L2 socio-cultural beliefs and norms seem to play a decisive role in multilingual development and language use. Consequently, an advanced nonnative speaker cannot be expected "simply to abandon his/her own cultural world" (Barro et al. 1993:56). Adamson (1988) pointed out that nonnative speakers are often reluctant to accept and share the values, beliefs, and presuppositions of an L2 community even if they have been living there for a long period of time and can speak the language quite well. The influence of L1 cultural expectations on communication patterns is so strong that even if the conceptual socialization process in L2 is very advanced and the individual has high proficiency and excellent skills in the L2, her/his interaction with Westerners can be severely blocked by the limits imposed by cultural factors. According to Lu (2001), the influence of the traditional Chinese culture is so far-reaching and persistent that even second- or third-generation Americans of Chinese descendants are unable to fully ignore it, even though their English proficiency is on a par with that of native English speakers. Many of these people do not speak Chinese any longer and totally depend on English as the tool of thinking and communication. "Nevertheless, their speech acts are still in the shadow of culturally governed modes of thinking, talking and behaving" (Lu 2001:216).

Based on the research reviewed above I argue that while developing L1 pragmatic competence socialization and language development are inseparable and decisive. However, in L2 it is not exposure and social interaction but individual willingness, motivation and acceptance that play the primary role in pragmatic development.

2. Pragmatic Competence in a Second Language

Pragmatic competence in L2 research is usually defined as the ability to produce and comprehend utterances (discourse) that is adequate to the L2 socio-cultural context in which interaction takes place (e.g., Rose and Kasper 2001; Thomas 1983). According to Barron (2003), who has researched study abroad programs in L2, "[P]ragmatic competence...is understood as the knowledge of the linguistic resources available in a given language for realising particular illocutions, knowledge of the sequential aspects of speech acts, and finally, knowledge of the appropriate contextual use of the particular language's linguistic resources."

As discussed in the "Introduction," speech communities differ in their assessment of speakers' and hearers' social distance and social power, their rights and obligations, and the degree of imposition involved in particular communicative acts (e.g., Rose and Kasper 2001). Bi- and multilingual speakers must be aware of the consequences of making pragmatic choices. Bialystok (1993:54) argued that bilingual "adults make pragmatic errors, not only because they do not understand forms and structures, or because they do not have sufficient vocabulary to express their intentions, but because they choose incorrectly." Although Bialystok identifies the cause of "incorrect choices" in adult learners' lacking ability to control attentional resources, another explanation may be that learners' sociopragmatic knowledge is not yet developed enough for them to make contextually appropriate choices of strategies and linguistic forms.

The interplay of pragmalinguistic resources for conveying communicative acts and sociopragmatic factors assuring social appropriateness of communicative behavior is especially important in intercultural communication where the participants have usually had more access to pragmalinguistics than to sociopragmatics, especially if they have acquired the target language in the classroom. This presupposes that L2 learners usually have higher pragmalinguistic skills than sociopragmatic skills. How pragmatic competence correlates with language proficiency is not yet known. However, it is a fact that while native speakers of a language are privileged by access to a range of linguistic devices from which they can draw, nonnative speakers are less so. The few studies that focused on the effect of L2 proficiency on pragmatic competence development have often presented different findings (Bardovi-Harlig 1999; Maeshiba, Yoshinaga, Kasper and Ross 1996). Language proficiency is, of course, a crucial factor, but not the only factor. It has been argued that learners of high grammatical proficiency will not necessarily show concomitant pragmatic skills. Bardovi-Harlig (1996) observed that the range of success among students with a high level of grammatical proficiency is quite wide. In a later study, Bardovi-Harlig (1999) argued that grammatical competence and pragmatic competence are independent of one another, though a lack of grammatical competence in a particular area may cause a particular utterance to be less effective. According to another view (e.g., Barron 2003), grammatical competence is the prerequisite of pragmatic competence, but Barron argued that these two aspects are interrelated, and the way they correlate with each other is not linear, but rather complex. More research is needed to investigate this complicated issue because the impact of low-level pragmatic competence of nonnative speakers may lead to serious consequences, especially in native speaker–nonnative speaker communication. Platt (1989) pointed out that when somebody speaks very little of the target language, s/he is usually considered to be an "outsider," so pragmatic mistakes do not generate any problem. However, when a nonnative speaker speaks English very well, native speakers tend to consider the person to be part of the speech community and interpret his/her behavior according to the socio-cultural rules of that community. So the tendency is to consider a misformulated utterance to have been deliberate rather than just an error. In lingua franca communication this issue is even more complex, as we will see later.

3. How does Pragmatic Competence of Bi- and Multilinguals Develop and Change?

The development of pragmatic competence is basically a part of language socialization in L1, L2, and Lx. Pragmatic skills develop through socialization in the given speech community. Linguistic and socio-cultural knowledge are constructed through each other. This interplay between language acquisition and socialization has been described by Ochs (1996:407) as follows: "the acquisition of language and the acquisition of social and cultural competence are not developmentally independent processes, nor is one process a developmental prerequisite of the other. Rather, the two processes are intertwined from the moment a human being enters society." Leung (2001:2) emphasized that language socialization basically deals with how novices "become competent members of their community by taking on the appropriate beliefs, feelings and behaviors, and the role of language in this process."

It was an important move in the development of the theory of language socialization when Ochs (1988) emphasized the role of activity in the process.

Linguistic knowledge <----------------➤Activity<------------------➤ Socio-cultural knowledge

This model of language socialization, where activity and knowledge construction are intertwined, underlines that interlocutors in verbal activities/practices draw on linguistic and socio-cultural knowledge to create and define what is taking place. On the other hand, these verbal activities and practices provide the means through which aspects of linguistic and social knowledge are developed (Ochs 1988).

Some studies (e.g., Blum-Kulka 1997; Li 2008) speak about pragmatic socialization defined by Blum-Kulka (1997:3) as "the ways in which children are socialized to use language in socially and culturally appropriate ways." Research that is done within the framework of pragmatic socialization reflects a more social, contextual, and cultural orientation in comparison with cognitive or psychological approaches to first- and second-language pragmatics (Ochs 1986; Schieffelin and Ochs 1986a, 1986b). Pragmatic development through language socialization in L1 depends mostly on the degree of active and purposeful involvement in interactions. In L1 socialization and language development go hand in hand. Language socialization relies on two processes: (1) socialization through the use of language, referring to "interactional sequences in which novices are directed to use language in specific ways"; and, (2) socialization to use the language, referring to "the use of language to encode and create cultural meaning" (Poole 1994:594). This view fits into the socio-cognitive approach (described briefly in the introduction and in details in Chapter 2) because on the one hand it emphasizes the importance of language use to develop socio-cultural behavior (appropriateness), and on the other hand it underlines the role of social processes in developing individual language skills (correctness). The appropriate use of language within a speech community depends on conventions, norms, beliefs, expectations, and knowing the preferred ways of saying things and preferred ways of organizing thoughts, as will be discussed in the following chapters. People can get to learn all these only if they go through the socialization process with the other members of the speech community. Pragmatic socialization is a lifelong process (e.g., Duff 2003; Schieffelin and Ochs 1986a, 1986b), as people keep entering new socio-cultural contexts and take up new roles in society.

The language socialization paradigm built mainly on the works of Ochs and Schieffelin has had a strong ethnographic orientation, and has paid close attention to contextual dynamics of language behavior and human agency in L1. Following the traditions of language socialization research, interlanguage pragmatics has aimed to identify deviations from native speakers' norms (Kasper 2001) and emphasized the dynamism and ever-lasting change of the individual's pragmatics competence that is modified under the new socio-cultural environments, situations, and challenges. *Intercultural pragmatics* takes into account the results of language socialization research both in L1 and L2. However, its concerns are slightly different from those of interlanguage pragmatics. The main issue for intercultural pragmatics concerning pragmatic socialization can be summarized as follows: How will the existing, L1-based conceptual system change under the influence of the newly emerging language, and how will the new strategies, behavior patterns, and socio-cultural knowledge blend and/or interact with the existing ones? These questions presuppose that

the change is primarily conceptual, which is, reflected in the use of the
    linguistic code,
the process is dynamic with its ups and downs,
there is a bidirectional influence between languages and cultures,
subjectivity plays a leading role in what new elements are accepted and incorporated into the existing system.

In order to describe how language socialization takes place in L2 and subsequent languages, Kecskes (2003) proposed the term "conceptual socialization," which he defined as "the transformation of the conceptual system which undergoes characteristic changes to fit the functional needs of the new language and culture." During the process of conceptual socialization, the L1-dominated conceptual base is being gradually restructured, making space for and engaging with the new knowledge and information coming through the second language channel (e.g., Kecskes 2003; Ortactepe 2012). This leads to the development of a conscious awareness of how another culture is different from one's own culture, the ability to reflect upon this difference in language production, and the development of an identity that is the reflection of the dual culture.

The term "conceptual socialization" has been used to distinguish the process of socialization in L2 or Lx from "language socialization" (c.f. Ochs 1988; Willett 1995; Mitchell and Myles 1998), which has its roots in anthropological linguistics. With this term, I wanted to underline that changes in pragmatic competence are primarily conceptual in nature. They are reflected in the functioning of the dual language system so conceptual socialization has its roots in cognitive linguistics studies. Language socialization research represented by a limited number of studies (c.f. Ochs 1988; Ochs and Schieffelin 1984; Willett 1995) has underlined that language and culture are inseparable because they are acquired together: each supports the development of the other. Here is what Ochs said about this issue:

> It is evident that acquisition of linguistic knowledge and acquisition of socio-cultural knowledge are interdependent. A basic task of the language acquirer is to acquire tacit knowledge of principles relating linguistic forms not only to each other but also to referential and nonreferential meanings and functions...Given that meanings and functions are to a large extent socioculturally organized, linguistic knowledge is embedded in sociocultural knowledge. On the other hand, understandings of the social organization of everyday life, cultural ideologies, moral values, beliefs, and structures of knowledge and interpretation are to a large extent acquired through the medium of language...Children develop concepts of a socioculturally structured universe through their participation in language activities (Ochs 1988:14).

Ochs's and Schieffelin's work has focused on L1 development. They did not pay much attention to L2 socialization. There are only a restricted number of studies that extend the paradigm to second language acquisition (e.g., Willett 1995; Platt 1989). Willett (1995), for instance, conducted a longitudinal study with young classroom learners of ESL in an elementary school with an international intake. Based on her results she argued that language socialization is a complex process in which participants construct and evaluate shared understandings through negotiation. This process leads to changes not only in their identity but also in social practices. Ortactepe (2012) conducted a longitudinal, mixed-method study that relied on the assumption that international students, as newcomers to the American culture, experience bilingual development via conceptual socialization that enables them to gain competency in the target language through exposure to the target language and culture. By collecting qualitative and quantitative data three times over a year, the study examined the linguistic and social development of Turkish bilingual students as a result of their conceptual socialization in the United States. Socio-cultural and linguistic features of the language socialization process were analyzed together to emphasize the interplay between them in shaping the social and linguistic behavior of the subjects. Ortactepe provided evidence that L2 learners' conceptual socialization relies predominantly—contrary to what previous research says—on learners' investment in language rather than only on extended social networks.

3.1. DIFFERENCES BETWEEN CONCEPTUAL SOCIALIZATION AND LANGUAGE SOCIALIZATION

Conceptual socialization broadens the scope of the paradigm of language socialization, which has its main focus on language developmental issues. Conceptual socialization has a second/foreign language perspective and differs from language socialization in that it emphasizes the primacy of mental processes in the symbiosis of language and culture, and aims at explaining the bidirectional influence of the two languages in second language development. The process of conceptual socialization is strongly tied to the emergence of the common underlying conceptual base that is responsible for the operation of two language channels (Kecskes and Papp 2000; Kecskes 2009). The child acquiring his/her first language lives in the socio-cultural environment that is responsible for the development of the encyclopedic knowledge base, social skills, image system, and concepts that give meaning to all linguistic signs used in the given language. This is not exactly the case if the target language is acquired as a second or foreign language. The main differences between L1 language socialization and conceptual socialization can be summarized as follows:

   Partial consciousness of the process,

L1 language socialization is basically a subconscious and partly automatic process through which the child gradually integrates into her/his environment and speech community both linguistically and socially. In the L2, however, much more consciousness is involved in the process in which age is a decisive variable. Several researchers have noted that nonnative speakers make deliberate, conscious choices about pragmatic strategies and/or features of the target language. Taguchi (2011:303) claimed that when learners' L1 and L2 cultures do not operate under the same values and norms, or when learners do not agree with L2 norms, linguistic forms that encode target norms are not easily acquired. Research has indicated that not all language learners wish to behave pragmatically just like native speakers of the target language (e.g., Li 1998; Siegal 1996). Li (1998) reported that Chinese immigrant women sometimes resisted more expert peers' pragmatic socialization based on their personal values and cultural beliefs. *The important thing here for intercultural pragmatics is that nonnative speakers may know target language norms and expectations but do not wish to act accordingly.* In intercultural communication (especially in lingua franca) this fact may support rather than hamper the smoothness of the communicative process. The too frequent use of "thank you," "I am sorry," "have a nice day" type of expressions may be annoying for nonnative speakers.

Age and attitude of language learner,

The older the L2 language users are, the more they rely on their L1-dominated conceptual system, and the more they are resistant to any pragmatic change that is not in line with their L1-related value system and norms. Ochs (1988:14) argued that "not only are language practices organized by the world views, they also create world views for the language users carrying out these practices." For second/foreign language users, the crucial question is whether those existing world views will be modified in any extent under the influence of the new language and culture, and how this new blend (if any) will affect language production in both languages. Gee (1999:63) argued that the situated and local nature of meaning is largely invisible to us. It is easy for us to miss the specificity and localness of our own practices and think that we have general, abstract, even universal meanings. We come to think, when we have learned no other languages, that "standing" is just standing, "eating" is just eating, "over there" is just over there. In fact, the situated, social, and cultural nature of meaning often becomes visible to us only when we confront language-at-work in languages and cultures far distant from our own. This "confrontation" often occurs at the level of fixed expressions, as will be discussed below.

Direct or indirect access to the target culture and environment,

As argued earlier, in L1 language and social development go hand-in-hand because people have direct access to the socio-cultural environment that shapes their norms, values, conventions, and beliefs. This is not the case in L2. Language learners have usually limited access to the target culture and environment. Even if they live in the target language environment, it is not certain that they have full access to it because of personal or external reasons. In L2 acquisition, pragmatic socialization is more about discourse practices as related to linguistic expressions than how these practices relate to cultural patterns, norms, and beliefs. Language learners may have direct access to the linguistic material they need but not to the socio-cultural background knowledge that gives sense to the particular linguistic expressions in the L2. Therefore, I found it important to make a difference between the *skill-side* and the *content-side of conceptual socialization* (Kecskes 2003). They are two sides of one and the same phenomenon. The skill-side means that conceptual socialization will be reflected in the actual language skills: structural well-formedness, language manipulation, sentence-structuring, lexical quality, and formulaic language use. Changes in both sides are qualitative rather than quantitative. The skill-side of the conceptual socialization process is measurable. The content of the language production is expected to give information about metalinguistic awareness, interactional style, pragmatic strategies, knowledge base, and multicultural attitude. Changes in the content-side, however, can hardly be measured. They are qualitative changes in the content of what the language learner says, and the way the language learner behaves in communication.

4.2. MOVING ON THE DYNAMIC CONTINUUM OF CONCEPTUAL SOCIALIZATION IN L2

From the perspective of conceptual socialization it is important to mention Lave and Wenger's (1991) legitimate peripheral participation. Their approach is based on the assumption that cognition is built from experience through social interaction in communities of practice. It is a process of "incorporation of learners into the activities of communities of practice, beginning as a legitimated (recognized) participant on the edges (periphery) of the activity, and moving through a series of increasingly expert roles as learners' skills develop" (Watson-Gegeo 2004:341). In the activities in the language community, while nonnative speakers adopt various communicative and social roles in temporarily and spatially situated activities and practices, at the same time they also develop grammatical, discourse, socio-cultural, and general cognitive structures of knowledge. This is how the skill-side and content-side of conceptual socialization are ideally intertwined. Second language learners, who begin peripherally, should be exposed to mutual engagement with the members of the community until they are granted enough legitimacy to be a potential member (Wenger 1998). Moving through this dynamic continuum, with its ups and downs, second language users can get from the status of a beginner to advanced roles through gaining and/or being allowed access to social interaction in the dominant language community. However, movement on this dynamic continuum depends both on individual and social factors. *Exposure, quality, and quantity of input can be effective only as much as the individual learner allows them to be.* As mentioned above, there can be much control here from the perspective of the individual L2 user.

In her longitudinal study, Ortactepe (2011) examined both the skill-side and content-side of conceptual socialization. In the qualitative analysis of the content-side that she connected to the dynamic changes of social identity, she found evidence against the language myth according to which students learn by osmosis when in the target speech community. Learning through osmosis is the natural way to acquire a language. To learn through osmosis means to learn by immersing oneself in a language and culture. Most of the literature in second language acquisition takes for granted that this is the best and most efficient way of acquiring another language. This way of thinking does not take into account the decisive role of the individual learner in the process. An important element of Ortactepe's work is that analyzing the conceptual socialization process of her subjects one by one she provides evidence that L2 learners' conceptual socialization relies predominantly—contrary to previous research—on learners' investment in language rather than on extended social networks. This finding fits into the socio-cognitive approach very well because it demonstrates that not only in language use but also in language development and socialization, the role of individual cognition is as important as the role of the socio-cultural environment and social networking.

5. How is Pragmatic Competence Reflected in Language Use?

Kecskes argued that using a particular language and belonging to a particular speech community means having preferred ways of saying things and preferred ways of organizing thoughts (Kecskes 2007a). Preferred ways of saying things are generally reflected in the use of formulaic language and figurative language. Selecting the right words and expressions, which is directly tied to pragmatic competence, is more important than syntax. Language socialization depends on the acquisition of what is expected to be said in particular situations, and what kind of language behavior is considered appropriate in the given speech community. That is why conceptual socialization in L2 requires direct access to the target culture.

Formulaic language will be discussed in Chapter 5. However, it is necessary here to deal with one type of formulaic expressions that are especially tied to pragmatic competence and language socialization: situation-bound utterances (SBU) whose use is tied to particular social events and situations. They behave like conversational routines and/or rituals and are usually understood in the same way by members of a speech community, such as "how are you doing?," "have a nice day," "be my guest," and so on. Formulaic language is the heart and soul of native-like language use. In fact, formulaic language use makes language use native-like. The reason why formulaic language is a reoccurring topic in this book is that they reflect the social behavior of members of speech communities. So what will happen if there are no social communities in the traditional sense? Dell Hymes (1968) said that "a vast proportion of verbal behaviour consists of recurrent patterns, . . . [including] the full range of utterances that acquire conventional significance for an individual, group or whole culture" (Hymes 1968:126-127). Coulmas (1981:1-3) argued that much of what is actually said in everyday conversation is by no means unique. Rather, a great deal of communicative activity consists of enacting routines making use of prefabricated linguistic units in a well-known and generally accepted manner. Successful coordination of social interactions heavily depends on standardized ways of organizing interpersonal encounters because conventional ways of doing things with words and expressions are familiar to everyone in the speech community—thus, speakers are expected to be understood according to their communicative intentions and goals. *Pragmatic competence is directly connected to and develops through the use of formulaic expressions*, mainly because use of formulas is group identifying. They reflect a community's shared language practices, and so they discriminate those who belong to the group from those who do not (Yorio 1980). This is so because, as Wray and Namba (2003:36) claimed, "speech communities develop and retain common ways of expressing key messages."

The language socialization studies highlighted the importance of prefabricated chunks in the socialization process both in L1 and L2 development. Ochs and Schieffelin (1984) pointed out that there is much direct teaching of the interactional routines ("elema") among the Kaluli in Western Samoa. Willett (1995) argued that in the first months, ESL students relied heavily on prefabricated chunks that they picked up from their fluent English-speaking peers or from adults during routine events. Coulmas (1979:256-260) gave an excellent summary of difficulties L2 learners have when using routine formulae. He categorized pragmatic interferences according to the respective process or structural phenomenon giving rise to the mistake in question. The socio-cognitive framework, however, requires a different approach to these pragmatic errors. SCA emphasizes that errors in the use of formulaic language are the results of pragmatic rather than structural problems deriving from the incomplete process of conceptual socialization during which second language users have to deal with the problems of culture-specific communicative functions, the formula-specific pragmatic properties of expressions, and differences in communication patterns.

From the perspective of conceptual socialization and change in pragmatic competence, the development and use of situation-bound utterances (SBU) are especially important because they are the reflections of socio-cultural patterns, cultural models, and behavioral expectations in a speech community. Situation-bound utterances are highly conventionalized, prefabricated pragmatic units whose occurrences are tied to standardized communicative situations (e.g., Coulmas 1981a; Kiefer 1985, 1995; Kecskes 1997, 2000). Many nonnative speakers have an excellent command of the language system and do not make grammatical errors. Besides pronunciation there are only two things that can reveal that they are not native speakers: word choice and use of SBUs. Situation-bound utterances are direct reflections of what is considered appropriate language use in a speech community. Here is an example given by Roberts Sanders (personal communication).

(2)

> He was ordering a pizza on the phone. The woman who answered was fluent in English but had an accent.
> SANDERS: I'd like to order a medium pizza.
> WOMAN: Is that pickup or delivery?.
> SANDERS: Pickup.
> WOMAN: *Is that it?*
> SANDERS: What?
> WOMAN: *Is that it?*
> SANDERS: Is that what?
> WOMAN: (No response. Silence)

SANDERS: We want three toppings: pepperoni, mushroom, cheese
WOMAN: OK, you want pepperoni, mushroom and cheese
SANDERS: Right.
WOMAN: Okay, about 20 minutes.

Although the woman at Pizza Hut was fluent in English, her inappropriate use of the SBU "is that it?" caused a slight breakdown in the interaction. Normally, "is that it?" is a formula used to close this part of the transaction and move on to something new or closing. But for Sanders, the transaction shouldn't have been moving on, because they were still in the middle of the ordering process. He hadn't yet told the assistant what toppings he wanted. The woman repeated, "is that it?" and Sanders said "is that what?" This was followed by silence from the woman, who must have been confused. After Sanders told her what toppings he wanted, she understood perfectly, and they closed the transaction properly. The confusion was caused by the nonnative speaker's inappropriate use of SBU.

HOW ARE SBUS TIED TO PRAGMATIC COMPETENCE?

Situational obligatoriness is culture-specific[1]

Situational obligatoriness of SBUs varies across cultures. This means that certain situations require the use of SBUs in a particular culture, which might not be the case in another culture. There are, for instance, cases when Americans easily can opt for a freely generated phrase while Japanese or Turks may not do so. This is true the other way around. It is almost impossible to find a Russian, Japanese, or Hungarian equivalent to the SBUs: "have a good one," "you are all set," or "I'll talk to you later" in English. Nonnative speakers have not only to memorize SBUs as linguistic units but also understand the socio-cultural background (cultural customs, values, attitudes, etc.) these routine expressions are applicable in. This is where most of the transfer from L1 occurs. Sometimes the communicative function is culture-specific, which makes it quite difficult to give the functional equivalent of the English "you bet," "welcome aboard," or Turkish "gülü gülü oturun" ("stay laughingly"), "gözünüz aydın" ("your eye bright"), "güle güle büyütün" ("raise laughingly"), and the like, in other languages because these phrases are the result of specific socio-cognitive development in the given language and have specific pragmatic features that are usually nonexistent or different in the other language(s). For instance, the Turkish "gülü gülü oturun" ("stay laughingly") is said to someone who has just bought, rented, or moved into a new house. "Gözünüz aydın" ("your eye bright") is said to someone who has had the good fortune to be visited by a loved one who was far away. It is not that these situations are nonexistent in other languages. However, other languages may not find it important to introduce a special SBU in those cases. Hungarians, for instance, also say something when a friend

---

[1] This part is based on Kecskes (2003).

or relative tells them that s/he has bought or moved into a new house. But they do not insist on the use of a particular SBU in that situation. What they say is usually freely generated. It is hardly possible to find equivalents to these Turkish SBUs in American English, Hungarian, Russian, or other languages because they are the representatives of Turkish culture, which finds it important to give voice to one's feelings in the situations described above. "Güle güle büyütün" ("raise laughingly") differs from the other two expressions in that it refers to an event that is considered joyful and very special in many cultures: birth of a child. This expression is said to the parents of a newborn infant. This situation is usually lexicalized differently in many cultures. Conceptual socialization means, among other things, that the L2 learner becomes aware of these differences, not searching for an equivalent SBU where there is none, and not trying to use the communicative customs of one language in another language.

Socio-cultural values expressed by SBUs

SBUs very strongly relate to socio-cultural values. According to Albert (1968), a value system represents "what is expected or hoped for, required or forbidden. It is not a report of actual conduct but in the system of criteria by which conduct is judged and sanctions applied (Albert 1968:288)." Even the slightest differences in the socio-cultural value system may result in differences in cognitive mapping and, as a consequence, in lexicalization (Kecskes 2003). For instance, guests are equally valued in American, French, and Hungarian society. But the SBUs that are used to welcome them demonstrate interesting differences:
(3)

ENGLISH: Make yourself at home.
FRENCH: Faites comme chez vous. ('Do as [you do] at home.')
HUNGARIAN: Érezze magat otthon. ('Feel yourself at home.')

Although these expressions can be considered as functional equivalents, the use of different verbs (French "faites" is the imperative of the French equivalent of "to do," and the Hungarian "érezd" is the imperative of the Hungarian equivalent of "feel") demonstrates that each language highlights something else as important in one and the same situation.

Coulmas (1979:262) argued that from the perspective of values it is important to analyze the original and literal meaning of SBUs because they may be quite revealing with respect to social values and past and present history of the given group of people. Coulmas also claimed that "the more tradition-oriented a society is, the more its members seem to make use of situational formulae (Coulmas 1981:11)." We, however, must be careful to not accept this claim at face value because it raises the question of how the content of SBUs relates to the situation(s) they are used in. Depending on whether SBUs directly say something about the action, and/or participants or relate them to other situations or agents, Kecskes (2003) made a difference between *situation-bound routines* ("nice to meet you"; "you bet";

"take care"; "you are all set"; welcome aboard"; etc.) and *situation-bound rituals* ("God bless you," "thank you"). Situation-bound rituals are close to what Goffman called "interaction rituals," a term with which Goffman (1967) referred to SBU-like expressions. Situation-bound rituals generally relate the actual situation to other situations, events, or agents. They are especially frequent in tradition-oriented cultures such as Japanese, Arabic, Chinese, and Turkish. The use of situation-bound rituals is almost obligatory and usually no freely generated phrases are acceptable instead. They behave like Yiddish psycho-ostensives, about which Matisoff claimed that "often it is not so much that the speaker is using an emotive formula that actually belies his true feelings, as that the formula has become a surrogate for the true feeling, an almost automatic linguistic feature that constant usage has rendered as predictable and redundant as the concord in number between subject and verb (Matisoff 1979:6)." Yiddish psycho-ostensives, just like SBUs, refer to the speaker's attitude to what s/he is talking about. Tannen and Oztek (1981), however, called our attention to the fact that while in Yiddish culture the priority is on verbal inventiveness (consequently, these emotive expressions are productive), in Greek and especially in Turkish culture situation-bound rituals are fixed sets and are usually complete utterances. In tradition-oriented cultures situation-bound rituals are not considered insincere because these cultures seem to have agreed to accept the surrogate as evidence for the true feeling (Tannen and Oztek 1981). For instance, in Turkish:

(4) If someone mentions a bad event or disaster, this should be followed by
an expression to erase the effect:
"Agzindan yel alsin"   'May the wind take it from your mouth.'

Tannen and Oztek (1981) argued that in Turkish many formulaic expressions deal with human powerlessness, and usually two sources of power are appealed to God and the magic power of words. For instance, when asking for God's aid Turks say:

(5) "Allah kolaylik versin"   'May God give ease'

In contrast to situation-bound rituals, situation-bound routines generally do not sound sincere, and interlocutors are aware of this. They usually say something that is directly related to the actual situation, participants, or actions. *They are standardized solutions to coordination problems where no negotiations are necessary.* Kecskes (2003) argued that situation-bound routines serve an important function in giving people confidence and behavioral certainty in conversation because they can usually be interpreted only in one particular way, which excludes misunderstanding. Future-oriented cultures (like the American culture) as opposed to tradition-oriented cultures generally prefer the use of situation-bound routines to situation-bound rituals. This is one of the reasons that it is so difficult to find the English equivalent to Turkish, Chinese, or Japanese situation-bound rituals. However, this does not mean that there are no situation-bound rituals in American English. Of course there are—for instance, "(God) Bless you" when someone sneezes. The situations that prompt the use of SBUs in tradition-oriented cultures, in many cases, are not even recognized by native speakers of English as events that demand any verbal reaction (c.f. Bear 1987). To illustrate this point Bear (1987) listed several situations where the English native speakers usually have nothing to say while the Turks find it necessary to use an SBU:

> (6) "sihhatler olsun"   ["may (it) be healthy"]   To address someone who has just taken a bath.
> (7) "helal"   ["(it is) lawful, legitimate"] To someone who choked.
> (8) "güle güle giy"   ["wear laughingly"]   To someone who has acquired a new article of clothing.
> (9) "güle güle otur"   ["stay laughingly"]   To someone who has moved into a new house.

(Examples from Kecskes 2003)

In contrast, English SBU routines are more "down-to-earth," and there is less attempt in them to establish rapport between participants of conversation. For the future-oriented Americans, expressions, such as "See you soon," "I'll talk to you later," "Look forward to seeing you again," "Why don't we have lunch tomorrow?," and others are quite natural. Zaharna (1995) argued that in Arabic culture, envisioning future activities as certainties sounds very unnatural. When Arabs speak about an action in the future, they often use the situation-bound ritual "In sha allah" ("God willing") because it is only God who knows for sure what will happen in the future.

It is especially SBU rituals that give us information about the value system of a language. Kecskes (2003) argued that lexical choice is correlated with socio-cultural relevance. The richness of a language in a particular type of SBU suggests that the particular domain of life that the given SBUs refer to plays an important role in the life of those people who use the SBUs. As we saw, the Turkish language is full of SBUs that are connected with religious thinking, or in Japanese several situation-bound rituals are attached to "omoiyari," which Lebra defines as follows: "Omoiyari refers to the ability and willingness to feel what others are feeling, to vicariously experience the pleasure or pain that they are undergoing, and to help them satisfy their wishes (Lebra 1974:38)."

SBUs and phatic communication (small talk)

Malinowski defined phatic communication as "[...] language used in free, aimless, social intercourse" (1923:476). It is small talk, a nonreferential use of language to share feelings and sympathy, or establish social rapport rather than to communicate information. Phatic communication is characterized by the use of routinized and ritualized formulas, mainly situation-bound utterances. This term refers to all kinds of acts including greetings, welcomes, questions about work, health, well-being, family and other aspects of life, leave-takings, well-wishes, farewells, compliments about obvious achievements or personal traits of the interlocutors, complaints about things or events with which they are familiar, or those narrations or chitchat about trivial facts or comments about topics that may seem obvious (Malinowski 1923:476-479). Why does intercultural pragmatics need to deal with small talk? Because it is part of what we referred to as preferred ways of saying things and preferred ways of organizing thoughts. This is what makes language native-like, and this is where nonnative speakers struggle most because of limited conceptual social-ization in the L2. Their erroneous choices of words and expressions in particular social contexts may have undesirable consequences not only on the relationship they wish to establish or maintain with their partners, but also on their addressees' perceptions of their personality, identity, attitudes, intentions, or level of politeness. More recently, Mugford (2011) has shown that his Mexican learners of English transferred local norms and practices and did not adhere to those of the L2 when engaging in phatic exchanges. For instance, unaware of the role of status and dis-tance in the target community, on some occasions Mexican learners made overly personal comments to their instructors, as if assuming they were talking to very close subjects. On other occasions, their small talk displayed local practices, such as lack of expected greetings when entering classrooms, very extended greetings with a profusion of self-disclosure, or the transfer of L1 idiomatic phatic expressions—e.g., "fresh as a salad" instead of "fresh as a daisy" as a reply to a how-are-you ques-tion. An effective management of small talk in any language requires an awareness of subtle issues such as when and with whom to engage in it, the underlying reasons and purposes to do so, the topics that can be addressed, or the effects achievable by means of it. Consequently, language teachers should devote part of their efforts and teaching activities to this area of communicative interaction, which, even if often regarded as unproblematic, may turn out to be quite risky and troublesome.

We might not be aware of how important the appropriate use of phatic expres-sions can be, especially when nonnative speakers talk to native speakers. For instance, Goffman (1967) said that the gestures (referring to small talk) that we sometimes call empty are perhaps in fact the fullest things of all. A "thank you," "I am sorry," or "I know what you mean" type of expression goes far in establishing rapport in communication.

6. Is There Anything like Pragmatic Transfer?

6.1. THE TERM "PRAGMATIC TRANSFER"

The phenomenon of pragmatic transfer is widely analyzed within the confines of interlanguage pragmatics and cross-cultural pragmatics. The term "pragmatic transfer" usually refers to the carryover of pragmatic knowledge from one language and culture to another language and culture. According to the socio-cognitive approach speakers can hardly "transfer" anything. "Transfer" may not exactly be the right term to describe what takes place in the bi- and multilingual mind. What really happens is that the nonnative speakers use their L1 (or Lx) cultural models, norms, and way of thinking about the world to formulate or interpret an utterance in another language, which may result in grammatical, lexical, and pronunciation errors at a lower level proficiency, and grammatically correct but odd utterances or inappropriate use of expressions and formulaic units at a higher level of proficiency. So "transfer" does not seem to be the best way to describe this phenomenon. Here are some examples that are traditionally considered transfers.

> (10) Grammatical transfer
> No plural form after a number (Chinese, Spanish)
> "There are three new student."
> No distinction between subject and object pronouns (Chinese, Spanish)
> "I gave the forms to she."

> (11) Lexical transfer
> A sign in a Serbian hotel (source: Octopus, October 1995, Champaign,
>   IL, p. 144): "The flattening of underwear with pleasure is the job of the
>   chambermaid."

> (12) Conceptual transfer
> DUTCH: What do you know about Kemal's mother?
> TURKISH: His mother was a house woman. Every job used to come from her
>   hand. In making food there was no one on top of her.
> DUTCH: You mean she was a good cook?
> TURKISH: Yes, yes…

Sharwood-Smith and Kellerman (1986:1) argued that the term *transfer* is inadequate and, therefore, suggest an umbrella term, *cross-linguistic influence*, that allows "to subsume under one heading such phenomena as 'transfer,' 'interference,' 'avoidance,' 'borrowing,' and L2-related aspects of language loss." They recommended that the term *transfer* should be restricted "to those processes that lead to the incorporation of elements from one language into another." In second language acquisition research Ellis's definition has been widely used: "Transfer" is to be seen as a general cover term for a number of different kinds of influence from languages other than the L2. The study of transfer involves the study of errors (negative transfer), facilitation (positive transfer), avoidance of target language forms, and their over-use (Ellis 1994:341)."

Kasper (1992:207) defined pragmatic transfer as "the influence exerted by learners' pragmatic knowledge of languages and cultures other than L2 on the comprehension, production and learning of L2 pragmatic information." Kasper (1992) revised the two types of pragmatic transfer that Thomas (1983) had spoken about. According to that revision, pragmalinguistic transfer refers to those cases in which the functional and social meanings of certain linguistic forms in the L1 affect the comprehension and production of "form-function mappings in L2" (Kasper 1992:209). Sociopragmatic transfer occurs when "the social perceptions underlying language users' interpretation and performance of linguistic action in L2 are influenced by their assessment of subjectively equivalent L1 contexts" (Kasper 1992:209). Bou-Franch (e.g., 1998; 2012) has given a very useful summary of the understanding of pragmatic transfer in interlanguage pragmatics.

6.2. BIDIRECTIONAL PRAGMATIC INFLUENCE

As discussed above, "pragmatic transfer" may not be the best term to describe what happens with pragmatic knowledge and skills in the language use of nonnative speakers. In interlanguage pragmatics and cross-cultural pragmatics this phenomenon is usually described as a unidirectional process. However, in the case of bilinguals, the two languages mutually affect each other. Pragmatic influence appears to be bidirectional (Kecskes and Papp 2000). Consequently, the term "bidirectional pragmatic influence" appears to better describe what happens in the language use of bilinguals.

An interesting example of bidirectional influence is what is called "the intercultural style hypothesis" (Kasper and Blum-Kulka 1993). It refers to a unique development of the common underlying conceptual base in multilingual people. According to this hypothesis (Blum-Kulka 1991; Kasper and Blum-Kulka 1993), speakers fully competent in two languages may create an intercultural style of speaking that is both related to and distinct from the styles prevalent in the two substrata, a style on which they rely regardless of the language being used (Kasper and Blum-Kulka 1993). Kasper and Blum-Kulka claimed that the hypothesis is supported by many studies of cross-cultural communication, especially those focusing on interactional sociolinguistics (e.g., Gumperz 1982; Tannen 1985) and research into the pragmatic behavior of immigrant populations across generations (e.g., Clyne, Ball and Neil 1991). In a later study Cenoz (2003) investigated the request behavior of fluent Spanish-English bilinguals. The result shows that these bilinguals make requests in their first language and second language essentially in the same way.

According to research in interlanguage and cross-cultural pragmatics, the effect of L1 pragmatic competence is overwhelming, especially if L2 was introduced at a later stage. Several researchers (cf. Schachter 1983; Gonzalez 1987; Schmidt 1993) have found that world views, beliefs, pragmatic assumptions, and values are almost always "transferred" from the L1 to the L2 environments. This strong L1 pragmatic influence is demonstrated by He (1988) with the use of the expression "Never mind" by Chinese-English bilinguals when responding to "Thanks a lot. That's a great help." According to Liu (2010), in Chinese, people use "没关系" (méi guānxi) or "不用谢" (búyòng xiè) in response to "Thank you." Thus, some Chinese-English bilinguals fail to see the slight differences among the three English expressions: "Never mind," "Not at all," and "You are welcome," as in Chinese they could all be translated as "没关系" (méi guānxi).

These findings are very important for intercultural pragmatics because as it was briefly discussed in the "Introduction," intercultures that are co-constructed in the course of intercultural communication are the results of modification and adjustment of the interlocutors' existing pragmatic competence to the actual situational context. To what extent the shaping of intercultures relies on existing cultural norms, beliefs, and pragmatic assumptions and to what extent it absorbs co-constructed, relatively new elements is a crucial issue in intercultural pragmatics analysis. The question is whether the effect of L1 pragmatic competence in this process is really as overwhelming as it was found in interlanguage pragmatics, where focus is on how particular speech acts are used in different languages and what the difference is in their use—whether it is just moderate or almost nonexistent, as some scholars say. This is one of the issues that will be discussed in the next chapter.

In sum, intercultural pragmatics considers pragmatic competence a very dynamic and flexible phenomenon whose development and functioning depends on several different variables including, among others, age, individual motivation, quality and quantity of input, and socio-cultural environment. Pragmatic strategies applied by individuals in intercultural interactions have both universal and culture-specific elements. The real differences between language users appear to be in the way they implement those strategies linguistically and distribute them accordingly in actual intercultural interactions. A unique feature of this kind of bi- and multilingual pragmatic competence is that individuals control what they find acceptable from the norms and conventions of the L2. Having a system of pragmatic norms already in place, adult sequential bilinguals may have some kind of resistance toward the use of certain pragmatic norms and speech conventions of the L2. Consequently, the language socialization process in subsequent languages may not take place through osmosis. Contrary to previous research, bilingual conceptual socialization relies predominantly on learners' investment in language rather than just on extended social networks.

This primarily individual control of pragmatic socialization is most clearly demonstrated in the use of situation-bound utterances because these formulaic expressions represent cultural models and ways of thinking of members of a particular speech community. Pragmatic competence is directly tied to and develops through the use of formulaic expressions, mainly because use of formulas is group identifying. These expressions reflect a speech community's shared language practices, and so they discriminate those who belong to the group from those who do not. This is so because speech communities develop and retain common ways of expressing key messages.

It was argued that bilingual pragmatic competence shows a unique symbiosis of pragmatic rules and expectations of both languages. Since a bilingual is not two monolinguals in one body (e.g., Grosjean 1989) there is hardly any transfer of pragmatic skills between the two languages. Rather, what we can see is that bilinguals have preferences in the pragmatic rule systems of both languages and act accordingly. The next chapter discusses what role encyclopedic knowledge and cultural models play in selecting and/or developing those preferences.

4

Encyclopedic Knowledge, Cultural Models, and Interculturality

In the socio-cognitive approach, language is defined as a system of signs resting upon a conceptual system that is relatively unique to each culture (Kecskes 2009). After discussing the theoretical framework of intercultural pragmatics and the pragmatic competence of bi- and multilinguals who participate in intercultural interactions, we need to have a closer look at the conceptual system that underlies language use and describe how it relates to intercultures. In the definition of intercultures, it was underlined that they are situationally emergent and co-constructed phenomena that rely both on relatively definable cultural norms and models as well as situationally evolving features (Kecskes 2011). Thus, in this chapter we will need to discuss cultural models that affect the shaping of intercultures.

1. Encyclopedic Knowledge

1.1. DEFINITION

As mentioned in the introduction, culture is seen as a socially constituted set of various kinds of knowledge structures that individuals turn to as relevant situations permit, enable, and usually encourage. Culture has fuzzy boundaries and is characterized by dynamic changes both synchronically and diachronically. The conceptual system includes encyclopedic knowledge that refers to the knowledge of the world as distinguished from knowledge of the language system. The encyclopedic view represents a model of the system of conceptual knowledge that underlies linguistic meaning. Cognitive linguistics holds that there is no clear-cut distinction between linguistic knowledge and encyclopedic knowledge. This is not the case in SCA that acknowledges that the linguistic system is rooted in the conceptual system but considers encyclopedic knowledge and linguistic knowledge as two inseparable sides of the conceptual system, both playing a profound role in how human beings make sense in communication.

Traditionally, the division between ontology and lexicon illustrates the distinction between encyclopedic and dictionary knowledge. Dictionary knowledge is supposed to cover the idiosyncrasies of particular words, whereas encyclopedic knowledge covers everything regarding the underlying concepts. In cognitive linguistics, however, meaning, emerging from language use, is a function of the activation of conceptual knowledge structures as guided by context. Consequently, there is no principled distinction between semantics and pragmatics (e.g., Evans 2006; Fauconnier 1997). This approach is not supported in intercultural pragmatics, as will be discussed later. In cognitive approaches, practically no sentence encodes a complete thought. Certain processes of contextual filling-in are required before anything of a proposition nature emerges (Carston 1998).

Encyclopedic knowledge is considered a structured system of knowledge, organized as a network. Rosch's (1977) view of category structure and its implications for reasoning (e.g., Lakoff and Johnson 1980) have had an important impact on the emergence of Schema Theory. Schema Theory is a theoretical framework that has been developed in the cognitive sciences over the last two decades. The central concept, "schema," has gone by a number of other names, including "cultural model" (D'Andrade 1992; Holland and Quinn 1987), "frame" (Minsky 1975; Fillmore 1982), "mental model" (Johnson-Laird 1983), "idealized cognitive model" (Lakoff 1987), "folk model" (D'Andrade 1987), and "script" (Schank and Abelson 1977). Encyclopedic knowledge is mostly represented in cultural models and schemas that provide scenarios or action plans for individuals of how to interpret speech situations and behave in a particular circumstance or how to interpret the behavior of others in one or another circumstance. Cultural schemas for social interaction are cognitive structures that contain knowledge for face-to-face interactions in a person's socio-cultural environment.

1.2. MEANING IN THE ENCYCLOPEDIC VIEW

Because the encyclopedic view is fully fleshed out in cognitive linguistics, we should review the main tenets briefly in order for us to explain where SCA differs from the approach in cognitive linguistics. The study of meaning in cognitive linguistics relies on an encyclopedic view on semantics that has some core assumptions (Evans 2007):

1.2.1. There Exists no Principled Distinction between Semantics and Pragmatics

Cognitive semanticists usually reject the idea that there is a distinction between "core" (dictionary) meaning on the one hand, and pragmatic, social, or cultural meaning on the other. According to this approach there is no autonomous mental lexicon that contains semantic knowledge separately from other kinds of (linguistic or nonlinguistic) knowledge. Consequently, there is no distinction between dictionary knowledge and encyclopedic knowledge. There is only encyclopedic knowledge, which incorporates both linguistic and extralinguistic knowledge.

In the SCA encyclopedic knowledge motivates linguistic knowledge. It is the background to linguistic meaning. Intercultural interactions demonstrate very clearly that knowing the "core" (dictionary) meaning of an expression is one thing, but knowing both the core meaning and the pragmatic, socio-cultural load attached to that expression in a given culture is another matter. The difference in the encyclopedic knowledge tied to an expression in different languages may cause misunderstanding. A case like this was described in example (6) in Chapter 2, where two different culture-specific conceptual properties were attached to the expression "patronize" in English and Korean.

1.2.2. Encyclopedic Knowledge is Structured

In cognitive linguistics encyclopedic knowledge is viewed as a structured system of knowledge, organized as a network. *Frames* are preconceived understandings of a new situation (we have a faculty meeting). *Scripts* are sequences of activities that we associate with a particular situation (we have procedures to follow when having a faculty meeting). *Scenarios* are sets of organized units in cognitive processes. They are components we anticipate for any new situation that has been given a label that we understand (we have an understanding of who and what should be present during faculty meeting). *Schemata* are higher level knowledge that help us understand a situation (our knowledge of practice in a faculty meeting). Mental or cultural models are logical sequences of thought that explain a situation, give sense to a situation. There is some overlap between these terms, but they give us some perspective from which to analyze our data.

1.2.3. Encyclopedic Meaning Emerges in Context

Encyclopedic meaning arises in context(s) of use. The "selection" of actual situational meaning is informed/determined by contextual factors. In the dictionary view of meaning, there is a separation of core meaning (semantics) from noncore actual meaning (pragmatics). The encyclopedic view, however, claims that encyclopedic knowledge is included in semantics, and meaning is determined by context. According to this approach there is no definable, preexisting word meaning, because the meaning of a word in context is selected and shaped by encyclopedic knowledge.

As we will see later, this view is not accepted in the SCA, which emphasizes the difference between prior context and actual situational context and the separation of core meaning (semantics) from noncore actual meaning (pragmatics).

1.2.4. Lexical Items are Points of Access to Encyclopedic Knowledge

In the encyclopedic view lexical items are *points of access* to encyclopedic knowledge (Langacker 1987). Consequently, words are not containers that present neat, prepackaged bundles of information (Evans 2006). Instead, they selectively provide access to particular parts of the huge network of encyclopedic knowledge.

There are several theories in cognitive linguistics that adopt the encyclopedic view, such as Frame Semantics (Fillmore 1982; Fillmore and Atkins 1992), the approach to domains in Cognitive Grammar (Langacker 1987), the approach to Dynamic Construal (Croft and Cruse 2004), and the Theory of Lexical Concepts and Cognitive Models—LCCM Theory (Evans 2006). One of the basic theories of the encyclopedic view is frame semantics, which has been applied to several latter cognitive theories such as construction grammar and LCCM. Originally, frame semantics is a specific approach to natural language semantics developed by Charles Fillmore. The main idea is that we cannot understand the meaning of a word (or a linguistic expression in general) without access to all the encyclopedic knowledge related to that word. According to frame semantics, meaning in natural language is not separated from other forms of knowledge. Consequently, it does not make sense to maintain a strict separation between world knowledge and knowledge of linguistic meaning. Frame semantics relies on the specific structures of encyclopedic knowledge that are called "frames." They are things occurring together in reality. The internal structure of word meaning is not autonomous but exists against a background of our general assumptions about the world (socio-cultural beliefs, assumptions, etc., included). In this approach, word meaning cannot be fully analyzed into features, since the meaning and its frame are inseparable from one another. The frame may not be part of the lexical meaning itself, but our understanding of meaning crucially involves analysis of both the frames and the lexical senses that depend on them. Frames can either be created by or reflected in the language. An example of a frame created by the language itself would be the case of grading detergent packages. The framing device allows the consumer to properly interpret the label <u>large</u> on the package; knowing that the other sizes are <u>economy,</u> <u>family size,</u> and <u>jumbo</u>, the consumer is led to the correct conclusion that <u>large</u> signifies the smallest package.

These core assumptions are not always maintainable in the socio-cognitive approach, as we will see in the following sections.

2. Crossing, Merging, and Blending Cultures

Before discussing cultural models and interculturality in intercultural pragmatics, we should look at current approaches to culture and explain what crossing cultures, merging cultures, and blending cultures means. Research in the last three decades has focused mainly on crossing and merging cultures according to the positivist (crossing) and constructivist (merging) approaches. Blending, however, is a relatively new development.

We live in a world in which most people speak more than one language and are affiliated with and/or affected by more than one culture. Speaking more than one language and crossing cultures is an essential part of our life. Technology and people's global mobility bring together representatives of cultures from all over the world. The frequency and variety of such encounters have changed our understanding of culture and communication. Gumperz (1982) and Gumperz and Roberts (1991) called our attention to the fact that "culture" is not present in communication in the "old" sense of a transcendent identity, which is composed of values and norms and linearly related to forms of behavior. Cultural phenomena in speech are contingent, situational, and emergent in nature. Blommaert (1998:4) claimed that what we can observe and analyze in intercultural communication are "different conventions of communication, different speech styles, narrative patterns, in short, the deployment of different communicative repertoires. As far as 'identity' is concerned (cultural, ethnic identity), it can be an inference of these speech styles: people can identify selves or others on the basis of such speech styles. But in actual fact, not 'culture' is deployed, but communicative repertoires."

Gumperz (1982) and Hymes (1996) have offered an alternative to simplistic views of cultural differences. They developed an analytical framework to study culture in communication. This framework emphasizes two important things: (1) the highly critical role of context in intercultural communication, and (2) the importance of social differences, power relations, and different value systems in assessing the role and function of culturally marked varieties of communication. These factors occur at all levels of linguistic-communicative structuring, including grammar (Errington 1998; Irvine and Gal 2000), deixis and gesture (Hanks 1990; Haviland 1998), narrative conventions (Hymes 1996; Blommaert 2000), and literacy (Collins and Blot 2003; Blommaert 2003). In recent years, they have led to the development of a research paradigm focusing on "language ideologies": culture- and society-specific views of language and communication that appear to dominate and organize the pragmatics of language (Schieffelin, Woolard and Kroskrity 1998).

The situational nature and contextual dependence of culture and the dynamism of ethnic style are amply demonstrated in Rampton's work (1996). Rampton investigated small groups of adolescents in urban areas in Britain. They were ethnically mixed groups consisting of Anglo youth and youngsters of Caribbean, Indian, or Pakistani descent. Rampton observed them in a variety of situations. He conducted interviews with the groups and with their members individually. He recorded their speech in sports events, music performances, and group meetings in private and public contexts. Rampton's multidimensional fieldwork offered very important insights into the relation between language and ethnicity (i.e., ethnic identity and its symbolic attributes, such as accents in speech, behavior, dressing). The group members performed what Rampton called "crossing." They switched codes with remarkable ease: sometimes switched into the ethnically marked varieties of English of other members of different ethnic descent. Anglos occasionally switched into Jamaican Creole or used a Panjabi word. This way, they moved out of their "Angloness" and temporarily took on their friends' ethnic identity. In most cases, these crossings worked smoothly. The boundaries of ethnicity appeared to be flexible and permeable. Moving in and moving out of these boundaries was not much of a problem.

The main argument of the research line represented by Gumperz, Hymes, Blommaert, Rampton, and others is that there is no single language, culture, or communicative style. What we have is language, culture, and communicative style instantiated in several group and individual varieties. In intercultural communication, speakers have a "repertoire" of varieties of styles and a combination of styles that are deployed according to communicative needs in the changing context. The nationality or ethnic membership of people may suggest the possibility of ethnic or cultural marking in communicative behavior. However, the interplay of several different factors affects the emergence of "ethnically" or "culturally marked" aspects of communicative behavior, which is most frequently dominated by other than cultural factors. Frustration and anger, powerlessness, or a feeling of threat may trigger ethnic style (cf. Giles and Johnson 1986; Blommaert 1998). The shift into an ethnic style may go hand-in-hand with the shift into a particularly emotional and highly sensitive domain of experience, as was demonstrated in Bulcean and Blommaert's research on immigrant females in refuges for battered women in Belgium; most of the younger Turkish women spoke near-native Dutch when they were interviewed (Bulcaen and Blommaert 1997). Rampton's data showed that, depending on who is addressed, when, and in what particular type of activity (e.g., playing, discussing, listening to music), the role and function of ethnically marked communication styles may change.

Both Blommaert's and Rampton's findings point to the fact that there is no single strategy associated with the use of ethnic styles. These styles are like a repertoire in the common underlying conceptual base of the multilingual and multicultural speakers, which can be activated in different circumstances, for different purposes, and with different effects. In the summary of his findings, Rampton underlined "how crossing varied in character according to the kind of event...in which it was embedded" (1995:265) and how it "involved the active ongoing construction of a new inheritance from within multiracial interaction itself" (1995:297).

According to Blommaert (1998:3) it is a mistake to consider intercultural communication only as a matter of colliding cultures and cultural gaps, something that is abnormal. He argued that the "abnormalization of intercultural communication is based on a gross hypostasis of 'culture' as the all-eclipsing contextual factor, and a massive overestimation of the degree and the nature of differences in speech styles. The way in which empirical answers can be found for patterns and problems in intercultural communication is a detailed and nuanced analysis of concrete communicative events."

Bulcean and Blommaert's and Rampton's data demonstrate that "culture" is situational in all its meanings and with all its affiliated concepts, and depends on the context in which concrete interactions occur. In their view culture cannot be seen as something that is "carved" in every member of a particular society or community. It can be made, changed, manipulated, and dropped on the spot. (In fact, it is not culture that can be changed, manipulated, and dropped in talk, but its manifestation.) This argument has close connections with the claim of theorists of meaning, who say that meaning is a situated, fluid, and online phenomenon (e.g., Evans 2009; Wittgenstein 2001). Thus, researchers in two different paradigms seem to have come to similar conclusions. This makes sense if we think about how the interaction is governed by communicative need affected by social dynamics and cultural crossing. Blommaert (1998), following the line of argument developed by Gumperz, Hymes, and others, claimed that culture is rarely unified, and new contexts generate new cultures and new forms of intercultural communication. Rampton's research (1995) provided empirical substance for the old Sapirian claim that one society can hide many societies, one culture can hide many cultures, and one language can hide many languages.

This, however, does not mean that there is nothing relatively stable and unifying in culture. On this issue there is a significant difference between the constructivist view represented by Blommaert, Gumperz, and Rampton, and intercultural pragmatics. According to Blommaert, Rampton, and others, there is no single language, culture, or communicative style. What we have is language, culture, and communicative style instantiated in several group and individual varieties. Interlocutors have a repertoire of varieties of styles and a combination of styles that are deployed according to communicative needs in changing contexts. The difference between the constructivist view and intercultural pragmatics lies in the understanding of the nature *of existing "communicative repertoires" and the ways these repertoires are deployed.* Existing communicative repertoires have been developed from prior experience and communicative encounters. What the online creation of culture means is similar to what online, actual meaning construction means: the bringing about of something needed in the actual situational context by using the existing repertoires and newly emergent elements. Culture, just like meaning, is characterized by both regularity and variety. It certainly is more than just an online created and co-constructed phenomenon. In communication, interactants can rely on two types of repository of prior experience and encounters: lexical units and communicative styles. Like lexical items, cultural patterns (often expressed in different communicative styles) code prior experience and encounters, i.e., relatively standard cultural behavior models and expectations that are activated in a given situational context. In the course of interaction, these existing models are modified and blended with situationally emergent new elements. This process of blending, which relies both on existing and emerging factors, constitutes the communicative encounter. Blending means joining these elements/factors into new intercultures. In the interaction the communicative repertoires of speakers are not just deployed but are actually modified and blended with emerging elements as the process develops. Intercultural pragmatics emphasizes that "third culture" creation means not just putting together what we have and bringing about a third phenomenon that is neither this or that, but giving sense to the communicative repertoires and changing them by relating them to the actual situational context, which also adds to or takes away something from what is existing. This process is very similar to linguistic creativity, which will be discussed in the next chapter.

3. Cultural Models

3.1. THE NATURE OF CULTURAL MODELS

Cultural models are cognitive frames or templates of assumed or implicit knowledge that assist individuals in interpreting and understanding information and events. Encyclopedic knowledge includes cultural models that are usually defined as "a cognitive schema that is intersubjectively shared by a social group (D'Andrade 1992:99)." There exist certain mental 'schemas,' which are activated when an individual experiences similar new situations or linguistic tasks. When we interact with members of the same culture in certain situations many times, or talk about certain information with them many times, cultural schemas are created and stored in our brain (cf. Nishida 1999). The development of these schemas is based on repeated prior experience, and they guide our behaviors in similar and familiar situations. The notion of "schema" was first introduced by Immanuel Kant to account for the mediation between logical concepts and sensory information, which gives "significance" to our mental representations. Research exploring the intersection of culture and the individual claims that cognition consists of subsets of shared *cultural models* that organize much of how people make sense of the world (e.g., D'Andrade 1992; DiMaggio 1997; Shore 1996). D'Andrade (1992:29) argued that a cultural model can be understood as "an interpretation which is frequent, well organized, memorable, which can be made from minimal cues, contains one or more prototypic instantiations, and is resistant to change." In cognitive linguistics the cultural models underlying reasoning and argumentation are considered to some extent idealized entities (see, for instance, the notion of Idealized Cognitive Models as introduced in Lakoff 1987). Geeraerts argued that actually occurring phenomena and actual situations usually differ to a smaller or greater extent from the models that act as cognitive reference points. The models themselves appear to be somewhat abstract, general, or even simplistic, because we use them to make sense of phenomena that are oftentimes more complicated (Geeraerts 2006:274).

Cultural models become internalized by individuals through everyday shared processes (e.g., DiMaggio 1997). These processes are cognitive patterns that develop from different types of inputs, such as instruction, activities, communication, observation, practices, and so on. Each human being is exposed to various aspects of the socio-cultural life, which leads to membership of a subset of socio-cultural speech communities (Shore 1996). Each speech community is identified by a variety of dominant cultural models that provide certain assumptions and outlook on the world. Because cultural models are a part of a person's cognitive resources, they influence his/her world view and behavior, as well as how s/he interprets and reacts to other people's behavior, information, and situations.

We must be careful, however, because although cultural models usually create a harmonizing effect, people are not cognitive clones of culture. In the socio-cognitive paradigm collective cultural models are internalized and privatized by individuals through their own experience and developed into private mental models. However, any sharp distinction between private mental models and collective cultural models is purely analytical. Cultural models stand out as standards and prototypes that are used to interpret and assess conduct, not to guide and direct it. Actual situations and personalities then lead interlocutors to act in accordance with or deviate from those prototypes, and may even lead them to claim a special virtue if they adhere to them or guilt or shame if they don't. But whether someone adheres or not does not depend on the cultural model itself. In real life much depends on an individual's cognitive dispositions and preference. For instance:

(1) Car rental
CLERK: What can I do for you, sir?
CUSTOMER: I have a reservation.
CLERK: May I see your driver's license?
CUSTOMER: Sure. Here you are.

Most people are familiar with the cultural frame of renting a car. Certain situation-bound utterances (see Kecskes 2000; 2003) such as "what can I do for you?," "I have a reservation," "May I see your driver's license?," and the like are expected to be used in this frame. However, how exactly this frame is played out depends on various factors, including the individuals' prior experience, who participated in its activation, environment, time-constraints, and so on.

Social and cultural routines result in recurring activities and institutions. However, these institutions and routinized activities have to be rebuilt continuously in the here and now. The question is whether these cultural models, institutions, and frames exist outside language or not. The social constructivists insist that models and frames have to be rebuilt again and again, so it is just our impression that they exist outside language. However, the socio-cognitive approach argues that these cultural mental models have some kind of psychological reality in the individual mind, and when a concrete situation occurs, the appropriate model is recalled, which supports the appropriate verbalization of triggered thoughts and activities. Of course, building and rebuilding our world occurs not merely through language but through the interaction of language with other real-life phenomena such as nonlinguistic symbol systems, objects, tools, technologies, and so forth.

The individual is not only constrained to some extent by collective cultural models but also participates in creating them. Private models may originate from a person's creative (and even unintended) combination of existing cultural models as well as unique cognitive dispositions (self-reflection, critical thinking, etc). Some private models always remain idiosyncratic (i.e., private), while others may enter into the socio-cultural framework and establish new cultural trends (e.g., Berger and Luckmann 1967). Both private and cultural models help people organize events, make actions easier, and, as such, free up cognitive resources that can be applied to less familiar issues and experiences.

3.2. THE "REALITY" OF CULTURAL MODELS

Language and culture are usually considered "collective representations," i.e., socially constituted systems (e.g., Saussure 2002; Durkheim 1947; Kronenfeld 2008). There are two main approaches to the debate about the actual existence of these systems. According to one of them, these systems have been considered to be merely epiphenomenal, which means that they have no actual direct existence (e.g., Kronenfeld 2008). However, they have the appearance of direct existence insofar as they are the byproducts of a group of individuals with similar minds confronting similar situations in similar contexts. The problem with this approach is that human beings usually talk about and rely upon language and culture as if they actually exist, as if they exist externally to them as individuals. Our individual understandings of language and culture are quite consistent across individuals. Generally, this is greater than our sense of our own individual patterns. We have highly shared senses of the collective patterns, and each of us is capable of describing where we ourselves deviate, or are somewhat idiosyncratic.

The opposing view to nonexistence has been that these systems have some sort of objective existence outside the individual. Culture is "real," and deals with the problems of the relationship between the individual and the given community. This approach that is adopted by SCA sees a child's socialization or enculturation as a process by which basic cultural structures and schemata represented out there in the world in the behavior of others are "internalized" deeply into the individual psyche. However, these cultural models and schemata keep changing both diachronically and synchronically. Definitely there is a great difference between cultural models that existed a hundred years ago and the ones that we have in our time. Besides, the internalization process is not mechanical, i.e., enculturation occurs as a bidirectional interaction between the individual and the social environment (Kecskes 2009).

When we talk about culture, we usually mean "subjective culture" (cf. Triandis 2002), which is a community's characteristic way of perceiving its social environment. However, there are generally two basic aspects of culture distinguished. When this distinction is not clarified, confusion may occur about whether culture exists "out there" or not. One aspect of culture is subjective culture—the psychological feature of culture including assumptions, values, beliefs, and patterns of thinking. The other is objective culture, which includes the institutions and artifacts of culture, such as its economic system, social customs, political structures and processes, arts, crafts, and literature. Objective culture can be treated as an externalization of subjective culture, which usually becomes reified. This means that those institutions that are properly seen as extensions of human activity attain an independent status as external entities. They seem to exist "out there," and their ongoing human origins are usually forgotten. The study of objective culture is well established because institutions and external artifacts of behavior are more accessible to observation and examination. Subjective culture is usually treated as an unconscious process influencing perception, thinking, and memory, or as personal knowledge that is inaccessible to trainers or educators.

Simmel (1972) also pointed out a difference between subjective culture and objective culture, with the latter referring to the cultural level of social reality. In his view, people produce culture, but because of their ability to reify social reality, the cultural world and the social world come to have lives of their own and increasingly dominate the actors who created them. We may also think about language like this.

Language has been created and is being created by people, but appears to have a life of its own as an institution "out there." Simmel identified a number of components of objective culture, including tools, transportation, technology, the arts, language, the intellectual sphere, conventional wisdom, religious dogma, philosophical systems, legal systems, moral codes, and ideals. The size of objective culture increases with modernization. The number of different components of the cultural realm also grows.

Simmel was concerned about the effect of objective culture on the individual's subjective existence. Postmodernists have taken that concern to another level. In the past, most of the culture was produced by people situated in real social groups that interacted over real issues. This grounded culture created real meanings and morally infused norms, values, and beliefs. In the postmodern era, a new, powerful shaping influence is from business producing or colonizing much of the culture by business advertising and mass media. According to Simmel, this important historic shift implies that culture has changed from a representation of social reality to representations of commodified images. In our time culture is produced rather than created, and people have changed from culture creators to culture consumers.

4. Cultural Models at Work

4.1. DEVELOPMENT OF CULTURAL MODELS

Each of us has rich individual experiences, and the cognitive structuring that pertains to them may differ, whether coded linguistically or not. When communicating with other people through language or otherwise, we need to interrelate our separate experiences and cognitive structures. When we routinely, repeatedly do things with other people, we usually develop some standardized way of doing those things. These shared action plans may emerge as cultural models. Kronenfeld (2008) argued that language gets involved when we need to verbally communicate, and then only with regard to those aspects of the action plan that need to be discussed and talked about or coded in memory. He emphasized that language is a socially constructed tool that can be exceedingly helpful to thought, but in no sense does it form the basis for individual thought, and it need not provide the basis for (much of) the shared or coordinated thought that makes up culture.

I think language plays a more important role than the one Kronenfeld assigns to it in culture. In fact, language supports both the development and reinforcement of cultural models, mainly through formulaic language, which is the heart and soul of the language use of a speech community and the basis of what we often call "native-like language use."[1] Both cultural models and formulaic expressions are the

---

[1] We all know that "native-like language use" is an abstraction that nobody knows how to define. We use the term in its traditional sense, referring to language proficiency that L1 speakers usually have.

results of reoccurring actions and behaviors. Formulaic language generally serves as a core for language use in a speech community because prefabricated linguistic expressions are usually the results of doing things in a particular way and mean the same for each member of the community. As mentioned in Chapter 3, languages and their speakers have preferred ways of saying things (cf. Wray 2002; Kecskes 2007a). Native English speakers *shoot a film*, *dust the furniture*, *make love*, or ask you to *help yourself* at the table. The use of these expressions creates scenarios and gives a certain kind of idiomaticity to language use. For instance:

(2)

>   JIM: Let me tell you something.
>   BOB: What...? Is something wrong?

The expression *"Let me tell you something"* usually has negative connotation, creating a scenario that anticipates trouble. Our everyday communication is full of prefabricated expressions and utterances, because we like to stick to our preferred ways of saying things. They trigger similar scenarios and familiar cultural models.

Cultural models provide a kind of reference library for possible plans of action for oneself or possible interpretation of actions of others. These models are not learned directly as models, but are inferred by each of us from what we see and experience with those other people around us. But what we see and experience are never the models themselves. What we infer from experience are pieces of information, images, features that keep a model together. What we infer depends directly on what parts of the given scenario are saliently and repetitively present in the messages we experience for us to pull out the regularities on which we will base our construction of the model behind them. Thus, systematic and repeated changes in speech or cultural behavior in one generation will be learned by the next generation as part of the givens of language or culture.

The cultural models that we actually experience (that is, cultural models, in the form in which we actually experience them) acquire specificity through the process of their instantiation in the concrete situations in which the models were realized. Much of our application of cultural models (instantiation and then realization) is in situations that represent some kind of extension from the prototypical, unmarked default situation. The core of cultural models that people in the same speech community share changes diachronically through systematic and repeated shifts that can come from socio-political changes, technological changes, environmental changes, and the like. For instance, at the beginning of the 1990s, we could usually see the following sign at construction sites: "Men at work." However, by the end of the '90s this sign was replaced by "Crew at work," a gender-neutral reference. This shift was the result of a socio-political practice that prefers the use of gender-neutral terms in language.

The application of the core of a cultural model, however, changes synchronically. No situation occurs exactly the same way as we have experienced it in any previous time. See, for instance, example (1) above, where the cultural frame (car rental) can be filled in with different utterances. In the socio-cognitive paradigm, action is always performed by individuals, and individuals are always adapting cultural models to the situation at hand to fit their needs. People use cultural models as devices to facilitate effective interaction with others in the various communities to which they belong. In this way, individuals not only shape cultural models but also are constrained by them. Most of these cultural models come from people's past experience, but they are constantly recreated in use. It is important to note that people are not required to follow cultural conventions (whether in the use of cultural models or in other ways). In any given time, they can ignore or modify cultural models that kick in in their mind when they get into a typical situation. Given that cultural models can (and often do) show slight variations across groups to which we all belong—groups that can be formal or informal, long-lived or evanescent, imposed or voluntary, and so forth.

4.2. INSTANTIATING CULTURAL MODELS

Cultural models are abstract plans at varying degrees of specificity. They relate knowledge, goals, values, perceptions, emotional states, and so on to actions in different contexts. Kronenfeld (2008) argued that these conceptual models do not directly or automatically apply to any specific situation. First they have to be "instantiated" by having their general generic details replaced with the specific details of the situation at issue. The instantiated cultural model is still only a conceptual structure, and several different (even mutually contradictory) ones may be taken into consideration for any given situation. Finally, one particular instantiated model is "realized" in the actual situational context. This can be an action plan for one's own behavior, or a device for interpreting the behavior of some other people. It is important to note that at any given moment, only one instantiated model can be realized. But we can quickly jump back and forth between different realizations.

The relationship between the abstract collective cultural model and the private realization of the model by interlocutors in a concrete situation is the same as in linguistics between "phonemes" and "phones" or between "morphemes" and "morphs." We consider "phones" as the actual phonetic realization of "phonemes," and morphs as the actual forms used to realize morphemes. In his pragmatic acts theory, Mey (2001) speaks about "pragmemes" that are instantiated in pragmatic acts in speech situations. A particular pragmeme can be substantiated and realized through individual pragmatic acts. In other words, a pragmatic act is an instance of adapting oneself to a context, as well as adapting the context to oneself. For instance:
(3)

> MARY: She is after my money.
> BILL: *Like I care.*

"*Like I care*" is a pragmatic act that expresses the pragmeme "I do not care," which can also be substantiated by several other concrete pragmatic acts such as "*I do not care," "I do not mind," "it's none of my business,"* and so forth. According to Mey, pragmatic acts are situation-derived and situation-constrained. There is no one-to-one relationship between speech acts and pragmatic acts because the latter does not necessarily include specific acts of speech. For instance (the same example was used as example #5 in Chapter 1):

(4)

> MOTHER: Joshua, what are you doing?
> JOSHUA: Nothing.
> MOTHER: Will you stop it immediately. (Mey 2001:216)

The pragmeme represented by the pragmatic act "nothing" can be described as "trying to get out (opt out) of a conversation" that may lead too far. But pragmemes in the sense as Mey uses the term are not cultural models. They are more like scenarios within cultural models. However, the process of instantiation happens similarly both in the case of pragmemes and cultural models.

This is where we can also demonstrate the difference between intercultural communication and intracultural communication. Cultural models are usually language specific, generally with some universal core. Instantiation of cultural models is even more language specific. The following conversation between an American professor and a Turkish student shows how cultural models are instantiated in intercultural communication.

(5)

> PROFESSOR: Is there anything else you want to tell us about yourself?
> AYSA: Uh,...no, nothing.... When can I call for the result?
> PROFESSOR: There is no need to contact us. We'll call you.
> AYSA: OK, but.., uhm,...when?
> PROFESSOR: Very soon.

The frame (job interview) has a universal core. However, how the expressions and utterances are formulated and selected refers to two different underlying cultural conventions. The Turkish student is eager to find out about the result of the interview.

In American culture, no hint is given after an interview. The expression "There is no need to contact us. We'll call you." demonstrates that the interviewee has no control of what happens after the interview. Still, the Turkish student continues insisting on getting at least some information about time. This does not happen.

4.3. PRACTICES

Culture includes many practices or routines. Feldman and Pentland (2003) argued that routines (i.e., practices) consist of two elements: the ostensive and the performative. The ostensive element comprises individuals' cognitive understanding of the processes, while the performative element consists of behavior in the actual situational context. From a socio-cognitive perspective both of these elements should be of interest for us. Cognitive understanding relies both on cultural and private models, and on how these models are applied by cognitive processing, spanning from automatic (as in categorical) thinking to self-reflective (as in reflective) thinking (see Ringberg and Reihlen 2008). When categorical thinking is applied, people establish meaning by automatically integrating incoming stimuli based on existing cultural and private models. Thinking in categories (male-female; marriage; university; etc.) helps people make sense of the world, although we know that categories have fuzzy boundaries. Categorical thinking allows us to transfer meanings and associations from a known context to one that is unfamiliar and uncertain to us. In intercultural communication, categorical thinking may be a source of misunderstanding because not all categories are universal, and in one language a particular category can be either broader or narrower than in another. For instance, in American English, the category "school" can include "university" as well, while this is not the case in Spanish, where "escuela" has a narrower scope.

Research in social cognition indicates that several epistemic factors can affect the applicability of categorical thinking. For instance, people usually apply categorical thinking in everyday routines, when they have high cognitive load, are under pressure to make quick decisions, have limited cognitive capacity, and/or are distracted. Categorical thinking generally leads to efficient processing of regular socio-cultural interactions and stimuli. As a consequence of relying on categorical thinking, environmental stimuli are "pushed" into existing mental models. This may prevent the person from adjusting to divergent inputs and unusual circumstances. For instance:

(6)

> ASSISTANT: *Can I help you*, Madame?
> CUSTOMER: Thank you. *I am just looking.*

In this exchange, the expressions "Can I help you?" and "I am just looking" function as plain situation-bound utterances. The customer is distracted because she is looking at clothes and the assistant appears to have disturbed her with his question.

Reflective processing works in a different way. It requires the ability of people to sustain a high level of cognitive responsiveness and combine, or broaden internalized cultural and private models in thoughtful and creative ways to improve their sense making. Reflective thinking means active connection making, which involves actively seeking connections between newly learned information and existing knowledge—a crucial element in the socio-cognitive approach.

The degree of application of categorical versus reflective thinking varies across situational contexts, and life experience and general acumen are also important variables. In reflective thinking, cultural and private models are applied in nonautomatic fashions. Ringberg & Reihlen (2008:923) argued that reflective thinking is a proactive process that occurs when a person has the cognitive capacity and need for deliberate cognition to engage with stimuli that are not easily or use-fully made sense of by a categorical application of private and/or cultural models. Category-inconsistent information may activate reflective thought processes among some people, through which they recombine cultural and private models in deliber-ate ways to improve the relevance of their sense making of a particular situation (e.g., Bodenhausen, Macrae and Garst 1998; Sperber and Wilson 2004).

(7)

Let us consider the following excerpt from the film *Coogan's Bluff*. Clint Eastwood is talking to his partner in a restaurant. They are about to pay the bill.

> GIRL: I have to be going…(putting some money on the table)
> CE: What are you doing?
> GIRL: Go Dutch.
> CE: You are a girl, aren't you?
> GIRL: There have been rumors to that effect.
> CE: Sit back and act like one.
> GIRL: Oh, is that the way girls act in Arizona?

In this conversation there is a clear difference between the man's private con-text and the woman's private context tied to the scenario "paying the bill." The collective cultural model attached to "paying the bill" is that it is the man's respon-sibility to take care of it. The man wants to act according to that "requirement." However, the woman appears to have a private gender-motivated model that may be different from the collective model.

The socio-cognitive approach incorporates cultural and private models into categorical and reflective processing. This means that most of the time a cognitive system is neither fully closed nor fully open, neither fully determined nor indepen-dent of external sensory inputs, and people are neither autonomous processors nor cultural dopes. Consequently, meaning creation and knowledge transfer are located somewhere on a continuum between fully automatic and fully idiosyncratic. This depends on several variables that include the nature of people's private and cultural models, level of categorical and reflective thinking, and environmental feedback mechanisms. The socio-cognitive approach broadens traditional positivist and social constructionist positions by situating sense making within the mind (and body) that may be influenced but rarely determined by environmental feedback mechanisms (Bandura 1986; Bunge 1996).

5. Interculturality

In the center of intercultural pragmatics is the concept of interculturality. Interculturality as was defined in the "Introduction" is a situationally emergent and co-constructed phenomenon that relies both on relatively definable cultural norms and models as well as situationally evolving features. This is a "third space" phenomenon that fits into the socio-cognitive approach very well. The important thing is that co-construction can occur only if participants have something to co-construct from. This "something" in communication is double-sided. On the one hand it contains normative elements such as cultural models, frames, and beliefs that the interlocutors have prior to the actual speech situation. The other side of this "something" is represented by novel emergent elements in the situational contexts that are blended with normative elements during the co-construction. This is how individual elements blend with social factors, and in the process co-construct each other, which creates the dynamism and ever-changing nature of intercultural encounters. Intersubjectivity (Rommetveit 1992) that develops between interlocutors is an essential part of the process. It refers to the development of a shared understanding or focus on particular elements of the communicative process between speaker(s) and listener(s). This development serves as a basis for common ground building and mutual understanding, as we will see later. As discussed in the Introduction, cultural constructs and models change diachronically, while cultural representation and speech production by individuals change synchronically.

It is important to note that there are understandings of "interculturality" out there, other than the one we have defined for intercultural pragmatics. They refer to "interculturality" as capacity and/or awareness rather than something that is created in language use. For instance, Barrett (2008) considers interculturality "the capacity to experience cultural otherness and to use this experience to reflect on matters which are normally taken for granted within one's own culture and environment.... in addition, interculturality involves using this heightened awareness of otherness to evaluate one's own everyday patterns of perception, thought, feeling and behavior in order to develop greater self-knowledge and self-understanding."

In this chapter we need to clarify the relationship of interculturality with intraculturality, and explain the normative side of the co-construction process, focusing mainly on cultural models.

5.1. INTERCULTURAL AND INTRACULTURAL

When defining interculturality in communication, we should make an attempt to separate it from intraculturality. There have been several attempts (e.g., Samovar and Porter 2001; Ting-Toomey 1999; Gudykunst and Mody 2002; Nishizaka 1995) to explain the difference between the two. According to Samovar and Porter (2001), "intracultural communication" is "the type of communication that takes place between members of the same dominant culture, but with slightly different values," as opposed to "intercultural communication," which is the communication between two or more distinct cultures. This approach has led to a common mistake that several researchers have committed. They have considered interculturality as the main reason for miscommunication (e.g., Thomas 1983; Hinnenkamp 1995; Ting-Toomey 1999). In fact, some researchers' findings show the opposite (e.g., House 2003; Kecskes 2008). The use of semantically transparent language by nonnative speakers results in fewer misunderstandings and communication break-downs than expected. The insecurity experienced by lingua franca speakers causes them to establish a unique set of rules for interaction that may be referred to as an interculture, according to Koole and ten Thije (1994:69): a "culture constructed in cultural contact."

Blum-Kulka et al. (2008:164) defined interculturality as "a contingent inter-actional accomplishment" from a discursive-constructivist perspective. They argued that a growing literature explores interculturality as a participant con-cern (e.g., Higgins 2007; Mori 2003; Markee and Kasper 2004). Nishizaka (1995) pointed out that interculturality is a situationally emergent rather than a norma-tively fixed phenomenon. As we have seen, the socio-cognitive approach (Kecskes 2008; Kecskes and Zhang 2009; Kecskes 2010a) goes one step further and defines interculturality as a phenomenon that is not only interactionally and socially con-structed in the course of communication but also relies on relatively definable cultural models and norms that represent the speech communities to which the interlocutors belong.

As far as the relation between intracultural and intercultural communication is concerned, I will argue that it is more like a continuum than a dichotomy. It is not necessarily very clear where intracultural communication ends and intercul-tural communication begins if we look at their main characteristic features only. However, the degree of difference between the two ends of the continuum depends mainly on how proficient the interlocutors are in the language that is used as the medium of communication. There is hardly any proficiency issue affecting intra-cultural communication. Of course, there are several other variables that affect this degree, such as cultural sensitivity, identity, familiarity, topic, and so forth. But all of them appear to be secondary to language proficiency since high proficiency and relative fluency in language use presupposes more attention to the communi-cative process itself rather than just to language use issues (word choice, fluency, correctness, etc.).

intracultural comm.----------------------------------intercultural comm.

Within the socio-cognitive paradigm it is hypothesized that the higher the pro-ficiency level of the interlocutors is in the lingua franca, the more the communica-tive process resembles intracultural communication. (This issue will be revisited in the chapter on formulaic language.) The real problem for intercultural communica-tion research is that it seems to have been focusing more on the right side of the continuum rather than the left side that represents communication between highly proficient speakers of the target language. For instance, the editorial of a 2006 edi-tion of the *Journal of Intercultural Communication Research* claimed that "during intercultural communication, the message sent is usually not the message received" and that "intercultural communication necessarily involves a clash of communica-tor style" (Neuliep 2006:1). It is quite difficult to agree with this claim if we think about the huge amount of successful international/interethnic/intercultural interactions that occur on a daily basis all across the world.

Another crucial issue in the discussion about intracultural and intercultural communication is blending. Co-constructing and blending in intercultural interactions rely on two sources: previously existing cultural models and frames tied to the L1 culture of the interlocutors plus novel elements emerging in the course of the intercultural interaction. The difference is that while in intracultural communication the first source (L1 socio-cultural background) is relatively common for language users, in intercultural communication this is not so. How much interlocutors are familiar with the target language culture encoded in the expressions of the L2 is usually unknown. Speakers enter into the intercultural communicative process and are supposed to adjust to cultural models and norms tied to the target language they use, which is not the L1 of any of them. They do not know what they can expect from the other(s). Mismatch in knowing culturally loaded expressions may lead to misunderstandings, as in the following conversation between a Chinese and a Turkish student.

(8)

> CHINESE: I think Peter drank a bit too much at the party yesterday.
> TURKISH: Eh, *tell me about it*. He always drinks too much.
> CHINESE: When we arrived he drank beer. Then Mary gave him some vodka. Later he drank some wine. Oh, too much.
> TURKISH: Why are you telling me all this? I was there.

The expression "tell me about it" actually means the opposite of what it says: don't tell me about it because I know it, I have been there, I have experienced it, and so on. Native speakers often use this situation-bound utterance. However, nonnative speakers who do not know the socio-cultural load of the expression can easily misinterpret it. The problem is that in intercultural interaction neither party can be sure whether the other is familiar with the socio-cultural load of the expression or not. This problem would not occur in intracultural communication.

5.2. INTERCULTURES

Intercultures are ad hoc creations. They are produced in a communicative process in which cultural norms and models brought into the interaction from prior experience of interlocutors blend with features created ad hoc in the interaction in a synergetic way. The result is intercultural discourse in which there is mutual transformation of knowledge and communicative behavior rather than transmission. The emphasis is on transformation rather than on transmission.

Interculturality has both an *a priori side* and an *emergent side* that occur and act simultaneously in the communicative process. Consequently, *intercultures* are not fixed phenomena, but are created in the course of interaction. The following conversation (source, Albany English Lingua Franca Dataset collected by PhD students) among a Brazilian girl, a Colombian student, and a Hong Kong student illustrates this point well.

(9)

> B: Have you ever heard about au pair before?
> COL: No, what is au pair?
> H-K: It's a French word.
> B: ...we come as an exchange to take care of kids.
> COL: What kids?
> B: Kids in the host family. We live with the host family.
> H-K: By the way, how about the kids? How do you know what to do with them?
> B: We have to go to training.

In this conversation interlocutors represent three different languages and cultures (Brazilian, Colombian, Hong Kong Chinese), and use English as a lingua franca. This is the prior knowledge that participants bring to the interaction. They create an interculture, which belongs to none of them but emerges in the course of conversation. Within this interculture, the three speakers have a relatively smooth conversation about the job of "au pairs" (domestic assistants). Neither of them is sure what, exactly, the term means, with the exception of the Brazilian girl, who actually works as an au pair. There are no misunderstandings in the interaction because intersubjectivity develops gradually and each participant is careful to use semantically transparent language in order to be as clear as possible.

Intercultures come and go, so they are neither stable nor permanent. They just occur. They are both synergetic and blended. But isn't this a phenomenon that also occurs in intracultural communication? Why and how should we distinguish intercultural communication from intracultural communication? Basically, the currently dominant approach to this issue is that there is no *principled* difference between intracultural and intercultural communication (e.g., Winch 1997; Wittgenstein 2001). This is true as far as the mechanism of the communicative process is concerned. However, as was discussed above, language proficiency is an issue in intercultural communication while it is not in intracultural interaction. There is also a qualitative difference in the nature and content of an intracultural interaction and an intercultural interaction. Speakers in intracultural communication rely on prior knowledge and culture of a relatively definable speech community, which is privatized by individuals belonging to that speech community. No language boundaries are crossed, although subcultures are relied upon and representations are individualized. What is created in the actual intercultural interaction enriches the given culture, contributes to it, and remains within the fuzzy but still recognizable confines of that language and culture. In the case of intercultural communication, however, prior knowledge that is brought into and privatized in the communicative process belongs to different cultures and languages, and what participants create in the actual situational context will disappear and not become an enrichment and/or addition to any particular culture or language. Intercultures are ad hoc creations that may enhance the individual and the globalization process, but can hardly be said to contribute to any particular culture. Of course, intercultures can exist for a shorter or longer time depending on the length and intensivity of encounters among the participants

5.3. COMMUNITIES OF PRACTICE

The socio-cognitive approach is against those contemporary endeavors that try to bundle languages and cultures into a big globalized whole where there are no boundaries at all, everything is "malleable and porous," and nothing is definable. This is what Hall et al. (2006:232) write about this issue:

"What are needed, we suggest, are new concepts and terms that capture contemporary understandings of language knowledge as emergent and provisional constellations of structures, whose shapes and boundaries are as malleable and porous as the social actions in which they are grounded. For example, like Pavlenko (2000), we suggest replacing the notion of language groups with that of 'communities of practice' (Chaiklin and Lave 1993; Lave and Wenger 1991). Communities of practice are social groups composed of individuals who come together for shared purposes that are organized around, for example, social, familial, or professional goals. Locating theoretical and conceptual concerns with language knowledge in communities of practice rather than in groups defined by language codes moves the focus away from acontextual language systems and toward communicative activities comprising particular communities of practice. Likewise, it defines individual language knowledge not in terms of abstract system components but as communicative repertoires—conventionalized constellations of semiotic resources for taking action—that are shaped by the particular practices in which individuals engage, be they interpersonal, that is, practices that involve others, or intrapersonal, that is, practices such as thinking, planning, and self-reflecting that involve just the individual (Vygotsky 1986). Terms like reorganization, redirection, expansion, and transformation, then, become useful in describing the continual evolution of individuals' language knowledge as they move into different contexts and appropriate different means for taking action."

The main problem with the usage-based approach is that individual language knowledge in L2 is not necessarily the result of language socialization and participation in communities of practice as is the case in L1. Much of this knowledge (especially in a foreign language environment) may originate through studying the linguistic code itself rather than just emerging in lifelike social experience through language use. Besides, as argued in Chapter 3 individual wiliness to accept certain community practices may vary.

Another issue with the usage-based approach is that it just does not work very well in intercultural communication in which, as it was discussed earlier, intercultures do not give much opportunity for conventionalization the way language use in communities of practice does. The communicative expertise that characterizes intercultural interactions usually lacks the most crucial element of the definition of communities of practice: repeating the experience in similar circumstances and sharing knowledge for a longer time. In communities of practice there is reoccurrence of frames and language, which is rarely the case in intercultural interactions. While rare, however, it is not impossible, since the same group of nonnative speakers can, on occasion, meet regularly and create a community of practice.

Hymes (1974:51) defines a speech community as "a community sharing knowledge of rules for the conduct and interpretation of speech. Such sharing comprises knowledge of at least one form of speech, and knowledge also of its patterns of use."

Lave and Wegner's (1991:98) concept of community of practice refers to "a set of relations among persons, activity, and world, over time and in relation with other tangential and overlapping communities of practice" through which learners move from "legitimate peripheral participation" to full membership in the socio-cultural practices of a particular community. Wenger, McDermott, and Synder (2002:4) also explain communities of practice as "groups of people who share a concern, a set of problems, or a passion about a topic, and who deepen their knowledge and expertise in this area by interacting on an ongoing basis." Each of these definitions contains an element of "over time," which is only partially there in intercultural communication.

5.4. CROSSING LANGUAGE BOUNDARIES

An example of intracultural communication would be if a dentist in the dominant culture, say, in the United States, spoke about dental issues with a plumber belonging to the same US culture. Their negotiation may not be entirely smooth because the plumber might not be very knowledgeable about dental terms. If, however, the American dentist speaks with another American dentist about dental issues, they would certainly understand each other's language use quite well, although still there might be individual differences. This is what prompts the argument that a US dentist would understand an English-speaking French dentist better than she would understand an English native-speaker plumber. However, we must be very careful with judgments like this. One intercultural situation may differ from another intracultural situation to a great extent. I have argued elsewhere (Kecskes 2009) that it is important to make a distinction between *a quantitative change* and *a qualitative change*, and between changes occurring within a culture or across cultures. If a person moves from Albany, New York, to New Orleans, Louisiana, and makes adjustments to the new Louisiana subculture, he may start to say things like "I might could do this." This scenario, however, cannot be compared *qualitatively* to a case where a person moves from Albany, New York, to Lille, France. In the first case we can speak about peripheral rather than core changes in the language use of the person. Louisiana culture and Upstate New York culture can be considered subcultures of American culture, and Louisiana dialect and the Upstate New York dialect are dialects of American English. However, the change is different when a person moves from Albany, New York, to Lille, France. Upstate New York dialect compares to the Picard dialect of Lille (rural area) differently than to the Louisiana dialect. In this case we speak about dialects of different languages (English and French) while in the first case we speak about dialects of the same language (English). *There is a qualitative difference between crossing language boundaries and crossing dialects* (but staying within the confines of the core of one particular language).

The same is true for cultures. The relationship between American and French cultures qualitatively differs from the relationship between Louisiana subculture and Upstate New York subculture. English-French bilingualism may create qualitatively different changes in the mind and behavior of a person than Louisiana-Upstate New York bi-dialectalism (Kecskes 2009). I would like to emphasize that this view does not represent a homogenous approach to language and culture. Languages and cultures are never homogenous. *What is temporarily and relatively homogenous-like is the linguistic faculty (language system) that changes diachronically while language use changes synchronically.*

There is another major difference between intracultural and intercultural communication. As it was mentioned several times in the previous chapters, intracultural communication is dominated by preferred ways of saying things (Wray 2002) and preferred ways of organizing thoughts within a particular speech community (Kecskes 2007). This is not the case in intercultural communication because the development of "preferred ways" requires time and conventionalization within a speech community. Human languages are very flexible. They can lexicalize whatever their speakers find important to lexicalize. There are preferred ways of lexicalizing certain actions, phenomena, and things. Americans "shoot a film," "catch cold," "make money," "do the dishes," and so on. One language names something directly while the other prefers a metaphorical expression. In Russian they have the word "spargal'ki" to denote notes for cheating in school. In Hungarian the same phenomenon is denoted by the word "puska," which can be translated into English as "gun." These words are used metaphorically in Russian and Hungarian, not naming the purpose of use directly. However, in American English we have "cheat sheets" and British English has "cribs," or "crib notes," where the expression's literal meaning describes its goal. In other cases one language has a word for a phenomenon that is important in that culture, and the other does not. For instance, there is no equivalent word in English for "schadenfreude" (German), which refers to the feeling of pleasure derived by seeing another's misfortune.

Knowing what expressions to select, what is appropriate or inappropriate in different situations, may be an important sign of *group-inclusiveness*, and "native-likeness," which is a notion with negative connotation nowadays, as stated earlier. In intercultural communication this group-inclusiveness is created on the spot by speakers with different linguistic and cultural backgrounds who can hardly rely on the advantageous use of formulaic and figurative elements of a common language. In an empirical study (discussed in detail in the next chapter) Kecskes

(2007) demonstrated that in lingua franca communication the use of formulaic language by the participants was less than 10 percent. Lingua franca speakers relied on semantically transparent language to make sure that their interlocutor could follow what they said. They also do this because they may not have had enough encounters with the target language and culture to be able to conventionalize the "preferred ways of saying things" and "preferred ways of organizing thoughts."

In this chapter we discussed how encyclopedic knowledge, cultural models, and intercultures relate to one another, and how they affect the language use of interlocutors.

Special attention was paid to the interplay of cultural models and situationally evolving features in the co-construction of intercultures. We emphasized that it would be erroneous to think that intercultural communication differs from intracultural communication because the former is more complicated than the latter, and the former leads to more miscommunication than the other. As we saw above, the dissimilarity is qualitative rather than quantitative, because there is a qualitative difference between crossing language boundaries and crossing dialects within a language. It was argued that formulaic language may be a crucial factor in distinguishing intracultural communication from intercultural communication. This issue will be further explored in the next chapter.

5

Formulaic Language Use

Formulaic language is not among the favorite topics of pragmaticians. Researchers, especially those working in the Gricean paradigm, usually ignore it. The explanation is quite simple. Formulaic language just does not fit into the "what is said—what is communicated" modular view. Besides, it is a real reflection of the social rather than structural side of language, with most formulaic expressions being ready-made units of social functions. In intercultural pragmatics, however, we cannot ignore this category because, as we saw in Chapter 3, these expressions are essential parts of pragmatic competence, reflections of native-like behavior and often express cultural values, social expectations, and speaker attitude.

By formulaic language we usually mean multiword collocations that are stored and retrieved holistically rather than being generated de novo with each use. Collocations, fixed semantic units, frozen metaphors, phrasal verbs, speech formulas, idioms, and situation-bound utterances can all be considered as examples of formulaic language (Howarth 1998; Wray 1999, 2002, 2005; Kecskes 2000). These word strings occurring together tend to convey holistic meanings that are either more than the sum of the individual parts, or diverge significantly from a literal or word-for-word meaning and operate as a single semantic unit (Gairns and Redman 1986:35).

Formulaic language is the heart and soul of native-like language use. In intercultural communication one of the major issues is to decide how exactly we expect interlocutors to use the common language, the lingua franca. Is it enough for the participants to simply use the common language as a system of linguistics signs (sticking mainly to the literal meanings of lexical units) with possible meanings that are disambiguated and negotiated in the process of interaction? Or do we expect that the interlocutors stick to the rules of the game and act similarly to what the native speakers of that language do, i.e., rely on both prefabricated chunks and ad hoc generated elements, combining them in a creative way? I know that with this question I have opened Pandora's jar (originally it was a "jar," not a "box"). Now readers may want me to define what I mean by "native speakers," "how I determine what language" is in the era of "community practices," and why I think that nonnative speakers should follow what the native speakers do when they are speakers in their own right. Well, let's just put these issues aside for the moment and turn to formulaic language whose use (or not use) is a crucial issue in intercultural pragmatics.

1. Much of What We Say Consists of Formulaic Units

Coulmas (1981:1) argued that much of what is actually said in everyday conversation is by no means unique. "Rather, a great deal of communicative activity consists of enacting routines making use of prefabricated linguistic units in a well-known and generally accepted manner." He continued claiming that "successful co-ordination of social intercourse heavily depends on standardized ways of organizing interpersonal encounters (Coulmas 1981:3)." Howarth (1998) also talked about the fact that native speaker linguistic competence has a large and significant phraseological component. This means that the ability to sound idiomatic (achieving "nativelike selection," in the words of Pawley & Syder, 1983) plays a very important role in language production and comprehension. This fact has a profound effect on how we explain intercultural interaction because both figurative and formulaic language is the result of conventionalization and standardization that is supported by regular use of certain lexical units for particular purposes in a speech community. This is usually what nonnative speakers have limited access to in the target language. Therefore, discussion on the use of formulaic language appears to have special importance in intercultural pragmatics.

As mentioned in the previous chapters, people using a particular language and belonging to a particular speech community have *preferred ways of saying things* (cf. Wray 2002; Kecskes 2007a) and *preferred ways of organizing thoughts* (Kecskes 2007a). Preferred ways of saying things are generally reflected in the use of formulaic language and figurative language, while preferred ways of organizing thoughts can be detected through analyzing, for instance, the use of subordinate conjunctions, clauses, and discourse markers. Selecting the right words and expressions, and formulating utterances in ways preferred by the native speakers of that language ("nativelike selection"), is more important than syntax. The following examples demonstrate this clearly:

> (1) A sign in an Austrian hotel catering to skiers (source: *Octopus*, October 1995, Champaign, IL, p. 144):
> "Not to perambulate the corridors in the hours of repose in the boots of descension."
> Correctly: "Don't walk in the halls in ski boots at night."

The sentence shows absolutely bad word choices but acceptable syntax.

2. Linguistic Creativity

Since Hudson (1984) a number of linguists have come around to the view that the lexicon is the central component of a person's internal grammar, with the syntax as subsidiary. Linguistic general relativity signifies that every meaning element depends synchronically on every other (Ross 1992:158), and the "value" (or sense) of a meaning element (its particular meaning) depends on what it is combined with and in what perlocutionary role. Ross (1992:145) suggested that widely accepted views of the componentiality of utterance-meaning be rejected because "we are not combining fixed meaning-values (like fixed quantities) under a single structural syntax, but are combining varying values in a syntax-affecting way. Instead of the notion of units of meaning combined by insertion into syntactical slots to make sentential wholes, we have meaning units whose identity depends reciprocally on which meaning-units they combine with, so as to determine a semantic whole that has a definite syntactic structure as a result of the semantic adjustment. Thus, the explanatory order is exactly the reverse of what is usually supposed."

The proper use of formulaic language is one of the conditions for linguistic creativity. In my book on situation-bound utterances (Kecskes 2003:135-136) I argued that linguistic creativity in language use is not a sentence level phenomenon. Creativity in communicative behavior means much more than just combining words, or meaning-units, in a syntax-affecting way. When language is used for communication it usually works with meaning-units that are qualitatively and quantitatively more complex than sentences: oral and written texts or discourse. Creativity in the production of these higher level units can be regarded as an interplay of grammatical rules, lexical choice, functional adequacy, situational appropriateness, stylistic preference, and norms of use. *Combining prefabricated units with novel items (newly generated items) to express communicative intention and goals is what makes language use really creative and native-like.* Van Lancker and Rallon (2004) came to a similar conclusion when they noted that creativity in language consists of artfully mixing formulaic (thus, inherently noncreative) with creative novel items.

Linguistic creativity is closely related to blending, as discussed in the previous chapter. Formulaic expressions behave like "communicative repertoires" that are activated, and according to needs, generated by the actual situational context and blended with ad hoc created lexical units to form utterances. In intercultural communication the real question is if interlocutors with different L1s and socio-cultural background need these prefabricated units or not to communicate successfully with people of similar backgrounds.

3. Psychological Saliency and the Formulaic Continuum

3.1. PSYCHOLOGICAL SALIENCY OF WORD SEQUENCES

The importance of formulaic language was noticed in earlier linguistic research. Hymes (1962) pointed out that an immense portion of verbal behavior consists of linguistic routines. Bolinger suggested that "speakers do at least as much remembering as they do putting together" (Bolinger 1976:2). Fillmore also found that "an enormously large amount of natural language is formulaic, automatic and rehearsed, rather than propositional, creative or freely generated" (Fillmore 1976a:24). However, with the appearance of huge corpora, understanding formulaic language has become more complicated. Working with large corpora Altenberg (1998) went so far as to claim that almost 80 percent of our language production can be considered formulaic. Whatever the proportion actually is, one thing is for sure: speakers in conventional speech situations tend to do more remembering than putting together. Our everyday conversations are often restricted to short routinized interchanges where we do not always mean what we say. So a typical conversation between a customer and a store assistant may look like this:

(2)

> A: What can I do for you?
> C: Thank you, I am just looking.
> A: Are you looking for something particular?
> C: No, not really.
> A: If you need help, just let me know.

None of the expressions used by the speakers looks freely generated. Each of them can be considered a formula that is tied to this particular kind of situation. However, if we consider the following conversation, we may see something different.

(3) Sam and Bob are talking.

> S: **If you want** to see me again you will need to do **what I tell you** to.
> B: OK, **my friend.**

Can the expressions in bold be considered formulas? Are they in any way different from the ones in example (2)? There is no doubt that the expressions in bold consist of words that are frequently used together. But are they formulas here? Do they have some kind of psychological saliency as formulas for the speakers? We must be careful with the answer because frequency is only one of the criteria based on which we can identify formulaic expressions. The problem is that the role of frequency seems to be overemphasized in present-day linguistics, especially in corpus linguistics. Recent research analyzing written and spoken discourse has established that highly frequent, recurrent sequences of words, variously called lexical bundles, chunks, and multiword expressions are not only salient but also functionally significant. Cognitive research demonstrated that knowledge of these ready-made expressions is crucial for fluent processing. The recurrent nature of these units is discussed in the relevant literature (Biber et al. 1999; McEnery and Wilson 1996). Simpson-Vlach and Ellis (2010) confirmed that large stretches of language are adequately described as collocational streams where patterns flow into each other. Sinclair (1991; 2004) summarized this in his "idiom principle": "a language user has available to him or her a large number of semi-preconstructed phrases that constitute single choices, even though they might appear to be analyzable into segments." (Sinclair 1991:110). However, this principle is based not primarily on frequency that results in long lists of recurrent word sequences (e.g., Biber et al. 2004; Biber et al. 1999), which hardly give any chance to distinguish where we have conventionalized formulas or where we have just frequently occurring word chunks that lack psychological saliency. Biber et al. (1999:990), in their study of "lexical bundles," defined formulaic language as "sequences of word forms that commonly go together in natural discourse," irrespective of their structural make-up or idiomaticity, and argued that conversation has a larger amount of lexical bundle types than academic prose. However, there seems to be a clear difference from the perspective of psychological saliency between sequences such as "to tell the truth" and "as a matter of fact" on the one hand, and "I think you…" and "to make it" on the other, although all these expressions are high on any frequency-based list. *This is why we need to distinguish between groups of prefabricated expressions that have psychological saliency for speakers of a particular language community and loosely tied, frequently occurring word-sequences (usually consisting of common words)* such as "if they want," "to do with it," "and of the," "tell them to," and so on. Simpson-Vlach and Ellis (2010) argued that psycholinguistically salient sequences like "on the other hand" and "suffice it to say" cohere much more than would be expected by chance. They are "glued together" and thus measures of association, rather than raw frequency, are likely more relevant to these formulaic expressions.

Second language studies show something different. They emphasize the importance of frequency in processing formulaic language. Ellis et al. (2008) argued that formula processing by nonnatives, despite their many years of ESL instruction, was a result of the frequency of the string rather than its coherence. For learners at that stage of development, it is the number of times the string appears in the input that determines fluency. Ellis et al. said that tuning the system according to frequency of occurrence alone is not enough for nativelike accuracy and efficiency. According to those authors, what is additionally required is tuning the system for coherence—for co-occurrence greater than chance. Ellis et al. (2008) claimed that this is what solves the two puzzles for linguistic theory posed by Pawley and Syder (1983), nativelike selection and nativelike fluency. Native speakers have extracted the underlying co-occurrence information, often implicitly from usage; nonnatives, even advanced ESL learners with more than ten years of English instruction, still have a long way to go in their sampling of language. These learners are starting to recognize and become attuned to more frequent word sequences, but they need help to recognize distinctive formulas.

Why is this issue important for intercultural pragmatics? It is because the development of psychological validity/saliency of these expressions is a matter of not only frequency and exposure to the language use but also immersion in the culture and the preference of the nonnative speaker in whether s/he wants to use them or not. Frequent encounters with these expressions for nonnative speakers help but are not enough to develop psychological saliency, as the following encounter between a Korean student and a clerk at the Registrar's office demonstrates:

(4)

> LEE: Could you sign this document for me, please?
> CLERK: *Come again...?*
> LEE: Why should I come again? I am here now.

In spite of the distinctive intonation used by the clerk when uttering "come again," the Korean student processed the expression not as a formula but a freely generated expression with literal meaning. So what really counts is the "measures of association, rather than raw frequency." What creates psychological saliency is the discursive function in a particular context of that expression. The functional aspect is what makes immersion in the culture important for nonnative speakers, because that is where those functions come from.

The difference in developing and using formulaic language in native and non-native speakers raises two questions: (1) Do we need to split "lexical bundles" into two groups: one with prefabricated lexical units with psychological saliency (such as "you are all set," "I'll talk to you later," "don't hold your breath," "on the other hand," etc.), and another whose components do not have this psychological saliency as a formula but are very frequently put together in speech ("if you want," "but it is," "how would you?," etc.)?, (2) Not having "nativelike selections" skills and "nativelike fluency," how much can interlocutors stick to the original rules of the game in intercultural interactions? We will return to these questions later in this chapter.

3.2. THE FORMULAIC CONTINUUM

Certain language sequences have conventionalized meanings that are used in predictable situations. This functional aspect, however, is different in nature in each type of fixed expression, which justifies the hypothesis of a *continuum* (Kecskes 2003; 2007a) that contains grammatical units (for instance: *be going to*) on the left, fixed semantic units (cf. *as a matter of fact*; *suffice it to say*) in the middle, and pragmatic expressions (such as situation-bound utterances: *welcome aboard; help yourself*) and idioms ("make ends meet," "spill the beans") on the right. This continuum (see below, Table 5.1) categorizes only those expressions that are motivated and have some psychological saliency for the speakers of a speech community.

The more we move to the right on the functional continuum, the wider the gap seems to become between compositional meaning and actual situational meaning

TABLE 5.1.
Formulaic Continuum

Gramm. Units	Fixed Sem. Units	Phrasal Verbs	Speech Formulas	Situation-bound Utterances	Idioms
going to	as a matter of fact	put up with	going shopping	welcome aboard	kick the bucket
have to	suffice it to say	get along with	not bad you know	help yourself	spill the beans

of expressions. Language development often results in a change of function, i.e., a right-to-left or left-to-right movement of a linguistic unit on the continuum. Lexical items such as "going to" can become grammaticalized, or lexical phrases may lose their compositionality and develop an "institutionalized" function, such as *I'll talk to you later*, *Have a nice day, Welcome aboard, Be my guest,* and the like. Speech formulas such as *you know, not bad, that's all right* are similar to situation-bound utterances (SBU). The difference between them is that while SBUs are usually tied to particular speech situations, speech formulas can be used anywhere in the communication process where the speakers find them appropriate. See, for instance, the difference between "*nice to meet you*" and "*you know*" or "*have a nice weekend*" and "*kinda.*"

As discussed above, corpus studies have broadened the scope of what can be regarded as formulaic expressions. Researchers working with large corpora talk about formulaic sequences that are defined by Wray (2002:9) as: "a formulaic sequence [is] a sequence, continuous or discontinuous, of words or other elements, which is, or appears to be, prefabricated: that is, stored and retrieved whole from memory at the time of use, rather than being subject to generation or analysis by the language grammar." Based on this definition we could say that much of human language is formulaic rather than freely generated, which hardly is the case. Most of human language is freely generated, but formulaic language plays a very significant role in most of them. In intercultural pragmatics not all prefabricated units play an equally important role. Focus is on fixed expressions that are usually motivated, have psychological saliency, and allow relatively few structural changes (fixed semantic units, speech formulas, phrasal verbs, idioms, and situation-bound utterances).

4. Why do Speakers Like Using Formulaic Expressions?

Linguistic models, especially generative linguistics, have emphasized combinatorial creativity as the central property of human language. Although formulaic language has been mostly overlooked for years in favor of models of language that center around the rule-governed, systematic nature of language and its use, the climate has been changing as a result of corpus linguistics and corpus-based studies. There is growing evidence that these prefabricated lexical units are integral to first- and second-language acquisition and use, as they are segmented from input and stored as wholes in long-term memory (Wood 2002; Wray 2002; Miller and Weinert 1998). Formulaic expressions are basic to fluent language production. Speakers of a language like using formulaic expressions for several reasons (see Kecskes 2003):

FORMULAS DECREASE THE PROCESSING LOAD

There is psycholinguistic evidence that fixed expressions and formulas have an important economizing role in speech production (cf. Miller and Weinert 1998;

Wray 2002). Sinclair's *idiom principle* says that the use of prefabricated chunks "may...illustrate a natural tendency to economy of effort" (Sinclair 1991:110). This means that in communication we want to achieve more cognitive effects with less processing effort. Formulaic expressions ease the processing overload not only because they are "ready-made" and do not require of the speaker/hearer any "putting together" but also because their salient meanings are easily accessible in online production and processing.

PHRASAL UTTERANCES HAVE A FRAMING POWER

Frames are basic cognitive structures that guide the perception and representation of reality (Goffman 1974). Frames help determine which parts of reality become noticed. They are not consciously manufactured but are unconsciously adopted in the course of communicative processes. Formulaic expressions usually come with framing. Most fixed expressions are defined relative to a conceptual framework. If a policeman stops my car and says *License and registration, please*, this expression will create a particular frame in which the roles and expressions to be used are quite predictable. Or, if my wife starts our conversation with "*Let me tell you something*," I know that something "bad" is coming.

FORMULAIC UNITS CREATE SHARED BASES FOR COMMON GROUND IN COORDINATING JOINT COMMUNICATIVE ACTIONS

The use of formulaic language requires shared experience and conceptual fluency. Tannen and Öztek (1981:54) argued that "cultures that have set formulas afford their members the tranquility of knowing that what they say will be interpreted by the addressee in the same way that it is intended, and that, after all, is the ultimate purpose of communication."

This feature is especially important in intercultural pragmatics because nonnative speakers in intercultural interactions usually share neither limited common ground and few similar experience. The question is whether the use of formulaic language also gives international interactants the "tranquility of knowing that what they say will be interpreted by the addressee in the same way that it is intended." As we will see, this is not exactly the case.

5. Formulaic Language in Pragmatics Research

As mentioned at the beginning of the chapter, formulaic language (prepatterned speech) has not received much attention within any subfield of pragmatics, with the exception of interlanguage pragmatics. Certain groups of formulas such as idioms, phrasal verbs, and others have been discussed in figurative language research. But with a few exceptions (e.g., Coulmas 1981; Bardovi-Harlig 2009, 2010; Overstreet and Yule 2001; Wray 2002; Van Lancker-Sidtis 2003, 2004; Kecskes 2000, 2003), not much has been written about formulaic language in pragmatics.

Why is it that pragmaticians almost ignore this topic, even though our everyday conversation is full of formulaic expressions? I can think of three reasons:

"WHAT IS SAID" IS NOT WELL DEFINED FOR FORMULAIC UTTERANCES.

In the Gricean paradigm listeners determine "what is said" according to one set of principles or procedures, and they work out (calculate) what is implicated according to another. Implicatures are based on "what is said," the combinatorial meaning of the expression as it was discussed in the previous chapters. But listeners often have to calculate certain parts of "what is said," too. This somewhat contradicts the basic assumption of major pragmatic theories (neo-Gricean approach, relevance theory) according to which "what is said" is usually well defined for every type of utterance. If this weren't so, we would have no basis for working out implicatures. However, in formulaic language there are many counterexamples, especially in phrasal utterances. Clark (1996:145) argued that when you tell a bartender, *Two pints of Guinness*, it is unclear what you are saying. Are you saying in Grice's sense, *I'd like* or *I'll have* or *Get me* or *Would you get me* or *I'd like you to get me a glass of beer*? There is no way in principle of selecting among these candidates. Whatever you are doing, you do not appear to be *saying* that you are ordering beer, and yet you cannot be implicating it, either, because you cannot cancel the order—it makes no sense to say *Two pints of Guinness, but I'm not ordering two pints of Guinness*. "What is said" simply is not well defined for formulaic, phrasal utterances. This is one more reason why the role of "what is said" in pragmatic theories has been reexamined as discussed in the previous chapters. As a further example for problems with "what is said":

(5)

>   To the cashier in a store: "*Are you open?*"
>   Customer to sales assistant: "*Do you carry batteries?*"

LINGUISTIC UNITS ONLY PROMPT MEANING CONSTRUCTION.

The leading thought in present-day linguistic research on meaning is that linguistic stimuli are just a guide or trigger in the performing of inferences about each other's states of minds and intentions. Linguistic units only prompt meaning construction (see discussion in Chapter 4). Formulaic expressions do not fit very well into this line of thinking because they usually have fixed meanings that are not context-sensitive. They are like frozen implicatures. The modular view rarely works with fixed expressions. When situation-bound utterances such as *Nice meeting you; You're all set; How do you do?* are used, there is usually just one way to understand their situational function. In fact, this is what is good about them, as Tannen and Öztek (1981) discussed in their paper.

But we have to be careful with the context-sensitivity of formulaic expressions. It is true that formulas such as "*it's not my cup of tea,*" "*you are all set,*" or "*be my guest*" are not necessarily context-sensitive in the sense that they are tied to particular contexts and are never (or rarely) used in other contexts. However, some of these expressions may be used both as formulas or freely generated expressions such as "*I'll talk to you later,*" "*give me a hand,*" etc. This issue will be discussed later in the chapter.

GRICE'S WORK APPLIES TO INFORMATION EXCHANGE

Grice made it clear that his work applies to information exchanges only and that it would be for future work to see how other kinds of exchange work. Admittedly, formulas aren't of great concern for Gricean scholars because they primarily have social and discourse functions.

6. Formulas in English Lingua Franca

In 2007 I conducted a cross-sectional survey to investigate how English lingua franca speakers use formulaic language in order to answer the following question: With no native speakers participating in the language game how much will the players stick to the original rules of the game?" (Kecskes 2007a). I thought the best way to answer this question was to focus on formulaic expressions that are the reflections of nativelikeness, best defined as knowing preferred ways of saying things and organizing thoughts in a language.

Data were collected in spontaneous lingua franca communication. Participants consisted of 13 adult individuals in two groups with the following first languages: Spanish, Chinese, Polish, Portuguese, Czech, Telugu, Korean, and Russian. All subjects had spent a minimum of six months in the US and had at least intermediate knowledge of English before arriving. None of them had English as their first language. Both Group 1 (7 students) and Group 2 (6 students) participated in a 30-minute discussion about the following topics: housing in the area, jobs, and local customs. The conversations were undirected and uncoached. Subjects said what they wanted to say. No native speaker was present. Conversations were recorded and then transcribed, which resulted in a 13,726-word database.

Data analysis focused on the types of formulaic units given in Table 5.1, above. The questions I sought to answer can be summarized as follows:

> How does the use of formulas relate to the ad hoc generated expressions in the data?
> What type of fixed expressions did the subjects prefer?
> What formulas did speakers create on their own?

TABLE 5.2.
Number of expressions that represent the six types of units

Gramm.Units	Fixed Sem. Units	Phrasal Verbs	Speech Formulas	Situation-bound Utterances	Idioms	Total
102	235	281	250	57	115	1040

6.1. FINDINGS

The database consists of 13,726 words. Table 5.2, above, shows the number of words that represents the six types of formulaic units that I focused on in the database. Words were counted in each type of formulaic chunk in the transcripts. Following are samples for each unit:

> Grammatical units: *I am **going to** stay here; you **have to** do that*
> Fixed semantic units: ***after a while, for the time being, once a month, for a long time***
> Phrasal verbs: *They were **worried about** me; **Take care of** the kids*
> Speech formulas: ***not bad; that's why; you know; I mean; that's fine***
> Situation-bound utterances: ***How are you?; Have a nice day; You are all set.***
> Idioms: ***give me a ride; that makes sense***

What is striking is the relatively low occurrence of formulaic expressions in the database. There were 1,040 formulas total used as formulaic expressions out of 13,726 in the corpus, which is only 7.6 percent. Even if we know that this low percentage refers only to one particular database and the results may change significantly if our focus is on other databases, it is still much less than linguists speak about when they address the issue of formulaicity in native speaker conversation. Even if our database is very limited and does not let us make generalizations about lingua franca communication, one thing seems to be obvious. *As far as formulaic language use is concerned, there seems to be a significant difference between native speaker communication and lingua franca communication.* Nonnative speakers appear to rely on prefabricated expressions in their lingua franca language production to a much smaller extent than native speakers. The question is why this is so. But before making an attempt to give an answer to the question, we should look at the distribution of formula types in the database displayed in Table 5.2.

Most frequent occurrences are registered in three groups: fixed semantic units, phrasal verbs, and speech formulas. It is interesting to mention that Ortactepe (2012) also found in her study that these three types of formulaic expressions are the ones most used and preferred in nonnative speaker language production. However, we have to be careful with speech formulas that constitute a unique group because if we examine the different types of expressions within the group we can see that three expressions (*you know; I / you mean; you're right*) account for 66.8 percent (167 out of 250) out of all units counted in this group. The kind of frequency that we see in the use of these three expressions is not comparable to any other expressions in the database. This seems to make sense because these particular speech formulas may fulfill a variety of different functions such as back-channeling, filling a gap, and the like. They are also used very frequently by native speakers, so it is easy for nonnative speakers to pick them up.

If we disregard speech formulas for the reason explained above, formulas that occur in higher frequency than any other expressions are fixed semantic units and phrasal verbs. We did not have a native speaker control group but we can speculate that this might not be so in native speaker communication. It can be hypothesized that native speakers use the groups of formulas in a relatively balanced way, or at least in their speech production fixed semantic units and phrasal verbs do not show priority to the extent shown in lingua franca communication. How can this prefer- ence of fixed semantic units and phrasal verbs by nonnative speakers be explained? How does this issue relate to the first observation about the amount of formulas in native speaker communication and lingua franca communication?

As the "think aloud" sessions (in which subjects talked about their own lan- guage production) demonstrated, the two issues are interrelated. English Lingua Franca (ELF) speakers usually avoid the use of formulaic expressions, not nec- essarily because, as they explained, they do not know these phrases, but because they are worried that their interlocutors—who are also nonnative speakers—will not understand them properly. They are reluctant to use language that they know or perceive to be figurative or semantically less transparent (see also Philip 2005). ELF speakers try to come as close to the compositional meaning of expressions as possible because they think that if there is no figurative and/or metaphorical mean- ing involved their partners will process the English words and expressions the way they meant them. Since lingua franca speakers come from different socio-cultural backgrounds and represent different cultures, *the mutual knowledge they may share is usually restricted to the knowledge of the linguistic code.* Consequently, semantic analyzability seems to play a decisive role in ELF speech production. This assump- tion is supported by the fact that the most frequently used formulaic expressions are the fixed semantic units and phrasal verbs in which there is semantic transparency to a much greater degree than in idioms, situation-bound utterances, or speech for- mulas. Of course, one can argue that phrasal verbs may frequently express figura- tive meaning and function like idioms such as *I never hang out*, or *they will kick me out from my home.* However, when I found cases like this in the database, I listed the phrasal verb among the category "idioms" rather than "phrasal verbs." So the group of phrasal verbs above contains expressions in which there is usually clear semantic transparency.

Our subjects were more advanced speakers. This is important because there is a difference in formulaic language use between less and more proficient nonna- tive speakers. Based on longitudinal studies both Howarth (1998) and Ortactepe (2011) came to the conclusion that less proficient learners pick up formulaic expres- sions and overuse them, while more advanced learners prefer to "generate" their own sentences rather than resorting to prefabricated units, a process that Howarth (1998:29) refers to as "deliberate creativity." Formulaic expressions provide non-native speakers with "survival phrases that achieve basic socio-interactional functions" (Wray and Perkins 2000:23). They have automatic access to prefabricated chunks, and this eases communication, especially in the early stages of language learning (cf. Wray 2002; Nattinger and DeCarrico 1992). According to Segalowitz and Freed, at later stages of language development formulaic expressions function as a database for nonnative speakers from which "learners abstract recurrent patterns, leading to the mastery of grammatical regularities" (Segalowitz and Freed, 2004:403). Wray considers this creative tendency of advanced learners as a major problem resulting from "the production of perfectly grammatical utterances that are simply not used by native speakers" (Wray 2002:147). This claim is in line with my finding about the language use of lingua franca speakers. Pawley and Syder (1983) referred to this deliberate creativity of relatively advanced L2 learners as a process of over-generating and producing grammatical, nonidiomatic utterances due to not having accumulated the native repertoire of formulaic expressions as "nativelike competence and fluency demand such idiomaticity" (Ellis 2003:12).

The danger for lingua franca speakers in the use of formulaic language is that they often pick up these expressions without comprehending the socio-cultural load that they carry. This is especially true for situation-bound utterances in which it is usually the figurative meaning that is dominant rather than the literal meaning. In lingua franca communication if one of the interactants does not know this figurative meaning and processes the utterance literally, misunderstanding may occur, such as in the following conversation between one of my Japanese students and me: (6)

NORITAKA: Hi Professor Kecskes.
KECSKES: Hi Noritaka. How are you? *Why don't you sit down?*
NORITAKA: Because you did not tell me to.
KECSKES: OK, I am telling you now.

Here, I used the expression "why don't you sit down?" figuratively as a formula, while the Japanese student processed it literally. In order to avoid cases like this, *lingua franca speakers stick to literal rather than figurative production.* The use of semantically transparent language resulted in fewer misunderstandings and communication breakdowns than expected in my survey. This finding of my study corresponds with House's observation about the same phenomena (House 2003).

Another example of this interesting phenomenon in the database is the endeavor of speakers creating their own formulas that can be split into two categories. In the first category we can find expressions that are used only once and demonstrate an effort to sound metaphorical. However, this endeavor is usually driven by the L1 of the speaker in which there may be an equivalent expression for the given idea. For instance:

(7)

> it is almost skips from my thoughts
> *you are not very rich in communication*
> *take a school*

The other category comprises expressions that are created on the spot during the conversations and are picked up by the members of the ad hoc speech community. One of the participants creates or coins an expression that is needed in the discussion of a given topic. It becomes a part of the interculture being created. This unit functions like a *target language formula,* the use of which may be accepted by the participants in the given conversation, as demonstrated by the fact that other participants also pick it up and use it. However, this is just a temporary formula that may be entirely forgotten when the conversation is over. This is a typical example of how intercultures are created. For instance:

(8)

> we connect each other very often
> *native American* (in the sense of native speaker of American English)

Lingua franca speakers frequently coin or create their own ways of expressing themselves effectively, and the mistakes they may make will carry on in their speech even though the correct form is there for them to imitate. For instance, several participants adopted the phrase *native Americans* to refer to native speakers of American English. Although in the "think aloud" conversation session, the correct expression (*native speaker of American English*) was repeated several times by one of the researchers, the erroneous formula "native Americans" kept being used by the lingua franca speakers. They even joked about it and said that the use of target language formulas coined by them in their temporary speech community was considered like a "joint venture" and created a special feeling of camaraderie in the group.

The avoidance of genuine formulaic language and preference for semantically transparent expressions can be explained by another factor. The analysis of the database and the "think aloud" sessions shed light on something that is hardly discussed in the literature. It seems that multiword chunks might not help L2 processing in the same way they help L1 processing. In discussing native speaker communication, Wray (2002) pointed out that if processing is to be minimized, it will be advantageous to work with large lexical units where possible, storing multiword strings as a whole as if they were single words. In some cases this will make it possible for speakers to go to their mental lexicon and pull out a single entry that expresses a complete message meaning (e.g., *Are you enjoying your day today?; Fancy meeting you here!*). However, lingua franca speakers usually do not know how flexible the formulas are linguistically, i.e., what structural changes they allow without losing their original function and/or meaning. Linguistic form is a semantic scaffold; if it is defective, the meaning will inevitably fall apart. This is one of the things lingua franca speakers worry about, as was revealed in the "think aloud" sessions. The "unnaturalness" of their language production from a native speaker perspective is caused more by imperfect phraseology than by inadequate conceptual awareness. These imperfections differ from the kind of alteration and elaboration of conventional phrases that native speakers produce, because there is flawlessness to native-speaker variation that ELF speakers usually fail to imitate. If native speakers do alter conventional expressions, they make any necessary changes to the grammar and syntax as a matter of course. This way they ensure that the expression flows uninterruptedly from word to word and expression to expression, and this really helps processing. However, this does not appear to work the same way for lingua franca speakers, who may not be able to continue the expression if they break down somewhere in the middle of its use.

We can say that formulaic language use in ELF communication points to the fact that with no native speakers participating in the language game the lingua franca interlocutors can't always keep the original rules of the game. Kecskes (2007a) argued that actual speech situations in lingua franca communication can be considered open social situations that do not encourage the use of formulaic language. In native speaker communication we have much more closed social situations defined by the parameters and values taken for granted in them (see Clark 1996:297). The result of these closed social situations is a highly routine procedure. For instance:

(9)

> BAR: Two vodka tonics.
> MUSEUM TICKET BOOTH: Three adults and one child.

In close social situations the participants know their roles. Clark (1996) claimed that the interlocutors' rights, duties, and potential joint purposes are usually quite clear. All they need to establish is the joint purpose for that occasion that they can do with a routine procedure. The first interlocutor initiates the conversational routine, often with a phrasal unit, and the second interlocutor completes it by complying. Use of conversational routines and formulas requires shared background knowledge, of which there is very little in lingua franca communication. Therefore, it is quite clear why lingua franca communicators avoid formulaic language. For them literality plays a powerful role.

6.2. LITERAL MEANING AND NONLITERAL MEANING

One of the major findings of the investigation of formulas in ELF was connected with how lingua franca speakers handle the difference between literal and nonliteral meaning. In the lingua franca data an overwhelming number of expressions used in their literal meaning were observed. This supports the assumption that literal meaning has both linguistic and psychological saliency for nonnative speakers because for them, the most salient meaning of lexical units in the lingua franca is almost always the literal meaning. This finding may have relevance to the ongoing debate in the pragmatics literature about the content of "what is said" and the semantics–pragmatics interface.

Currently, there has been a heated debate going on about literal meaning that has usually been defined as a type of pretheoretical semantic or linguistic meaning (Ariel 2002). The classical definition (see Katz 1977; Searle 1978) says that linguistic meaning is direct, sentential, specified by grammar, and context-free. Being fully compositional, linguistic meaning is generated by linguistic knowledge of lexical items, combined with linguistic rules. According to Grice literal meaning is also "what is said" (Grice 1978). He actually claimed that "what is said" is "closely related to the conventional meaning of words" (Grice 1975:44).

As briefly discussed in previous chapters, in recent pragmatic theories there is a tendency to distinguish three levels of interpretation instead of the Gricean two: the proposition literally expressed (compositional meaning), explicitly communicated content ("explicature" or "impliciture"), and implicitly communicated content (implicature). There is no consensus on the explicit nature of pragmatically enriched content. The debate is about whether the pragmatically enriched content is explicitly communicated or not. The relevance theorists argue that the pragmatically enriched content is explicitly communicated, so they use the term "explicature." However, most neo-Griceans (e.g., Bach 1994; Horn 2005) resist the term "explicature" because they do not consider the pragmatically enriched content explicitly communicated. Therefore, they prefer to use the term "impliciture" for these cases. For Bach (1999), impliciture is the implicit component of what is said, and it is not explicitly communicated. Recanati (2001) speaks about "what is said-max" in these cases. The pragmatically enriched content is a partially pragmatically determined proposition that may accommodate different degrees of explicitness and implicitness. It appears to be necessary to distinguish this level because in most cases the proposition literally expressed is not something the speaker could possibly mean. For instance:

> (10) At a gas station:
> – *I am the black Mercedes over there. Could you fill me up with diesel, please.*
> – *Sure.* (Example from Clark 1996)

Berg (1993:410) goes so far to say that: "What we understand from an utterance could never be just the literal meaning of the sentence uttered." Actual communicative behavior of native speakers in many cases points to the fact that Berg may be right.

Bach (2007:5) said that (actual situational) context does not literally determine, in the sense of constituting, what the speaker means. What the speaker really means is a matter of his communicative intention, although what he could reasonably mean depends on what information is mutually salient. Bach further argued that taking mutually salient information into account goes beyond semantics, for what a speaker means need not be the same as what the uttered sentence means.

This claim raises an important question from the perspective of lingua franca speakers. What is the "mutually salient information" for them? Salience is based on familiarity, frequency, and common prior experience (Giora 1997, 2003). Mutually salient information (unless it is connected with the ongoing speech situation as we saw it when ELF speakers created their own formulas) is something ELF speakers lack because they speak several different L1s and represent different cultures. For them mutually salient information should be directly connected with the actual speech situation, tied to some universal knowledge and/or encoded in the common linguistic code (lingua franca) so that it can be "extracted" by the hearer without any particular inference based on nonexisting common prior experience in lingua franca communication. *Inferencing for the lingua franca hearer usually means something close to decoding.* It is essential, therefore, that pragmatics for lingua franca interlocutors not be something "they communicate over and above the semantic content of the sentence," as King and Stanley (2005:117) assumed. For lingua franca speakers the semantic content is usually the conveyed content. Pragmatics is present in there. If this is not clear from their utterance they try to reinforce it with repetition, paraphrasing, or other means. So for nonnative speakers (especially with lower language proficiency) participating in intercultural interactions pragmatics is very close to semantics. This is not quite so for native speakers, at least based on what Bach said:

> It is generally though not universally acknowledged that explaining how a speaker can say one thing and manage to convey something else requires something like Grice's theory of conversational implicature, according to which the hearer relies on certain maxims, or presumptions (Bach and Harnish 1979:62–65), to figure out what the speaker means. However, it is commonly overlooked that these maxims or presumptions are operative even when the speaker means exactly what he says. They don't kick in just when something is implicated. After all, it is not part of the meaning of a sentence that it must be used literally, strictly in accordance with its semantic content. Accordingly, it is a mistake to suppose that "pragmatic content is what the speaker communicates over and above the semantic content of the sentence" (King and Stanley 2005:117). Pragmatics doesn't just fill the gap between semantic and conveyed content. It operates even when there is no gap. So it is misleading to speak of the border or, the so-called 'interface' between semantics and pragmatics. This mistakenly suggests that pragmatics somehow takes over when semantics leaves off. It is one thing for a sentence to have the content that it has and another thing for a speech act of uttering the sentence to have the content it has. Even when the content of the speech act is the same as that of the sentence, that is a pragmatic fact, something that the speaker has to intend and the hearer has to figure out (Bach 2007:5).

What Bach means is that if I say "You are late," I could mean a complaint (action), an implicature such as "you missed dinner," or I could mean just what the sentence says (in answer to your question, "am I on time?"). If I mean the latter, it is not because that is what the sentence literally means, but is a matter of the pragmatics that applies just then in that situation. Thus, pragmatics is what is always there for the native speaker. Even if the content of the utterance is the same as that of the sentence, the fact that the speaker uttered it constitutes a pragmatic act that the speaker has to intend and the hearer has to figure out. Inference does not kick in just when something is implicated. It is always there. The same is true for intercultural communication. Although interlocutors stick to the literal meaning of expressions most of the time when the content of the speech act is the same as that of the sentence, that is a pragmatic fact, something that the speaker must have intended and the hearer has to figure out.

7. Situation-bound Utterances (SBU)

When pragmatic competence was discussed, it was argued that situation-bound utterances play a very important role in the development of pragmatic competence because they usually express what is expected to be said in particular social situations and what kind of language behavior is considered appropriate in a given speech community. Now we return to SBUs because of their specific role in intercultural interactions.

7.1. WHAT ARE THEY? WHY ARE THEY IMPORTANT FOR INTERCULTURAL PRAGMATICS?

As defined earlier, situation-bound utterances are highly conventionalized, prefabricated pragmatic units whose occurrences are tied to standardized communicative situations (Coulmas 1981a; Kiefer 1985, 1995; Kecskes 1997, 2000). *If, according to their obligatoriness and predictability in social situations, formulaic expressions are placed on a continuum where obligatoriness increases to the right, situation-bound utterances will take the rightmost place because their use is highly predetermined by the situation* (Kecskes 2000). SBUs are unique lexical units because they demonstrate the distinction between conventions of language and conventions of usage. This division has been made by several researchers including Searle (1979) and Morgan (1978). Searle said: "It is, by now, I hope, uncontroversial that there is a distinction to be made between meaning and use, but what is less generally recognized is that there can be conventions of usage that are not meaning conventions (Searle 1979:49)." This distinction is expressed even more clearly by Morgan: "In sum, then, I am proposing that there are at least two distinct kinds of convention involved in speech acts: conventions of language...and conventions in a culture of usage of language in certain cases...The former, conventions of language, are what make up the language, at least in part. The latter, conventions of usage, are a matter of culture (manners, religion, law....) (Morgan 1978:269)." This is exactly why SBUs have particular interest for intercultural pragmatics: they represent conventions of usage that are a matter of culture. Their use is a question of appropriateness rather than correctness.

To complicate things even more for nonnative speakers, many SBUs can be used either as SBUs or freely generated expressions because the pragmatic functions are not always encoded in them, but "charged" by the situation they are used in (conventions of usage). It is generally this situational charge that distinguishes SBUs from their freely generated counterparts. Compare the following situations:
(11)

> SALLY: Bob, can I talk to you for a minute?
> BOB: Sorry, I must run, but *I'll talk to you later* when I return.

(12)

> JANE: OK, this is all for today.
> PAUL: Fine, *I'll talk to you later*.

In (11) the expression "*I'll talk to you later*" appears to be freely generated as opposed to (12) where it is an SBU rather than a freely generated utterance.

Several labels have been used to refer to these types of expressions in the relevant literature: "*interaction rituals*" (Goffman 1967) "*routine formulae*" (Coulmas 1981) "*énoncés liés*" (Fónagy 1982), "*situational utterances*" (Kiefer 1985; Kiefer 1995), "*bound utterances*" (Kiefer 1997), "*institutionalized expressions*" (Nattinger and DeCarrico 1992), and *"situation-bound utterances"* (Kecskes 1997, 1998, 2000). This variety of terms can be explained not only by the difficulty of defining this particular type of pragmatic units but also by the fact that these expressions are discussed in different subfields of theoretical and applied linguistics, and sometimes authors seem to care relatively little about research on SBUs made outside their own respective field. I prefer the term "situation-bound utterances" to any other term because this label refers to the main characteristic feature of these utterances: their strong tie, their boundedness to a particular situation. "Routine formulae" is too broad a category, "situational utterances" presupposes that there are utterances other than situational, and "institutionalized expressions" seems to be too specific a term. "Conventional expressions" (Bardovi-Harlig 2009; 2010) is too broad, too "faceless." The French term "énoncés liés" used by Fónagy (1982) expresses best what these expressions are all about. Kiefer (1995) refers to Fónagy when explaining "situational utterances" but I regard the term "situation-bound utterances" as being a closer equivalent to "énoncés liés" than "situational utterances."

7.2. HOW DO SBUS RELATE TO OTHER FIXED EXPRESSIONS?

It is important to clarify the relation of SBUs to "conversational routines" (cf. Coulmas 1981; Aijmer 1996) on the one hand, and to idioms on the other. Fixed semantic units and idioms ("*make both ends meet*"; "*kick the bucket*") are stored as unanalyzed chunks in memory just like words, and are retrieved as a whole. They are not tied to particular situations and can occur in any phase of a conversation where speakers find their use appropriate.

Conversational routines (Coulmas 1981) have an inclusive relation to SBUs. Conversational routines constitute a much broader category than SBUs. Aijmer argued that conversational routines are expressions that, as a result of recurrence, have become specialized or "entrenched" for a discourse function that predominates over or replaces the literal referential meaning (Aijmer 1996:11). Conversational routines include fixed semantic expressions ("*suffice it to say*," "*as a matter of fact*"), speech formulas ("*you know*," "*I see*," "*no problem*"), and SBUs. All SBUs are conversational routines, but this is not so conversely because not all expressions labeled as conversational routines are SBUs. For instance, "*you know*," "*I see*," and "*no problem*" can be considered conversational routines, but they are not SBUs. They are more like *speech formulas*. The difference between SBUs and speech formulas is socio-cultural and usage-based rather than linguistic. Speech formulas are function-bound rather than situation-bound. They can express one and the same particular function in any situation while SBUs frequently receive their charge from the situation itself. Fixed semantic units such "*after all*" or "*to tell you the truth*" and speech formulas such as "*I see*,"and "*you know*," can be uttered in any situation where they are considered appropriate. However, SBUs such as "*how do you do?*" upon acquaintance, or "*welcome aboard*" as a greeting to a new employee make sense only in particular well-definable situations.

The tie of SBUs to a specific situation that prescribes their particular meaning may become so dominant that the functional–situational (SBU) meaning may take over as the most salient meaning of the expression. For instance: "*piece of cake*," "*help yourself*," "*give me a hand*," "*not my cup of tea*." Conversational routines other than SBUs tend to have discourse functions rather than a situation-bound function. Discourse functions are not necessarily tied to particular situations. They can be expressed by conversational routines including not only SBUs but also expressions of turn-taking, internal and external modifiers, discourse markers, connectors, and others.

SBUs differ from idioms in origin, purpose, and use. The likelihood of occurrence of lexico-semantic idioms is usually unpredictable while the use of situation-bound utterances is generally tied to particular social contexts. Idioms, just like metaphors, arise from a creative act. They are used to represent complex content in a tangible way that can hardly be analyzed conceptually. Situation-bound utterances are repetitive expressions whose use saves mental energy. Idioms are like words while SBUs are more like pragmatic markers. SBUs fulfill social needs. People know if they use these prefabricated expressions they are safe: nobody will misunderstand them because these phrases usually mean the same to most speakers of a speech community (see above discussion). However, there is a price for repetitiveness. SBUs often lose their compositional meaning and become pure functional units denoting greetings, addressing, opening, and so on. This is where we can draw the dividing line between idioms (*spill the beans*, *kick the bucket*, *pull one's leg*, etc.) and SBUs (*see you later*; *it's been a pleasure meeting you, say hello to*, etc.). While semantic idioms are not transparent at all, pragmatic idioms (SBUs) remain transparent and usually have a freely generated counterpart (see examples 11 and 12, above). In contrast to idioms, SBUs do not mean anything different from the corresponding free sentences: they simply mean less (Kecskes 2003). They refer to a particular social and/or situational function. For instance, when the nurse says in the waiting room at the doctor's office: *"The doctor will be in in a few minutes,"* everybody knows that this will not happen—"a few minutes" could be half an hour or more. The function of the expression is to indicate to the patient that his/her presence is acknowledged, and s/he will be taken care of soon.

Kecskes (2003) argued that the loss of compositionality is a matter of degree. When SBUs are frequently used in a particular meaning they will encode that meaning, and develop a particular pragmatic function. This pragmatic property is becoming conventionalized when it starts to mean the same thing for most native speakers. That is to say, when native speakers are asked what comes into their mind first when they hear a given expression, and their responses are very similar, we can say that the SBU has already encoded a specific pragmatic property. SBUs are both selective and completive. They are selective because they are preferred to be used to a number of utterances, both freely generated and idiomatic, which equally could be used in the given situation. SBUs are completive because they evoke a particular situation, which freely generated utterances usually do not do. For instance, *"let me tell you something"* generally creates a negative expectation by the hearer, or *"step out of the car, please"* is something that most people identify with police stops. In freely generated utterances, the sense of the utterance is defined by the interplay of linguistic meaning and context, situation, and background knowledge. In SBUs, however, the communicative meaning, or the sense of the utterances, is encoded, and fixed by pragmatic conventions. Consequently, prior context encapsulated in them can create actual situational context. For instance, *"be my guest,"* *"can I help you?,"* *"you are all set."* All these expressions can create their own context.

7.3. CHARACTERISTICS OF SBUS

SBUs are usually transparent and have psychological saliency. They are idiomatized in the sense that the words in them as a whole constitute a pragmatic unit with a particular function. Nattinger and DeCarrico (1989:128) referred to them as "idioms with a pragmatic point." The weaker an SBU is motivated, the stronger it is idiomatized. According to the degree of motivation we can distinguish three types of SBUs: *plain, loaded, and charged* (Kecskes 2003). Plain SBUs have a compositional structure and are semantically transparent. Their situational meaning may only differ slightly from their propositional meaning because their pragmatic extension is minimal, if any. Their meaning can be computed from their compositional structure. For instance:

(13)

> MARY: *Do you have a minute?*
> BILL: *Yes, what can I do for you?*

In this exchange both expressions function as situation-bound utterances.

On the other end of the continuum we find *loaded SBUs* that are the closest to semantic idioms because they may lose their compositionality and are usually not transparent semantically any more. Their pragmatic function is more important than their original literal meaning, which is difficult to recall if needed. These SBUs are "loaded" with their pragmatic function that remains with them, and usually cannot be cancelled by the actual situational context because it is encoded in the expression as a whole. They are pragmatic idioms whose occurrence is strongly tied to conventional, frequently repeated situations. We think of a particular situation even if we hear the following expressions without their routine context: "*Nice meeting you,*" "*Help yourself,*" "*Not my cup of tea,*" and so forth, because their most salient meaning is the one that is extended pragmatically.

Charged SBUs come in between plain and loaded SBUs. An SBU may exhibit pragmatic ambiguity, in the sense that its basic function is extended pragmatically to cover other referents or meanings (c.f. Sweetser 1990:1). For instance, this is the case with a phrase such as "*See you soon,*" which retains its original sense but can also be conventionally (situationally) interpreted as a closing, a way to say goodbye to one's partner. So this expression has two interpretations: a literal and a situation-bound one. However, the situation-bound function ("closing") is charged by the actual situation only. If the expression "*See you soon*" is given without a particular actual situational context, it may be ambiguous because it can create one of two situations in the mind of a hearer: (1) closing, a way to say goodbye, and (2) what its compositional meaning says: the speaker will see the interlocutor soon. Here is another example with the expression "come on."

(14)

> JENNY: *Come on*, Jim, we will miss the train.
> JIM: Relax, we have plenty of time.

(15)

> JILL: Bob, I think I can't go with you.
> BOB: *Come on*, you promised to come with me.
>
> In (14) "*Come on*" is transparent and functions like a speech formula while in (15) it is more like an SBU that serves to press the interlocutor to do something.

7.4. SBUS AS PRAGMATIC ACTS

It is important to explain how SBUs relate to what Mey (2001) calls "pragmemes" in his Pragmatic Act Theory (PAT). By the term "pragmeme" he means a generalized pragmatic act that is concretely realized by "practs" in situational use. Defining pragmemes Capone (2005) referred to Geis's view of speech acts, according to which there are broad mappings (or correlations) between sentence types and illocutionary forces (or types of illocutionary force). The appeal to the context serves to determine the specific meaning accruing to the situated use of a literal speech act (Geis 1995). However, in addition to the defeasible aspects of meaning (identified as the "point" of an utterance; Dummett [2003:210]), Capone also considered certain nondefeasible aspects of meaning deriving from the interaction between the context, the discourse type, and the utterance type in question, and so on. He emphasized that pragmemes involve both defeasible and nondefeasible inferences (Capone 2005). This is in line with Mey's approach (2001) that I also agree with.

Kecskes (2010c) argued that SBUs can be considered "practs" because they function as concrete realizations of a pragmeme that may refer to a general situational prototype, a socio-cultural concept that usually has several possible realizations. This is where SBUs may be used to clarify the relationship between pragmemes and practs. In my understanding, pragmemes represent situational prototypes to which there may be several pragmatic access routes (practs). An SBU can be one of several possible pragmatic access routes to a pragmeme. For instance:
(16)

> PRAGMEME: [inviting someone to take a seat]
> PRACTS: Why don't you sit down?; Please take a seat; Sit down, please, etc.

There are several practs through which this pragmeme can be realized. All these expressions can be considered SBUs. However, there are many cases where an SBU is only one of the possible realizations of the given pragmeme. See example (17), below.
(17)

> PRAGMEME: [greeting a new employee]
> PRACTS: Nice to have you with us; *Welcome aboard*; Hope you will like it here.

Two of these expressions have some kind of prepatterned structure in which elements can be changed. However, "*Welcome aboard*" appears to be an SBU with an unanalyzable structure, definitely tied to the situation represented by the pragmeme.

As we have seen above, context plays a major role in defining what expressions we can consider an SBU and how pragmemes relate to SBUs. The next chapter will have a closer look at the understanding of context.

6

Context

There are three crucial factors in intercultural pragmatics that determine how we see and think about intercultural communication: context, common ground, and salience. These phenomena are intertwined and bring together the individual and societal features of intercultural interaction. The next three chapters will be committed to the "big three."

In linguistics context usually refers to any factor—linguistic, epistemic, physical, social, and so on—that affects the actual interpretation of signs and expressions. This is too broad a definition, one that does not reflect the complexity of the issue. Intercultural pragmatics calls for the revision of how we understand the role of context in communication in general and in intercultural communication in particular. This revision is needed because context does not exactly affect meaning production and comprehension in the way it does in intracultural communication. There are several reasons for this. One of them is that actual situational context cannot play the role of catalyst in intercultural communication the way it does in intracultural communication because the participants' different socio-cultural background ties them to culturally different L1 communities. Besides, context-sensitiveness may also work differently due to the increasing number of "interpretation sensitive terms." Cappelen argued that "[N]atural languages contain what I'll call *interpretation sensitive terms*: terms the correct interpretation of which varies across interpreters (or, more generally, contexts of interpretation). An interpretation sensitive sentence can have one content relative to one interpreter and another content relative to another interpreter (Cappelen 2008a:25). When Cappelen talks about "interpretation sensitive terms" he does not think about nonnative speakers of a natural language. He refers to native speakers of a natural language. However, he is right that this notion is important in natural languages no matter whether the given language is used by a native speaker or a nonnative speaker. What these *interpretation sensitive terms* are and how they function for nonnative speaker language users is an important matter in intercultural interaction. The content of an utterance should be understood relative to a speaker and a hearer. The same utterance can express several distinct propositions depending on who the hearer/s is/are. The question is what makes those "terms" interpretation sensitive in intercultural interactions and how the nature of interpretation sensitive terms may depend on the culturally diverse background of interlocutors. Before we discuss that question, we need to survey current approaches to context and explain how it is understood in the socio-cognitive paradigm that underlines intercultural pragmatics.

1. Context as Declarative and Procedural Knowledge

The socio-cognitive approach argues that context is a dynamic construct that appears in different formats in language use both as a repository and/or trigger of knowledge. Consequently, context represents both declarative and procedural knowledge. It has both a selective and a constitutive role. Several current theories of meaning (e.g., Coulson 2000; Croft 2000; Evans 2006) claim that meaning construction is primarily dependent on actual situational contexts. The SCA, however, claims that the meaning values of linguistic expressions, encapsulating prior contexts of experience, play as important a role in meaning construction and comprehension as actual situational context. So what SCA attempts to do is bring together individual cognition with situated cognition. It recognizes the importance of an individual's background and biases (prior context) in information processing (Starbuck and Milliken 1988; Finkelstein Hambrick and Cannella 2008), but at the same time also suggests that the context in which individuals are situated is equally strong in shaping attention and interpretation (Ocasio 1997; Elsbach et al. 2005). In other words, the context in which individuals are located has a major effect on what they notice and interpret as well as the actions they take.

Context represents two sides of world knowledge: one that is in our mind (prior context) and the other (actual situational context) that is out there in the world. These two sides are interwoven and inseparable. Actual situational context is viewed through prior context, and vice versa. Their encounter creates a third space. According to this approach, meaning is the result of the interplay of prior experience and current, actual situational experience, which are both socio-cultural in nature. Prior experience that becomes declarative knowledge is tied to the meaning values of lexical units constituting utterances produced by interlocutors, while current experience is represented in the actual situational context (procedural knowledge) in which communication takes place, and which is interpreted (often differently) by interlocutors. Meaning formally expressed in the utterance is co-constructed online as a result of the interaction and mutual influence of the private contexts represented in the language of interlocutors and the actual situational context interpreted by interlocutors.

In current pragmatic theories, it is widely accepted that meaning is both socially constructed and context-dependent and is therefore the result of cooperation in the course of communication. This process is unproblematic if the speaker's intentions are recognized by the hearer through pragmatic inferences. Consequently, pragmatics aims to explain how exactly the hearer makes these inferences, and in turn determines what is considered the speaker's meaning.

Contextualism is one of the dominant approaches according to which context-sensitivity (in various forms) is a pervasive feature of natural language.

Literalism, according to which (many or most) sentences express propositions independent of context (declarative knowledge), has been almost completely extinct for some time. Carston claims that, "linguistically encoded meaning never fully determines the intended proposition expressed" (Carston 2002a:49). Consequently, according to this view, linguistic data must be completed by nonlinguistic, contextual interpretation processes.

I think the overemphasis on context-dependency gives a lopsided perspective. Dependency on actual situational context is only one side of the matter. As claimed above, prior experience of individuals with recurring contexts expressed as content in their utterances also plays an important role in meaning construction and comprehension. We can assume that both the traditional semantic view (literalism) and the novel pragmatic view go wrong when they leave prior context out of the picture. According to the traditional view that goes back to Frege and Russell, we must distinguish between the proposition literally expressed by an utterance ("what is said" by the utterance, its literal truth conditions) and the implicit meaning of the utterance ("what is communicated" by a speaker producing the utterance): the former level is the object of semantics, the latter of pragmatics. Followers of the pragmatic view underline the importance of semantic underdetermination: the encoded meaning of the linguistic expressions used by a speaker underdetermines the proposition explicitly expressed by the utterance. According to Bianchi (2004:4), this means that every utterance expresses a proposition only when it is completed and enriched with pragmatic constituents that do not correspond to any syntactic element of the sentence (neither an explicit constituent, as in cases of syntactic ellipsis, nor a hidden indexical present at the level of the logical form of the sentence) and yet are part of the semantic interpretation of the utterance. For instance:

(1)

Bob and Mary are engaged (to each other).
Some (not all) girls like dancing.
I need to change (clothes).

According to the traditional view, truth conditions may be ascribed to a sentence (of an idealized language), independently of any contextual considerations. The opposing pragmatic view says that a sentence has complete truth conditions only in context. The semantic interpretation of utterances, in other words the propositions they express, their truth conditions, is the result of *pragmatic processes of expansion and contextual enrichment*. The followers of the semantic view may not be right when they think that any linguistic sign can be independent of any contextual considerations. No linguistic sign or expression can be independent of context because they carry context (prior context), encoding the history of their prior use (prior context) in a speech community. The supporters of the pragmatic view may go wrong when they do not emphasize that expansion and contextual enrichment are the results of the individual's prior experience. Suffice it to say that both sides appear to be mistaken to some extent because they talk about *context* without making a distinction between its two sides: *prior context* and *actual situational context*. The proposition literally expressed (sentence meaning) is the result of collective prior experience of speakers of a given speech community. This is expanded and/or enriched by prior experience, present situational experience, and/or need of a concrete speaker when s/he uses that utterance (speaker's meaning). The speaker privatizes the collective experience by enhancing/enriching the content with his private experience. Inferred meaning (implicature) is the reflection of the interplay between prior experience of the speaker and prior experience of the hearer in an actual situational context. Prior context as understood in the socio-cognitive paradigm is declarative knowledge, while actual situational context represents procedural knowledge. Anne Bezuidenhout (2004) claimed that parallels exist between the declarative/procedural divide, the semantics/ pragmatics interface, and the competence/performance distinction. She proposed that a clear-cut distinction must be made between procedural knowledge, which belongs to the performance system and is pragmatic, on one hand, and lexical conceptual knowledge, which belongs to the competence system and is semantic, on the other. This is in line with what the SCA claims: lexical conceptual knowledge is the basis for prior context that is encapsulated in the lexical items whie procedural knowledge, which is pragmatic, is triggered by the actual situational context. Returning to the sentences in example (1), the SCA says that all of those sentences are complete without the parentheticals, and express a truth conditional, actual situational context-independent, proposition. I want to emphasize *actual situational context-independent* because what those sentences are not independent of is prior context. Prior context, reoccurring use (without the elements in parenthesis) makes their meaning clear even without actual situational context. This issue is directly connected to speaker meaning, as was already discussed in Chapter 2 and will also be discussed in the next chapter. Here it suffices to say that the speaker can declare Bob and Mary are engaged true or false without concern for "to whom." The speaker can say some girls like dancing true or false without concern for whether all do, and can say she needs to change true or false without considering in what way (clothes? diet? priorities? career?). The parentheticals add what that speaker was talking about specifically, an added propositional element based on actual situational context. But it's a new proposition. The one it supplants is still adequate in itself as the expression of a proposition, so I argue that *it is a mistake to claim that no sentence is complete without context.* It is more the case that speakers can something different than the sentence itself means, because context supplies the rest. But the sentence does say something, completely, and sometimes it is exactly what the speaker means, too.

2. Externalist and Internalist Perspective on Context

Context-dependency is one of the most powerful views in current linguistic and philosophical theory going back to Frege (1884), Wittgenstein (1921), and others. The

Context Principle of Frege (1884) asserts that a word has meaning only in the context of a sentence. Wittgenstein (1921) basically formulated the same idea, saying that an expression has meaning only in a proposition. Every variable can be conceived as a propositional variable. This external perspective on context holds that context modifies and/or specifies word meanings in one way or another. Context is seen as a selector of lexical features because it activates some of these features while leaving others in the background. Some versions of externalist contextualism take this line of thinking to the extreme and claim that meanings are specified entirely by their contexts, and that there is no semantic systematicity underlying them at all (e.g., Barsalou 1993, 1999; Evans 2006). According to this view, the mind works primarily by storing experiences and finding patterns in those experiences. These patterns shape how people engage with, and store in their minds, their subsequent experiences.

According to Sperber & Wilson's theory (1986), relevance is something that is not determined by context but constrained by context. A context-driven pragmatic process is generally top-down. It is usually not triggered by an expression in the sentence, but occurs for purely pragmatic reasons: that is, in order to make sense of what the speaker says. Such processes are also referred to as "free" pragmatic processes. They are considered free because they are not mandated by the linguistic expressions but respond to pragmatic considerations only. For example, the pragmatic process through which an expression is given a nonliteral (e.g., a metaphorical or figurative) interpretation is actual situational context-driven because we interpret the expression nonliterally in order to make sense of a given speech act, not because this is required by linguistic expressions.

The opposite view on context is the internalist perspective. This perspective considers lexical units as creators of context (e.g., Gee 1999; Violi 2000). Violi (2000) claimed that our experience is developed through the regularity of recurrent and similar situations that we tend to identify with given contexts. The standard (prior recurring) context can be defined as a regular situation that we have repeated experience with, about which we have expectations as to what will or will not happen, and on which we rely to understand and predict how the world around us works. It is exactly these standard contexts that linguistic meanings tied to lexical units refer to. For instance:

(2)

> You are all set.
> Be my guest.
> What can I do for you?

These and similar expressions create their own context. We called them situation-bound utterances in the previous chapters. They can actually create their own contexts. Gumperz (1982) said that utterances somehow carry with them their own context or project a context. Referring to Gumperz's work, Levinson (2003) claimed that the message versus context opposition is misleading because the message can carry with it or forecast the context.

As discussed in Chapter 1 the main problem with the externalist and internalist views of context is that they are both one-sided because they emphasize either the selective or the constitutive role of context. However, the dynamic nature of human speech communication requires the development of a model that recognizes both regularity and variability in meaning construction and comprehension, and takes into account both the selective and constitutive roles of context and declarative and procedural nature of context at the same time. Millikan (1998) claimed that the conventional sign (lexical unit) is reproduced or "copied," not discovered or invented anew by each producer–processor pair. This is only possible if the linguistic unit has some kind of regular reference to certain contexts in which it has been used. Consequently, we need an approach to communication that recognizes both the selective and constitutive role of context, and distinguishes the two sides of context as prior context and actual situational context.

3. Interplay of Prior and Actual Situational Context

Through the interplay of prior context and actual situational context, individual and social factors of communication are intertwined. In Kecskes (2008) and Kecskes & Zhang (2009), we argued that meaning and common ground are dynamic constructs that are mutually constructed by interlocutors throughout the communicative process, and that this process of co-construction relies on both prior context and actual situational context. Mey (2001:218) also emphasizes the dynamic nature of conversation when he speaks about the fact that our acting is determined by what the scene can afford, and by what we can afford in the scene, which is to say, the scene not only determines our acting but also our actions determine and reaffirm the existing scene. I can agree with him on this. However, he may not be correct in overemphasizing the role of social contexts and actual situation context. He seems to have overlooked two important facts. First, as I claimed above, lexical items encode the history of their use, which basically creates a record of prior contexts. They trigger frames and cultural models that the interlocutor has experienced before. Mey's (2006a) claims that the explanatory movement in a theory of pragmatic acts is from the outside in, gives too much weight to actual situational context, and appears to ignore the fact that utterances, as linguistic units (which encode prior contexts), play as important a role in meaning construction and comprehension as actual situation context.

Linguistic units encapsulate the history of their use, i.e., the situations in which they have been used (Kecskes 2008). What happens in communication is that prior context encoded in the utterances interplays with the actual situational context, and this interplay results in what we call "meaning." There is movement in both directions: from the outside in (actual situational context--→ prior context encoded in utterances used) and from the inside out (prior context encoded in utterances used--→ actual situational context). Two sides of world knowledge interact in a meaning-creating way. Second, words encode the experience of individuals.

Consequently, when individuals enter into conversation with other individuals, the words and utterances they use are selected and formulated according to their prior communal experience. This means that *a conversation is a unique interplay of individual and societal factors.* Individuals are not only constrained by societal conditions, but also shape them at the same time. As claimed in the previous chapters, communication is driven by the interplay of *cooperation* required by the actual situational/societal conditions and *egocentrism* rooted in the prior socio-cultural experience of the individual. They are both present in all stages of communication to varying degrees because they represent the individual and societal sides of the dynamic process of communication (Kecskes 2008; Kecskes and Zhang 2009). A speaker always tries to use those utterances that s/he thinks will best convey his/her intention in the given situation, and vice versa, a hearer will always rely on those prior experiences with the linguistic items (and the encapsulated activity, relationship, practice, etc.) used that s/he thinks best match the speaker's intention expressed in his/her utterance in the given situation. As stated several times in the previous chapters utterances are thus not underspecified, and they do not get their full specification only from the actual situational context, because these linguistic units usually bring much into the situation. What gives specification to utterance meaning is neither the actual situational context nor the prior context encoded in the utterances, but both (Kecskes 2008): the interplay of situational context and prior context specifies meaning in a given situation. Mey (2006) is right that speech acts are situated. But this does not mean that their linguistic and/or socio-cultural load tied to the linguistic units constituting the utterance becomes of secondary importance when they get situated. Rather, the extent of the contribution of prior context and actual situational context to meaning construction and comprehension keeps changing in the process of communication. At certain stages (segments) of the communicative process actual situational context seems to be dominant, while at some other stages prior context tied to the utterances overrides actual situational context. This constitutes the dynamics of communication.

SBUs discussed in the previous chapter are an ideal means to demonstrate the interplay of actual situational context and prior context in meaning construction and comprehension because they are often linguistically transparent and carry a socio-cultural load at the same time. They are typical "interpretation sensitive terms." Consider the two conversations:

(3)

> SAM: Coming for a drink?
> ANDY: Sorry, I can't. *My doctor* won't let me.
> SAM: *What's wrong with you?*

(4)

> Sam: Coming for a drink?
> ANDY: Sorry, I can't. *My mother-in-law (my wife)* won't let me.
> SAM: *What's wrong with you?*

The situation-bound utterance "*What's wrong with you?*" has two different meanings in (3) and (4) even though the only difference between the two conversations is that "*My doctor*" is changed to "*My mother-in-law.*" It is not the actual situational context that creates this difference in meaning. Rather, it is the stigmatic load that is attached to the use of the lexical phrase "*My mother-in-law,*" which has a negative connotation in most contexts. If we use a third option, "*My wife,*" the meaning of "*What's wrong with you?*" will depend on the actual situational context, i.e., on how the hearer processes his friend's expression "*My wife,*" based on his knowledge about the relationship between Andy and his wife. In this case, because of the "weakness" of the conceptual load tied to the expression "*My wife,*" dominance of the actual situational context becomes obvious.

In these three situations, dominance seems to be changing and depends on what interpretation the encoded conceptual load of the expression makes possible. If the load is very strong and deeply conventionalized, the actual situational context can hardly cancel it. Some "interpretation sensitive terms" are interpretation sensitive because of the interplay of prior context and actual situational context. Let us consider another example:

(5) In one of his films ("The Survivors") Robin Williams says the following:
- "I had to sleep with the dogs. Platonically, of course . . . . "

Why does he feel that he should add "platonically, of course"? In the context of that movie, the utterance "I had to sleep with the dogs" had no sexual overtone at all. Still, the actor added "platonically, of course" because the sexual connotation of the expression "sleep with" is so strong that the actual situational context itself can hardly cancel it. This shows that not only conventionalized, prefabricated expressions but also ad hoc created expressions can dominate meaning construction and comprehension if the expression put together in the course of conversation refers to some phenomenon that is strongly carved in the mind of interlocutors for some reason. Interesting, too, is that some people more than others fixate on certain meanings, e.g., some people are more attuned to any possible sexual innuendo (what they call "a dirty mind"). This also supports the argument that although individuals may be the members of a speech community, collective salience is distributed individually.

Mey (2006) argued that quoting out of context is a well-known means of manipulating a conversational partner. Based on what is discussed above, we have to be careful about how we understand "quoting out of context." What this refers to is quoting out of *the actual situational context* in which the given linguistic expression has been used. This does not mean that there is no context, because the linguistic expression, if "quoted out of context," will create a context itself. This context, however, will not necessarily match the original situational context. In fact, the problem usually is that the expression or utterance creates its own context. We are referring to two different meanings here. The original one is created as the result of the interplay of the actual situational context and the given expression. In the second case ("out of actual situational context"), meaning construction is based only on prior context encoded in the linguistic expression (Kecskes 2010a). Mitt Romney's aforementioned utterance "I am not concerned about the very poor" can serve as a good example here. As a presidential candidate in 2012, Romney was speaking to a group of investors. In that actual situational context, he was trying to imply that the poor are usually taken care of in the US due to the great variety of programs helping them. However, the wording of the utterance was so powerful that it created its own context that overrode the actual situational context. So the problem was not that the utterance was "quoted out of context". In almost any situational context the utterance would have caused the same problem.

4. The Dynamic Model of Meaning (DMM) and Context

The dynamic model of meaning proposed by Kecskes (2008) argues for a broad understanding of context that includes both prior and present experience with the world. According to the dialectics of context, both sides of world knowledge (encoded private context and actual situational context) participate in meaning construction and comprehension. The degree of their respective contributions keeps changing depending on which stage of a concrete speech situation the interlocutors happen to be in. The DMM serves to demonstrate this dynamism. It is built on two assertions:

1) The dynamic behavior of human speech implies a reciprocal process between language and actual situational context as demonstrated in Figure 6.1.

Language encodes prior contexts and is used to make sense of actual situational contexts, so *language is never context-free*. There are no meanings that are context-free because each lexical item is a repository of context (s) itself; that is to say, it is always implicitly indexed to a prior recurring context(s) of reference. Even when an explicit context (actual situational context) is not available, one is constructed from stored knowledge originating in prior experience during the process of comprehension (cf. Katz 2005). Suppose we hear or read the sentence, "I want to sleep with you" without any actual situational context. With no difficulty at all, we can create a context based on the meaning of the words in the sentence. The interesting thing is that we all will probably make up the same context that is based on the figurative rather than the literal meaning of "sleep." This is how powerful collective salience encoded in lexical units can be.

2) The fact that communication is increasingly intercultural (cf. Rampton 1995; Blommaert 1998; Kecskes 2004a) requires the development of a

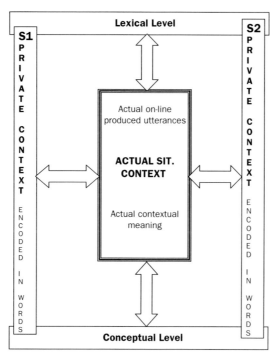

FIGURE 6.1 Understanding context

theory of meaning that can explain not only unilingual processing but also bi- and multilingual meaning construction and comprehension. Fauconnier (1997:188) wrote that when we deal with a single language the complexities of modeling meaning do not necessarily stand out. However, when we compare two or more languages, or translate something from one language to the other, we realize that different languages have developed different ways of prompting the required cognitive constructions. Furthermore, different cultures organize their background knowledge differently. Translating from one language to another requires a reconstruction of cognitive and cultural configurations that were prompted by one language and a determination of how another language would set up similar configurations with an entirely different meaning prompting system and pre-structured, pre-wired background.

Processing contexts and establishing repositories of contexts in the mind have both individual-specific elements and common elements. That is why communication is full of misunderstandings. In Rapaport's words, "We almost always fail [....]. Yet we almost always nearly succeed: This is the paradox of communication (Rapaport 2003:402)." Why do we both fail and succeed? We have difficulties in speech communication because individual socio-cultural experience with lexical items and actual situational contexts may be different even within one speech community. Prior experience creates private context that gets encapsulated in lexical items in the mind of speakers of a particular speech community. This private context incorporates core knowledge (tied to the prior experience), which is the public part of the private context, and individual-specific knowledge that may not be shared by the other members of the speech community because it is the individualized reflection of the socio-cultural context. The public context, that is to say, the public part of the private context, however, is available to each speaker of that speech community because it refers to relatively similar conceptual content that is conventionalized. The paradox of communication is caused by the fact that private and public are both present all the time. However, people must be relying on communally shared rather than individual knowledge and experience. Even when a person has quite personal experiences with something (an alcoholic with drinking liquor) so that an utterance can have a private meaning ("let's have a drink"), the person knows the difference between what people generally mean by that and what it means to him/her personally (and perhaps to other alcoholics). The important point here is that the meaning value of a lexical unit refers to both relatively static and dynamic elements that are the results of actual use of the given lexical unit in different actual situational contexts. Political correctness is a matter of the private becoming public—some faction's sensitivity or private meaning brought to the awareness of the larger speech community. The "language police" capitalize on this to impose their political vision.

Figure 6.1 demonstrates the different ways context is understood in the DMM. A speaker's private context encoded in lexical units and formulated in an utterance (actual linguistic context) is uttered (or written) "out there" in the world by a speaker in a situation (actual situational context) and is matched ("internalized") to the private cognitive contexts "inside" the head of the hearer (prior knowledge). Meaning is the result of interplay between the speaker's private context and the hearer's private context in the actual situational context as understood by the interlocutors.

4.1. MEANING VALUE OF WORDS

The DMM serves to explain not only relations between prior contexts encoded in lexical units and actual situational contexts, but also the meaning values of words and bigger lexical units such as situation-bound utterances (Kecskes 2003), speech formulas, and fixed expressions. Here I will focus mainly on the meaning values of words and emphasize that the word functions as an interface that links the phonological, syntactic, lexical, and conceptual structures in working memory in the course of perceiving or producing an utterance (cf. Culicover and Jackendoff 2005).

4.1.1. Do Words have Meanings?

In fact, they do, although Evans (2006) and others argue that they do not. This is what Evans (2006:496) says: "I argue that meaning is not a property of language per se, but rather is a function of language use, and thus, a characteristic of a process of meaning construction, rather than relating to mental entities/units stored in memory. Meaning construction is not an unpacking of stored information, as assumed in more traditional accounts. Rather, it is a constructive process, in which integration of lexical units involves differential access to the conceptual knowledge to which lexical entities potentially afford access."

I agree with Evans that meaning production is a constructive process. The question is, however, what situational meaning is constructed from, if "meaning is not a property of language per se." The DMM claims that language is meaningful, and we need to make a difference between the meaning values of lexical units on the one hand, and their situational meaning on the other. The process of situational meaning construction includes both "unpacking" (stored private contexts expressed in meaning values of lexical units) and "constructing" (interplay of private contexts of interlocutors with the actual situational context). Current work in cognitive psychology appears to support this view (e.g., Swinney 1979; Gibbs 1996; Giora 1997, 2003). Gibbs (1996:33) argued that "context becomes operative only at a post-access stage, guiding the selection of the contextually relevant meaning of the ambiguous words." The main claim of the graded salience hypothesis of Giora is that salient meanings are processed automatically (though not necessarily solely), irrespective of contextual information and strength of bias in the first phase of comprehension when lexical processing and contextual processing run parallel (Giora 2003:24). This assumes that while situational context can be predictive of certain meanings, it is deemed ineffective in obstructing initial access of salient context encoded in lexical units based on prior experience. We will return to this issue in the chapter on salience (Chapter 8).

According to Evans, words are purely linguistic units that make access to conceptual knowledge structures. These structures represent only "semantic potentials" that are realized in language use. He acknowledges that words have some kind of "meaning," whatever it may be called. Evans (2006:493) says the following: "What a word 'means,' which is to say, which part of its encyclopaedic knowledge potential is activated will always be a function of how it is being used in any given context." I have several problems with this approach. Evans ignores that words encapsulate prior contexts of their use, so when he uses the term "context," he means actual situational context only. Evans's claim is that words do not mean anything without them being filtered through actual situational context. There are two ways to demonstrate that this is not quite so, and that words happen to have more than just "semantic potential": (1) When a word is uttered or written down without any actual situational context (this is what Evans means by "context"), it can actually create its own context based on prior experience encoded in it as was discussed above. Kecskes (2001) gave a list of words and expressions to a group of native speakers of English and a group of nonnative speakers, and asked them to write down what came to their mind first when they saw or heard the given lexical unit. None of the subjects asked for actual situational context to execute the task. The native speakers' responses showed a remarkable similarity in most of the words and expressions such as "break," "welcome," piece of cake," "get out of here," and so on. As the lexical units were polysemic in some cases, however, there were deviations in subjects' responses, or they gave two or three "stored contexts" in a hierarchical order. Certain deviations in subjects' responses were essential because their first response was the most salient context that came into their mind based on their prior individual experience with the use of that word. The "context-free" exercise has pointed to the fact that words have meaning values without actual situational context. Uttered or written without any situational context, words create a context in the mind of the hearer/reader. These meaning values, however fuzzy they may be, are the results of prior experience with, and prior use of, the given lexical unit; (2) Research in second language acquisition (e.g., Kroll and Stewart 1994; Jiang 2000; Kecskes and Cuenca 2005) demonstrated that in the first phase of L2 development, when encountering a new word in L2, the learner tries to reach into the conceptual base to find the concept that the word in the L2 stands for. Since the conceptual system of the learner is L1-based, the closest concept that can be reached through an L1 word is the concept in the L1, which may be different from the L2 concept. The problem, however, is that concepts are culture-specific. Consequently, there can hardly be any direct route between the L2 word and the L2 concept at this stage of development, since the L2 concept is just being developed in relation to the existing L1 concept. The obvious way for the L2 learner to reach the concept, then, is through the L1 translation equivalent. This is called the "word association model" by Kroll and Stewart (1994), and most recently "the first language (L1) lemma mediation stage" by Jiang (2000:47). For instance:

(6) L2 (Spanish) word -----> L1 translation equivalent -------> L1 concept
    almuerzo   "lunch" (English)   [LUNCH]
    escuela   "school" (English)   [SCHOOL]

The higher the fluency in L2, the less the learner has to rely on L1 word association because the growth of L2 proficiency brings about changes in the conceptual system, which starts to accommodate socio-cultural knowledge and concepts gained through L2 use and experience. This makes it possible for the learner to reach the appropriate conceptual structures directly without associating them with L1 translation equivalents. Second language learning and bilingual experience show that in the first phase of development there is an interaction of L2 and L1 lexical equivalents on the linguistic level. This interaction relies on linguistic rather than conceptual knowledge, which points to the fact that what Evans calls "linguistic knowledge" comprises not only an abstract network of grammatical rules but also lexico-semantic information that derives from conceptual information. A wrong word choice by L2 learners often occurs because they believe that (relative) lexical equivalency also means conceptual equivalency, which is not the case, as we can see in the following example: In a Bucharest hotel lobby: "The lift is being fixed for the next day. During that time we regret that you will be unbearable." (*The*

Octopus. Oct. 1995.) These types of sentences are the results of so-called "mirror translation," when the second language learner translates a thought from L1 into L2 by taking the dual language dictionary and translating each L1 word into its L2 dictionary equivalent.

Evans is right when he makes a distinction between "linguistic knowledge" and "encyclopedic knowledge" (the semantic potential). The problem is, however, that he considers linguistic knowledge an abstract network of grammatical rules only: "lexical concepts constitute the semantic units conventionally associated with linguistic forms, and form an integral part of a language user's individual mental grammar" (Evans 2006:496). Linguistic knowledge in the DMM is the result of not only grammaticalization but also lexicalization, a process of language change broadly defined as the adoption of concepts into the lexicon, as the "development of concrete meanings" (Brinton and Traugott 2005). As a result of lexicalization words may have "word-specific semantic properties" (Cruse 1992), which are the results of recurring use of words in particular contexts. Some part of the "encyclopedic knowledge" may become lexicalized and developed into a part of linguistic knowledge. The meaning properties that differentiate cognitive synonyms like "GIVE UP," "CAPITULATE," "SURRENDER," and "CHICKEN OUT" can be viewed as properties of the individual lexical units, as distinct from properties of the common concept. Word-specific semantic properties will include such things as emotive coloring, stylistic value, and various kinds of contextual affinities (see Cruse 1990 for a more detailed discussion of word-specific semantic properties).

4.1.2. Two Sides of Word Meaning

According to the DMM (see Figure 6.2) there are two facets of the meaning value of a word (lexical unit): coresense and consense (actual contextual sense). Coresense is a denotational, diachronic, relatively constant (for a period of time), and objective feature that reflects changes in the given speech community, while consense is actual, subjective, referential, and connotational, and changed by actual situational context (cf. Kecskes 2004a). In the DMM, a lexical item represents world knowledge based on prior contextual experience. Figure 6.2 shows how "privatized" world knowledge may be represented in a lexical unit as a blend of coresense (general world knowledge tied to the given concept), word-specific semantic properties (lexicalized part of world knowledge), and culture-specific conceptual properties (culture-specific part of world knowledge). The dynamism of language use may result in changes in the relationship of these constituents of the blend.

Coresense is abstracted from prior contextual occurrences of a word. It is neither conceptual nor lexical, but the interface between the two linguistic and conceptual levels. Coresense is not the sum of the most essential properties of the given category, but a summary of the most familiar, regular, typical, and (generally, but not always) frequent uses of a word. It reflects the history of use of the word and is the common core information that was called *public context* above, usually shared by members of a speech community. Coresense is not a pure linguistic phenomenon

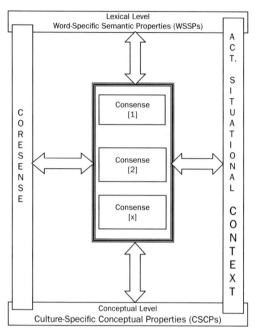

FIGURE 6.2 The Dynamic Model of Meaning

because it depends on extralinguistic factors such as familiarity, conventionality, and frequency. It is an essential feature of the word that pulls together conceptual semantic and lexical semantic information when a word is uttered. Coresense grows as a generalization from the most common conceptual features of contexts the word has been used in through various interactions. This set of core features is abstracted from speakers' usage of the given lexical item. It changes in time by losing some features and/or adding new ones. Just think about the historical change in the coresense of words such as "candy," "kidnap," "school," "snack," and so on.

Coresense has a unique relationship with the *word-specific semantic properties* (WSSP) and *culture-specific conceptual properties* (CSCP). Word-specific semantic properties link the coresense to the lexical level while culture-specific conceptual properties tie it to the conceptual level. Culture-specific conceptual properties belong to conceptual pragmatics, while word-specific semantic properties are features of the word itself, hence are a matter of lexico-semantics. It is within these two types of properties that individual differences occur, where individual speakers' private contexts tied to a particular word may differ.

As noted above, culture-specific conceptual properties tie coresense to the conceptual level. They are the basis for figurative, metaphorical meaning and the development of word-specific semantic properties. Culture-specific conceptual properties can be revealed relatively easily if we compare words from different languages that show lexical equivalency but differ as to their culture-specific conceptual properties. For instance, let us take the concept denoted by the word "lunch" in English and "almuerzo" in Spanish. "Lunch" for a native speaker of American English refers to a light meal consisting of a sandwich, soup, and/or salad, or something else that is consumed in a 30- to 60-minute break around noon. "Almuerzo," for a Spaniard, denotes the main meal of the day (usually consisting of three courses) that s/he consumes between 1 and 4 o'clock (Spanish restaurants will generally not serve "almuerzo" before 1 p.m.). The coresense of the two words is relatively the same; there is no word-specific semantic property attached to either. However, they differ in culture-specific conceptual properties. Bilingual people will have the same coresense for each word with different culture-specific conceptual properties, which will result in a synergic concept whose content may change depending on the extent of exposure to the two languages and cultures (for more on this issue see Kecskes 2007b).

Not all concepts have culture-specific conceptual properties. For instance, the concept denoted by the English word "salt" as a noun has hardly any culture-specific conceptual property, nor do its lexical equivalents in other languages. However, a derivative of "salt," the adjective "salty" can have culture-specific conceptual property. Swearing is sometimes called "salty" language, possibly as a reference to sailors (on the salty sea). This is related to "swear like a sailor." Or again, there's the expression "not worth his salt," meaning worthless. The word "pumpkin," however, is different. It has a culture-specific conceptual property that usually has a positive value in American culture: a pumpkin is a popular symbol of autumn and Halloween, and parents often use the word as a nickname for their children:

(7) FATHER: Listen, Pumpkin, how about going for ice cream?
    MARGIE: Cool, let's go.

As also seen in the English-Spanish example ("lunch" versus "almuerzo"), these culture-specific conceptual properties do not apply across cultures. An exchange like the one in (7) could hardly take place in Hungarian, where the lexical equivalent of the English word "pumpkin" is "tök," which carries a culture-specific conceptual property with a negative value. Hungarian children would not be happy if addressed by the word "tök," which has the connotation of "stupid."

Culture-specific conceptual properties are very dynamic features of words and keep changing all the time. They are sensitive to socio-cultural changes in the given language community. Culture-specific conceptual properties represent the cognitive base for word meaning value, and are responsible for changes in the coresense of a word and its word-specific semantic properties. *When culture-specific conceptual properties get fully lexicalized, they may turn into word-specific semantic properties.* This is why native speakers of English do not have to check with the conceptual system when they use words such as "chicken out," "kidnap," "blackmail," and so on.

On the linguistic side we have word-specific semantic properties. The term "word-specific semantic properties" (WSSP) was coined by Cruse (1992) to denote specific semantic properties that belong to the lexical rather than the conceptual level. Word-specific semantic properties make it possible for speakers to have alternative lexical access routes to a single concept: for instance, "run," "dash," and "rush"; or "sleep," "doze," and "nap." Cruse (1992:291) argued that cognitive synonyms map onto identical concepts. The meaning properties that differentiate such cognitive synonyms as "die," or "pass away," can be viewed as properties of the individual lexical units, as distinct from properties of the common concept. Word-specific semantic properties are the result of the recurrent use of words in particular contexts. Originally word-specific semantic properties derive from the interplay of the given lexical unit and actual situational contexts, and they are the best evidence for category stability and variability. They usually develop from metaphors or other figures of speech, and over time they become lexicalized and conventionalized. Cruse (1992) argued that words with word-specific semantic properties can create a more emotive, more "colorful" context than words without word-specific semantic properties. Compare the following sentences:

(8) Peter ate the steak. --------------> Peter devoured the steak.
    John repaired the car. ----------------> John overhauled the car.

It should be emphasized that word-specific semantic properties (that is, "semantic loads"), just like culture-specific conceptual properties, are not mandatory features that are attached to each lexical unit in use. There are lexical units that have neither word-specific semantic properties, nor culture-specific conceptual properties (such as "division," "example, "depart," etc.) no matter what actual situation context they are used in. Actual situational context can suppress culture-specific conceptual properties. This is, however, hardly the case with word-specific semantic properties encoded in the word, such as "pass away," "chicken out," "dash," and so forth. Actual situational context cannot cancel word-specific semantic properties.

The process of diachronic development of culture-specific conceptual property into word-specific semantic property can be well demonstrated through the word "patronize." The primary dictionary meaning of "patronize" is "to act as patron of: provide aid or support for." However, with time the word has developed two additional senses. One of its senses is closely related to the primary meaning of the word. When the direct object after the verb refers to an organization, firm, hotel, or store the verb means "give one's regular patronage, support; trade with." In the other sense, when the direct object after the verb refers to a person, the word has developed a negative cultural load: "adopt an air of condescension toward, behave in an offensively condescending manner toward." This latter sense may have arisen from focusing on the superior position that a patron in the other senses has. This meaning might be a reflection of American way of thinking: Don't patronize me, I know how to do that. You patronize me because you think that I am unable to do (something). In intercultural communication this may lead to serious misunderstandings. A case like this was described in example (6) in Chapter 2, where two different culture specific conceptual properties were attached to the expression "patronize" in English and "huwonhada," its closest equivalent in Korean. As already established, in American culture the word "patronize" usually has quite a negative culture-specific conceptual property if the object of the verb is animate, referring to a person or persons ("patronize someone"). In Korean, on the other hand, "huwonhada" has a positive culture-specific conceptual property. For Koreans, if they are patronized, it means that they receive a favor.

The other side of word meaning in Figure 6.2 is *consense* should be distinguished from corsense. Coresense is the invariant, while consense represents the possible variants. Consense realizes a particular aspect or aspects of the coresense by uniting it with the appropriate word-specific semantic property and/or culture-specific conceptual property when the word is uttered in an actual situational context. Consense is a mental representation consisting of a variable set of conceptual features compositionally related to the syntactic structure of the lexical unit. (This appears to be similar to what Evans [2006] understands by word meaning.) This set may vary with every use of the given expression in actual situational contexts. There is a dialectical relationship between coresense and consense. Coresense changes diachronically, while consense changes synchronically. Systematic, repeated changes in consenses (actual uses) over time will result in changes of coresense. Change in the coresense of the following words over time clearly supports this point: "mouse," "gay," "google."

Figure 6.2 demonstrates how coresense and consense fit within the dynamic model of meaning. As the diagram shows, coresense is the interface between the conceptual and lexical level. Word-specific semantic properties are links to the lexical level, while culture-specific conceptual properties are ties to the conceptual level. Consenses are the variations of coresense in context. The actual contextual interpretation of coresense is expressed in a consense connected to consenses of other lexical units to form an utterance.

4.2. USE OF DYNAMIC MODEL OF MEANING FOR UTTERANCE INTERPRETATION

The dynamic model of meaning can also be used to explain the meaning structure of lexical units bigger than a word. Using situation-bound utterances (SBU), Kecskes (2003) demonstrated that the dynamic model of meaning can be adjusted to accommodate pragmatic acts. The coresense of an SBU is an abstraction of communicative, pragmatic functions that an SBU can execute in a particular situation. As we discussed earlier, in this sense it is similar to Mey's (2001) "pragmeme," which he uses in his pragmatic act theory to refer to a generalized pragmatic act that is concretely realized by "practs" in situational use. Situation-bound utterances possess communicative functions that represent socio-cultural concepts. Their culture-specific conceptual properties are represented by their frames. When an SBU is used, a particular frame is activated. There are several possible pragmatic access routes to each socio-cultural concept. These pragmatic access routes may be represented by functionally synonymous SBUs. The relationship of these SBUs to the socio-cultural concept they represent is similar to the relationship of words to concepts. Consider the following examples:

(9) Socio-cultural concept: [when meeting someone, you know you are expected to greet the person] Some SBUs expressing this concept are as follows:

How are you doing?
How are you?
How is it going?
What's up?
Howdy?

Each SBU has a coresense that represents the same concept. The several different pragmatic access routes are distinguished from one another by "formula-specific pragmatic properties" (Kecskes 2000) that function the same way as the word-specific semantic properties do in the case of words. Like words, SBUs can either be neutral, have no modulatory effect ("how are you?"), or have formula-specific pragmatic properties ("what's up?" or "howdy"). Consequently, consenses representing the same coresense are not always interchangeable. Interchangeability depends on the actual situational context.

Meeting your professor.

(10) – How are you doing, Professor Patrick? ("What's up?" would not fit.)
(11) – Professor Patrick, how are you? ("Howdy" would not be appropriate.)

According to the dynamic model of meaning, formula-specific pragmatic properties can be either permanently present or situationally activated elements of an SBU's meaning. They are either encoded in SBUs or charged by the situation. However, several SBUs have these pragmatic properties without the situation, such as "howdy," "you bet," "what's up?," and so on. However, many SBUs are not like this. Their formula-specific pragmatic properties are not encoded in them, but rather are charged by the situation, as in the following case:
(12)

ROBERT: I think Ray was really rude to you yesterday.
DEBRA: Tell me about it.
(Source: *Everybody Loves Raymond*. Sitcom. CBS. 3/12/2002)

"Tell me about it" can be a freely generated expression. It means what it says. However, in the actual situation above, context gives a figurative meaning to the expression, which denotes the opposite of what the expression says: "don't tell me about it, I already know."

5. Context in Intercultural Communication

We need to refer back to two important issues that were discussed in the previous chapters: Bach's thoughts about actual situational contextual constrains and my claim about the role of semantic analyzability in intercultural interactions. Kent

Bach (2005) argued that context does not determine what is meant by an utterance. It does not even constrain what a speaker actually means. Context can constrain only what the speaker can reasonably mean or reasonably be taken to mean. That is to say, the context constrains what communicative intention the speaker can have in uttering a given sentence while reasonably expecting to get recognized. The contextual constrains that Bach speaks about function in a similar way for speakers of a given speech community. The reason for this is that common ground, mutual knowledge, and collective salience work in a relatively harmonious way based on shared prior experience. What if speakers are from different language communities? How will these actual situational contextual constraints work?

The DMM is built on the interplay of prior context encoded in lexical units and actual situational context. Nonnative speakers' prior experience with lexical items in the target language significantly differs from that of native speakers because they have gone through either a limited socialization process in the target language or none whatsoever. Their limited exposure to lexical items in L2 can hardly encode coresense the way it does in L1. Rather, the coresense of expressions in L2 for nonnative speakers relies on L1-dominated knowledge. What is common in lexical items for interlocutors in intercultural encounters is based on universal elements and/or literality of the expression. The following excerpt illustrates this issue clearly. An American student and a Korean student are discussing the Korean's experience with bagels.

(13)

NNS: So:: (0.7) to me, s- uh: when I first came in here, ·hh when I <eat some::>
       (0.2) when I ate some bagels?
       (1.2)   *:30*
NNS: ·hhBa(h)gels (though/so) (1.0) ah, give me a *pressure* h-h- [to eat [because
       there is so many=
NS: [hh   [h-h-
NNS: =cream cheese in [(there)
NS: [I k<u>now</u>::, the <cr<u>ea</u>m ch<u>ee</u>[:::se>
NNS: [Y<u>e</u>:::s (.) Now I can
       (.) eat but- at that time? (0.2) at that point I can't, I couldn't ea::t (0.5)
       cuz it's- a little bit *burden*, it was a little *burden* (0.2) to ea::t? (0.5) An:d
NS: When you say *burden*, what do you mean?
NNS: *Pr<u>e</u>ssure*, I m[ean::
NS: [Oh:: (0.5) Okay=
NNS: Yeah:::
NS: (I::)
NNS: It's too mu:ch.

The Korean student is talking about her experience with eating bagels in the US, and tries to explain that the cream cheese on the bagel was too heavy for her. She does not find the right word to express this, however, so she first goes with "give me a pressure." This is a literal translation of the Korean expression "*boo darm.*" She knows that this might not be the best way to put it, so she self-initiates a repair in her next sentence and replaces that with the expression "a little bit burden." She is still not sure that she has prevailed, however, and thus repeats "a little burden" with a raising intonation. She wants to continue explaining, when the American student interrupts her with a question about the word "burden." It is very clear that their prior experience with the word "burden" is absolutely different. The Korean student may have used that word as the closest possible equivalent to what she actually wanted to say. When that evidently failed (indicated when NS asked what she meant by "burden"), she returned to "pressure." Her second use of that word seems to be more successful. It is not the best way to express what she intends to, but this time the American student gets it. This is a typical illustration that the actual situational context does not necessarily help to fully clarify meaning in intercultural interactions because the interlocutors are not on equal terms as far as conceptual load attached to lexical items is concerned. The reason for this is that English words do not mean the same or similar things for them due to their limited prior experience with them.

The discrepancy in culture-specific conceptual properties of expressions in intercultural interaction is even more noticeable with highly conventionalized expressions. This is because the interlocutors' limited prior experience with such expressions in the target language does not give them enough background knowledge to move away from the literal meaning of the expression and acquire the meaning of conventionalized routines that derives from the symbiotic relationship of prior situational contexts and actual situational contexts of use. Doi's account of these expressions confirms the assumption above: "The 'please help yourself' that Americans use so often had a rather unpleasant ringing in my ears before I became used to English conversation. The meaning, of course, is simply 'please take what you want without hesitation,' but literally translated it has somehow a flavor of 'nobody else will help you,' and I could not see how it came to be an expression of good will" (Doi 1973:13).

Context-sensitivity, which in the socio-cognitive paradigm means *actual situational context-sensitivity*, seems to work differently in intercultural encounters. As we said earlier, context usually refers to any factor—linguistic, epistemic, physical, social, and so on—that affects the actual interpretation of signs and expressions. There are universal contextual factors that affect language processing similarly no matter what language is actually used. These factors are connected with general knowledge of the world such as weather, landscape, human relations, and so forth. When I say "have a good one," it is not necessary to name whether I mean day, night, afternoon, or morning. The actual situational context does that. Or in Russian when we say Саша и Света поженились (Sasha and Sveta got married), we do not have to refer to the fact that they got married to each other.

However, most actual contextual factors are language and culture-specific. Each language has interpretation-sensitive lexical items, expressions, and utterances where a part or whole of the knowledge that is necessary for processing is taken for granted in the given culture. No wording is needed because actual situational context does the rest. For instance, when in Russian we say "Как дела?" (How are things?), speakers know what the word "дела" (things) refers to. Basically, the closest equivalent of this expression in English is "how are you doing?" This is where the major problem of intercultural communication with context occurs. Whose context are we talking about? The prior context of the L1, the prior context of the L2, or the actual situational co-constructed context or all three? If we go back to the definition of interculturality, then our answer should be "all three." However, we should know that the lower the proficiency of speakers is in the target language, the more they will be affected by the prior context of the L1 and ignore or pay little attention to the actual situational context. So context-sensitivity in these cases cannot work the way it does *in intracultural communication where salience and common ground are governed by the (relatively) similar culture.* However, this does not mean that there is much more misunderstanding in intercultural communication than in intracultural encounters. Interlocutors negotiate meaning and with relying more on semantics than context, they work out their differences, as in the example below in which a Japanese student and an American student are talking through Skype (Data collected by Emiko Kamiya).

(14)

A: ..You know (.) I used to play tennis myself
J: Oh really
A: Yeah I (..) I just I used to play ( ) the first serve? ((gesture))
J: [Mm hm?
A: [You know? then (.) you know? ( ) a couple of ( ) [( )
J: 　　　　　　　　　　　　　　　　　　　　　[Ahhhhhh
A: I never ( ) but played a little bit (here and there?)
J: Ahahaha
J: [I
A: [Hahaha
J: I can just play (0.3) SOFT tennis?
A: Sof (..) now soft tennis (.) you play with a racket and a tennis ball though right?
J: Ah (1.2) white ball↑
　(1.4)
A: White ball↓
J: Yeah (.) gom? (.) gom ball?
　(1.4)
A: gom ball
J: a (.) I don't know
A: HAHAHA
J: ((laugh))
A: Are you using a (gumball?)? to play tennis? hehehe

J: Mmm (..) Yyeah (.) maybe hahaha
A: I use my ( ) hehe=
J: =fffff

The Japanese student is explaining to the American that she also played some game similar to tennis. However, she does not know the right word in English for softball and so uses the ad hoc constructed phrase "soft tennis" and tries to explain to the American what she really means by describing the ball they used. However, "gom ball" (instead of "rubber ball") does not get her meaning across, due to two things: (1) wrong pronunciation, and (2) wrong choice of word ("gum" instead of "rubber"). She uses "gom" (gum) because she has prior experience with that word rather than with "rubber." Actual situational context does not help the interlocutors much in this situation. What they rely on is their prior context, prior experience. However, there is discrepancy between those experiences that is worked out after all in the actual situational context.

The nature of the interplay of prior context and actual situational context in intercultural communication makes it important for us to rethink exactly what it means to be cooperative, a concept that is at the heart of most theories of language use. For one, the assumption that speakers want to be maximally informative in lexical selection does not seem to fit what they actually do. Perhaps a better description of what they do is that they simply rely on their past and current discourse experience and select the terms that are most salient and easily available to them in the actual situational context. Of course, this does not mean that they are uncooperative. Actually, they are eager to be cooperative. They are sufficiently cooperative to manage to get through the interaction successfully. But this cooperativeness needs further analysis. The next two chapters will continue examining this issue by discussing two important phenomena that are immediately connected with the role and functioning of context: common ground and salience.

7

Common Ground

1. What is Common Ground (CG)?

Co-constructing intercultures leads to common ground in intercultural communication. According to Clark (1996), in order for one person to understand another, there must be a "common ground" of knowledge between them. Duranti (1997) argued that even comparatively simple exchanges such as greeting are organized according to complex socio-historic cultural knowledge and are dependent for their interactional accomplishment on participants "sharing" that knowledge, having it as part of common ground. Where this knowledge is not shared, one might expect breaches to these taken for granted linguistic forms, with all kinds of interactional consequences. The more common ground we share with another person, the less effort and time we need to convey and interpret information. Enfield (2008:223) uses the term "economy of expression" for this phenomenon. Common ground refers to the "sum of all the information that people assume they share," (Clark 2009:116) which may include world views, shared values, beliefs, and situational context. People usually infer this "common ground" from their past conversations, their immediate surroundings, and their shared cultural background and experience. We can distinguish between three components of common ground: information that the participants share, understanding the situational context, and relationships between the participants—knowledge about each other and trust, and their mutual experience of the interaction. According to current research, if people have common or similar prior experience, participate in similar actions and events, know each other, and have been in similar situations before, all that will result in common ground. Similar prior contexts, prior experience, and similar understanding of the actual situational context will build common ground. Does this common ground exist in intercultural communication? Of course it does. However, it exists in a smaller degree than in intracultural encounters. Understanding between interlocutors with similar histories, experiences, and world knowledge is believed to be much easier than between those who lack common backgrounds (Gumperz 1982; Scollon and Scollon 2001; Tannen 2005). As discussed in Chapter 3 communication conventions are usually acquired through a long-lasting history of socialization and usage in the first language. They are generally processed unconsciously during interaction and thus not easily subject to repair procedures. However, the participants of intercultural communication do not share much of that type of common ground, which has led to a "problem approach" in second language and intercultural communication research. Gass and Varonis (1985:340) summed up the various issues associated with "shared background" and described in their study what can be termed a problem approach to the study of cross-cultural, cross-linguistic communication: "NSs [native speakers] and NNSs [nonnative speakers] are multiply handicapped in conversations with one another. Often they may not share a world view or cultural assumptions, one or both of which may lead to misunderstanding. In addition, they may not share common background…that would permit them to converse with shared beliefs about what Gumperz and Tannen (1979) call the "semantic content" of the conversation. Furthermore, they may have difficulty with speaking and interpreting an interlocutor's discourse as a result of a linguistic deficit."

So the main problem in intercultural interactions is that interlocutors do not and cannot have the type of common ground that L1 speakers have because of lack of shared prior experience. Consequently, since they have little mutual knowledge to activate and seek, they have to create common ground in the course of conversation. This results in the utmost importance of emergent common ground in intercultural communication, which will be discussed later in this chapter. Prior to that, however, we will need to investigate what is included in the understanding of the term "common ground."

Much of the success of natural language interaction is caused by the participants' mutual understanding of the circumstances surrounding the communication. This mutual understanding of perceived context that is termed "common ground," is made up of all of the background and shared information that will lead to the success of communication (e.g., Clark 1996; Stalnaker 2002). According to Stalnaker (2002) the expression "common ground" as a term for the presumed background information shared by participants in a conversation has its origin in Paul Grice's William James lectures. Grice did not define or explain the term in the published text, but described certain propositions as having "common ground status" (See Grice 1989, page 65 and page 274). There are several terms referring basically to the same phenomenon, such as *common knowledge, mutual knowledge, shared knowledge, assumed familiarity, presumed background information, and common ground.* Although we may find differences among them (e.g., Lee 2001) all those terms describe basically the same thing, and it is what defines the pragmatic competence of an L1 speaker: the knowledge and application of how and when to use utterances appropriately that combines with grammatical knowledge (of semantics, syntax, morphology, phonology) in the production of utterances to generate a coherent text comprehensible to its intended audience (Alan forthcoming). Clark et al. (1983) defined common ground as follows: "The speaker designs his utterance in such a way that he has good reason to believe that the addressees can readily and uniquely compute what he meant on the basis of the utterance along with the rest of their common ground (Clark, Schreuder and Butterick 1983:246)." This means that the speaker assumes, or estimates the common ground between speaker and hearer with respect to the utterance. However, this is not something the speaker is normally conscious of, except, maybe, if s/he communicates with a stranger. However, even then this is not always the case. Assumed common ground from the speaker's perspective is based on an assessment of the hearer's competence to understand the utterance. This assumption affects such things as choice of language and language variety, style, and level of presentation. For instance, addressing a police officer or a neighbor must be differently handled from addressing a doctor or a professor. *Common ground makes it possible for speakers to be economical in wording utterances.* As a consequence, language understanding is a constructive process in which a lot of inferencing is expected from the hearer. However, if this common ground is very limited, as is the case in intercultural communication, speaker meaning is expected to be less underspecified, so as to require less inferencing. This is why nonnative speakers usually rely on semantic analyzability—literal meaning of expressions, as discussed in the previous chapters.

Common ground is directly related to prior context (core common ground) and actual situational context (emergent common ground) as well as cultural models, cultural beliefs, and intercultures. Cultural models make up a "container" of scenarios that individuals can choose from in any given situation. They provide options for possible plans of action for the individual or possible interpretation of actions of other individuals. The choice is driven by a number of factors, including prior experience, the possible alternative outcomes different choices lead to, the degree of similarity of the application situation to the prototypic situation for the given cultural model, and so on. Kronenfeld (2008) argued that there is no guarantee that different individuals involved in a given situation will all be working off the same cultural models. This is especially true in intercultural communication in which the participants' cultural models and norms attached to their first language (core common ground) significantly differ from each other. This requires that they all mutually adjust (or negotiate), and modify their separate models and norms while creating an interculture (intercultures) in order to ensure the desired degree of mutual interpretability and interactive reciprocity. This is where interculturality and interplay of cooperation and egocentrism become important from the perspective of common ground. I will argue that emergent common ground is the result of creating and co-constructing intercultures in intercultural communication. In this sense the result of emergent common ground can be considered interculture or intercultures.

What intercultural pragmatics calls attention to with its emphasis on emergent common ground is that current pragmatic theories (e.g., Stalnaker 1978; Clark and Brennan 1991; Clark 1996) may not be able to describe common ground in its complexity because they usually consider much of common ground as the result of prior experience and pay less attention to the emergent side of common ground. In the meantime, current cognitive research (e.g., Arnseth and Solheim 2002; Barr 2004; Barr and Keysar 2005a, 2005b; Colston and Katz 2005; Koschmann and Le Baron 2003) may have overestimated the egocentric behavior of the dyads and argued for the dynamic emergent property of common ground while devaluing the overall significance of cooperation in the process of verbal communication and the a priori side of common ground. Intercultural pragmatics attempts to eliminate this conflict and proposes to combine the two views into an integrated concept of common ground, in which both core common ground (assumed shared knowledge, a priori mental representation) and emergent common ground (emergent participant resource, a post facto emergence through use) converge to construct a socio-cultural background for communication.

Both cognitive and pragmatic considerations are central to this issue. While attention (through salience, which is the cause for interlocutors' egocentrism) explains why emergent property unfolds, intention (through relevance,) explains why presumed shared knowledge is needed. Based on this, common ground is perceived as an effort to merge the mental representation of shared knowledge that is present as memory that we can activate, shared knowledge that we can seek, and rapport, as well as knowledge that we can create in the communicative process. The socio-cognitive approach emphasizes that common ground is a dynamic construct that is mutually created by interlocutors throughout the communicative process from prior and emergent elements. The core component (shared based on the knowledge of target language, let it be either L1 or L2) and emergent components join in the construction of common ground in all stages, although they may contribute to the construction process in different ways, in various degree, and in different phases of the communicative process.

As said above, in intercultural communication the core common ground that participants bring into the interaction is limited. People having different first languages and being motivated by norms and cultural models rooted in different cultures possess limited shared knowledge and presumed background information (core common ground) that may comprise more universal than language-specific factors. Consequently, relying on limited core common ground, interlocutors need to seek, create, and co-construct common ground (emergent common ground) in the process of communication. There appears to be a basic difference between intracultural communication and intercultural communication from the perspective of common ground. While the former usually builds on existing core common ground that is the result of relatively similar prior experience of interlocutors and less on emergent common ground, intercultural communication relies more on the emergent side of common ground. This is because of the limited availability of core common ground resulting from the little or no mutual prior experience. As we will see later, limited core common ground and stronger reliance on emergent common ground have a profound effect on how intercultural encounters take place.

2. Current Approaches to Common Ground

Presently there are two main approaches to common ground: the pragmatic view and the cognitive view. The dominant *pragmatic view* (e.g., Stalnaker 1978; Clark and Brennan 1991; Clark 1996) considers common ground a category of specialized mental representations that exists in the mind a priori to the actual communication process. Current pragmatic theories attach great importance to cooperation in the process of communication. Communication is considered an intention-directed practice, during which the interlocutors mutually recognize the intentions and goals, and make joint effort to achieve them (Clark 1996). Grice's (1975) four maxims formulate the overall rules to regulate the speaker's production of an utterance, and it is on the basis of a mutual agreement of these maxims that cooperation is recognized and comprehension is warranted. As we said earlier, this looks like an ideal abstraction of verbal communication, in which cooperation and effect of intention are greatly valued. Under such a communication-as-transfer-between-minds construal, common ground is considered an a priori mental state of interlocutors that facilitates cooperation and successful communication (e.g., Stalnaker 1978; Clark and Brennan 1991; Clark 1996). The mental representations of (assumed) shared knowledge exist in the speaker and hearer prior to a conversation, and contribute to it as this mutual knowledge relates to and facilitates comprehension of the intentions and goals that direct the conversation in a desired way. However, Arnseth and Solheim (2002) pointed out that Clark and Brennan's joint action model (1991) and Clark's contribution theory (1996) retain a communication-as-transfer-between-minds view of language, and treat intentions and goals as preexisting psychological entities that are later somehow formulated in language. In these theories, common ground is considered as a distributed form of mental representation and adopted as a basis on which successful communication is warranted.

The other approach to common ground that can be called *the cognitive view* has emerged as a result of recent research in cognitive psychology, linguistic pragmatics, and intercultural communication. Investigating how the mind works in the process of communication, cognitive researchers (Barr 2004; Barr and Keysar 2005a; Colston and Katz 2005) revealed that a priori mental representation of common knowledge is not as significantly involved in the process of communication as pragmatic theories have claimed; instead, they form a more dynamic, emergence-through-use view of common ground that conceptualizes it as an emergent property of ordinary memory processes (also see Arnseth and Solheim 2002; Koschmann and Le Baron 2003). This dynamism is also emphasized in other studies (e.g., Heritage 1984; Arundale 1999; Scheppers 2004), which reported that real everyday communication is not conducted as a relatively static practice of recipient design and intention recognition—something current pragmatic theories tend to claim. In fact, communication is more like a trial-and-error, try-again process that is co-constructed by the participants. It appears to be a nonsummative and emergent interactional achievement (Arundale 1999, 2008). While this is all true, we must be careful not to overemphasize the importance of co-construction and forget about the role of existing cultural models and norms of the participants with which they enter into the communicative process.

With this revision of common ground, the role of cooperation has also been challenged. As discussed in the previous chapters, several researchers (e.g., Keysar and Bly 1995; Barr and Keysar 2005a; Giora 2003) have indicated that speakers and hearers are egocentric to a surprising degree, and individual, egocentric endeavors of interlocutors play a much more decisive role in the initial stages of production and comprehension than current pragmatic theories envision. Their egocentric behavior is rooted in the speakers' or hearers' prior individual experience and more reliance on their own knowledge instead of mutual knowledge and common ground. Recent research in intercultural communication also affiliates with cognitive dynamism. Kecskes (2007a) argued that especially in the first phase of the communicative process, instead of looking for common ground, which was basically missing, lingua franca speakers articulated their own thoughts with linguistic means that they could easily use.

Barr and Keysar (2005a) claimed that speakers and hearers commonly violate their mutual knowledge when they produce and understand language. They called this behavior "egocentric" because it is rooted in the speakers' or hearers' own knowledge instead of in mutual knowledge. Other studies in cognitive psychology (e.g., Keysar and Bly 1995; Giora 2003; Keysar 2007) also have shown that speakers and hearers are egocentric to a surprising degree, and that individual, egocentric endeavors of interlocutors play a much more decisive role—especially in the initial stages of production and comprehension—than is envisioned by current pragmatic theories. This egocentric behavior is rooted in speakers' and hearers' relying more on their own knowledge than on mutual knowledge. People turn out to be poor estimators of what others know. Speakers usually underestimate the ambiguity and overestimate the effectiveness of their own utterances (Keysar and Henly 2002).

Findings about the egocentric approach of interlocutors to communication are also confirmed by Giora's (1997, 2003) graded salience hypothesis and Kecskes's (2003, 2008) dynamic model of meaning. Interlocutors seem to consider their conversational experience more important than prevailing norms of informativeness. Giora's (2003) main argument is that knowledge of salient meanings plays a primary role in the process of using and comprehending language. She claimed that "privileged meanings, meanings foremost on our mind, affect comprehension and production primarily, regardless of context or literality" (Giora 2003:103). Kecskes's dynamic model of meaning (2008; previous chapter) also emphasizes that what the speaker says relies on prior conversational experience, as reflected in lexical choices in production. Conversely, how the hearer understands what is said in the actual situational context partly depends on his/her prior conversational experience with the lexical items used in the speaker's utterances and the familiarity with the situational frame. Smooth communication depends primarily on the match between the two. Cooperation, relevance, and reliance on possible mutual knowledge come into play only after the speaker's ego is satisfied and the hearer's egocentric, most salient interpretation is processed. Barr and Keysar (2005b) argued that mutual knowledge is most likely implemented as a mechanism for detecting and correcting errors, rather than as an intrinsic, routine process of the language processor. Example (1), taken from Norton (2008:189), illustrates this point. The excerpt is from the Call Home Corpus, which is a collection of telephone conversations between friends and family members collected by the Linguistic Data Consortium (Kingsbury et al. 1997):

(1)

    A: And one of her students showed her how to get into the X-500
      directories.
    B: Which are?
    A: Hm?
    B: What are the X-500 directories?
    A: Oh um where you put- your um- How c- How can you not know?

The excerpt contains an infelicitous referring expression. Speaker "A" seems to attribute too much knowledge to his addressee, referring to the "X-500 directories" without further identifying information. This prompts "B" to seek clarification about what is meant.

The studies mentioned above and many others (Giora 2003; Arnseth and Solheim 2002; Koschmann and Le Baron 2003; Heritage 1984; Arundale 1997, 2004; Scheppers 2004) warrant some revision of traditional pragmatic theories on cooperation and common ground. However, a call for revision of the ideal abstraction does not mean the absolute denial of it. If we compare the pragmatic ideal version and the cognitive coordination approach, we may discover that these two approaches are not contradictory but complementary to each other. The ideal abstraction adopts a top-down approach. It works for a theoretical construct of pragmatic tenets that warrant successful communication in all cases. In contrast, the cognitive coordination view adopts a bottom-up approach. It provides empirical evidence that supports a systematic interpretation of miscommunication, and further is applied to all cases in general. From a dialectical perspective, as was emphasized several times in the previous chapters, cooperation and egocentrism are not conflicting, and the a priori mental state versus post facto emergence of common ground may converge to a set of integrated background knowledge for the interlocutors to rely on in pursuit of relatively smooth communication. So far no research has yet made an attempt to combine the two, at least to my knowledge. Intercultural pragmatics attempts to do that by eliminating the ostensible conflicts between common ground notions as held by the two different (pragmatic and cognitive) views, and proposing an approach that integrates their considerations into a holistic concept of assumed common ground. This approach to common ground is substantiated by adopting a socio-cognitive view that, as we saw earlier, envisions a dialectical relationship between intention and attention in the construal of communication.

3. Common Ground in the Socio-cognitive Approach

Intercultural pragmatics needs the socio-cognitive view to explain why prior context and inherent salience (based on prior experience) play a decisive role in the communicative behavior of participants in intercultural interactions, and how these features join actual situational context and emergent salience in creating emergent common ground. I argued above that there is some difference in how native speakers of a language community rely on common ground and how nonnative speakers participating in intercultural communication use and create common ground. In the first case there seems to be a stronger reliance on core common ground, while in the second case emergent, co-constructed common ground appears to be dominant. Why is that so?

The notion of common ground necessitates a community that observes social norms such as that speakers and hearers are mutually aware of and that, normally, their interlocutor is an intelligent and aware being (Allan forthcoming). This means that each interlocutor believes of him/herself and fellow interlocutors that they are intelligent and aware beings and believes of fellow interlocutors that they, too, consider themselves and fellow interlocutors (including him/herself) to be intelligent and aware beings. There is also a mutual assumption of communicative competence, which refers to the knowledge and application of how and when to use utterances appropriately and combines with grammatical knowledge (of semantics, syntax, morphology, phonology) in the production of utterances in order to create a relatively coherent text comprehensible to its intended audience. This works very well in intracultural communication because interlocutors have communality, relatively common conventions, norms, and beliefs that basically constitute a firm common ground for their interactions. They need to seek and create new common ground to that extent that is immediately connected with the actual situational context in which the interaction occurs. However, in intercultural communication, assumed core common ground is rather limited and most of common ground should be created and co-constructed by the participants in the communicative process. The main reason for this difference should be sought in conventionalization and normativity. *Long-term speech communities* are characterized by using the linguistic system of a given language according to certain socio-cultural norms conditioned by conventionalization. However, this is not exactly the case in *short-term speech communities* that are established in intercultural interactions in which the participants spend a relatively short time together, which is usually not enough for any kind of long-term conventionalization or development of norms. In these cases the assumed core common ground on which the interlocutors can rely on is quite limited and thus emergent common ground becomes dominant in the communicative process.

3.1. TWO SIDES OF COMMON GROUND

Common ground is both an a priori existing and a cooperatively constructed mental abstraction. It is assumed by interlocutors in a sense that none will know for sure that it exists. The multidimensional concern of the dynamic model of meaning presented in Chapter 6 facilitates the construction of common ground in communication. From the time dimension, common ground derives from the interlocutors' information gained from prior communicative experience and current communicative experience (actual situational context). From the range dimension, common ground derives from the interlocutors' shared information that belongs to a community (a macro concern) and that pertains to their individual experiences (a micro concern). The distinction between macro-concern and micro-concern resembles Clark's (1996:100) distinction between communal and personal common ground. However, there are some differences. The socio-cognitive approach has been influenced by the Durkheimian view that claims that collective belief is not a summative one. Durkheim (1982) expressed the view that anything properly called a collective belief will be "external to individual consciousness." This means that a collective belief is "external to individual consciousness" insofar as it is not necessary for any individual member of a group to believe that "p" in order for the group to believe that "p." It is possible that most members of the committee do not personally believe what the group believes. SCA says the same about a priori common ground that is supposed to be shared by the speech community as a group. However, individual members of the community may function without what is assumed to be common ground.

According to Kecskes (2008:390), prior experience of speakers creates private contexts that get encoded in lexical items in the mind of speakers of a particular speech community. These private contexts incorporate *core knowledge* (tied to prior experience), which is the public part of the private context shared by the other members of the speech community and *individual-specific knowledge* that is the individualized reflection of the socio-cultural context. The public context (something like common belief), that is to say, the public part of the private context, however, is available to each speaker of that speech community because it refers to relatively similar conceptual content that is conventionalized. To illustrate this, here is a conversation between Jill and Jane from a British sitcom.[1]

(2)

> JILL: I met someone today.
> JANE: Good for you.

---

[1] The example looks similar to the excerpt from the film *Angel Eyes* used in Chapter 2, but it has nothing to do with that text, except that both refer to "police officer."

> JILL: He is a police officer.
> JANE: Are you in trouble?
> JILL: Oh, no.

The utterance "I met someone today" sets the scene, creating the actual situational context. The utterance sounds like an opening to talk about a romantic involvement. However, after Jill says that the man is a police officer, Jane wants to know if she is in trouble. They clearly have a different understanding of "police officer," which usually has a negative culture-specific conceptual property tied to it. According to common belief, "police officer" usually means some kind of trouble. It is clear that the public context (collective salience) is changed (privatized) for Jill as a consequence of her positive experience with a police officer. Thus, Jill does not seem to stick to the common belief anymore. As a result of her positive private experience, the term "police officer" loses its negative connotation for Jill.

Common ground is inevitable in communication. The more common ground we activate, share, and create, the better we are supposed to understand each other, and the more efficiently we achieve our desired effect. However, common ground is not something that is already there as a reliable repertoire for interlocutors, nor is it something that comes about as a loose contingent subsequence of the conversation. Neither the pragmatic nor the cognitive approach of common ground suffices to offer us a complete picture of common ground, although certain dynamism of common ground is emphasized by the pragmatic approach. Clark (1996:116) said that "common ground isn't just there, ready to be exploited. We have to establish it with each person we interact with." Similar thoughts are formulated by Stalnaker (2002). The difference between Clark's contribution theory (Clark 1996) and the socio-cognitive approach is that while the former considers communication as a constant search for common ground following a contribution-by-contribution sequence in a relatively idealized way, the latter adds to that picture the "untidy," chaotic nature of communication that does not necessarily follow a contribution-by-contribution sequence and is not just recipient design and intention recognition, as most theories that have grown out of Grice's approach claim. The SCA emphasizes that speakers do not always seek common ground, and they are both egocentric and cooperative in the communicative process in a varying degree. This requires that we integrate the pragmatic and cognitive approaches to communication and, as a consequence, distinguish two sides of common ground: *core common ground* and *emergent common ground*. *Core common ground* refers to the relatively static (diachronically changing), generalized, common knowledge and beliefs that usually belong to a certain speech community as a result of prior interactions and experience, whereas *emergent common ground* refers to the dynamic, particularized knowledge created in the course of communication and triggered by the actual situational context. The former is a repertoire of knowledge that can be assumed to be shared among individuals of a speech community independent of the actual situational context, such as when and where the conversation occurs, between whom it occurs, and so on. This can be split into three subsets: common sense, cultural sense, and formal sense. In contrast, the actual contextual part is knowledge that is aroused or evolved as shared enterprises in the particular situational context that pertains to the interlocutors exclusively. This contingent circumstance draws attention of the interlocutors to the same entities or states and, with the formation of particular intentions therein, activates some of their prior individual experiences that join in this intention-directed action. This actual contextual part can be split into two subsets: shared sense and current sense, which will be explained in 3.1.2.

3.1.1. Core Common Ground

There are three subcategories that compose core common ground: common sense, culture sense, and formal sense (Kecskes and Zhang 2009). *Common sense* (of generality of the world) entails the generalized knowledge about the world. This is based on our observation of the objective world and our cognitive reasoning of it; the knowledge of natural science that is most available and accessible to us in our daily life contributes to this sense. *Culture sense* (of society, community, nation, etc.) entails the generalized knowledge about cultural norms, beliefs, and values of the human society, a community, a nation, and so on. People form and observe certain norms in social life, such as customs and ethics; the knowledge of social science that is available and accessible to us in our daily life contributes to this sense. *Formal sense* (of linguistic system) entails the generalized knowledge about the language system that we use in our social interaction. We rely on a shared language system, sometimes more than one language system (i.e., bilinguals or multilinguals), to put through our meaning to each other and achieve certain desired effects, such as informing others, performing an action, or expressing our emotions. The knowledge of linguistic system that is available and accessible to us in our daily life contributes to this sense.

Core common ground is a general assumption in two ways. First, although core common ground is relatively static and shared among people, it can change diachronically. During a certain period, say a couple of years, we may safely assume that the interlocutors have access to relatively similar common knowledge as components of core common ground will not change dramatically. However, in the long run, it definitely will change. People's social lives, both material and spiritual, will experience some changes over a long period, and as a consequence their core common ground will also be changed. Transformation in contents of lexical items demonstrates this diachronic change. The most salient meaning of the following expressions has gone through significant changes in the last 40 to 50 years: *gay; piece of cake; kidnap; awesome; patronize*. For instance, the sense of the word "gay" in the fifties and sixties was entirely different from what we have today. Irwin Shaw had a short story published in the fifties, titled "Wistful, delicately gay" where the word "gay" is used throughout the story but has nothing to do with the current most salient meaning of the word. At that time, the most salient meaning of the word was "joyful." It is this sense in which Shaw used the word. However, gradually the meaning of the word has transformed from "joyful," to denote a homosexual person. Presently, that is the most typical, regular, and salient meaning of the word. It is the meaning that comes to the mind of most English native speakers if they hear the word out of actual situational context. In addition, core common ground may also vary among different groups of individuals. Type of knowledge and scope of a community determined by different factors such as geography, lifestyle, and educational, financial, and racial factors restrain the accessibility of common ground to a community that is characterized in a particular way.

3.1.2 Emergent Common Ground

Emergent common ground is the part that is more sensitive to contingent situational context. There are two subcategories that emergent common ground relies on: shared sense and current sense. *Shared sense* entails the particularized knowledge about personal (not of community) experiences that interlocutors share. *Current sense* entails the emergent perception of the current situation. This is more private a part of common ground; interlocutors perceive and evaluate the current situation from their own perspective. The following conversation between a Turkish student and the department secretary demonstrates how common ground emerges between the two speakers (the excerpt is from Deniz Ortactepe's dissertation.)
(3)

> BEDRO: Hi, how are you?
> BOBBIE: I'm fine. Thank you and you?
> (0.5)
> BEDRO: Thank you, I'm fine. oh, I'm just looking for a course - a writing course, you know, uh I'd like to (.) improve my writing skills (.) so I need a- I need to take a writing course so: uh do you have such a course in your department?
> BOBBIE: Oh, yes = We do = We have one for uh at 687 and uh then we have a 500 level one (.) One is probably- the 500 level one is for umm (1.2) speakers that are not as well (.) equipped to speak English [as]
> BEDRO: [huh]
> BOBBIE: The other one is advanced- as more
> BEDRO: [huh]
> BOBBIE: Advanced, the 687. I'm not sure which-you speak pretty good English.
> BERDO: [Huhha]
> BOBBIE: [you're looking for the 687 one (1.0) perhaps
> BERDO: Yeah, (.) actually I'm an international student so: you know in my home country we don't have so-so intense (.) writing (.) [classes]
> BOBBIE: [Huhha]
> BERDO: So here graduate study I have some difficulties in my writing papers.

BOBBIE: [OK]

BERDO: [Soo (.) do these courses, you know, o:h contribute to my: writing as an international s or do they, do they—or are they offered to you know, native speakers?

BOBBIE: Now they're umm, normally offered, the native speakers can take the course but it's normally international students like yourself.

The emergent common ground is evolving around the "writing course" that Bedro is looking for. He explains to Bobbie, the department secretary, why he needs a writing course and what course would be suitable for him. The important thing here is that both speakers talk about the same thing: "writing course." Although one of them is Turkish and the other is American, they share some core common ground, which is the understanding of "writing course" based on the fact that both know university life and what basic courses are like. However, as individuals they have their own particularized knowledge about "writing course." Bobbie knows the department offerings and their approximate contents and goals while Bedro knows what his needs are as far as the type and/or contents of a writing course. During the conversation, common ground emerges as a result of both parties communicating their knowledge to the other about the core ("writing course"). In this type of intercultural communication, emergent common ground equals to intercultures.

Emergent common ground is assumptive in that it is contingent on the actual situation, which reflects a *synchronic* change between common grounds in different circumstances. *Shared sense* varies according to the relationships of the interlocutors (see above), and their mutual knowledge based on their personal experiences (Bobbie as a secretary, Bedro as a student). For example, the shared sense Bedro enjoys when talking to his fellow student is not the same that he has when talking to the department secretary. Even about the shared experience, such as a "writing course," the two people involved may have different aspects they find important, i.e., Bobbie represents the department view (contents, level, etc.) while Bedro is preoccupied with his individual needs in regard to the course. There is no perfect match between them, and shared sense is achieved only after their joint effort to construct it. *Current sense* also enjoys this dynamic assumptive feature. Interlocutors may share this sense since they are involved in the same actual situation. It may, however, often be the case that they need to co-construct this sense when they perceive the current situation differently, which is caused by their different angles of perception, available attentional resources, and other factors. For example, Bobbie and Bedro co-construct the "ideal" writing course for Bedro's needs based on the information they discuss, and as a result, share. In brief, both shared sense and current sense can vary from case to case according to the identification of relations and/or roles of interlocutors, their memory of prior experiences, and their cognitive perception of the actual situational context available to them.

3.2. COMMON GROUND IS AN ASSUMPTION

Common ground is an assumption that we make in the course of actual communication. Both core common ground and emergent common ground are integrated parts of this assumed common ground. While core common ground is generalized from prior experience of a certain community, emergent common ground derives from blending individuals' prior personal experiences with perceptions of the actual situational context.

There is a dialectical relationship between core common ground and emergent common ground. First, the core part derives from macro socio-cultural information of a community (or any groups of people divided by nations, regions, etc.) that is accessible to all individuals in that community, whereas the actual part derives from micro socio-cultural information that pertains to individuals solely. Second, the core part changes *diachronically*, whereas the actual part changes *synchronically*. Third, the core part may affect the formation of the actual part in that it partly restricts the way the actual part occurs. In most cases the actual part involves instances of information that are predictable in the core part. On the other hand, the actual part may contribute to the core part in that the contingent actual part in a frequent ritual occurrence potentially becomes public disposition that belongs to the core part. In other words, they are different components of assumed common ground, which have internal connections and constant interplay between them.

In the socio-cognitive view *assumed common ground (both core and emergent common ground) works as a dynamically changing background on which the interplay of intention and attention occurs and communication takes place.* According to Kecskes and Zhang (2009) there are three different ways the two components (intention and attention) contribute to common ground in the process of communication. One is that the *interlocutors activate mental representations* of shared information that they already have. For example, Ann talks to her husband:
(4)

ANN: Please check why the baby is crying.

The common ground of "the baby," which is represented in the form of presupposition, is the shared part from their experience and activated in this utterance. This belongs to the actual part of common ground. Besides, other components of common ground including the core part are also activated, such as a baby's physiological needs (common sense), the parents' social roles and responsibilities (cultural sense), and their competence of language use (formal sense). Upon her utterance, Ann is fully confident that her husband has a good knowledge of the above and thus they share the same common ground that facilitates the achievement of the goal of the conversation.

A second way of constructing common ground occurs when *interlocutors seek information* that potentially facilitates communication as mutual knowledge. Before the speaker makes the seeking effort, the piece of information is not salient in the hearer as background underlying the upcoming conversation. Because the piece of information may or may not be accessible to the hearer, the speaker pronounces it explicitly so that this information becomes salient and joins in the conversation as a relevant part. For example, when walking on campus, Sally is talking to Bill while a woman with blonde hair passes them:

(5)

> SALLY: See the woman with blonde hair? She's our new English teacher. She's pretty, isn't she?

Sally seeks their mutual perception of the woman because her seeing the woman passing by doesn't necessarily guarantee a mutual perception, and/or she aims at building up the same salient knowledge in Bill so as to start a relevant conversation.

In other cases, a piece of information is mutually known to the interlocutors but doesn't appear as most salient in the particular moment when the conversation takes place. This occurs when the speaker attempts to talk about past experience or information that she shared with the hearer earlier. In order to involve the information as salient, the speaker will state it explicitly in the conversation. The instance of a teacher's utterance illustrates this situation:

(6)

> TEACHER: As you well know, I am leaving soon, . . . (Giora 1997:24)

Before he proposes a make-up-lecture timetable, the teacher starts with the statement of information that is publicly known to the students. We won't comment on whether Giora's coherence or Wilson and Sperber's relevance works best for the above situation. Rather, we argue that the assumed common ground is superior to both of them in that it identifies common ground as a set of knowledge that is salient and pertinent to the current situation. The information that is commonly known to the interlocutors doesn't necessarily become a part of common ground in the current conversation if it is neither salient nor relevant to the social action involved.

The third contribution to common ground is when the speaker brings in her private knowledge and makes it a part of common ground. Here, the speaker has some private information that she knows is nonaccessible to the hearer and adopts it as common ground in the belief that it facilitates the conversation and that the hearer will accept it willingly. For example, Nancy responds to Jack's invitation to dinner:

(7)

> JACK: Nancy, can you have dinner with me tonight?
> NANCY: I'd love to, but I'll have to pick up my sister at the airport.
> JACK: Oh, you have a sister, do you?

The knowledge that Nancy has a sister and that she plans to pick her up wouldn't have become publicly known to the interlocutors if Jack hadn't made that invitation for dinner. It was not necessary for Nancy to tell Jack this piece of information except when the actual situational context required so. Nancy had to tell Jack about her sister because her sister was Nancy's excuse for not having dinner with him. In other words, the relevance of this piece of knowledge to the intention of the conversation makes it available as a part of common ground.

Assumed common ground is an integral part of the socio-cognitive view of communication. The three ways of constructing common ground occur within the interplay of intention and attention, and in turn the interplay of the two concepts is enacted on the socio-cultural background constructed by common ground. The processes in which we activate, seek, and create shared information are driven by relevance to the intention and realized with salience to attention. On the other hand, shared knowledge that we enjoy affects the formation of intention as well as the interplay of intention and attention as has been explained in the socio-cognitive view.

4. Common Ground in Intercultural Interactions

4.1. BOTH SUCCESS AND FAILURE

In intercultural communication we cannot be sure what we, interlocutors, can consider or assume as core common ground. So we can do less activation and should do more seeking and creating of common ground. When representatives of different cultures communicate with each other, most of common ground is emerging in the process of creating intercultures. This process is full of both failures and successes. However, these successes and failures do not always have direct connection with the existing cultural differences. It would therefore be a mistake to consider intercultural communication as a process that is full of misunderstandings and misinterpretations because of cultural differences.

Intercultural pragmatics rejects the "problem approach" that was described above by Gass and Varonis (1985). Instead, it supports the "normal communication approach" that was emphasized in the Introduction. The interlocutors in intercultural communication are not "multiply handicapped." They are normal communicators who have their own problems and difficulties, which may be different from those of interlocutors in intracultural communication. Interactants in intercultural communication also have their successes and failures, just like any human beings who communicate, as the following conversation demonstrates. A Brazilian girl, a Colombian girl, and a girl from Hong Kong discuss their experience about using a car in America.

(8)

> HK: Errh. I remember when I first came to this country, first thing I did . . . second day . . . errh . . . is to buy a car.
> (All giggle.)

HK: I came here on Friday. I bought a car on Saturday. (Giggle a little.) Just
   look around, you know...

CB: But...how about your license, driving license?

HK: I have the international...

CB: Oh. The international license will work here.

HK: Errh...of course after a time, you can get a US license.

BR: It is really easy.

HK: It is not a big deal...It is very easy.

HK: You want to say something.

BR: I just wanted to say I don't have a car. That's kind of...not so nice taking
   the bus, all the time, going shopping by bus, so whatever, so...

In the conversation, participants create an interculture, a common ground, i.e., an understanding of driver's license in the US. The interaction goes relatively smoothly. The important thing here is that coming from different cultures and not knowing how American society works, they need to establish common ground about the concept of a driver's license, which is unnecessary in intracultural communication where Americans share that knowledge. Of course, each interlocutor has an idea about what a driver's license is. That can be considered core common ground. However, what type of driver's license is accepted in the US and how and when you can obtain it are issues that are part of the emergent common ground.

Current research has been supporting the "normal communication approach." Kidwell (2000) proposed using a "success approach" in the study of cross-cultural, cross-linguistic communication that has as its aim explicating the resources that enable participants to accomplish their communicative tasks. Koole and ten Thije (2001) argued that rather than working deductively from cultural differences to communication, an inductive analysis of interaction should be applied to discover whether actors orient to group differences at all, and if so, in what terms these groups and their boundaries are defined. Preexisting images that interlocutors have of each other, as for instance prejudice, images (resulting, maybe, from intercultural communication training), false beliefs, hearsays, must also be accounted for in the analysis of intercultural communication (e.g., Hinnenkamp 1991; Meeuwis 1994).

4.2. "NOT SURE" APPROACH

I argue that an approach that I call "not sure" exists among interlocutors in intercultural communication that has a significant effect on how common ground is deployed and emerges. This approach means that the speakers have some kind of predisposition toward their communicative partners but are not exactly sure what they can expect from their counterparts. However, the origin and nature of this "not sure" approach differs in native speakers and nonnative speakers. In nonnative speakers this "not sure" approach derives from the fact that they share limited core common ground, have little knowledge about each other's proficiency in the target language, and can rely on the meaning-specifying function of actual situational context less than in intracultural communication. Since nonnative speakers can't be sure that they can count on these factors (common ground, relatively equal language competence, actual situational context) in that degree that they can in intracultural communication, they monitor production, consciously cooperate, anticipate problems, give more information than needed, and so on. This "not sure" behavior goes back to concrete past events where something went wrong with the use of a concept, an expression, an utterance, or some kind of misunderstanding happened. So the nonnative speakers occasionally anticipate trouble that s/he would like to avoid.

For the native speaker when talking to a nonnative speaker or speakers this "not sure" behavior is something like a general, top-down phenomenon that is associated with language proficiency issues. The native speaker's expectation and assumptions in a conversation with a nonnative speaker differ from that in an interaction with another native speaker. They usually do not formulate these feelings for themselves but behave accordingly with the nonnative speakers, generally subconsciously and automatically. The following conversation between a Korean student and a Chinese student shows that the nonnative speakers are aware of this different approach and attitude of native speakers.

(9)

> KOREAN: And then language problem. Sometimes I obviously look like a foleign...foreign person...foreigner here...so they assume I don't speak English so they sometimes...I don't know...they sometimes don't understand what I'm saying...even though I'm speaking English. It hurts me a lot...I don't know.
>
> CHINESE: Could you follow them?
>
> KOREAN: Of course.
>
> CHINESE: But they find it hard to follow you?
>
> KOREAN: Mhmm I don't know why. I think it's because of my...how I look like you know. I don't know it hurts me a lot.
>
> CHINESE: I don't think it matters very much because just for your physical appearance. Did you try slowing down your space?
>
> KOREAN: *Yes eventually they understand I can speak English but still in their mind they have strong strategy ...I mean ...I'm sorry ...stereotypes prejudice like ...you look foreign.*
>
> CHINESE: Foreigner.
>
> KOREAN: And you probably don't speak English so they don't even bother themselves to speak to me.

This "not sure" approach in native speakers is usually not connected with concrete prior events or actions. It is more like the result of a general picture that a native speaker has about a person who does not speak his/her language as a first language. It is important to note that this is not necessarily a negative expectation. It is often instantiated in supporting gestures, repetitions, providing background information, let-it-go behavior, and so on. Lüdi (2006:30) posited that the manifestation of an outsider status can generate particular attention and willingness to help. "The interlocutor knows s/he cannot take for granted that the speaker will adhere to usual comportment norms, which are inherent to the group membership. If somebody addresses me with the familiar 'Du' in German where the formal 'Sie' would be appropriate, I'll perceive this behaviour as impolite. But if s/he has a strong foreign accent, I'll debit this behaviour to her/his lack of language control and local rules and accept it. As it is, translinguistic markers are usually interpreted as indicators of lack of competence in the exolingual situation." The following conversation between an American student and a Thai woman contains several instances of this "not sure" approach on both sides. (Transcription done by Robert Sanders)

(10)

NS: So:: (1.2) the question, is what do you do: to stay healthy? in alb- in the
       Albany area? Like- (0.7) So do you like sports?
NNS: °I love sports.°
NS: What sports do you love?
NNS: I love football: (0.5) op- in here we call soccer.
NS: ↑Oh okay.
NNS: Yeah, (I love) soccer, (like) badwinton, swim.
          (0.7)
NS: What was the second one? (0.2) "I love soccer::"
NNS: Badmin. ((mimics swinging racket overhead))
NS: Oh badminton. ((mimics swinging racket))
NNS: Ye[ah:
NS: [I like Badminton too.
NNS: But in here it's windy, difficult to play badmin.
NS: T- t'day especially.
NNS: ((lau[ghs))
            00:30
NS: [The hurricane ((tape made 10/30/12 when Hurricane Sandy had
       moved inland))
NNS: Y[eah
NS: [Ahm- do you play on ↑teams? (0.7) Like soccer ↑team?
NNS: No, I (0.2) I like to watch (.) soccer [game.
NS: [Oh: okay. Okay.
NNS: °Yeah:°
NS: You like to swim. ((mimicking swimming/breaststroke with arms))
NNS: Yeah, normally. (0.2) In my country I (.) swim (.) almost every day, [but in
       here we have to wait (ti'-) (0.2) summer::
NS: [(Oh::)

NS: Right, (0.2) °right.°=Where you ↑from?
NNS: I'm from Thailand.
NS: Oh okay, is it warm there?
NNS: It'sa hot.
NS: Yeah.
NNS: ((laughs))
NS: So he:re, ((pointing downward to "here")) you're cold °all the time.°
   ((arms around self mimicking being cold))
NNS: Yeah::. Like a summer in here. (0.[2) (The) same weather.
            1:00
NS: [↑mm
NS: ↑Okay:. (0.7) ·hh Um, I run.((arms pumping like runner)) hh Like (0.2)
        really fa::r? ((extending arms in forward movement as if covering dis-
        tance)) Like marathons?
NNS: °Oh:::° I cannot do that.
NS: ((laughs)) Well::, I did my first one. (0.2) °(↑on my) ↑shirt?° ((pulls front
        of her shirt outward to show marathon logo))
            (1.2) ((NNS studying shirt))
NNS: ↑Oh ↑yeah, is maraton, right?
NS: Mm ↑hm
            (0.5)
NNS: Awesome::.
NS: Um:: (0.5) do you (.) eat healthy food? ((NNS makes facial grimace as
        if she tasted something unpleasant, shakes head slowly)) Or do you like
        junk food?
NNS: I love junk food, >I don't like healthy food, I don't like sahlahd.< I love
        chocolaht. (0.5) I lo::ve (0.5) sna:ck. (0.5) I love fried (.) chicken:: (.) ski::n
        chicken:: ((la[ughs))   *1:30*
NS: [Mmm
NNS: I don't like healthy food, (0.2) I love (0.2) to drink (0.2) beer:: (0.5) I eat a
        lot (.) chocolate (.) (from here).
NS: °Mm hm°
NNS: °(No)° ((shaking head))
NS: Well, if you: (.) exercise, it doesn't matter (.) if you:: (.) you can eat junk
        food if you exercise.
            (0.7)
NNS: Ah:: I'm au pair, do you know:? down here, (all [ )]
NS: [Yeah,] I know [au pair
NNS: [Yeah. (0.2) I have five kid. [This mean I play wit dem:
NS: [Oh my goodness
            (0.5)
NNS: all day:
NS: Ss-
NNS: I don't care what I (c-),

NS: Yeah, [you eat
NNS: [just bur::n.
NS: Right, you will [burn those calories.=
NNS: [(um)
NNS: =Yeah, after class (0.2) at night right. I can have dinner at
              2:00
         ten:: (0.5) [or midnight, I don't care.
NS: [((exaggerated facial display of disbelief))
NS: Oh my goodness.
NNS: That's fine for me. hhh
NS: Do the k<u>i</u>ds like sports?
              (0.7)
NNS: ↑Yeah, b- I have (0.5) f<u>ou</u>r girls
NS: °mm°
NNS: a::nd they have one baby who's boy.
              (0.5)
NS: Ok[ay.
NNS: [(This) mean I have to:: (.) take care of baby all day.
NS: Oh my good[ness.
NNS: [An::d (0.2) the baby (come and) run (.) all day.
NS: Okay.
NNS: That's good for me:, like I- I don't need (.) Gym:: (0.2)
         o[r:: sport. ↑('Kay?). Play with him.
NS: [NohǝHH
NS: Ye:ah
NNS: Yeah, that's good exercise and fun, (.) and w<u>or</u>k.
              2:30
NS: I work at a preschool (0.7) so
NNS: Ye↑ah, I think [you kn<u>ow</u> that. ((laugh))
NS: [there
NS: there are twe::lve (0.2) um k<u>i</u>ds in there three and f<u>ou</u>r (0.2) so:: it's the
         sa(h)me, I [move (0.2) lifting and running
NNS: [(It isn't), I have tw<u>o</u>::
NNS: >Wait wait wait< is two: four: (0.2) ·hh six seven (0.7) n<u>i</u>ne.
NS: ↑Oh okay- = so they go t' schoo:l, (.) the girls.
NNS: The <u>gi</u>rls go to school [(0.5) (every day). (0.5)] (Just baby).
NS: [°(↑Oh::   nice)°]
NNS: Sometime they come back from schoo=but- (0.2) we da:nce, together.
NS: Oh you dance? How fun, [( )?
NNS: [(Y<u>ea</u>h: that is) f<u>un</u>, I try to: (0.2) find (0.2)
         activity for them, it fun, (but   boring).
              3:00
NS: Oh↑oo::
NNS: ↑°Yeah:°

NS: Do they: um (0.5) are you teaching them any Thai? (0.2) Do they speak
       °Thai°?

NNS: So:metime=it difficult (to) them, sometime they (like a copy) me::?
          (0.5)

NS: Oh::

NNS: <When they heard> me talk on phone or something.

NS: Oh [okay.

NNS: [Some girl- (0.2) just <u>one</u> girl (love) to learn Thai language.

NS: ↑Oh that's so ↑cool.

NNS: Just <four years old>, she love Thai foo::d

NS: Oh↑oo

NNS: She love to speak Thai:: hh

NS: Do they- is she good?

NNS: She count one to ten in Thai.

NS: ↑Wow::, that's so [goo:d
          3:30

NNS: [Yeah:: heh, she so cute, I love her.

NS: Yeah::? Um I'm tryin' t' think of other he<u>a</u>lthy stuff.
          (1.2)

NS: We have to talk [about what's health- Oh:: you <u>look</u> healthy.

NNS: [(I'm not healthy) ((laughs))

NNS: ( ) not ( ). You know, I never diet

Instantiation of the "not sure" approach in the conversation above
Nonnative Speaker

1) <u>Anticipates problem because of the two different concepts or unfamiliar
concept</u>

NNS: I love *football*: (0.5) op- in here we call *soccer.*

xxx

NNS: Ah:: I'm *au pair*, do you know:? down here, (all [ )]

NS: [Yeah,] I know [au pair

NNS: [Y<u>ea</u>h. (0.2) I have five kid. [This mean I play wit dem:

2) <u>Starts with background information to explain how she remains fit by looking
after kids.</u>

NNS: Ah:: I'm *au pair*, do you know:? down here, (all [ )]

NS: [Yeah,] I know [au pair

NNS: [Y<u>ea</u>h. (0.2) I have five kid. [This mean I play wit dem:

NS: [Oh my goodness
          (0.5)

NNS: all day:

NS: Ss-

NNS: I don't care what I (c-),

NS: Yeah, [you eat

NNS: [just bur::n.

NS: Right, you will [burn those calories.=

3) Verbose, gives more information than needed

NNS: I love junk food, >I don't like healthy food, I don't like sahlahd.< I love
          chocol<u>aht</u>. (0.5) I lo::ve (0.5) sna:ck. (0.5) I love fried (.) chicken:: (.) ski::n
          chicken:: ((la[ughs))   *1:30*

NS: [Mmm

NNS: I don't like healthy food, (0.2) I love (0.2) to drink (0.2) beer:: (0.5) I eat a
          lot (.) chocolate (.) (from here).

NS: °Mm hm°

Native Speaker:

1) Gesturing

NS: You like to swim. ((mimicking swimming/breaststroke with arms))

2) Gesturing plus descriptive explanation

NS: ↑Okay:. (0.7) ·hh Um, I r<u>un</u>.((arms pumping like runner)) hh Like (0.2)
          really fa::r? ((extending arms in forward movement as if covering dis-
          tance)) Like marathons?

3) Helping NNS with asking more than one question

NS: Um:: (0.5) do you (.) <u>eat</u> healthy food? ((NNS makes facial grimace as
          if she tasted something unpleasant, shakes head slowly)) Or do you like
          junk food?

4) Let-it-go

NS: Oh you dance? How fun, [( )?

NNS: [(Y<u>ea</u>h: that is) f<u>un,</u> I try to: (0.2) find (0.2)
          activity for them, it fun, (but boring).
             3:00

NS: Oh↑oo::

NNS: ↑°Yeah:°

4.3. FORMULAIC LANGUAGE USE AND COMMON GROUND

In this book we keep returning to formulaic language. This is because formulaic expressions clearly represent the ways of thinking of a speech community and serve as group identifying means. Formulaic language use is a significant indicator of core common ground as well. Holtgrave (2002:148) argued that when common ground among participants is high, indirect speech acts and figurative language are more likely to be understood, and probably more likely to be used, while literal interpretations tend to be preferred when common ground is low. This coincides with what Kecskes (2007a) reported about lingua franca communicators who used the linguistic code, semantic analyzability as common ground to make sure that they understand each other properly.

In his paper reviewing the last 30 years of formulaic language, Pawley (2007:22) stated: "Speaking a language idiomatically is a matter of conforming to established ways of saying things." As was discussed in Chapter 5, formulaic expressions are usually claimed to be group-identifying since they indicate a speech community's preference in certain interactional situations (Tannen and Oztek 1981; Kecskes 2007). However, the evidence for this hypothesis has not been conclusive due to the lack of empirical data. Ortactepe (forthcoming) conducted a study to investigate whether the use of formulaic expressions can be an indicator of nativelikeness. Contrary to previous studies where nativelikeness refers to nativelike fluency, in her study, nativelikeness was operationalized as the extent to which the utterances reflected the native speaker's preferred ways of saying things and preferred ways of organizing thoughts (Kecskes 2007a). Ortactepe emphasized that while her study acknowledges the native speaker fallacy and agrees to "the need to abandon the native speaker as the yardstick and to establish empirically some other means of defining an *expert* (and *less expert*) speaker of English" (Jenkins 2006:175), her study also underlines that language learners' use of formulaic language can only be compared to those speakers of English whose use of formulaic language is the result of their language socialization in L1 and who, as a result, are competent in using formulaic expressions in a variety of situations. She thus adapted Davies's (1991:1) definition of native speaker as people who have an "insider knowledge about 'their' language." This insider knowledge, in Ortactepe's study, refers to the use of formulaic expressions. Hence, "nativelikeness" is not imitation of the native speakers, nor abandoning one's social identity to acquire another (Byram 2003), but adopting native speakers' preferred ways of saying things and preferred ways of organizing thoughts (Kecskes 2007a).

Ortactepe's nativelikeness analysis supported the view that the acquisition of formulaic expressions is an indicator of nativelike selection of words and expressions. As a result of their conceptual socialization experiences, the subjects in her study not only increased their use of formulaic expressions but also sounded more nativelike by producing formulas preferred by the native speakers. Ortactepe's findings are in line with the research examining the functions of formulaic expressions in ESL learners' development of speech fluency. For example, Wood's (2006) study argued that the use of formulaic expressions facilitated the learners' speech fluency over time. Boers et al.'s (2006) study also revealed significant relationship between perceived oral fluency and perceived range of formulaic expressions.

All these studies are very important from the perspective of common ground because they have proven that formulaic language use constitutes a significant part of core common ground. In fact, this is the part of core common ground that speakers can rely on for sure, and if they are familiar with it the use and proper understanding of these expressions can help avoid misunderstandings. From this perspective, it is interesting to look at Kidwell's (2000) example where the native speaker receptionist is speaking with a nonnative speaker student:

(11)

Example 15 ELP 2-4 (Kidwell (2000:31)

S is waiting at the desk as another student finishes up. He is waiting to the side, looking down. When the other student leaves, he slides over and takes his place and talks to the receptionist.

```
1 S: [°hi::°
2 R: [What's up.
3 (0.2)
4 S: Hi how are you? ((smiles))
5R: Okay ((smiling)) [and you?
6-S: [he-he-he
7-S: [(goo'(d)) ((nods head affirmatively))
8-R: [=thhh! ((laughing sound))
9 S: Uh cam you give me the telephone for m: [y=uhh conversation partner?
```

In the conversation the international student comes to the desk and says "hi," which is in overlap with the receptionist's solicit, "what's up?" Rather than answering "what's up" with a business-directed response, however, the student repeats "hi" in a louder voice and adds "how are you?," initiating a sequence that pushes back his disclosure of business to line 9. The international student tried to stick to the formulas he learned, although he looked to be confused by the right sequence. However, there was no misunderstanding and the interaction went smoothly because the formulas the speakers used were part of both interlocutors' core common ground.

The socio-cognitive view on assumed common ground offers a transparent description of sources and components (core and emergent) of common ground, and the specific manners in which they join to influence the process of communication. In the dynamic creation and constant updating of common ground, speakers are considered as "complete" individuals with different possible cognitive status, evaluating the emerging interaction through their own perspective. Constructing common ground occurs within the interplay of intention and attention, and in turn the interplay of the two concepts is enacted on the socio-cultural background constructed by common ground. In this sense common ground plays not only a regulative but also a constitutive role in communication.

Common ground is tied not only to context as discussed above but also to salience. What is considered core common ground in a speech community is supposed to be also salient for community members. However, as we will see in the next chapter, this issue is more complex than it appears at first sight.

8

Salience

The third element of the "big three" in intercultural pragmatics is salience. As a semiotic notion, salience refers to the relative importance or prominence of signs.[1] The relative salience of a particular sign when considered in the context of others helps an individual to quickly rank large amounts of information by importance and thus give attention to that which is most significant. We tend to overestimate the causal role of information (salience) we have available to us both perceptually and linguistically. In psychology, attention represents the process that enables organisms to select, among different sources of information, those that will receive cognitive processing. Information is selected according to its salience. Thus, salience denotes a feature of an object (both contextual and subjective) whereas attention is a process. In pragmatics when we speak about salient information we mean given information that the speaker assumes to be in central place in the hearer's consciousness when the speaker produces the utterance. It is the most probable out of all possible.

As discussed in the previous chapters, on the societal side intercultural pragmatics focuses on how actual situational context affects relevance and cooperation, and how those two trigger and shape intention. From the perspective of individual cognition, research in intercultural pragmatics deals with the unique symbiosis and interplay of attention, salience, prior context/experience, and common ground. It seeks to explain how prior experience and actual situational experience affects salience, and how salience governs attention and common ground building. These processes have a profound effect on the language production and comprehension of interlocutors in communication in general and in intercultural communication in particular. Because linguistic salience is the result of prior experience, familiarity, conventionalization, and frequency—none of which are shared by interlocutors in intercultural interactions—it is especially important to discuss in this book how salience operates in those types of communication. Research in intercultural pragmatics emphasizes three important factors that have received less attention in salience research: (1) There is a bidirectional influence between linguistic salience and perceptual salience; (2) Salience plays a crucial role not only in comprehension but also in production. It is important to emphasize this because current research

[1] This chapter is based on Kecskes (2013).

on salience in communication has focused mainly on comprehension (e.g., Giora 1997, 2003; Osgood and Bock 1977); (3) Salience is language- and culture-specific (Kecskes 2006). First, we will look at the relationship of linguistic salience and perceptual salience. Then, a review of previous research will follow.

1. Linguistic Salience and Perceptual Salience

The motivation for salience does not come from the language itself but is external to it. This distinction allows the separation of cognitive salience and linguistic salience from one another for analytic purposes. The former pertains to the mental representation and the latter to the possible observable effects on language at the structural and semantic level. However, when we talk about linguistic salience in pragmatics it includes conceptual salience as well. Linguistic salience describes the accessibility of entities in a person's memory and how this accessibility affects the production and interpretation of language. Several theories of linguistic salience have been developed to explain how the salience of entities affects the form of referring expressions and information structure, as in the Givenness Hierarchy (Chafe 1976; Givón 1992; Gundel et al. 1993), or how it affects the local coherence of discourse, as in Centering Theory (Grosz and Sidner 1986; Grosz et al. 1995), which was further developed into a Meta-Informative Centering by Wlodarczyk and Wlodarczyk (2006), or in Giora's Graded Salience Hypothesis (1997, 2003), just to mention a few. Jaszczolt's (2005) concepts of "primary meaning" and "pragmatic default" also belong to this list, because they, too, deal with salience, albeit from a somewhat different perspective. Most of the work on salience in pragmatics focused on encoded lexical meaning (cf. Giora 1997, 2003; Gibbs 2002; Jaszczolt and Alan 2011; Kecskes 2006) rather than on perceptual salience (e.g., Landragin et al 2001; Watts 1989). Thus, what is meant by linguistic salience in pragmatics is basically salience of lexical meanings that is defined according to its consolidation in the mental lexicon. Salient meanings are the encoded lexical meanings of a word or expression that are high in usage frequency, familiarity, conventionality, and prototypicality (Giora 1997, 2003). Giora argued that only consolidated and lexicalized meanings are salient. The graded salience hypothesis considers lexical saliency as a matter of degree rather than an absolute attribute of a word or expression. Lexical units can have more than one salient lexical meaning, and if these meanings are similarly salient they will all be accessed simultaneously (Giora 2003:37).

Perceptual salience is about how the state or quality of information on an entity stands out relative to neighboring items. Perceptual salience (or physical salience) comes from the perception of the relative prominence of some external features of an object. This type of salience is computed automatically, with no effort, and in real-time. In natural environments, objects with high saliency tend to automatically draw attention toward them. Designers and advertisers usually create objects, pictures, and texts that would appear highly salient to others in a wide range of viewing conditions. An object can be considered salient when it attracts the user's visual attention more than other objects in the environment. Visual salience depends on visual familiarity. When a painter enters a room, the pictures on the walls might be more salient for him than the piano, whereas the opposite might be true for a musician. Human beings acquire their own sensitivities to objects and happenings in their environment, the same way as they do to lexical items. Visual salience also depends on intentionality. When you invite people into your office, you search for chairs in your visual space, so chairs are more salient than the rest of the furniture. The same thing in language: when you introduce a topic on soccer, you search for lexical items connected with soccer. Visual salience depends on the physical characteristics of objects. Following the Gestalt Theory, the most salient form is the "good form," i.e., the simplest one, the one requiring the minimum of sensorial information to be treated. This principle has been first described by Wertheimer (1923) to determine contours, but it is also suitable for the organization of forms into a hierarchy. In language we also look for the simplest possible lexical items to express our thoughts about the subject matter.

The socio-cognitive approach claims that there is a bidirectional influence between linguistic salience and perceptual salience. This claim differs from the traditional view. There are two approaches to the issue of how language interacts with perceptual processing. According to the traditional view, language is "merely the formal and expressive medium that is used to describe mental representations" (Li and Gleitman 2002:290). Language is just a tool for reporting perceptual or conceptual representations, rather than shaping and modulating them (Bloom and Keil 2001; Gleitman and Papafragou 2005; Pinker 1994). According to this view, linguistic-perceptual interactions are seen in terms of recoding perceptual experiences into verbal ones (e.g., Dessalegn and Landau 2008; Munnich and Landau 2003). Lupyan and Spivey's work (2010) represents an opposing view, which argues that language dynamically modulates visual processing. Although they focused only on one aspect of this interaction—the degree to which processing spoken labels facilitates the visual processing of the named items—I agree with their claim and speculate further that there is a bidirectional influence between linguistic salience and perceptual salience, which will be discussed later. Recent studies seem to support this claim and have shown that language processing interacts with perceptual processing in various ways, indicating that linguistic representations have a strong perceptual character (e.g., Pelekanos and Moutoussis 2011).

2. Previous Research

Clark Hull (1943:229) was likely to be the first to have tackled salience in production with his principles of behavior. He argued that in both comprehension and production, more salient meanings would be processed first. In their studies, Osgood and Bock (1977) and MacWhinney (1977) entertained the idea that the attentional processing of the cognized world may somehow be reflected in how people organize their production and comprehension of sentences. Osgood and Bock's study (1977) explicitly suggested that the referents' salience status acting as an exogenous determinant of the distribution of a speaker's attention should promote the referents currently in focus to the prominent positions in a spoken sentence. MacWhinney (1977) presented the "Starting Point" hypothesis. Although it is not specifically geared toward sentence production, the hypothesis predicts that one of the main factors determining the assignment of the prominent positions in a sentence is the interlocutor's perspective or attentional focus.

Osgood and Bock (1977) distinguished three principles of salience: naturalness, vividness, and motivation of the speaker. All three principles are based on the assumption that more prominent or more salient items appear earlier in a sentence. Osgood and Bock argued that *naturalness* is exhibited in the fact that subjects almost always come before objects in languages around the world because the subject is more prominent than the object. This prominence often arises naturally from a series of relations. It should be noted here that there are subject-prominent and topic-prominent languages. Li (1976) distinguished topic-prominent languages, like Chinese and Japanese, from subject-prominent languages, like English. Topic-prominent languages have morphology or syntax that highlights the distinction between the topic and the comment (what is said about the topic). Topic-comment structure may be independent of the syntactic ordering of subject, verb, and object, as in Chinese. See for instance (1):

(1) Yuàn zi lǐ tíng zhe yī liàng chē.
    yuànzi lǐ tíng zhe yī liàng chē
    courtyard in parked a car
    In the courtyard is parked a car.

The topic of the sentence (defined as "old" information) takes precedence in the sentence. The sentence does not follow normal subject-first word order, but adheres perfectly to the topic-comment structure.

Vividness refers to the affective features of a particular element. The more emotional intensity a unit carries, the more likely it will appear earlier in the sentence. Emotional intensity naturally raises the level of prominence for the speaker, making it only natural that such a movement should occur. See for instance (2) and (3):

(2) Never have I got such a slap in the face.
(3) To grandma's house we go.

Motivation relates to the prominence a speaker gives to a particular unit that otherwise may carry no special significance. This principle has been thought to carry the largest effect of the three principles. However, Osgood and Bock's study claimed otherwise. Naturalness was found to be highly regulatory in terms of ordering. The earlier occurring elements of an utterance will be more salient because they have more prominence in the mind of both the speaker and the hearer. Ordering is influenced by the salience prominence of the agent (for active relations) or figure (for stative relations).

Orderings occurred as predicted in the various test situations. The basic hypothesis was that speakers around the world promote the more salient elements of an utterance to the beginning of that utterance. According to Osgood and Bock this phenomenon derives originally from the unconscious forward movement of items that have inherent salience. *Their study showed that the effects of inherent salience consistently trumped those that would need to gain salience from speaker motivation.* Speakers naturally fronted items that occur in a number of situations that inherently comprise an element of increased salience. These situations included cases of actors and instruments, which were found to be more active or potent (increasing their salience); animateness, for which living elements were always evaluated as more active and more meaningful than nonliving ones; and for mobility, where mobile pieces were more salient than nonmobile ones (tongue vs. tooth, animal vs. vegetable, etc.). Palpability did not hold the same effect, as the more palpable elements were not found to be significantly more salient than their impalpable partners (cube vs. square, ball vs. smoke, etc.). Subordinates (September as compared to month, baby as compared to human, tarantula as compared to spider, etc.), however, were found to be considerably more salient. Since inherently salient items naturally move to the beginning of utterances, it makes sense that this trend would not be continued when the salience of the element in question is not inherent. Human speech production is expected to follow a principle that is already naturally in place. The claim made by this principle has effects that reach well beyond these observations.

The analysis of the experimental data in Osgood and Bock (1977) revealed several important things. First, speakers tended to use naturalness as the main determinant of the order of mentioning in the sentence (in other words, they relied heavily on the natural event causality and the canonical grammar of English). Second, Agents were more likely to be mentioned before Patients. Third, referents of a higher vividness status were more likely to be mentioned before ones of a lower vividness status. Osgood and Bock (1977) contrasted their findings to the well-known tendency of the old discourse information to appear before the novel material. They claimed that control of the ordering through givenness is not as powerful as the same process driven by the factors related to "naturalness" and "vividness." They, however, acknowledged that the problem with this interpretation is that the "perceptual" properties of the referents, such as vividness, were derived solely from the lexical ratings. Whether such vividness reflects a tendency for a preferential perceptual treatment of corresponding world referents is not at all clear.

Languages around the world further demonstrate the fronting of salience-high elements through topicalization (see example 1), which very frequently is manifest through forward movement. This means that the element intended to have the greatest salience or importance is placed at the beginning of the sentence, regardless of its grammatical category. In configurational languages, a syntactic change accompanies this movement; in nonconfigurational languages, such a change is unnecessary as the relevant morphemes still clarify the meaning of the sentence (cf. Chomsky 1981; Hale 1982).

(4) English (configurational)
Peter likes dogs. It is Peter who likes dogs. (structural change)
(5) Russian (nonconfigurational)
Petr ljubit sobak. Ljubit Petr sobak. Sobak ljubit Petr. (word order change)
Peter likes dogs. Likes Peter dogs. Dogs likes Peter.

In configurational languages such as English, Dutch, and Spanish, word order plays a central role in sentence building. Function of words depends on their position in the sentence. In nonconfigurational language such as Russian, Hungarian, and Turkish, words receive grammatical markers (endings, suffixes) that show how the words are related to each other grammatically within the sentence. Word order in these languages serves pragmatic purposes. Configurationality–nonconfigurationality of languages constitutes a continuum rather than a dichotomy.

Movement to the beginning of the sentence appears to follow the theory of naturalness primarily through generative effect. Speakers consider whatever they have topicalized to be most salient in their utterance, and therefore simply follow the standard rules of the principle of naturalness and promote that item to position prominence. Although this explanation makes some sense, Osgood and Bock (1977) made an interesting distinction. They claimed that elements whose high salience is the result of speaker cognition rather than inherent attribution are categorized differently. Osgood and Bock proposed a theory concerning motivation of the speaker, which includes a host of salience effects that closely mirror those of the principle of naturalness in many aspects but were shown to differ in some key ways. Their study indicated that differences might exist between the processes that apply to inherently or motivationally salient items. (This finding will be very important in some further discussion.) Osgood and Bock (1977) found that *elements of inherent salience have a stronger effect on ordering than elements of motivated salience.* This claim basically coincides with what Giora said in her graded salience hypothesis (Giora 1997, 2003). Of course, she spoke about linguistic salience and comprehension. However, further research is needed, especially in production, because a speaker's emergent motivation (which I call "emergent situational salience") could easily overcome the effects of inherent salience in ordering in the process of communication. We can topicalize any element of a sentence that we feel is most important, so shouldn't what we feel is important trump whatever effect naturalness has? I will return to this question later.

Continuing on the work of Osgood and Bock, Rosemary Stevenson (2002) studied referent generation from the perspective of salience. Her findings were rather clear in demonstrating that salience does affect the choice of whether someone will refer to an entity in an utterance, though they went into further detail in a number of areas. Osgood and Bock's principles of vividness and naturalness are again confirmed in this study, though Stevenson adds to the idea some relatively new elements. Animacy was found to be a deciding factor in salience—verb-evoked salience (from implicit causality verbs and the like) and proximity salience are only applicable when the subject is animate. Inanimate subjects failed to carry the salience required to properly trigger the naturalness or vividness principles.

Stevenson (2002) also proposed a theory of salience effects blended with the Centering Theory (Grosz and Sidner 1986). Her work dealt primarily with the generation of pronouns. Centering Theory posits two local discourse centers: Cf (which is forward-looking) and Cb (which is backward looking). The Cf is used to introduce entities, whereas the Cb is used to refer back to previously mentioned entities. Since multiple Cfs can occur in a single utterance, the most salient of these is also identified. This is labeled as the Cp, or "preferred center." Several methods have been proposed for ranking Cfs, but current research is trending toward structure being the main factor, with ranking determined by order of occurrence—that which comes first is ranked highest. This fits very well with Osgood and Bock's (1977) theory of naturalness.

So what do Cfs (forward looking centers) and Cbs (backward looking centers) have to do with salience and production? Stevenson (2002) claimed that the Cb will be present in the choice of what referent a pronoun takes. Whatever realized Cf in the previous utterance (U_n-1) is the highest ranked element, so this will be the referent for the Cb in the current utterance (U_n). Gordon et al. (1993) made the claim that the pronominalization of the Cb actually increased the coherence of the discourse as it forced relational cohesion in the mind of the listener, because using a pronoun naturally makes the listener go back and relate the previous utterance to the current one. If the pronoun is left out in favor of an actual name, it may suggest to the listener that the sentences are somehow not meant to correlate, as the interpretation can be that this is a Cf instead of a Cb. In a study by Stevenson et al. (1994), it was found that the salience of the antecedent in U_{n-1} affected the choice of entity referred to in U_n, but not how it was referred to, which was chosen instead by the grammatical role of the entity. Stevenson also claimed that "the choice of who to refer to in an utterance depends on the salience of the entity in the speaker's mental model of the preceding utterance" (Stevenson 2002:188).

3. Salience in the Graded Salience Hypothesis (GSH) and The Socio-cognitive Approach

3.1. DIFFERENCES

The socio-cognitive approach relies on the Graded Salience Hypothesis (GSH) to a significant extent, but does not accept all of its tenets. GSH is basically hearer-centered, while SCA focuses on both production and comprehension. The focus of GSH is on linguistic salience, specifically meaning salience. GSH deals with lexical processing, whereas SCA's concern is both lexical (linguistic) salience and perceptual salience. While GSH uses "context" in the sense of actual situational context, SCA emphasizes the difference and interplay between prior context encoded in lexical items and actual situational context.

The main claim of the GSH is that salient information is superior to less salient information and often (Giora 2003:15), though not always, to unstored information, such as novel information or information inferable from context (see Giora 2003:10–11; Peleg, Giora, and Fein 2001). As a consequence, salient meanings of lexical units (e.g., conventional, frequent, familiar, or prototypical meanings) are processed automatically, irrespective of contextual information and strength of bias. Although context (actual situational context) effects may be fast, they run in parallel with lexical processes and initially do not interact with them (Giora 2003:24).

According to the GSH hypothesis, in language processing, both salient information and contextual knowledge run in parallel, and salient information may not be filtered out even when it is contextually inappropriate. This claim basically questions context-dependency, which is one of the main tenets of current pragmatic theories. The main concern if GSH is the storage of knowledge as a function of degree of familiarity, frequency, prototypicality and conventionality. Salience in SCA is understood as the contingent effect of salient knowledge that is the result of attentional processing of communication in a particular situation, which facilitates or hampers the expression of intention and the subsequent achievement of communicative effects. Another significant difference between GSH and SCA is that GSH emphasizes the importance of stored information, while SCA considers salience to be both a stored (inherent salience and collective salience) and an emergent entity (actual situational salience). According to the GSH (Giora 2003:15), for information to be salient—to be foremost on a person's mind—it needs to undergo consolidation, that is, to be stored or coded in the mental lexicon, which usually happens as conventionalization. Stored information is superior to unstored information, such as novel information or information inferable from the context: While salient information is highly accessible, nonsalient information requires strongly supportive contextual information to become as accessible as is salient information. At this point, Giora seems to equate salient information with consolidated/ stored information and nonsalient information with unstored information. This, in the SCA, is somewhat questionable because it considers salience as a relatively static entity that changes mainly diachronically. According to Giora, in order for something to be salient, it should be stored in the memory. What is ranked as "most salient meaning" at the present moment may die off after only a few decades. An example of such diachronical change is the word "gay," (as discussed earlier) whose most salient meaning in the '50s of the past century was "joyful"; nowadays, this meaning would rank below that of "homosexual." Salient information can be "disconsolidated" when its salience dies off and the information in question ends up as less salient or nonsalient. So the problem with Giora's approach is that it acknowledges mainly diachronic change, and does talk less about synchronic change. In contrast, SCA emphasizes that salience is in a continual state of change not only diachronically but synchronically as well (emergent situational salience) as a result of the interplay of linguistic salience and perceptual salience.

3.2. TYPES OF SALIENCE IN SCA

SCA distinguishes three types of salience: inherent salience, collective salience, and emergent situational salience. The notion of *inherent salience* is close to what Prat-Sala and Branigan (2000) called "inherent accessibility" and Pattabhiraman (1993) referred to as "canonical salience." Inherent salience is characterized as a natural preference built into the general conceptual and linguistic knowledge of the speaker. It has developed as a result of prior experience of the individual with lexical items, and changes both diachronically and synchronically. Inherent salience is affected by the two other types of salience. *Collective salience* is shared with the other members of the speech community, and changes diachronically.

As I discussed that earlier this type of salience has close connection with common ground. *Emergent situational salience* is similar to "derived accessibility" of Prat-Sala and Branigan (2000) and instantial salience of Pattabhiraman (1993). It changes synchronically and refers to the salience of specific objects and linguistic elements in the context of language production. Emergent situational salience may accrue through such determinants as vividness, speaker motivation, and recency of mention. In an actual situational context, inherent salience is affected and shaped both by collective and situational salience. The following example serves to show the role of salience both in production and comprehension. The excerpt is from the sitcom *Two and a Half Men*. Alan (the main character, Charlie's brother) and Berta (Charlie's housekeeper) are meeting in the kitchen in the morning.
(6)

> ALAN: Morning.
> BERTA: What is so good about it?
> ALAN: I did not say "good."

This exchange is interesting because the collectively salient expression in the morning is "good morning." Of course, many people say "morning" only, which serves as the shortened version of "good morning." Although "morning" is a short form, it still implies "good" without directly wording it. This is so obvious according to collective salience that people do not even notice (or care about) the omission of "good." This is what happened in Berta's case.

Emergent situational salience refers to the salience of situational constraints that can derive from factors such as obviousness, vividness, and recency of mention. A cashier's "How are you doing today?" question in a supermarket, for instance, requires only a short "Fine, thank you." The salience of the situation makes the function of the expression obvious, just like in example (6). However, actual situational salience can be overridden by both collective salience and inherent salience.

In the following example, situational salience is overridden by collective salience, individualized similarly by hearer-readers.

> (7) (Sign on the door of a department store)
> "Girls wanted for different positions."

Not even the actual situational context and environment (door of a department store) can subdue the sexual connotation of the sentence. As Giora (2003) claimed, both salient information and contextual knowledge run in parallel, and salient but contextually inappropriate information may not be discarded. A similar example (discussed in Chapter 6) comes from one of Robin Williams's films (*The Survivors*), where the hero (Williams) says, "I had to sleep with the dogs. Platonically, of course..." The speaker thinks that the sexual connotation of "sleep with" (collective salience) is so strong that a clarification is necessary.

3.3. COMPETITION BETWEEN INHERENT AND EMERGENT SITUATIONAL SALIENCE

From a theoretical perspective, it is difficult to reconcile the attended first (instantial salience, situational salience) with the given-before-new (canonical salience, inherent salience) hypothesis. Bock, Irwin, and Davidson (2004) provided a comprehensive account of this theoretical controversy. They claimed that "the focused first" and "the old first" proposals are contradictory because the information that attracts the focus of attention is typically the new elements of the scene, whereas givenness promotes the already established background. The lexical-semantic factors (e.g., old-before-new) and the perceptual factors (e.g., focused/attended first) should, therefore, produce competing effects. However, this is not necessarily so in the socio-cognitive paradigm. Prior experience also plays some role in attention-getting; i.e., it may determine what the focus of attention becomes. Inherent salience (old-before-new) and emergent situational salience (focused-first) are intertwined and affect each other continuously in the communicative process. The strongest communicative effect is reached when there is no competition between the two, as in the advertisement in Figure 8.1, below.

Not only actual situational salience but also perceptual collective salience directs (especially males') attention to the girl in the advertisement. However, this is just perceptual salience. Linguistic salience is another matter. The text "Wherever your destination we deliver" has nothing to do with the girl in the picture. The note "girl not included" aims to decrease the powerful perceptual saliency, and solve the discrepancy between perceptual salience and linguistic salience. Advertisements usually build on the harmonious cooperation of perceptual collective salience and linguistic salience. Female figures are usually used as attention-getters that direct attention to the product. The linguistic text is generally about the product itself. Perceptual salience is used to create actual situation linguistic salience.

FIGURE 8.1 Perceptual salience as actual situational salience

The interdependence of inherent salience (old-before-new) and emergent situational salience (focused-first) and their bidirectional influence is based on the assumption that inherent salience is dominated by linguistic salience, while emergent situational salience is usually governed by perceptual salience. The following example (8) demonstrates how the two different types of salience operate.

(8) Alan and Sherry (of the sitcom *Two and a Half Men*) are sitting in a restaurant. Alan's right eye is covered with a bandage, so he does not see Sherry very well.

> ALAN: You know, Sherry, I would really like to see more of you.
> SHERRY: *Maybe we should wait and see how the night goes.*
> ALAN: Oh, no. I mean I have only got one good eye. Can we change places?
> SHERRY: Sure.

The conversation demonstrates that Sherry completely misunderstood Alan's utterance "I would really like to see more of you." This may be due to the fact that she relied exclusively on linguistic salience and ignored perceptual salience in processing the utterance. Some studies referred to the fact that inherent linguistic salience seems to override perceptual salience in most cases. Osgood and Bock's study (1977) also showed that the effects of inherent salience consistently trumped those that would need to gain salience from speaker motivation. Lupyan and Spivey

(2010) also came to a somewhat similar conclusion when they argued that language dynamically modulates visual processing.

4. Utterance Generation in SCA

As we have seen in the former chapters, intercultural pragmatics promotes a speaker-hearer pragmatics approach that focuses both on production and comprehension where equal attention is given to the speakers' production. Consequently, it is important to discuss how utterances are generated. The reason why the focus is on production here is that we already know much about how salience operates in comprehension. SCA demonstrates a functional and cognitive view of utterance production, according to which utterance structures reveal the cognitive processes involved in the preparation and production of sentences. Basic cognitive operations, such as memory retrieval and attentional tracking of entities, therefore become important phenomena underlying aspects of utterance production.

By producing an utterance, the speaker makes a commitment to some information or action s/he can be held accountable for. However, the degree of the speaker's commitment and accountability varies between saying and implying. Haugh (2010a) argued that where two (or more) interlocutors co-construct what is said, the speaker generally holds him/herself accountable for that interpreting. However, in the case of implying, where two (or more) interlocutors co-construct an implicature, the degree to which the speaker should hold him/herself accountable for that interpreting is often more open to discussion. This is what happens in example (9).
(9) Chris's friend Peter arrived by plane and Chris met him at the airport.

> CHRIS: Are you hungry?
> PETER: I had something to eat on the plane. I am OK.
> CHRIS: All right. Let's go to a Wendy's.

In this conversation, Peter's utterance, "I had something to eat on the plane" can be interpreted in three different ways: kind of hungry, not hungry, and don't really know. However, his utterance, "I am OK," points to implying that he is "not hungry." Chris either misses this interpretation or thinks that his friend needs encouragement. Or, maybe, he is hungry himself. In any case, his suggestion to go to a Wendy's does not quite match Peter's intention.

Haugh added that he did not want to suggest that speakers are always held less accountable for meanings achieved through *implying*, because implicatures cannot always be legitimately cancelled (Burton-Roberts 2006; Jaszczolt 2009). Instead, he proposed that a richer understanding of speaker meanings may be derived through greater exploration of the ways in which interlocutors *create* meanings in interaction.

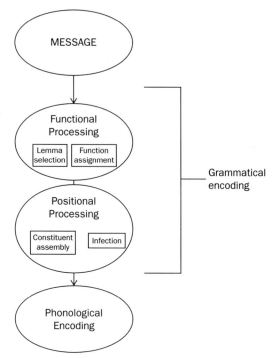

FIGURE 8.2 Bock and Levelt's production model

4.1. THE MECHANISM[2]

The SCA adopts Levelt's modular approach to explain perceptual, conceptual, and linguistic processes during production of sentences in different languages (Levelt 1989; Bock and Levelt 1994). The model (see Figure 8.2) includes three levels or stages of sentence generation distinguished as (1) MESSAGE component, (2) GRAMMATICAL component, and (3) PHONOLOGICAL component or ARTICULATOR (see Figure 8.2, adopted from Bock and Levelt 1994).

Accordingly, the production stages are as follows:

> PERCEPTUAL (from perceptual analysis to rapid apprehension) → CONCEPTUAL (from lemma selection to lexical access) → LINGUISTIC (from lexical retrieval to phonological encoding).

Each of the processing stages receives input from the preceding level. At the first step of producing an utterance, a communicative intention is created. This intention is called a message (cf. Garrett 1975). At the message stage, preverbal thought (intention) is processed and organized into a conceptual scheme of the event before any linguistic processing occurs. It is at this message level that salience comes in

---

[2] The mechanism explained here is based on the description in Kecskes (2013).

as an important factor. The perceptual effects are supposed to be the most active here, biasing conceptualization of the event according to the event's salience map. The message captures features of the speaker's intended meaning and provides the raw material for grammatical encoding. The grammatical component has two sub-stages: functional processing level and positional processing level. The functional level is responsible for word selection: selecting *lemmas*. Lemmas are "amalgams" of an individual lexical concept's properties, including its semantic representation and its morpho-syntactic features (cf. Myachykov 2007). However, lemmas are not yet lexical forms. This is also the level in which grammatical functions like Subject and Object are assigned. Lemmas and grammatical function information are fed into the positional subcomponent. At this sublevel, representations of words are sequentially inserted into a sentence structure that later becomes fixed as the order of the elements in an utterance. This ordering may not be imposed during functional processing. Evidence for this comes from different types of errors. For instance, according to Garrett (1982), quoted by Myachykov (2007), when sounds are exchanged, they originate in the same phrase 87 percent of the time, as opposed to whole word exchanges that occur within the same phrases only 19 percent of the time. Finally, at the phonological level, the phonological forms for the words are retrieved and an overt utterance is produced.

4.2. SELECTION AND ORDERING

What determines the selection of words into which the preverbal thoughts are placed? Past and current research has focused mainly on the formal and structural issues of selection and ordering, asking the question, *What facilitates the choice of a structure and the ordering of the sentence constituents during the production of utterances?* However, according to SCA, conceptualization and the concept/word (lemma) interface play a crucial role in shaping structures. Selected words require/facilitate particular structures and not vice versa. Structural variability depends on the selected words. Before this is explained, we need to review findings on the formal and structural selection and ordering.

Evidence from some previous studies points to the role of salience and the distribution of attention in planning and formulation of sentences (e.g., Myachykov 2007; Tomlin 1997; Stevenson 2002). Speakers seem to actively take into account the attentional status of the referents in the scene when they decide what to say first and, depending on that, what structure to use to organize the sentence (Myachykov and Posner 2005; Myachykov 2007; Garrod and Pickering 1999; Sanford 2001). But several other factors have also been found to influence the accessibility of words and, therefore, their ordering in sentences. Those factors comprise the ones that are related to the referent's conceptual status: novelty in discourse, animacy, concreteness, definiteness, imageability, and prototypicality.

The role of salience and distribution of attention as primary factors affecting selection and ordering somewhat contradicts the traditional view commonly shared in linguistics. As King says: "The [sentence] constituents move to certain positions because of their discourse function interpretation" (King 1995:63). This approach is based on the assumption that the assignment of the syntactic positions in a clause is based on the functional opposition between clause-level *theme and rheme*, *topic and comment*, and/or the referents' semantic roles, like *agent and patient*. Traditionally, starting from the Prague School of Linguistics (e.g., Mathesius 1929; Firbas 1965; Daneš 1970) and continuing with Halliday (1985), the notion of theme is associated with the element "what one is talking about, the topic," while the rheme is "what one says about it, the comment" (Daneš 1970). In this framework, the subject of a sentence frequently acts as the syntactic counterpart of the theme or topic of the utterance. But there may be other structures that highlight the theme through means such as clefts and dislocations.

Functional interaction between discourse elements is generally realized as the hierarchy of semantic roles. Fillmore (1968) used the term "agent" to denote a doer of the action, while the term "patient" referred to an experiencer of the agent's action. According to this view, the semantic agent is the most likely candidate to take the position of syntactic subject of a sentence. This is usually so in configurational language, such as English, as for example in (10):

(10) Because of the rain, **the driver** could hardly see the road.

However, this is not necessarily the case in nonconfigurational languages such as Russian, Turkish, and Hungarian. Example (11) comes from Russian:

(11) Mne nravits' a Masha.
     ('I like Mary')
     For me like Masha

In this Russian sentence, "Masha" is in the grammatical subject position while the agent is in the dative.

In order to understand what makes one referent more prominent than another, or why some referents (or, more broadly, concepts) receive preferential treatment by the processor, we need to attend to the notion of conceptual accessibility (Bock and Warren 1985), which is related to "codeability," "imageability," "retrievability," and so on. Bock and Warren said that "Conceptual accessibility is the ease with which the mental representation of some potential referent can be activated in or retrieved from memory" (Bock and Warren 1985:50). Sanford and Garrod (1981) developed a similar approach. They claimed that one important function of maintaining coherence in discourse is to constantly perform a successful search for discourse-relevant referents in the memory of the interlocutors. They called such referential situation a *scenario*. They argued that referents that form part of the current portion of the discourse, and, therefore, are actively maintained in the memory, are more easily (or quickly) accessible than the referents that do not correspond to the current topic of discussion (see Myachykov 2007). Levelt (1989) expressed a similar idea. He related the production of referring expressions to the level of the accessibility in terms of the addressee's mental state.

As mentioned above, the information flow in discourse can be divided into old or given information and new information. The term *givenness* represents the knowledge shared between the interlocutors. Consequently, the given information is that which the speaker believes to be known by the hearer. In contrast, the new information is the information with which the hearer is unfamiliar (cf. Clark and Haviland 1977; Halliday 1967/1968, Haviland and Clark 1974). A quasi-psychological view on givenness suggests that the given versus new distinction correlates with the notion of cognitive activation of the concept. Chafe (1976:30) said that, "Given (or old) information is that knowledge that the speaker assumes to be in the consciousness of the addressee at the time of the utterance. The so-called new information is what the speaker assumes he is introducing into the addressee's consciousness by what he says." In fact, here, Chafe implicitly referred to the issue of salience and memorial activation. Explaining what makes the referent given or new, he argued that the new information is "newly activated" at a given point in conversation, while the old information is the one that does not require such activation (Chafe 1994:72). Such activation status, among other things, depends on the speaker's perspective affected by the salience of the processed material.

5. Salience in Language Processing

The role of salience in language production involves a ranking relation of prominence of entities, as well as a preferred choice among alternatives. When the speaker is faced with having to choose a word or an expression, a ranking of the available choices is obtained on the basis of the degree of salience of entities in the context of generation. The word or phrase is then selected for utterance on the basis of maximum salience. Once a speaker has either an a priori or an emergent, co-constructed intention to communicate, s/he should find an appropriate linguistic representation to transfer this message to the hearer. The message of the preverbal thought is made up by combining the concepts that the speaker intends to *explicate*. Concepts are attached to several possible frames. When a preverbal thought is formulated, the related schemas will be activated. Jackendoff (2002) claimed that concepts have no direct, one-to-one connection with lexical items. A concept may be associated with several lexical expressions, and conversely the process of transforming preverbal thought into linguistic expressions varies among different speakers because they have several options to explicate their intentions.

Kecskes (2008:401) argued that there is a difference between speaker processing and hearer processing. When a lexical unit (labeled for private context) is used by a speaker, private contexts attached to this lexical expression are activated top-down in a hierarchical order based on salience. This hierarchical order works differently for the speaker and the hearer. For the speaker, there is primarily an inter-label hierarchy, while for the hearer the intra-label hierarchy comes first. The *inter-label hierarchy* operates in the first phase of production, when a speaker looks for words to express her/his intention. As a first step, s/he has to select words or expressions from a group of possibilities in order to express his/her communicative intention. These words or expressions constitute a hierarchy from the best fit to those less suited to the idea s/he is trying to express. The hearer, however, has to cope with a different type of hierarchy from her/his perspective. Thus, an *intra-label hierarchy* is in force when the hearer processes (a) lexical unit(s) in an utterance (or even an entire utterance). The label (word) uttered by the speaker hierarchically triggers the history of that particular label as used by the hearer (but not by the speaker). This may also be a reason for misunderstanding in the communicative process, both in intracultural and intercultural interactions. Compare the following (source: American sitcom) interchange in (12):

(12) BOB: Are you OK?
     MARY: I am fine.
     BOB: I know you are fine, but are you OK?

Bob had several options to ask about Mary's well-being: "Are you OK?," "Are you fine?," "Is everything all right?," and so on. His selection of "Are you OK?" caused a slight misunderstanding between the two because they interpreted "OK" differently.

The mechanism of putting preverbal thought into linguistic expressions is a process of privatization, subjectivization of the actual situational context. In fact, this process contradicts Grice's notion of "what is said." For how can a truth-conditional semantic meaning be transferred from speaker to hearer without any change? Both processes, the speaker's utterance production and the hearer's interpretation, are highly personalized/privatized/subjectived, and are the results of the interplay of inherent salience and emergent situational salience. Both speaker's production and hearer's inference comprise lexical processes and contextual processes that run parallel and are governed by salience. A speaker's utterance often undergoes corrections showing the speaker's attempts to adjust to the context en-route. Similar processes occur in comprehension. Utterance interpretation hardly consists of just those two modules, as the Neo-Griceans maintain. Inferencing/interpreting is a trial-and-error process on the part of the hearer, who tries to make sense of the speaker's intention.

As we have seen, salience is both an individual and a societal phenomenon. Prior and actual situational experience is privatized/subjectivized and prioritized in the mind of interlocutors. Their different prior experiences, varying evaluations of the actual situational context, dynamically changing intentions, and individual degrees of salience result in a subjectivized process of production and comprehension. As a result, there may be no single point in the recovery process at which a speaker's utterance *fully* matches a hearer's interpretation. This is because both a speaker's production and a hearer's interpretation are "contaminated" by individualized pragmatic elements. Pragmatic enrichment processes work differently for both speaker and hearer. Consequently, the match between the two sides keeps varying in the communicative process. This is why we think that, "we almost always fail. [. . .] Yet we almost always nearly succeed" (Rapaport 2003: 402). And this is why a pragmatic theory should be both speaker- and hearer-centered. Speaker's production should be analyzed in its own right.

6. Salience is Culture Specific

According to research on lexical salience, as stated above, stored information is more influential in processing than unstored information, at least in the first phase of processing (e.g., Giora 1997; 2003). Talking about meaning salience (which we called inherent salience, above), Giora claimed that "privileged meanings, meanings foremost on our mind, affect comprehension and production primarily, regardless of context or literality" (Giora 2003:103). Salient meaning encodes standard context in which the given lexical item repeatedly occurs, on which we build our expectations about what may or may not happen, and on which our ability to understand and predict how the world around us works is based (see Violi 2000). The more encounters we have with this coded meaning, the more familiar the situation(s) in which it occurs become. This is where salience connects to core common ground and the issue of culture-specific character of salience becomes important.

I argued above that besides the inherent salience that causes this effect, we also need to deal with emergent situational salience, which emerges for both the speaker and the hearer in the process of co-constructing the conversation. Inherent salience is based on stored information, while emergent situational salience is dominated by perceptual salience and thus basically serves as a trigger for all interlocutors. The question is how this emergent situational salience operates, what it is that it actually triggers in the mind of the participants of the conversation, and how all this relates to intercultural communication and nonnative speaker language use. Inherent salience for nonnative speakers is dominated by L1 prior experience and some limited experience with L2, while emergent situational salience is motivated by the common current experience for all interlocutors—so there is more chance for common ground building there. Stored information is built on prior experience, usually in the socio-cultural environment of one's speech community. What is on one's mind, i.e., inherent salience, is very much connected with encyclopedic knowledge, cultural models, and norms of the primary language and culture, and how all this is privatized, or subjectivized, by the individual in speech situations. In the meantime, emergent situational salience is the result of the momentum, the current experience that can be governed by both perceptual and linguistic factors, with the former being usually dominant if present. This was well-demonstrated with Figure 8.1 above.

6.1. DIFFERENT EXPERIENCE RESULTS IN DIFFERENT SALIENCE

The problem for L2 users is that what is salient for individuals belonging to the target language community will not necessarily be salient for the "newcomers," the L2 language users. When acquiring and/or using another language, learners do two things. First of all, they rely on prior knowledge that is the knowledge of the first language as a system and the socio-cultural background knowledge that the L1 is based upon. Second, they also give priority to certain knowledge and meanings they encounter in the target language, which is constituted by their limited prior experience with the target language. So the primary meaning that emerges in the mind of an L2 learner as the most salient meaning of a lexical unit or utterance in the target language (L2) is the result of experience with two languages and cultures (one full and one limited). Consequently, this salient meaning may significantly differ from what the native speakers of that language consider as the most salient meaning of a particular lexical item or expression. This may cause misunderstandings in communication. This is what happened in the next interchange between an American student and a Chinese student. They were looking for the Registrar's office.
(13)

> SALLY: Here is the door.
> XIAOLU: Who should go in first?
> SALLY: *Be my guest.*
> XIAOLU: We are not guests here.

The response of the Chinese student to Sally's utterance "Be my guest" shows that she may have misunderstood Sally's idiomatic expression. What Sally meant is that Xiaolu should go in first. However, Xiaolu may not have had any such experience with the idiom "be my guest." For her, the most salient meaning of the expression was the literal meaning.

It seems fair to say that in order for nonnative speakers to use the target language appropriately, they are expected not only to develop similar collective salience for lexical items and expressions that native speakers have but also to follow the changes in salience as the target language adjusts to the socio-cultural changes in the given language community. Is this not too much to expect of the language learner? Yes, it is. Thus, this is one of the reasons why nativelike competence, although theoretically feasible, in practice is highly unlikely. No two nativelike competencies in one body seem to be possible. This is confirmed by research on bilingualism and multicompetence. Grosjean (1989) argued that "a bilingual is not two monolinguals in one body." Discussing multicompetence, Cook (1997) concluded that L2 users process language differently, and have different knowledge of both their first and their second languages. Analyzing the results of a longitudinal experiment, Kecskes and Papp (2000) pointed out that the bidirectional influence between the L1 and L2 results in a language use that is not exactly the same as the language use of monolinguals of either language. This is because while the language channels are kept separate, thoughts originating in one and the same conceptual system are fed into two different language channels.

However, we should not forget one thing. For nonnative speakers to develop relatively the same collective salient meanings as those of native speakers is not a question of ability. Theoretically, L2 speakers can achieve this goal. What they are not able to do, however, is go through the same or similar linguistic and socio-cultural experience that the native speakers go through (as discussed in Chapter 3), and which results in similar salient meanings these native speakers collectively have encoded in their minds. When native and nonnative speakers were asked about the most salient meaning of the expression *welcome aboard*, the vast majority of native speakers referred to the same "standard context" in which the situation-bound utterance is used (greeting a new employee), while the nonnative speakers gave a variety of answers depending on their concrete experience (Kecskes, 2001:253). What becomes salient in the mind depends on conventions, familiarity, and frequency of encounters (Giora 2003), e.g., linguistic and socio-cultural experience. Research shows that what is carved in the mind is difficult to erase. As we discussed in Chapter 3 Barro et al. (1993:56) are right when they say that an advanced nonnative speaker cannot be expected "simply to abandon his/her own cultural world." The dual language system (see Kecskes 2009) seems to be a far more complex system than the interlanguage theory (e.g., Selinker 1972; Selinker and Douglas 1985) suggests, and therefore, further investigation into the interplay of conceptual and linguistic levels is needed.

6.2. LITERAL MEANING AND NONLITERAL MEANING

In a recent study (Kecskes 2007a) on formulaic language that was also discussed in Chapter 5, the lingua franca database analysis showed an overwhelming dominance of expressions used in their literal meaning. Based on these results I hypothesized that for nonnative speakers it is almost always the literal meaning that is the most salient meaning of lexical units in lingua franca communication. Nonnative speaker processing significantly differs from native speaker processing as far as salience is concerned. Nonnative speakers almost always process the literal meaning of lexical units first, and if it does not match the context they go on trying to figure out the actual situational meaning. Basically, they seem to be acting according to the Gricean modular view: literal first, inferencing next. However, this is not the case with native speakers. Their most salient meaning in the first phase of processing can be literal, figurative, or both (Gibbs 2002; Giora 2003). This leads us to the debate about the definition and nature of literal meaning in the pragmatics literature.

Recently there has been a heated debate going on about literal meaning, which has usually been defined as a type of pretheoretical semantic or linguistic meaning (Ariel 2002). The classical definition (see Katz 1977; Searle 1978) says that linguistic meaning is direct, sentential, specified by grammar, and context-free. Being fully compositional, linguistic meaning is generated by linguistic knowledge of lexical items, combined with linguistic rules. According to Grice, literal meaning is also "what is said" (Grice 1978). He actually claimed that "what is said" is "closely related to the conventional meaning of words" (Grice 1975: 44).

An important claim of the Graded Salience Hypothesis is that the most salient meaning is not always the literal meaning. Giora (2003:33) defines "literal meaning" as follows: "Literal meaning refers to what is denoted by individual words, as well as to what is said by the compositional meaning of the sentence made up of these words intended nonfiguratively." The most salient meaning(s) of a lexical unit can be either literal or figurative or sometimes even both. For instance, in the case of the expression *give me a break* or the word *patronize*, both the literal meaning and figurative meaning can be considered salient. Giora argues that "cognitively prominent salient meanings rather than literal meanings play the most important role in comprehension and production of language." The GSH requires that the Gricean standard pragmatic model therefore be revised: instead of postulating the priority of literal meaning, the priority of salient (e.g., conventional, familiar, frequent, prototypical) meaning should be postulated (Giora 1997). Consequently, it is not the figurative vs. literal split that matters, but the salient vs. nonsalient continuum that really counts when processing the meaning of words or utterances. The literal vs. figurative split has some psychological reality in the mind of native speakers, although this dichotomy has been problematic because native speakers often tend to identify literal meaning with the most frequent and familiar meaning of a lexical unit, which, as Giora claimed can be literal, figurative, or both. The following two sentences demonstrate this:

(14)

> John was literally glued to the television.
> She has literally driven me nuts lately.

The traditional linguistic approach claims that in most people's minds it is the literal meaning from which all other meanings derive (see Gibbs 2002). The belief about the primacy of the literal meaning is so strong that not everyone notices when there is a shift in the semantic structure of a word, and what was once the most familiar, most frequent, and most conventionalized of all possible senses gives way to another sense that takes over as the most salient sense but never as the literal meaning. The following example may shed some light on this phenomenon: I had scheduled a meeting with one of my doctoral students who is a native speaker of English. She was late. When she entered my office, she said "Hello," and gave the following explanation: "Sorry. I was held up at a gas station. Not literally, though." The explanation of the student raises the question, Why did she find it important to add "Not literally, though" after the use of the lexical unit "hold up"? Why did she think that her words could have been interpreted incorrectly? Was it because she knew I was a nonnative speaker? Not really. I confronted her with these questions. She said that she did not want me to think that there was actually a hold-up at the gas station. She actually thought that the literal meaning of the verb "hold up" was "rob," which is clearly the figurative meaning, but which appears to be more salient for the native speaker than the literal meaning "stop, prevent from doing something," because the verb "hold up" may be used more frequently in that figurative sense. According to The American Heritage Dictionary of the English Language (Morris 1976: 628), the lexical entry HOLD UP has the following readings:

1. to prevent from falling; to support,
2. to present for exhibit; to show,
3. to last; to stand up; to endure,
4. to stop or interrupt; to delay,
5. to rob.

So why was this confusion in the mind of this native speaker of American English? And was it really a kind of confusion or something else? It is likely that what happened was that she equated the most frequent and familiar meaning, that is, the most salient meaning, with the literal meaning.

What is important in the example above is that there must have been a shift in lexical representation, which may not have been followed by a shift in conceptual representation.[3] The literal versus figurative dichotomy makes sense for language analysis, but not for language processing, where it cannot be claimed that the literal meaning is always processed before the figurative meaning. Where does this leave intercultural pragmatics and nonnative language users? They are expected to be up-to-date not only in meaning use but also in meaning shift and/or meaning change that occurs in the target language. However, this looks like an unreasonable expectation. The application of GSH to intercultural communication demonstrates the critical split between native speakers and nonnative speakers in figurative language processing. Actually, this is a part of second language research where the GSH has already started to be applied. Recent studies on idioms and prefabricated pragmatic units use the GSH to demonstrate the difference between native speakers and nonnative speakers in figurative language processing (e.g., Kecskes 2001; 2004; Bortfeld 2002, 2003; Cieslicka 2004, 2006). These studies all concluded that native speakers tend to take a holistic approach toward idioms and consider their figurative meaning more salient, while nonnative speakers use an analytic approach toward idioms and usually take their literal meaning as more salient. Abel (2003) found that nonnative speakers showed a general tendency to judge idioms as being decomposable, whereas native speakers more often judged them as being nondecomposable. Abel's findings also showed that for native speakers the figurative meaning of an idiom is highly salient, which presupposes an idiom entry in the mental lexicon, whereas for nonnative speakers it is less salient, which points to the fact that they rely on constituent analysis rather than on a developed separate entry.

---

[3] These issues were first discussed in Kecskes (2006).

In Bortfeld's (2003) experiments, subjects classified idioms from three languages according to their figurative meanings. Response times and error rates indicated that participants were able to interpret unfamiliar (e.g., other languages') idioms depending largely on the degree to which they were analyzable, and that different forms of processing were used both within and between languages depending on this analyzability. Relying on her findings, Cieslicka (2004) advanced the proposition that literal meanings of idiom constituents enjoy processing priority over their figurative interpretations. She claimed that understanding L2 idioms entails an obligatory computation of the literal meanings of idiom constituent words, even if these idioms are embedded in a rich figurative context and if their idiomatic interpretation is well known to L2 learners. The literal salience model of L2 idiom comprehension proposed by Cieslicka ascribes a higher salience status to literal meanings, regardless of whether an L2 idiom is familiar to the learner or not, and regardless of contextual bias. Kecskes's analysis of "situation-bound utterances" (SBUs) is in accordance with the findings of the studies discussed above. While processing SBUs, the nonnative speaker subjects used an analytic approach and usually identified the literal meaning of pragmatic units as most salient. Kecskes (2001; 2002) argued that salience is culture-specific and nonnative speakers cannot be expected to approach figurative speech the way native speakers do because of their different linguistic and cultural experience.

L2 users, especially those who have studied the L2 in an instructional environment, are usually much more familiar with the literal meanings of lexical units than with their figurative meanings. This is mainly due to the bottom-up approach to instruction that is based on the belief that instruction should follow a path from the easier to the more complex. Literal meaning has been considered less complex because this is the level at which lexical equivalency between languages is believed to be working. (This is not quite true, though.) Development of figurative meaning, however, is facilitated by language socialization in L1, which is usually remote for the L2 learners. It is easy to find a lexical equivalent in many languages for the English word *shoot* at the literal level, such as "John shot the fox," or "she learned how to shoot with a gun." However, this is not the case with its figurative use of the word, such as, "give it a shot," "give me a shot of whiskey," or "they are shooting a film." The American culture is full of expressions that are related to *shoot*. One of the examples that has hardly any lexical equivalent in another language is as follows:

(15)

> Bob, I have some questions about this project.
> OK, *shoot.*

Languages may have much lexical equivalency at the literal level but much less equivalency exists at the metaphorical, figurative level. Words may have close lexical equivalents in the languages of bi- and multilinguals at the lexical level, while the metaphorical, figurative domain tied to those words in the respective languages may differ to a great extent. This is what affects interlocutors' language processing in intercultural interactions to a great extent.

Chapters 6, 7, and 8 discussed context, common ground, and salience. In the next chapter we will see how these factors affect politeness and impoliteness, which as yet are not very much explored territories in intercultural communication. In intercultural pragmatics, however, they need to be discussed because context, common ground, and salience do not work the same way as they do in intracultural communication. Consequently, what is polite and impolite in intercultural communication, and how nonnative speakers can be polite or impolite, appears to be a very complex issue.

9

Politeness and Impoliteness

Research in politeness and impoliteness in intercultural communication is almost an uncharted territory. This is not necessarily surprising because politeness and impoliteness are considered universal categories that are lexicalized differently in languages. Researchers have thus been busy investigating how these categories are expressed in different language and how they compare to each other. As a result, there is much research on politeness/impoliteness focusing on one language or cross-cultural comparisons, but much less about how politeness/impoliteness theories can be applied to intercultural interactions. Writing about intercultural (im) politeness, Haugh (2010b) found that no specific theory of intercultural politeness had yet been developed. The main reason for this situation may be that politeness and impoliteness are essential parts of cultural models, conventions, and norms in languages that bring about different expectations about what is polite or impolite in a given language. For instance, Culpeper (2005:38) suggested we should use Tracy and Tracy's definition of impoliteness (1998:227): "communicative acts perceived by members of a social community (and often intended by speakers) to be purposefully offensive." This definition clearly refers to the "members of a social community." However, interlocutors in intercultural interactions hardly make up a "social community" in the traditional sense of the expression. That social community is usually just temporary. As we discussed earlier, interlocutors can rely on factors such as common beliefs, cultural models, and community norms only to a limited extent in intercultural communication. The question for intercultural pragmatics is as follows: Will a person, with, let us say, a Bulgarian L1 sound polite enough or impolite to a, for instance, Colombian speaker when they use English as a lingua franca? Will the Bulgarian's nonnative speaker communication partner consider the utterance of the Bulgarian speaker impolite or polite enough in English? Will the actual situational context help them to process utterance appropriately? Will they have common ground that they can rely on while processing the given utterance? What does it mean for those international speakers to process the utterance "appropriately"? To illustrate what I mean here is an example from a dialogue at Fuzhou Airport between a Chinese waitress and an Australian traveler who was sitting at a table talking to two other travelers and drinking beer and coffee and eating something.

(1)

CHINESE:	Can I get you some more coffee, sir?
AUSTRALIAN:	*Who is stopping you?*
CHINESE:	You want to stop me?
AUSTRALIAN:	Oh no, just bring me the damned coffee.

The expression "*who is stopping you?*" in this actual situational context sounds very rude according to the norms of the English language. However, the Chinese waitress did not seem to realize that. She may have been misled by the literal meaning of the expression, which hardly fits into the actual situation context. Or she may not have found the utterance rude according to her L2 cultural models and expectations and/or the literal meaning of the expression. This means that the rudeness/impoliteness of the utterance may have been lost in this interaction, and the actual situational context did not help the Chinese interlocutor in any way to figure out the real meaning of the utterance The example shows very well what problems nonnative speakers face when they produce and process utterances in intercultural communication.

It is not the goal of this chapter to go into the details of the very complex debates about politeness and impoliteness theories that are all monolingual in nature. However, a basic understanding of the notions and leading current theories is necessary for us to explore what exactly is going on in intercultural communication with the politeness and impoliteness phenomena and how those theories of politeness/impoliteness should or could be modified (if needed) to accommodate intercultural interactions. Several authors (e.g., Garces-Conejos Blitvich 2010a; Wierzbicka 2001) emphasized that most models of politeness and impoliteness are Anglo-centered. At the same time, there are some studies that show a certain awareness regarding cultural and linguistic variation when theorizing about impoliteness-related concepts (e.g., Holmes et al. 2008; Bargiela-Chiappini and Haugh 2009; a special issue on impoliteness in the journal "*Intercultural Pragmatics*" 7/4, 2010). This is basically true for the field of politeness studies where there are a number of studies that focus on cross-cultural variations. However, impoliteness has just started to be explored in the last decade. Culpeper et al. (2010:598) claimed that "it makes sense to put notions that may assist in understanding how impoliteness works to the cross-cultural test as a matter of priority, the objective being to let the mechanisms of variation help define impoliteness, rather than let a definition of impoliteness obscure variation."

1. Politeness and Impoliteness Theories

Politeness theory has been with us since Brown and Levinson (1987), but only lately has impoliteness theory been separated from the former. Recently, both politeness and impoliteness theories, with some slight difference, have been following two lines. First-order politeness and impoliteness (or Politeness and Impoliteness 1) is based on the commonsense notion of politeness, and is defined as politeness perceived by members of different socio-cultural groups. Second-order politeness and impoliteness (or Politeness and Impoliteness 2) is based on Brown and Levinson's approach (1987), Gricean intention, maxims, and speech acts, and is a theoretical construct that is the scientific conceptualization of Politeness and Impoliteness 1. Politeness and Impoliteness 2 have traditionally applied Brown and Levinson's individualistically and cognitively focused formulation of face (Bargiela-Chiappini 2003: 1463) and viewed politeness as facework, i.e., as mitigation of face-threatening acts. Politeness and Impoliteness 1 is the result of the *discursive turn*, with particular focus on participants' own assessments of discourse as polite or impolite.

Because of its emphasis on dynamism and constructivist approach, the discursive turn is particularly important for intercultural pragmatics. We will thus briefly review its main tenets. According to Garces-Conejos Blitvich (2010a), the discursive turn was partly inspired by Eelen (2001), who identified three main problems with the theories of Politeness and Impoliteness 2, namely that: (1) they are conceptually biased toward the polite end of the polite/impolite distinction; (2) they conceptualize politeness and impoliteness as opposites; and (3) their conceptualizations of impoliteness are speaker-biased, focusing almost entirely on production. Using Bourdieu's (1991) notion of habitus, Eelen proposed an alternative model of politeness with three main tenets: argumentativity, historicity, and discursiveness. Her model put the evaluative role of the hearer into the center of attention. Its major advantage is that it accounts for both politeness and impoliteness, while providing a more dynamic approach to the individual-social relationship. According to Eelen's model, evolution and change are considered essential features of politeness and impoliteness, which are defined in constructionist terms. The evaluations of politeness and impoliteness are deemed constructions of reality rather than references to a factual reality (Eelen 2001:247).

Several researchers (e.g., Locher and Watts 2005; Mills 2003; Watts 2003) followed the lines of the Eelen approach and criticized the traditional politeness models. Watts (2003) claimed that the ontological status of politeness needs to be solved before a model is applied. The traditional models present stipulative definitions of politeness and are essentialist, governed by rationalist principles. They avoid dealing with conflict, communicative discord, and rudeness. In Watts's opinion, the construction and reproduction of mental concepts by means of language (such as polite, rude, aggressive, etc.) is carried out discursively, and so the right approach to politeness and impoliteness is constructivist rather than rationalist. As a result, the discursive line of research proposes a qualitative and nonpredictive approach to the politeness and impoliteness phenomena. This approach has not attempted to come up with an overarching theory of politeness and impoliteness as Brown and Levinson did.

From the perspective of intercultural pragmatics the Politeness & Impoliteness 1 approach has two important things to offer. First of all, in this discursive paradigm, analysis happens on the discourse level and one of the main arguments is that it is the speaker rather than the utterance that is impolite or polite. This claim puts emphasis on the individual. However, Politeness & Impoliteness 1 also relies on the notion of *communities of practice* (cf. Wenger 1998) that has been very popular lately in several other fields including sociolinguistics, second language acquisition, and bi- and multilingualism, as was discussed earlier. This notion focuses on language practices and styles developed by groups of people as they engage in a common task. Analyzing these practices, the researcher is expected to identify the norms of appropriateness for a given community of practice and then assess a given utterance as polite or impolite against those norms. However, the analyst's interpretation as an outsider's might not always coincide with that of participants' themselves. This approach raises several problems for intercultural pragmatics. For instance, can an intercultural interaction be considered a community of practice? Or can intercultures as described in this book be considered temporary norms and/or interim rules? We will return to these issues later.

As Mills's approach (2003) makes clear, norms and their sharedness have become a central aspect of politeness research in the discursive view. However, the discursive approach does not take norms as straightforward and preexisting entities, but as versatile argumentative tools, not necessarily shared across the board by individuals in the language community. This view is in line with what the socio-cognitive approach advocates about common beliefs and partly about common ground. Core common ground and collective salience are group phenomena, but this does not mean that each individual in the group will behave accordingly. Norms are seen as being relative to the practice to which they are part rather than informing it in an objective way (Eelen 2001:229–236). Thus, researchers' focus is on how norms are discursively co-constructed and how they may be resisted or contested. The discursive approach thus questions essentialist notions, such as the existence of "cultures" because they presuppose that norms guiding a particular group of individuals are fixed or unchanging (Mills 2003). Therefore, all attempts at universality or cross-cultural comparison are abandoned (Haugh 2007). This is not quite so in the socio-cognitive approach that emphasizes that cultures and cultural models exist with fuzzy boundaries and are distributed individual by individual. Norms are guides that we can deviate from. Mills (2009:1058) argued that the notion of communities of practice allows researchers to analyze groups of individuals "without falling prey to large-scale generalizations about all of the individuals in a particular language group or culture." At the same time, communities are not isolated, and therefore the focus should include the interplay among individuals, groups, and social norms.

According to Garces-Conejos Blitvich (2010a), a very positive outcome of the introduction of the discursive approach is that it has contributed to opening up the field, once limited to the study of face-threat mitigation, i.e., politeness as conceived by Brown and Levinson (1987), to target all types of relational work (Locher and Watts 2005), with impoliteness phenomena being among those receiving increased attention (Bousfield and Locher 2008; Bousfield and Culpeper 2008).

However, there is a major problem with Politeness & Impoliteness 1. The approach rejects prescriptive norms and relies on the minute-by-minute description of specific occurrences of politeness and impoliteness in individual encounters. Terkourafi (2005b:245) argued that if the predictive nature of any theory is disregarded, what we are left with are "minute descriptions of individual encounters, but these do not in any way add up to an explanatory theory of the phenomena under study." She further claimed that speakers involved in interactions commonly make predictions regarding appropriateness and what might be expected therein. Another problem with the Politeness & Impoliteness 1 view is that although it focuses on the descriptive rather than predictive level, it still uses the traditional descriptive tools of Politeness & Impoliteness 2 approaches such as conversational analysis terminology and face-related terms. Terkourafi proposed a data-driven approach to the study of politeness and impoliteness: the frame-based view. Her approach seeks to establish regularities between linguistic expressions and their contexts of use (frames). In this paradigm politeness and impoliteness is not seen as a property of linguistic expressions. It is those regularities and norms—the unchallenged co-occurrence of particular contexts and particular linguistic expressions—that create the perception of politeness and impoliteness. Terkourafi's frame-based approach combines conversational analytical and speech-act theoretic criteria. Haugh (2007) also criticized the discursive approach because it chose Relevance Theory, which is an intention-based model, as its model of communication. However, according to Garces-Conejos Blitvich (2010a), RT is incompatible with the constructivist view of communication.

From the perspective of intercultural pragmatics, Spencer-Oatey's (2002, 2005, 2007) rapport management model is worth mentioning because it was developed, in part, to offset what was deemed as the Western ethnocentric bias of other models. Spencer-Oatey's approach is both universal and extremely context-sensitive. Spencer-Oatey claimed that rapport management (the management of harmony-disharmony among people), besides the management of face needs, comprises two other components: the management of sociality rights and obligations, and the management of interactional goals. The rapport management model's fine-tuned categories—quality, relational and social identity, face and sociality rights (further subdivided into equity and association rights)—can be used as discerning tools in both qualitative and quantitative approaches. Spencer-Oatey's model is not compatible with the socio-cognitive approach being promoted in this book because it puts too much emphasis on the socio-cultural factors and almost completely ignores the individual factors. Besides, it is sociolinguistics with heavy emphasis on the social rather than on the cognitive, linguistic factors. The socio-cognitive approach underlines the importance of both the societal and individual elements in the analysis.

Several attempts have been made to solve the problem of the separation of the two lines of research and the relationship of the analyst and participants in the interaction. Our goal cannot be here to review these attempts. A summary can be found in Garces-Conejos Blitvich (2010a). Here I will just briefly mention some innovative attempts that, in my opinion, have already affected or will affect research in intercultural pragmatics.

Based on the work of Lachernicht (1980), some scholars (e.g., Culpeper 1996, Kienpointner 1997) have already started to explore impoliteness in its own right. Following the same lines as Lachernicht, Culpeper (1996) developed a model of impoliteness, which was a reversal of Brown and Levinson's politeness taxonomy. He expanded and revised the model in Culpeper et al. (2003), Culpeper (2005). Recently, Bousfield (2008) also added to the model and presented the latest version of the model that is based on two tactics, rather than strategies: on-record and off-record impoliteness, the latter including sarcasm, and withhold politeness. Individual strategies can all be deployable within the two tactics described.

Some scholars have argued that Politeness & Impoliteness 1 and 2 are inseparable. Eelen (2001) and Garces-Conejos Blitvich (2010b) opted for a theory that incorporates both aspects. They argued that an unequivocally one-sided position is, in practice, impossible. An approach that has special importance for intercultural pragmatics is Garcés-Conejos Blitvich's (2010a; 2010b) genre approach, which is a blended theory that fits into the socio-cognitive paradigm because it pays equal attention to individual and societal factors. The genre approach is based mainly on Fairclough's (2003) views on genre. Fairclough claimed that discourse is always situated, always shaped by genres. Genres in his work are seen as ways of (inter) acting or relating discursively, and constitute a mediating level between discourse, ways of representing, and style, ways of being. Genres, discourses, and styles are, respectively, relatively stable and durable ways of acting, representing, and identifying. Although they vary considerably in terms of their degree of stabilization, fixity, and homogenization—some are almost ritualized, others are quite variable and in flux (Garces-Conejos Blitvich 2010b). Discourse, genres, and style are considered dialectically related, constantly interrelating in top-down, bottom-up fashion. They are co-constructed at the level of style.

The important thing is that the application of the Fairclough's model to the study of politeness/impoliteness allows for a combination of top-down and bottom-up analyses just like it was suggested in the socio-cognitive approach. At the level of genre, there are top-down operating expectations and norms that are accepted, resisted, or modified at the level of style in the communicative process. Consequently, this works like the co-construction of intercultures where both prior experience and actual situational experience contribute to the "end product." The genre method also relies on the context view presented in the socio-cognitive approach in (Kecskes 2008; 2011). According to Garces-Conejos Blitvich (2010a:541), "the genre approach views context as a dynamic construct that appears in different formats in language use both as a repository and/or trigger of knowledge. Thus, according to Kecskes (2011), context represents two sides of world knowledge: prior context and actual situational context, which are intertwined and undividable. The actual situational context is viewed through the prior context, and this combination creates, as it were, a third space. Meaning is, in this view, seen as the outcome of the interrelation of prior and current experience. This dynamism is also the main feature of face, which is seen as interactionally and discursively constructed and emerging in interaction (Arundale 2006; Haugh 2009; Locher and Watts 2005; Terkourafi 2008)."

2. What is Polite and What is Impolite in Intercultural Interaction?

In intercultural pragmatics we cannot put more emphasis either on the individual factors or on the socio-cultural, contextual factors. They are equally important. However, as SCA argues, the extent to which they affect interaction at different stages may change. Intercultural (im)politeness research should integrate the micro level and macro level perspective on language, culture, and interaction by postulating that interlocutors, to some extent, rely and/or are under the influence of their own cultural models, norms, and conventions (macro) while co-constructing intercultures in the communicative process (micro). This extent can occasionally be minimal or even zero, i.e., no a priori cultural norms of L1 of participants are represented in a particular segment of conversation. Everything just happens according to the norms of the lingua franca (target language).

It is important to note that the politeness/impoliteness phenomenon itself lies within the micro-macro nexus, as Haugh (2010b) claimed. (Im)politeness comprises interactionally grounded evaluations that occur at the level of individual cognition (what X thinks Y shows what Y thinks of X). At the same time, it also encompasses normative expectations and conventions that are supposed to be shared by others in a particular speech community (what X thinks Y should show Y thinks of X; see in Haugh and Hinze 2003). In sum, following Kecskes (2010a, 2011) and Haugh (2007, 2009), we can say that (im)politeness is both constituted in interaction in the form of evaluations (micro) and constitutive of interaction in the form of expectations (macro).

In intercultural pragmatics it is crucial to define what factors affect the speaker in making his utterance sound polite or impolite, and what factors affect the hearer in processing an utterance as polite or impolite. In order to answer these questions we should look at three issues: (1) intention, (2) norms and cultural models, and (3) role of context.

2.1. ROLE OF INTENTION

There is a debate in the politeness & impoliteness paradigm about whether the speaker's intention plays a role in the hearer's assessment of a given discourse as polite or impolite. Most of the researchers appear not to be fully decided on this issue. Culpeper (2009), for instance, said: "I am not convinced that (full) intentionality is an essential condition for impoliteness." Holmes et al. (2008) claimed that speaker's intention may be irrelevant for the hearer to assess an action as impolite. Their view is supported by Locher and Watts (2008), who said that what really counts in establishing whether a communicative act is deemed impolite or not is the interlocutors' judgment rather than their intention. According to Haugh (2007), politeness is an evaluation of behavior. On the other side of the aisle is Terkourafi (2008), who argued that the recognition of intentions is linked to rudeness, not to impoliteness. According to Hutchby's view (2008), intentions are only seen as important because of researchers' methodological partiality toward the categorization of linguistic features that index (im)polite intentions.

To move the debate forward, it would appear necessary that the discussion on the role of intention in assessments of impoliteness be informed by current research on the role of intention in pragmatic theories. Haugh (2008b:102) pointed out that the evidence "against the continued placement of Gricean intentions at the centre of theorizing in pragmatics is now substantial, if not overwhelming." Others (cf. Tomasello 2008), however, still view the recognition of Grice's communicative intention as central to triggering inferential processes and comprehension. As it was argued earlier, the socio-cognitive approach does not question the central role of intention in communication. However, it emphasizes that intention is both a priori and emergent. We should therefore not question the central role of intention as Haugh and several other scholars do, but rather incorporate the dynamic element (emergent) into its understanding. Brown and Levinson's (1987), as well as Leech's (1983), approach is based on the Gricean notion of the speaker's a priori intention, that is, intention that exists before s/he produces an utterance. Currently, a priori intention appears to be superseded in the literature by its post facto counterpart (e.g., Haugh 2008b; Culpeper 2011). The post facto intention refers to cases when communicators use the notion of intention explanatorily, to account for their utterances and actions, especially when communication troubles or alleged violation of politeness norms occur (see Haugh 2008b). This is especially important in intercultural interactions where the techniques and strategies for resolving them are not fully shared by the interlocutors, as in the following excerpt, which demonstrates a case for communication trouble (and not for politeness) where the post facto intention of the Korean speaker is expressed in different ways so that the American speaker can process it properly.

(2)

In the conversation below, a Korean speaker and an American speaker are talking about air pollution. The Korean speaker tries to explain to her American counterpart what causes bad air in Seoul: "sand wind." However, she pronounces the word incorrectly, which causes misunderstanding. Several attempts follow to solve the misunderstanding, but each fails for similar reason.

8 NS: Did you wear the mask? ((moving hand back and forth in front of mouth))

9 (0.5)

10 NS: In Korea? =

11 NNS: =Yeah::. In (0.2) in ↑spring?

12 NS: Hm mm

13 NNS: There is a (0.5) um (0.7) how- how can I 'spl- ah:: how can I say::?
    (0.5) Send wind?

14 (1.7) ((NS displaying mental effort))

15 NS: Uh:::m

16 NNS: Sen::d (0.2) the wind? *0:30*

17 NS: ((now nodding)) Yeah::, it would blow around [the pollen?

18 NNS: [Yes.

19 NNS: Yeah yeah [yeah (0.2) yeah.

20 NS: [(from) the trees?

21 NNS: Ye[ah

22 NS: [Yeah::

23 NNS: Ah, the:: (0.7) the wind came from China?

24 NS: (0.7)

25 NNS: Do you know that wind?

26 (0.2)

27 NS: ↑No::.

28 NNS: The the:: (0.7) the- many sand? (("sand" sounds like "send"))

29 NS: (0.5) ((flashes little smile))

30 NNS: Sen:d in a: (0.5) desert?

31 NS: Oh, (.) sa:nd.

32 NNS: Yeah, [sand ((shift in pronunciation to match NS))

33 NS: [Oh:::, [god, yeah

34 NNS: [in deser::t. We've had- (0.2)wi:nd (0.2) go to- uh lan- (0.5) come- (0.2)
    over *1:00*

35 TO KOREA: also. (0.5) So in spri:ng, it's very difficult to (0.5) little bit dif-
    ficult to (0.7) hhh um::

The intention of the Korean speaker is to explain air pollution in Seoul. She aims to explain that the main reason of pollution is the sand wind that comes from China. However, her intention is derailed several times because of the bad pronunciation of the expression "sand wind." The American speaker tries to work with the Korean to figure out what she really intends to say. She knows that the Korean girl is speaking about some kind of wind but it is unclear what exactly that wind is like. The solution comes in line 30: NNS: Sen:d in a: (0.5) desert?., when the Korean speaker connects "sand" with the "desert." This connection makes it clear for the American speaker that the Korean is speaking about "sand wind."

Now back to the politeness/impoliteness perspective. Grice's (1989 [1957]) notion of *utterer's meaning* or *speaker meaning* seems to have an effect on those (im)politeness researchers who emphasize the importance of speaker's intention when expressing meanings and/or hearer's recognition of it (e.g., Culpeper et al. 2003; Culpeper 2005,

2008, 2011; Bousfield 2008a, 2008b, 2010). However, a number of scholars argued that intention recognition is irrelevant, and that discourse is co-constructed by interlocutors (Terkourafi 2005b; Locher and Watts 2008; Haugh 2007). As we saw in the excerpt above, this is not quite so in intercultural communication, where the recognition of the intention of the interlocutor is of primary importance. Co-construction of the intention often means finding the correct linguistic tools to express intention. The approach represented by Haugh, Terkourafi, Locher, and others may be understandable if we consider that intentions cannot be probed with full certainty. What is also a decisive factor in determining (im)politeness is how the hearer perceives the speaker's communicative intention, which may even take priority over the speaker's actual intention (see Locher and Watts 2008). In defense of the advocates of (im)politeness based on the speaker's intention, Dynel (forthcoming) argued that hearers need not consciously determine speakers' intentions (and their intentions to have those recognized, cf. Grice's notion of reflexivity) before gleaning meanings, but usually take it for granted that the meanings they infer are indeed speaker-intended.

Just like current pragmatics theories, the (im)politeness paradigm tends to support the decisive role of hearer interpretation in what is considered polite or impolite. Culpeper et al. (2003) rightly emphasized that the hearer's impoliteness strategies are dependent on context and the speaker's intentions (see also Bousfield 2008a, 2008b, 2010; Culpeper 2011). Dynel (forthcoming) claimed that whether particular instances of conventional formulae subscribe to the salient patterns or less typical uses must be judged individually in the light of particular speakers' intentions. *Present climate in the field seems to support the idea that no linguistic form invariably carries politeness or impoliteness* (cf. Watts 2003; Locher 2004; Locher and Watts 2005; Mills 2005). However, it cannot be denied that certain forms of expression are commonly associated with politeness or impoliteness. For instance, well-wishes like "have a nice day," "enjoy your coffee," "have a good one," and so on are generally associated with politeness, but they may also be used with a sarcastically ironic undertone for the sake of impoliteness, like "have a nice day" after a debate between a salesman and a customer. These well-wishes usually exist cross-culturally. However, the culture-specificity of politeness/impoliteness is also confirmed by the fact that certain cultures do not have them—such as, for instance, Russian, Chinese, and Arabic. Of course, they are translatable but just because you can say something in a language does not mean you should. For instance, the translation equivalent in Russian sounds awkward:

Хорошего Дня (Xaroševo dnja) "Have a nice day"

The phrase "Ich wünsche Ihnen einen schönen Tag!" (I wish you a nice day) in German also sounds rather odd. However, there is a tendency in certain European cultures, including German, Slovakian, and Hungarian to introduce these well-wishes in some form, such as *Schönen Tag! Pekný deň! Pekný deň prajem! Szép napot!* (Have a nice day). These short forms are accepted in the target culture and are more and more frequently used.

The use of conventional formulas is an especially problematic issue in intercultural communication. Kecskes (forthcoming) argued that nonnative speakers who may not have an impolite intention are nevertheless assessed as being impolite, as they are perceived as being in breach of local or socio-cultural norms of appropriateness. This is exactly how the American girl (Sara) evaluates the Serbian girl's utterance (Mira) in example (3).

(3)

> s: Mira, why don't you leave that letter on the table?
> M: 'cause I want to read it.
> s: It's not for you. Please don't touch it.
> M: *Screw you,* Sara.
> s: What did you just say?
> M: (LAUGHING NERVOUSLY) - Nothing.

Nonnative speakers in intercultural interaction may not feel the burden of impolite conceptual load of expressions, and use them freely, with no or low responsibility. This is what seems to have happened in this case. The Serbian girl did not really feel how rude the expression "screw you" can be in the target culture. This is in line with research on cursing (e.g., Dewaele 2004; Jay and Janschewitz 2008), which talks about the fact that if a person utters a curse word or expression in a second language, it will have less meaningful intent than a curse in the L1. Or vice versa—if a person hears a curse in L2, it will have less emotional impact on him than a curse in the native language.

2.2. THE IMPORTANCE OF SHARED CULTURAL ASSUMPTIONS AND NORMS

Only a few would deny that (im)politeness is culture specific. Although Brown and Levinson (1987) described the social implications of speech acts and the strategies available for performing them as universal, empirical research has demonstrated that the pragmatic impact of functionally close utterances differs across languages. In order for intercultural interactants to produce and interpret (im)politeness properly, they need to have not only appropriate language skills but also be familiar with the cultural models, norms, and expectations of their partners. However, in intercultural pragmatics, we should ask the question, whose cultural models, norms and expectations do the interlocutors have to be familiar with? Is it the cultural models, norms, and expectations of the target language speech community (L2, lingua franca) or the partners' cultural models, norms, and expectations (L1), or both? The right answer is "both," but is that not too much to expect from the nonnative communicators? Here is a funny way to present the problem:

(4)

Italians and Germans speaking English

Five Germans in an Audi Quattro arrive at the Italian border. An Italian police officer stops them and says: "Itsa illegala to putta five-a people in a Quattro!"

"Vot do you mean, it's illegal?" the German driver asks.

"Quattro mean-a four!" the policeman answers.

"Quattro iz just ze name of ze fokken automobile" the German shouts.
    "Look at ze dam paperz: Ze car is dezigned to carry 5 people!"

"You canta pulla thata one on me!" says the Italian policeman. "Quattro
    meansa four. You have a five-a people in a your car and you are therefore
    breaking the law!"

The German driver gets mad and shouts "You ideeiot! Call ze zupervizor
    over! Schnell! I vant to spik to zumvun viz more intelligence!!!"

"Sorry" the Italian says, "He canta comea. He'sa buzy with a two guys in a
    Fiat Uno."

This conversation demonstrates that although the participants use English as a lingua franca, they hardly follow any norms or expectations of the English language. They do almost everything according to their own cultural models and norms. However, we should not forget that the conversation is very heated emotionally, and it is precisely in this emotional state when co-constructed intercultures contain many more elements from the participants' own culture than newly created elements in the course of conversation. Even very fluent speakers of L2 fall back on their L1 norms and conventions when they are very happy or very angry and when they are tired.

As mentioned above, norms, conventions, and their sharedness have become a key issue in politeness research in the discursive view. However, the discursive approach does not consider norms straightforward and preexisting entities, but versatile argumentative tools, which are not necessarily shared across the board by individuals in the language community. Norms are seen as being relative to the practice to which they are part of, rather than informing it in an objective way (Eelen 2001:229–236). In other words, norms are not a priori, but co-constructed in the process of communication. As a consequence, researchers should focus on how norms are discursively co-constructed and how they may be resisted or contested. As discussed above, the discursive approach questions the existence of "cultures," because this view does not recognize preexisting norms and conventions. The rejection of prescriptive norms means that the discursive approach relies on the minute-by-minute description of specific occurrences of politeness and impoliteness in individual encounters. The socio-cognitive approach does not accept the radial approach of Politeness & Impoliteness 1. It maintains that interlocutors rely both on preexisting norms and conventions and co-constructed elements in both production and comprehension. The effect of prior experience cannot be ignored. As we said before, relying on Haugh (2010a), in the socio-cognitive approach politeness/ impoliteness is both constituted in the communicative process through on-the-spot evaluations and decisions and constitutive of the communicative process through expectations and norms. Prior experience with politeness and impoliteness expressions is especially important for nonnative speakers in intercultural communication. If those expressions are used according to the norms of the target language and interactants are familiar with them, no problem will occur in the interaction. The following conversation between a Turkish student and a Russian student illustrates this point.

(5)

> ALI: Sasha, come with me to the library.
> SASHA: Sorry, I cannot. I need to finish this essay.
> ALI: You really need to come. Peg will also be there.
> SASHA: *Knock it off, will you?* Don't you see that I am kinda busy?
> ALI: Okay, okay, just chill..

"*Knock it off, will you?*" used by the Russian student is quite rude, and this is how the Turkish student processed it. Both of them were familiar with the impolite load of the expression. However, this type of expression may cause trouble in intercultural interaction because we cannot be sure that our communicative partners know that particular formulation of a norm. There are several expressions like this. Although they usually express a polite approach if they are processed literally, they may be easily misinterpreted.

(6)

> Don't you look pretty,
> Not that I do not believe you, but…
> Tell me about it,
> Get out of here.

The co-constructed, negotiated norm relies on a more universal way of expressing politeness: *say directly what you expect the hearer to do and add a politeness marker ('please')*. The problem with the discursive approach denying the existence of a priori norms and expectations is that speakers involved in interactions usually make predictions regarding appropriateness and what might be expected therein. Therefore, the norms underlying expectations of politeness/impoliteness go back to generic constraints, and those generic norms are the ones the analyst needs to assess vis-à-vis assessments of politeness/impoliteness. Hong (2008) described an interesting example for this generic norm to illustrate how it may work in a speech community. "Where the bloody hell are you?" has been used as a catch phrase of Tourism Australia's marketing campaign encouraging tourists to visit Australia. The advertisement features images of Australians preparing for visitors to their country. It begins in an outback pub—the barkeeper says that he's poured a beer; moves on to a young boy on the beach—he says he's got the sharks out of the swimming pool;

and then to partygoers watching Sydney Harbour fireworks—they say that they've turned on the lights. The commercial ends with a girl stepping out of the ocean asking "So where the bloody hell are you?" There was quite a controversy about this phrase all over Australia. Some thought that the catchphrase demonstrated light-hearted play on stereotypical characteristics of Australia, such as "informality," "casualness," and "friendliness." Others said that, since the ad represents Australia, it should show more politeness and courtesy in standing for the country. Hong (2008), relying on Wierzbicka (2002) and his own survey, argued that "bloody" is generally considered to be a very mild expletive, unlikely to cause offense in most circles. Close to 80 percent of his respondents said that the expression "bloody hell" is acceptable and not impolite. Of course, this would not necessarily be the case if nonnative speakers were asked about the polite/impolite load of the expression because lacking the conceptual support, they would probably process the expression literally.

2.3. THE ROLE OF CONTEXT IN INTERCULTURAL POLITENESS AND IMPOLITENESS

Almost all politeness/impoliteness researchers seem to agree that no act is inherently polite or impolite, but depends on the context or speech situation. Culpeper (2009) argued that impoliteness involves (1) an attitude comprised of negative evaluative beliefs about particular behaviors in particular social contexts, and (2) the activation of that attitude by those particular in-context-behaviors. As proposed earlier in this book, the issue of context-dependency should be revisited in intercultural interaction because context may play a more complex role than just being a selector/activator. The interplay of prior context and actual situational context in meaning construction and comprehension is unique in intercultural interaction.

2.3.1. Context and Semantic Analyzability

Actual situational context may affect the processing of politeness and impoliteness differently from what actually happens in intracultural communication. As a result, the polite or impolite load of the expressions and utterances may be lost or an evaluative polite/impolite function may emerge where it should not. We saw an example for the first case at the beginning of the chapter.

The Chinese waitress did not recognize the rudeness of the Australian traveler when he asked "Who is stopping you?" as the waitress offered him more coffee. The waitress processed the utterance literally but seemed to be confused because it did not make sense in that context. So the actual situational context caused confusion rather than clarification because the rudeness of the expression was lost as the waitress could not process it properly.

Another case is when a politeness or impoliteness function emerges where it should not. This is what is happening in example (7) in which a Japanese student, Akiko, is talking to an American student, Melody.

(7)

      A: Melody, I have received the travel grant.

      M: *Nooou, get out of here!*

      A: You should not be rude. I did get it.

      M: OK, I was not rude, just happy for you.

The Japanese student processed the situation-bound utterance "get out of here" literally, although it is clear that if processed that way, the literal sense of the expression does not match the actual situational context. The interesting thing is that not even the intonation and enthusiasm of Melody helped the Japanese student to process the expression properly. In sum, in this short interaction all actual situation contextual factors were overridden by the student's prior experience with the use of "get out of here" and the strong semantic analyzability of the expression.

This issue is worth attention because, as we saw in the previous chapters, in intralingual communication the main tenet is that the context is everything: meaning is dependent on context because the linguistic sign is underdetermined. We argued that it is not quite so in intercultural communication, where the semantic analyzability of expressions often creates its own context as we saw in example (7). In discussing intracultural communication, all researchers seem to agree that no act is inherently polite or impolite, but such a condition depends on the context or speech situation. Yes, this may be true for intracultural communication. However, in intercultural interactions the actual situational context does not always work as a collective frame that helps interlocutors make similar sense of the linguistic signs. Oftentimes the actual situational context is interpreted differently by the interlocutors because their prior experience is rooted in different cultures. A possible example is the restaurant scenario in the US where the custom is that you stop at the receptionist's desk and wait to be shown to a table. Chinese students often get into trouble when they ignore the receptionist and run right away to the first (or best) available table. The situation frame is the same for both the Chinese and American guests, but is interpreted according to their own norms and prior experience. The issue of context-dependency should be revisited in intercultural pragmatics because prior context appears to be as powerful (and often even more powerful) as actual situational context in shaping meaning.

2.3.2. Context-dependency

In Chapter 6 we discussed the role of context in detail. What is important for us here is the interplay and role of prior context and actual situational context. It was argued that actual situational context usually modifies and/or specifies word meanings in one way or another. This side of context is seen as a selector of lexical features because it activates some features while leaving others in the background. Prior context representing the other side of context is based on our prior experience, so it develops through the regularity of recurrent and similar situations, which we tend to identify with given contexts. It is exactly these standard contexts that linguistic meanings are tied to and lexical units refer to.

Although mainstream approaches favor context-dependency, several research-ers have claimed that the message versus context opposition is misleading because the message can carry with it or forecast the context (Gumperz 1982; Levinson 2003; Kecskes 2008). Actual situational context is viewed through prior context. This has a profound effect on the evaluative function of language, including polite-ness and impoliteness, because prior, reoccurring context may cancel the selective role of actual situational context. We can demonstrate this through an example taken from Culpeper (2009).

(8)

> CULPEPER: Example 3: Creative deviation from the default context (cf. "mock impoliteness") [Lawrence Dallaglio, former England Rugby captain, describing the very close family he grew up in]
> "As Francesca and John left the house, she came back to give Mum a kiss and they said goodbye in the way they often did. "Bye, you bitch," Francesca said. "Get out of here, go on, you bitch," replied Mum. (It's in the Blood: My life, 2007)."

Culpeper explained that the reason the conversation between the mother and daughter does not hurt either of them is due to the context ("mock impoliteness"). However, a closer look at the example reveals that actual situational context hardly plays any role here. What we have in this brief interaction is the strong effect of prior context, prior experience that overrides actual situational context: "they said goodbye in the way they often did." *Reoccurring (prior) context, frequent use may neutralize the impolite conceptual load attached to expressions.* This is exactly what has happened here.

For nonnative speakers, prior context may have a stronger effect on meaning construction and comprehension than actual situational context when processing politeness or impoliteness functions of utterances. Interpretation generally depends on what the utterance says rather than on what it actually communicates. As a consequence, focusing on compositional meanings, interlocutors may sometimes be unaware of politeness or impoliteness because it is conveyed implicitly or through paralinguistic means. Here we should refer back to what was said about common ground. Core common ground is constituted by knowledge, expectations, and beliefs that members of a speech community have in common based on their prior experience while emergent common ground is mutual knowledge that emerges in the process of communication, and co-constructed by the participants. Core com-mon ground is usually attached to prior experience, prior context while emergent common ground is immediately related to actual situational context. Limited com-mon ground may restrict the interpretation process to the compositional content of an utterance, and may also decrease context-sensitivity.

2.3.3. Anti-normative politeness

From the perspective of context-sensitivity, we should discuss a unique occurrence of politeness/impoliteness that is called "anti-normative politeness" in the literature (see Mugford 2012). Anti-normative politeness has been described as "mock impoliteness" (Culpeper 1996) "banter" (Leech 1983), "sociable rudeness" (Kienpointner 1997:268) and "ritual abuse" (Parkin 1980:45). Mock impoliteness is often contrasted with impoliteness. Culpeper defined mock impoliteness as "impoliteness that stays on the surface, since it is understood that it is not intended to cause offence" (1996:352).

Anti-normative politeness makes it possible for interlocutors to establish their own interactional patterns without having to conform to conventional patterns of use. They use rude, aggressive, and/or impolite expressions in order to convey solidarity, friendship, group-inclusion.

Anti-normative politeness allows a subgroup of given speech community to express positive politeness in its own creative and unique way. It is often used cross-culturally, as the following example shows.

(9)

> AMERICAN ENGLISH: What's up, dudes?
> RUSSIAN: Kak dela, muzhiki?

Functionally, the Russian word "muzhiki" (meaning "peasants") is the equivalent of the American English "dudes."

Relating anti-normative politeness to the foreign-language use and participation, Mugford (2012) argued that foreign language users must be aware not only of linguistic features of expressions but also how they are used socially to achieve interpersonal goals and group understandings. Nonnative speakers need to understand that anti-normative politeness reflects phatic communion, mutual trust, group affiliation, and enhanced individual image of a given speech community subgroup. This is, however, very difficult for nonnative speakers to do because their prior experience, or prior context, usually overrides actual situation context, which may result in processing the utterance literally. Banters are especially hard to process. Discussing mock impoliteness, Culpeper refers to Leech (1983), who uses the term the Banter Principle: "In order to show solidarity with the hearer, say something which is (i) obviously untrue, and (ii) obviously impolite to the hearer" (1983:144).

However, we must be careful how we evaluate the role of actual situation context in anti-normative impoliteness. Culpeper argued that the role of actual situational context is neutralized in these cases. Analyzing example (8) above, I already claimed that this is not quite so. What neutralizes the actual situation context is prior context, which can also be the way the involved individuals are accustomed to speaking to each other. From this respect, we should look at another example of Culpeper (2009). He talks about a party to which he was late. He turned up at 7:00 pm, only to discover the party had started at 5:00 pm and had almost finished. Upon telling the host, a friend of his, the reason for his mistake, the friend replied, "You silly bugger." He used a conventionally impolite insult. But, of course, Culpeper did not take offense. For him this was a friendly banter. Banter involves mock or nongenuine impoliteness, as do some types of teasing and humor. The important thing in language processing is to recognize that it is indeed nongenuine. Culpeper (2009) argued that the recognition of this mock impoliteness relies on some degree of mismatch between the conventionally impolite formulae used and the context (e.g., "you silly bugger" vs. friendly relations), along with additional signals (e.g., laughter, smiling) that the impoliteness is not genuine. In fact, the additional nonverbal signals paired with the speakers' prior experience (not the actual situational context) cancel the impoliteness effect.

At another place, Culpeper (2009) acknowledges that "the neutralisation of impoliteness by any context is difficult to achieve." He then continues: "The main reason for this is that the context in many cases is likely to be overwhelmed by the salience of impoliteness behaviors. Research in social cognition would suggest that people do not carefully attend to contextual reasons why they should not take offence; they are more likely to focus on the impolite language or action and, with little thought, take offence." I think we can agree with this statement that fits how intercultural pragmatics handles these cases. The semantic content of expressions (that encodes prior contexts) is so powerful that the actual situational context cannot cancel that. But how would that work for a foreign language user who did not have enough encounters with the group of native speakers to establish this camaraderie? Probably not very well, as the following encounter demonstrates.

(10) Jerry and Bob are going to the movies. They want their Chinese friend, Zhang, to go with them.
JERRY (SMILING): Hey, duschbag, wana come with us?
ZHANG: What did you just call me?
JERRY: Forget it. Do you want to come with us?

The Chinese person was embarrassed to be called "duschbag." He may not have known what the word exactly means, but took it as an offense. Jerry, however, was using the expression as a banter. He wanted to sound funny and express a kind of camaraderie. When he saw it did not work out, he just let it go.

Mugford (2012) argued that young people convey solidarity and affiliation within their interpersonal discourse. They do this in nonconventional or anti-normative ways, which is often considered as negative although accepted social behavior. In the following example of Mugford, the use of *güey* [idiot] underscores camaraderie on the *frontenis* court:

(11)

A: *No sé con quién voy a jugar.*
(I don't know who I am going to play with.)

B: *¿Cómo que con quién? ¡Conmigo güey!*
(What do you mean with whom? With me, *güey [idiot]*!)

Zimmermann claimed (2003:57) that anti-normative politeness can be seen in the vocabulary of young people: "We can see it in the mechanisms that make up young people's lexis and we can see it even more clearly in the interactional behaviour between them and above all in what relates to identity. Therefore I think that the acts described as impolite are not in fact impolite but are part of this anti-normative behaviour. Therefore I call them anti-polite." Mugford rejected the use of the term "anti-polite" because he considered it as ideologically loaded, being that it reflects a very subjective and personal evaluation of acceptable and unacceptable behavior instead of examining politeness according to the standards and practices of a speech community subgroup.

As we saw in the previous chapters, intercultural pragmatics treats norms as dynamic phenomena. It acknowledges that norms are results of conventions within a bigger speech community. Within that community there exist subgroups that may have their own norms, which may differ from the norms of the given speech community as a whole. Bernal claimed that young people's language often indicates the need for belonging and consequently offers "a mechanism of affiliation to a group and possibly of identity cohesion" (2008:793). Therefore, nonauthentic impoliteness may reflect intra-group norms rather than a rejection of conventional language use. Bernal also made it clear that this kind of impoliteness appears to play a phatic function, as it involves "the use of expressions that show that 'everything is fine between us'" (Bernal 2008:797). The synchronic side of norm-formation is basically connected with intercultures. Once an interaction begins and intercultures are created, those intercultures themselves become a norm against which any potential impoliteness works. Referring to the classic research on norms by Sherif (1936), Culpeper (2009) said that people use norms as a frame of reference. Sherif demonstrated that when people made perceptual judgments alone in a context that was free from the influence of previously established norms (the judgment of light movement in a darkened room), their own judgments rapidly became the norm—the frame of reference. However, when people were in the same context but in a group, diverse individual assessments converged to become a common assessment, and people used that as the norm. Thus, the norm basically emerged from the interaction between the members of the group, and once established it acquired a life of its own, just like intercultures do.

After having discussed the main tenets and claims of intercultural pragmatics, we should turn to methods used in the paradigm to analyze language use. Not that we have not done that in the previous chapters in which a number of examples were used and analyzed to clarify the main points made. However, a kind of summary will help researchers to identify those methods that can be used most effectively to get a clear picture about the interplay of speakers, context, and language in intercultural interactions.

10

Methods of Analysis

1. What to Consider When Methods are Selected

Co-constructing intercultures means developing common ground between participants in intercultural discourse who have very little shared knowledge. When analyzing this process, we must be careful with selecting our methodology. Koole and
ten Thije (2001) argued that the qualification of a communication process as intercultural, though justified from an ethnographic perspective, may lend an unwanted
methodological direction to the analysis of this process. This may "lead the analyst
to disregard major characteristics of the discourse and to focus solely on cultural
differences (Koole and ten Thije 2001:572)." Sarangi (1994:409) also discussed this
phenomenon as "analytical stereotyping." Scollon and Scollon (1995:125) called
attention to possible overgeneralization when "culture" is applied to the analysis of
discourse. Thus, whatever method is selected to analyze intercultural discourse, the
main focus should be on the discursive process rather than just on culture.

There have been a great variety of research tools, data collection methods, and
data analysis used in intercultural pragmatics research. They all have at least three
features in common. First, the main focus of intercultural pragmatics is language
use in oral, written, and computer-mediated settings, and researchers select methods accordingly. Second, intercultural pragmatics is an inquiry that is discourse
segment-centered rather than utterance-centered. The focus of pragmatic theories is
on communicative actions (speech acts, pragmatic action, utterance) while intercultural pragmatics focuses on interaction. Pragmatic theories are utterance-centered,
which means that in these theories the most significant difference between a sentence and an utterance is that sentences are judged according to how well they make
sense grammatically, while utterances are judged according to their communicative
validity (Habermas 1979:31). Austin's work (1976) is widely associated with the
concept of the speech act and the idea that speech is itself a form of action. In his
opinion language is not just a passive practice of describing a given reality, but a
particular practice to invent and affect those realities. What can we do/achieve with
words and utterances? This question has been one of the main driving forces of
contemporary pragmatics research. Consequently, the main focus of pragmaticians
since Austin has been meaning conveyed by an utterance in its actual situational

context in intracultural, monolingual communication. However, utterance analysis in intercultural pragmatics may be problematic for two reasons. On the one hand, utterances in intercultural communication are often not quite properly formed because of language proficiency issues. On the other hand, as discussed earlier in an experimental study Kecskes (2007a) demonstrated that creativity of lingua franca speakers is detectable on the discourse level rather than utterance level. A similar claim was made in Prodromou (2008). Consequently, in intercultural communication, it makes more sense to analyze discourse segments rather than just utterances. And indeed, the criticism of intercultural interaction as characterized by miscommunication, lack of systematic coherence, and a low level of creativity is seen to be invalid when we analyze the phenomenon on a discourse segment rather than on utterance level. In the socio-cognitive paradigm, we treat creativity and coherence as discourse in progress. Third, the methodological approach should be reconstructive in nature that recreate the process through which interlocutors have successfully achieved their communicative goals.

According to Koole and ten Thije (2001) the reconstruction of intercultural discourse phenomena neither restricts itself to a bottom-up movement from utterances to social structures, nor to a top-down movement from social structures to the interpretation of utterances. Reconstructive process follows a hermeneutic interpretative strategy that is not unidirectional, but continuously moves from the sequentially ordered utterances to discourse segment structures and back.

Another important issue that the analyst should take into account is coherence. In intercultural pragmatics text coherence also receives a new interpretation. Current approaches to coherence emphasize that instead of considering coherence a formal text- and product-oriented concept, we should perceive it as an interactively negotiated process that is dependent on the context and interlocutors. Coates (1995) argued that much real language data are coherent without the application of any cohesive devices. Thus, coherence is closely connected to interpretability and acceptability in context, and involves both intra- and extra-textual factors. When ascribing meaning to utterances, it is not the text that coheres, but people. Understanding takes place when the speaker's and hearer's contributions cohere. All human communication underlies a "default principle of coherence" (Bublitz and Lenk 1999): a basic assumption that our interlocutors produce coherent discourse. In intercultural pragmatics this constructivist approach is modified according to the principles of the socio-cognitive approach—just as all other phenomena in intercultural pragmatics coherence is also the result of the interplay of the individual and social sides, prior experience, and actual situational experience. We have the language product (utterance, discourse-segment, etc.) that is construed by an individual to mean something. The person has encoded some message into the linguistic signs. Coherence is assured by the interplay of the used code, speaker's commitment encoded in the language product, hearer(s)' interpretation, and actual situational context. The following discourse segment demonstrates that coherence is more like a discourse-level phenomenon in intercultural communication than an utterance-level phenomenon.

(1)

A Polish woman is speaking about housing and English study with a man from Hong Kong and a Brasilian female.

> HKM: How about you?...circumstances...Where do you live? You rent...or?
>
> PAF: Mmm...I am live...not so far from the university.
>
> HKM: Hmm.
>
> PAF: It is a college...you don't know...It is not so far. It's Albany.
>
> HKM: Hmm.
>
> PAF: But I have 3 minutes...errh...to go to my work.
>
> HKM: Hmm.
>
> PAF: And this house is...errh...on our own so my husband and I ...
>
> HKM: Hmm.
>
> BIF: Doesn't have any kids?
>
> PAF: No. don't have...
>
> BIF: No?
>
> PAF: Yeah.
>
> BIF: Errh...Are your husband American or...?
>
> PAF: Errh...Actually he is...he is Polish. He is American but...
>
> BIF: OK.
>
> PAF: ...because he came into the United States when he was a child.
>
> HKM: Hmm.
>
> PAF: He was something like twelve.
>
> BIF: All right.

The whole conversation is quite segmented. If we analyze the utterances that the speakers produce, what we see is that they are full of mistakes, and occasionally do not seem to be directly relevant to the previous utterance, are quite short, and do not reflect much creativity. However, on the discourse-level, the segment appears to be coherent. The dialogue as a whole makes sense and the speakers understand each other perfectly.

This segmented and occasionally ungrammatical nature of intercultural communication requires us to revise our understanding of the role of contextualization cues, which represented central innovation in Gumperz's analysis of discourse and which have been so important and influential in any kind of oral and written text, dialogue, and discourse analysis. Using an interactional sociolinguistics approach, Gumperz (1982) analyzed gatekeeping encounters (such as job interviews) to shed light on sources of misunderstanding and miscommunication.

Contextualization cues have played a pivotal role in his analysis. These cues are any linguistic or paralinguistic signals that give meaning to an utterance. They are present in the surface structure of messages and so are empirically detectable

(Gumperz 1982, 1992). Gumperz (1982) underlined that suprasegmental features are crucial to the process of conversational inference. Levinson (2003) further developed our understanding of contextualization cues, arguing that cues are first of all prosodic or paralinguistic in nature. When contextualization cues are lexical or grammatical, they are a matter of fine-tuned distinctions not readily observable without particular analysis, such as word choice or register and/or minor grammatical structures like, for instance, particles. Levinson argued that contextualization cues are "nonpropositional content, e.g., affectual, rhetorical, or metalinguistic" and "reliant on a large dose of inferencing" (Levinson 2003:37), so cues are context-dependent. What cues depend upon is co-occurring expectation. Speakers develop these expectations through their prior experience, usually rooted in their own culture, and through their previous interactions (usually in their L1). The cues, thus help speakers make hypotheses about an interaction (contextual presuppositions) and then interpret meaning as the conversation moves forward. This is where the Gumperzian idea meets with one of the major tenets of the socio-cognitive approach: the message can carry with it or project the context. It is not necessarily the message content that does this, however, but the message background—the attached socio-cultural load, the culture-specific conceptual property whose presence can be triggered by conversational cues. The goal of these cues is to project the context in which the meaning of the message should be interpreted. The reason why semantically strong messages are occasionally interpreted out of the actual situational context is that the cues that could project the right interpretation are missing. If we have a contextualization cue, the semantic content of the message can be directed to the right interpretation. Just think about example (5) in Chapter 6 in which Robin Williams says the following: "I had to sleep with the dogs. Platonically, of course…" The lexical cue "platonically" directs the hearers to the correct interpretation of the utterance.

This is what Levinson said about the nature of contextualization cues:

> This is, I take it, the Gumperzian notion, in which the term "cue" denotes an encoded or conventional reminder, like a knot in a handkerchief, where the content of the memo is inferentially determined. Thus the "cue" cannot be said to encode or directly invoke the interpretative background, it's simply a nudge to the inferential process. Moreover, the interpretative process is guided more by a series of nudges now in one direction and now in another—thus "cues" come as complex assemblages where the result of the whole assemblage cannot be equated with the inferential results that each part alone might have. The interpretive process may be guided by general pragmatic principles of a Gricean sort, and thus be in many ways universal in character; but the "cues" are anything but universal, indeed tending toward sub-cultural differentiation. Hence the Gumperzian perspective on communication: at once potentially possible across cultural divides and inevitably thwarted by cultural nuances (Levinson 1997:27).

As far as the use of contextualization cues in intercultural interactions is concerned, the main issue is that, according to the Gumperzian approach, most of them are culture-specific, so "they can only be learnt by rich exposure to a communicative tradition, a deep immersion in social networks (Levinson 1997:29)." How, then, can interlocutors in intercultural interactions manage with or without these cues? Will their use or nonuse lead to misunderstandings or miscommunication? Well, in certain cases yes, in other cases no. Example (2) demonstrates a case of "yes."

(2) An American male student and a Korean female student are talking.

NS: But I've never °skiied before. Have you skiied before?°
NNS: (Oh yeah, in) Korea.
NS: Really?
                (0.7)
NS: Are there a lot of places to ski in Korea?
                (1.5)
NNS: Actually in in winter I don't like go to the gym.
NS: Ye[ah:
NNS: [So. And I don't like (0.7) to walk, (.) because (0.5) It's ↑too cold.
NS: Yeah.
                (0.7)
NS: >So you ski?<
                11:00
NNS: ((laughs)) It kind've not- doesn't make sense but- (0.7) ski::s (0.5)
      I like ski:s.
NS: It's exercise, right?
NNS: Yeah, exercise.

There is clear contradiction between two statements of the Korean speaker. First she said that she does not like walking in winter because it is cold. Then she said that she goes skiing instead. The NS notices that contradiction and refers to it in a very subtle way: "so you ski?" Both the intonation and the question can be considered as contextualization cues. The reaction of the Korean speaker shows that she perfectly understood what the American student has referred to.

In the socio-cognitive approach, contextualization cues are considered not always culture-specific. This is a significant difference from the Gumperzian use. There are individual ways of using contextualization cues in an interaction and these individual ways do not always derive from collective experience and standard prior context that is tied to the L1 culture of the speaker. Sometimes these contextualization cues are ad hoc creations of the individual in response to actual situational context, as it is demonstrated in example (2) where the two individuals representing two different cultures act according to neither. They select their wording and contextualization cues as they find appropriate in the actual situational context.

2. Types of Methods

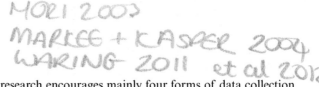

Intercultural pragmatics research encourages mainly four forms of data collection and analysis: conversational analysis, corpus methods, discourse segment analysis, and computer-mediated communication. The problem with all of them is similar. While there has been a great deal of work on intercultural interaction, very few studies have discussed naturally occurring casual conversation. If there are corpora at all, rarely are they large enough to shed light on interesting linguistic patterns. The other problem is that data may be so unnatural as to be of limited use for drawing conclusions about how real people converse in the real world (because, for instance, they are DCTs, role-plays, or directed conversations).

2.1. CONVERSATIONAL ANALYSIS

Recently, serious efforts have been made to introduce Conversational Analysis (CA) in second language acquisition and interlanguage pragmatics research. Although CA application received quite a critical response from second language acquisition researchers, it has become fully acceptable in interlanguage pragmatics. CA has been used mainly to analyze classroom talk (e.g., Mori 2003; Markee and Kasper 2004; Waring 2011; Waring et al. 2012) and institutional talk (e.g., Bardovi-Harlig and Hartford 2005; Félix-Brasdefer 2008). CA can also be used efficiently in intercultural pragmatics because it requires description and analysis of the sequencing of action and organization of turns at the micro level of verbal and nonverbal acts. CA is empirically based, and it has clearly defined methodological procedures for developing participant-relevant analyses of talk-in-interaction, and is concerned with the possibility of replication.

The word "conversation" in CA is used to indicate any activity of interactive talk, regardless of its purpose (ten Have 1999:4). Conversational Analysis as a discipline was founded by Harvey Sacks and his colleagues, including Emanuel Schegloff and Gail Jefferson. The main goal of CA is to investigate the norms and conventions that speakers use in interaction to establish communicative understandings. For CA, talk is organized as strings of mutually oriented actions. Traditional CA is concerned only with the speech of the interlocutors as an observable, external event. In their seminal work, Sacks, Schegloff, and Jefferson (1974) identified three basic facts about conversation: (1) turn-taking occurs, (2) one speaker tends to speak at a time, and (3) turns are taken with as little overlap between them as possible (the speakers coordinate their interactions as much as possible to avoid overlap). These fundamental tenets presuppose a continuity of shared time and space in conversations. This claim has been questioned recently by researchers who focus on virtual conversations and find it necessary to broaden this basic sense of CA through theory building and new methodologies based on how conversation and interaction continue to be redefined and reshaped by computer-mediated communication technologies (see Mazur 2004). Such revisions, according to Mazur, will enable researchers interested in the ever-proliferating worlds of online conversation to translate the traditions of CA to investigations of computer-mediated conversations.

From the perspective of intercultural pragmatics it is important to note that for the conversation analyst there does not exist a prescriptive definition of what constitutes a turn construction, as, for instance, a linguist may define a sentence or a pragmatician may define an utterance. Sacks (1974a, 1974b) and others were careful to emphasize that there are no prescriptive rules but, rather, rules that develop within and through the interaction. Thus, CA is considered a systematic method to observe the production of intention or the achievement of understandings in the turns of talk between human speakers. In CA, what the turn construction comprises in a situated segment of conversation is a concern for the interlocutors themselves. According to Mazur (2004) this tension between the technical methods of analyzing conversation and its socially constituted nature is a continual challenge to researchers working with CA. Talk-in-interaction is organized by turns that occur one after the other, i.e., in a serial order. But the relationship between turns is not serial but sequential. This distinction is very important because the talk does not just occur in a series of responses. The interaction is organized in sequences of two or more in which interlocutors demonstrate that they understand what kind of turn the prior one was supposed to be. This is called the adjacency pair sequence.

One of the issues on which the socio-cognitive approach does not agree with Conversational Analysis is the question of culture. SCA accepts that there are relatively definable a priori cultural models that reflect the core values and beliefs of a speech community, while CA rejects this idea. CA considers culture as a sociological artifact. Culture is not treated as a mechanism that drives action, but as an observable feature of it. According to this view (e.g., Schegloff 1999) culture can hardly be extracted from discursive contexts as a sociological explanation for conversational praxis but can merely be examined as an interactional event. In the CA paradigm, Mazur (2004) argues, culture cannot be privileged in intercultural exchanges as an abstracted conceptual concern, but must simply be an empirical focus and be shown to be of relevance and of issue within and through the analysis of conversation.

In spite of its approach to culture, CA has become very popular in analyzing native speaker–nonnative speaker and nonnative speaker–nonnative speaker interaction, especially in educational context (e.g., Taleghani-Nikazm 2002; Markee 2000; Mori 2003; Waring et al. 2012). Mori (2003) examined the achievement of intercultural discourse and the ways in which it is worked through in the moment-by-moment shifts of discourse. She investigated co-presence question-answer sequences between first- and second-language Japanese speakers in multiparty conversations and analyzed how participants dealt with cultural differences. She demonstrated that first language speakers, when asking questions, used strategies that served to categorize the intended second language speakers as linguistic novices. Mori's paper showed that cultural differences represented in linguistic ability are visible aspects of conversation. They are present in participants' attempts to understand the "other." Park's (2007) findings were similar to those of Mori. He examined the ways that the categories native speaker (NS) and nonnative speaker (NNS) are made "procedurally relevant" to and in conversational interaction. It was demonstrated that NS and NNS are related to identities (categories) of "expert" and "novice." These categories were treated as emergent, sequentially realized, and negotiated features of the talk.

Although CA research has argued and shown that the fundamental interactional apparatus (i.e., the underlying orderliness of turn-taking; Sacks, Schegloff, & Jefferson, 1974) is not culture-specific, there are also a number of phenomena that have been found to exhibit socio-cultural variation within conversations. For instance, telephone openings and closing (e.g., Pavlidou 1994, 1998; Sun 2004, 2005; Taleghani-Nikazm 2002), conversational fillers (e.g., Clark and Fox Tree 2002; Rendle-Short 2006), response tokens (e.g., Keevallik 2010; Sorjonen 2001), and so on. As these variations show, CA may provide a valuable resource for understanding how different socio-cultural norms are reflected in language use, and determine the universality or culture specificity of mundane interactions in language communication (Sidnell 2009).

CA can help intercultural pragmatics research in several different ways. In native speaker–nonnative speaker interaction, CA demonstrates that it is not always the nonnative speaker who creates misunderstandings and difficulties in the conversation, and what strategies the two sides use to overcome the lack of core common ground and achieve mutual understanding. In lingua franca communication the application of CA methods calls into question some of the major tenets of CA, such as turn and floor. Tannen (1989) [2007], for instance, argued that, contrary to Sacks et al.'s (1974) assumptions, "[c]onversation is not a matter of two (or more) people alternatively taking the role of speaker and listener, but [...] both speaking and listening include elements and traces of the other." Wolfartsberger (2011) said that this issue is crucial for interactions conducted in English as a lingua franca, because several researchers have found that ELF is jointly constructed and negotiated to an even greater extent than native speaker conversations in intracultural communication. She said that the fact that participants in ELF are communicating across different languages makes constant feedback by the listener(s) in the form of minimal responses, agreement tokens, clarification requests, and the like particularly important.

Wolfartsberger (2011) investigated collaborative as well as competitive turn-taking strategies used by business professionals in ELF workplace meetings. Her study focused on so-called "turn-interventions." This refers to any instance where one of the listeners interferes with what the current speaker is saying. The concept of intervention was defined by Watts (1991) as "any utterance by a member of the group which cuts into the ongoing speech of another, whether or not it causes overlapping speech" (Watts 1991: 4). Intervention may include interruptions, turn-completions, jointly produced utterances, and stretches of talk where so many utterances cut into the ongoing speech of an interlocutor that, Wolfartsberger argues, it becomes virtually impossible to distinguish interventions from turns at talk. Here is her example (Wolfartsberger 2011:3).

(3)

> S5: and if somebody says his highest objective is to retire early yeah? then we should next time call you and ask you is this really <1>what he talked to us</1> (.)
> S1: <1>and discuss it</1>
> S5: <2>because everybody here was</2> very er just er very curious (.)
> S3: <2>yeah which is not @@</2>
> S1: yeah
> S5: and and erm so <3>we (have) to ask you (.) and you should just take care</3>
> S3: <3>but it-it's it's really pity that you didn't mention this</3> earlier. right?
> S4: mhm
> S4: it's pity.
> S5: yeah (.) <4>yeah</4>
> S1: <4>yeah</4>
> S3: so: <5>please next time @ ask</5>
> S1: <5>so it was a mistake</5> yeah i-it was a mistake (.) and (.) so we

Wolfartsberger argued that she was struggling to decide who was intervening in whose turn, or even to decide whose turn it was in the first place. However, she also noticed that the participants in this interaction seem to be perfectly able to make sense of what was going on. They showed no sign of irritation or awareness of a "violation of turn-taking rules."

Wolfartsberger identified three points of criticism that have a direct relevance for the study of turn-taking in English as a lingua franca. They are as follows: (1) the somewhat unclear nature of the concepts "turn" and "floor"; (2) the model's failure to account for unproblematic overlaps and jointly authored turns that results from the one-at-a-time principle; (3) and the framework's supposedly ethnocentric foundation, which might make it unsuitable for analyzing turn-taking in intercultural communication. All three of these issues become acute when studying turn interventions in ELF interactions.

Edelsky (1981:401) argued that most of "the literature either ignores an examination of the floor or uses turn and floor interchangeably." This can be especially problematic in highly interactive exchanges that very often exhibit a lot of simultaneous speech, such as lingua franca communication. The other problem is the "one speaker at a time principle" according to which only one speaker occupies the floor, which automatically assigns all other participants the role of passive listeners. This is definitely not what happens in intercultural communication that is jointly co-constructed and negotiated with the listener through constant feedback in the form of back channeling, short response formulas, argument tokens, and so forth.

The third critical note deals with the framework's supposedly ethnocentric founda-tion and its unsuitability for analyzing turn-taking in intercultural communication. Wolfartsberger (2011) argued that studies investigating turn-taking in ELF have so far yielded quite contradictory results. Firth (1996), in his work on "let-it-pass" behavior in dyadic telephone conversations in a Danish company, found that par-ticipants produced very few sentence completions, and overwhelmingly applied a turn-taking distribution of "one party talks at a time." Other scholars, such as, for instance, Cogo (2007) reported about different findings. She found quite a num-ber of cooperative overlaps in casual ELF speech. In addition, House (2002, 2008) discovered that turn-taking management in ELF is "nonsmooth" and lacking in recipient design. She claimed that ELF speakers just start talking instead of waiting for the best point at which to "jump in" and "appear not to be able to wait for and/ or to project a suitable point of transitional relevance" (House 2008:359, see also House 2002:256). According to House, interlocutors failed to take account of their partners' utterances, "the result being an under-attuning of individual turns that leads to, or is the outcome of, a lack of mutual responsibility for the ongoing talk as a collective undertaking" (House 2008:355). This was not confirmed by Meierkord (1998, 2000), who said that "[c]onversations are built up collaboratively and speak-ers used a comparatively high amount of sentence completions and restatements" (Meierkord 1998: section 5).

All these somewhat contradictory findings demonstrate that more research is needed to investigate the nature of various forms of intercultural communication. In this endeavor, however, we need to find out if the existing frameworks, theories, and methodologies can cover and explain what actually happens in lingua franca communication, native speaker–nonnative speaker interaction, and other forms of intercultural communication. Ehrenreich pointed out that "there is general agree-ment that established notions and frameworks may no longer be able to capture the new (socio-) linguistic realities of ELF communication adequately" (Ehrenreich 2009:130). Similar thoughts were expressed by Seidlhofer (2009). However, we should be careful to remain fair to existing theories that also keep changing. For instance, in his latest book, Schegloff (2007) pointed out that turn-taking should not and cannot be studied in isolation from sequences of actions. Without taking into account the action being performed in and through the turn, and the condi-tionally relevant actions related to the action in the turn, an analysis of turn-taking would be insufficient. Schegloff (2007:2) said, "When we think of clumps of turns in 'action' terms, we are dealing with courses of action—with sequences of action that have some shape or trajectory to them, that is, with what we will call 'sequence organization' or 'the organization of sequences.'" He emphasized that sequences can be considered the vehicles for getting some activity accomplished. Then he continued (Schegloff 2007:3), "Just as parties to talk-in-interaction monitor the talk-in-a-turn in the course of its production for such key features as where it might be possibly complete and whether someone is being selected as next speaker (and, if so, who), so they monitor and analyze it for what action or actions its speaker might be doing with it.... And the parties monitor for action for the same reason they monitor for the other features we investigate; namely, because the action that a speaker might be doing in or with an utterance may have implications for what action should or might be done in the next turn as a response to it." This leads us to our next issue, discourse segment analysis, which is close to what conversational analysts call sequence organization or the dialogue researchers call "dialogue sequence."

2.2. DISCOURSE SEGMENT ANALYSIS

2.2.1. Discourse Segmentation Analysis Combined with CA

Recently, there have been attempts to develop a data analysis method that can be considered as the combination of discourse segmentation analysis and CA. In this bottom-up approach, the utterance-focused analysis of the discourse segment comes first, and the discourse unit types emerge from those patterns. Combining conversational analysis with discourse analysis looks like pairing apples with oranges at first sight. Discourse Analysis (DA) is very difficult to define because of the many approaches to it. For us here, DA means analyzing language in use above or beyond the utterance, focusing on language as meaning in interaction and language in situational and cultural context. There is a major difference in how DA and CA approach "culture." DA recognizes the importance of socio-cultural context, while CA has a distinctive orientation to the concept of "culture." In CA, empirical examination brackets out the assumption of "shared culture" in the shape of norms and knowledge that are held in common and that operates "behind the scenes" of social action. That is, it ignores the idea that this shared knowledge exists between the participants in a given action/community. Instead, it attempts to find that knowledge as visible and working practices in real social action. So, instead of explaining action relying on abstract cultural rules that operate as a normative framework for action, social action is investigated such that those rules can be made visible as features of social praxis. The aim of conversational analysis is to uncover the operations of the "stock of knowledge" as a feature of the "natural attitude of everyday reasoning" (ten Have 2002).

I want to emphasize that this method is not exactly the combination of CA and DA. It is neither this nor that but a third, as it is usually the case in the socio-cognitive paradigm that has been promoted in this book. DA researchers tend to choose more socially and politically relevant themes, while CA often works on very mundane issues and data. This means that while CA preserves its distance from convention (generally, but not always) by avoiding materials of obvious social importance, DA tends to focus on such materials. Intercultural pragmatics encourages the combination of the two approaches for a couple of reasons. First, analysis in intercultural pragmatics requires a rigorous approach to both the micro level and macro level because, as it was discussed earlier, the traditional utterance analysis cannot reveal much since the formulation of the utterances may be incorrect and thus misleading. Second, a broader, socio-cultural analysis encouraged by DA could also be problematic because socio-cultural patterns are not being represented but are rather being created in intercultural interactions.

The combination of CA methods and DA methods is not impossible even according to Schegloff (1997), who made the point that for any consideration of a "text" and its "context" (whether academic or "critical" in one or another respect), one should first analyze that "text" on its own terms. By doing this, any form of "critical discourse analysis" of an interactional segment would then require a CA-type of analysis as a first step. This type of analysis pays attention to the details of the interaction that are definitely relevant for the interlocutors, and which constitute practices that have been observed in other contexts. Schegloff argued that a basic analysis along these lines, focused on the participants' own relevancies, could serve "as a buffer against the potential for academic and theoretical imperialism which imposes intellectuals' preoccupations on a world without respect to their indigenous resonance" (Schegloff 1997:163).

The discourse segment analysis that I am proposing here can reveal important details about speakers' language processing in intercultural interactions. First we do a rigorous, detailed analysis of utterances in CA style, and then try to fit these pieces of information into the topic frame that the discourse segment focuses on. For instance, the analysis of example (4) demonstrates how a Korean female student and an American male student are teasing each other using very short utterances without any kind of misunderstanding.

(4)

NNS:	But someti:me, ↑someday:, (0.2) >I will go there.< (0.7) I- (0.2) >I have a question.<
	(0.7)
NS:	I hopefully have an answer.
NNS:	((laughs))=
NS:	=((laughs))
NNS:	I think you:: (0.5) have an answer.
	(1.5)
NNS:	°(You).°
	(3.5)
NNS:	So:::
	(0.7)
NNS:	Ski (resort)? (0.7) Ski? [Ski?
NS:	[Mm↑m!
	(0.5)
NS:	(Ski resorts? Yeah).
NNS:	Iss good? (0.2) In (Albany)?
NS:	I really don't know. ((lau[ghs))
NNS:	[(Oh) Okay hh
NS:	So I don't have [an answer.
	10:30

NNS: [O:::: kay::::
NS: No, i- it's really popular.
NNS: °Yeah.° (.) >Oh really?<
NS: Well, [yeah.
NNS: [Why- why popular?
NS: (There's) a lot[ta, a lotta people like ta: [(0.2) ski:, =

When the Korean student says "I have a question," she already knows that she wants to ask about skiing. However, in the next lines they are teasing each other. Both are aware of that. Then the NNS makes a question: "Ski resorts? Ski? Ski?" She repeats the word "ski" because she is not sure that the American student understood her. His first reaction shows that the pronunciation of "Ski resort?" was not clear for him. In the next line, he asks for clarification or confirmation. However, in response, the Korean asks another question: "Is good? In Albany?" The NS responds to this question with, "I really don't know." He does not know whether the resorts are good or not. He then refers back to their teasing each other with the statement: "So I do not have an answer." Following this, he continues his response to the question of NNS ("Is it good?") with "No, it's really popular." I think his "No" here still refers to the teasing, meaning something like "seriously." The second part of the utterance then basically says that he does not know whether the resorts are good or not but they are popular. Later he explains that he thinks the resorts are popular because many people go there.

This is a fairly sophisticated interchange between the native speaker and the nonnative speaker. However, the creative approach of both sides becomes detectable only if we analyze their utterance production within the whole discourse segment. Otherwise the utterances are very short and poorly formulated.

2.2.2. Centering Theory

Another analytical methodology that can be successfully used in intercultural pragmatics derives from the centering theory developed first by Grosz & Sidner (1986) to stress the role of purpose and processing in discourse. This theory is compatible with the socio-cognitive approach because it focuses on the interplay and change of intention and attention within discourse segments and underlines both a priori and emergent features in the discursive process. The theory attempts to relate focus of attention, choice of referring expression, and perceived coherence of utterances within a discourse segment. It provides a model of discourse structure and meaning well suited to intercultural interaction, where an understanding of the ways in which focus of attention affects both the production and the comprehension of various linguistic expressions in discourse is crucial. Centering Theory (Grosz and Sidner 1986) aims at accounting for coherence in discourse by explaining how speakers and hearers maintain the focus of attention in discourse. It is concerned with how both global and local discourse structure have an influence on the expressions used to refer to entities that are in the participants' focus of attention. Those entities are commonly known as centers of attention, hence the name Centering.

In the Centering Theory of Discourse, we distinguish among three components of discourse structure: linguistic structure, intentional structure, and attentional state. Linguistic structure groups utterances into discourse segments. Intentional structure consists of discourse segment purposes and the relations between them. The attentional state is an abstraction of the focus of attention of the participants as the discourse unfolds. The attentional state, being dynamic, records the objects, properties, and relations that are salient at each point of the discourse.

In the theory there are two levels of attentional state. The global level is concerned with the relations between discourse segments and the ways in which attention shifts between them; it depends on the intentional structure. The local level is concerned with changes of attention within discourse segments. Centering (Grosz, Joshi and Weinstein 1995), an element of the local level, pertains to the interaction between the form of linguistic expression and local discourse coherence. In particular, it relates local coherence to choice of referring expression (pronouns in contrast to definite description or proper name) and argues that differences in coherence correspond in part to the different demands for inference made by different types of referring expressions, given a particular attentional state.

The Centering Theory claims that discourses contain constituent segments, and each segment is represented as part of a discourse model. Centers are semantic entities that are part of the discourse model for each utterance in a discourse segment.

Cf: forward-looking center
Cb: backward-looking center
Cp: preferred center

Centering theory predicts four transition states:

CONTINUE: If the current Cb is not only the same as the previous one, but also the same as the current Cp.

RETAIN: If the current Cb is the same as the previous one, but different from the current Cp.

SMOOTH-SHIFT: If the current Cb is different from the previous one, but the same as the current Cp.

ROUGH-SHIFT: If the current Cb is neither the same as the previous one, nor the same as the current Cp.

I demonstrated how this works through the following simple example (Kecskes 2011):

(5)

U1   Brazilian: And what do you do?

          Cf: you

U2   Pole: I work at the university as a cleaner.

          Cf cb: you (I) Cf: cleaner   CONTINUE

U3	B:	As a janitor?	
		Cf cb: you; janitor (cleaner)	CONTINUE
U4	P:	No, not yet. Janitor is after the cleaner.	
		Cf cb: cleaner (janitor)	RETAIN
U5	B:	You want to be a janitor?	
		Cf cb: janitor	CONTINUE
U6	P:	Of course.	

Several researchers (e.g., Walker 1998; Hu and Pan 2001) argued that the restriction of centering to operating within a discourse segment should be abandoned in order to integrate centering with a model of global discourse structure. According to Walker (1998), the within-segment restriction causes three problems. The first problem is that centers are often continued over discourse segment boundaries with pronominal referring expressions whose form is identical to those that occur within a discourse segment. The second problem is that recent work has shown that listeners perceive segment boundaries at various levels of granularity. It is almost impossible that each listener will have the same segment boundaries within discourse process. The third issue is that even for utterances within a discourse segment, there are strong contrasts between utterances whose adjacent utterance within a segment is hierarchically recent and those whose adjacent utterance within a segment is linearly recent. Hu and Pan (2001) argued that the centering theory makes wrong predictions in center computation because the theory does not distinguish backward-looking center (Cb) from the Discourse Segment Topic (DST). Although Cb and DST share many properties, they are conceptually different, and should thus be differentiated from each other. Cb is used to process the local coherence of discourse between utterances, while DST is used to process the more global coherence of discourse between discourse segments. In our example the Discourse Segment Topic is "cleaner." The DST changes in U3 to "janitor." However, this is only a semantic change; the dialogue continues to be about the same thing (cleaner; janitor).

Centering Theory has not yet been used to analyze intercultural interaction. However, some studies were published that focused on two languages at a time, such as, for instance, Taboada & Wiesemann's paper (2010) that used centering as a way to distinguish between subjects (defined through verb agreement mostly) and topics (characterized as the backward-looking center) in English and Spanish. They showed that the majority of Cbs (backward-looking centers, i.e., topics) are also subjects, 80 percent of the time in English and 73 percent in Spanish. This means that, at least in their corpus, there is a strong preference for subjects that are topics, i.e., for conflating subjecthood and topichood. The authors argued that this is certainly not surprising, because it confirms previous research that assigns salience to subjects, and it validates the claim of Centering that the Cb realizes the most salient entity. The tendencies were quite similar for both English and Spanish.

We have no space here to go into a detailed explanation of how to use the centering theory to analyze intercultural interaction data. There is no doubt about the fact, however, that this type of analysis looks most promising in intercultural pragmatics.

2.3. CORPUS ANALYSIS

Corpus analysis is an important method in all kinds of language-oriented research. However, it is not commonly used in pragmatics research. Although the scene has been changing rapidly with the new book series "Pragmatics and Corpus Linguistics" (Springer; edited by Jesus Romero-Trillo) and the "Yearbook of Corpus Linguistics and Pragmatics, 2013 (Springer; edited by Jesus Romero-Trillo). Discussing corpus pragmatics, Knight and Adolph (2008) argued that corpus-based research into utterance function is a relatively underexplored area at present. They explained this with reference to problems related to assembling and accessing spoken corpora and partly due to the inevitable focus on lexical rather than functional units, concordance lines rather than extended discourse stretches, in corpus research. They also claimed that the fact "that spoken language is multi-modal in nature, and that meaning is created through an interplay of a range of semiotic modalities, contributes further to the unease that often accompanies this particular line of enquiry."

Pragmatics research increasingly makes use of corpus data and corpus linguistics analysis (e.g., Romero-Trillo 2008; Jucker et al. 2009; O'Keeffe et al. 2011). These works demonstrate how to bring together natural language processing and applied linguistics techniques. They usually focus on pragmatic markers, variations in language use, and teacher talk in the classroom and elsewhere. There have been some attempts to analyze nonnative speakers' language use with corpus methods (see Romero-Trillo 2008). This research line is very promising for intercultural pragmatics because it focuses on naturally occurring language production.

Biber et al. (2007:10) talked about the interface of corpus linguistics and discourse analysis as one of the current challenges of corpus linguistics: "Is it possible to merge the analytical goals and methods of corpus linguistics with those of discourse analysis that focuses on the structural organization of texts? Can a corpus be analyzed to identify the general patterns of discourse organization that are used to construct texts, and can individual texts be analyzed in terms of the general patterns that result from corpus analysis?" Few studies have attempted to combine these two research perspectives. Upton and Cohen (2009) argued that, on the one hand, most corpus-based studies have focused on the quantitative distribution of lexical and grammatical features, generally disregarding the language used in particular texts and higher-level discourse structure or other aspects of discourse organization. On the other hand, most qualitative discourse analyses have focused on the analysis of discourse patterns in a few texts from a single genre, but they have not provided tools for empirical analyses that can be applied on a large scale across a number of texts or genres. As a result, we know little at present about the general patterns of discourse organization across a large representative sample of texts from a genre.

Just like in the discourse segment with the CA approach above, in corpus-based discourse analysis the "units of analysis" must be well-defined discourse units: the segments of discourse that provide the building blocks of texts. Upton and Cohen (2009) argued that the first step in an analysis of discourse structure is to identify the internal discourse segments of a text, corresponding to distinct propositions, topics, or communicative functions. These discourse segments will become the basic units of the subsequent discourse analysis. For a corpus study of discourse structure, all texts in the corpus must be analyzed for their component discourse units.

Discourse segment identification makes the analysis of oral intercultural interaction easier because with a top-down approach we can identify what the segments are all about. I have used different segments of the same conversation between a Korean female speaker and an American male speaker to demonstrate different aspects of native speaker–nonnative speaker communication: in example (2) contradiction and in example (4) teasing.

Some of the existing corpus works that can be considered intercultural in nature are based on the International Corpus of Learner English (Granger 2003). Other works use different corpora. Belz (2004) discussed how learner corpus analysis can be used to demonstrate the development of foreign language proficiency. Waibel (2005) analyzed the use of phrasal verbs in learner English based on a corpus of German and Italian students' production. Tagnin (2006) reported about a multilingual learner corpus in Brazil.

The Vienna-Oxford International Corpus of English (VOICE) is probably the biggest presently available corpus for the study of lingua franca communication. VOICE provides a sizeable, computer-readable corpus of English as it is produced by this nonnative speaking majority of users in different contexts. As their website says, these speakers use English successfully on a daily basis all over the world, in their personal, professional, or academic lives. The project participants therefore consider them primarily not as language learners but as language users in their own right. Their purpose with the project is to find out how these nonnative speakers use the English language as their lingua franca.

The database can certainly be a good source for research in intercultural pragmatics, depending on what the focus of the researcher is. VOICE consists of transcripts of naturally occurring, nonscripted face-to-face interactions in English as a lingua franca (ELF). According to the website, VOICE currently comprises 1 million words of spoken ELF interactions, equaling approximately 120 hours of transcribed speech. In addition, 23 recordings of transcribed speech events can also be listened to. The speakers recorded in VOICE are experienced ELF speakers from a wide range of first language backgrounds. The database includes approximately

1,250 ELF speakers with approximately 50 different first languages (disregarding varieties of the respective languages). It is important to note that VOICE focuses mainly, though not exclusively, on European ELF speakers. According to the project description, the recorded interactions cover a wide range of different speech events in terms of domain (professional, educational, leisure), function (exchanging information, enacting social relationships), and participant roles and relationships (acquainted vs. unacquainted, symmetrical vs. asymmetrical). They are classified into the following speech event types: interviews, press conferences, service encounters, seminar discussions, working group discussions, workshop discussions, meetings, panels, question-answer-sessions, and different kinds of conversations.

As mentioned above, VOICE is a good source for research in intercultural pragmatics if we do not forget that English lingua franca is a "contact language" between persons who share neither a common native tongue nor a common (national) culture, and for whom English is the chosen foreign language of communication (Firth 1996:240). There is no doubt about the fact that ELF is being shaped mainly by its nonnative speakers. However, this can hardly lead to the development of a common core that may differ in any way from the common core of the English language because of the enormous variety of speakers that use ELF. Thus, no conventions, norms, and standardization can develop, with the exception of sporadic examples such as Jenkins (2000), who found that being able to pronounce some sounds that are often regarded as "particularly English" but also particularly difficult, namely the "th" sounds /u/ and /D/ and the "dark l" allophone [ɫ], is not necessary for international intelligibility through ELF. Seidlhofer (2007; 2011) also argued that analyses of ELF interactions captured in the VOICE corpus clearly show that although ELF speakers often do not use the third person singular present tense "-s" marking in their verbs, this does not lead to any misunderstandings or communication problems. However, these features do not demonstrate any process of normativization. It was known from error analysis research that nonnative speakers of English, no matter what their L1 is, often omit the third person singular "-s." This can either be a systematic error or just a one-time mistake even in the speech production of fluent speakers.

The rise of English to a position of a lingua franca in the present-day world has led to the emergence of something that has come to be called "Global English," i.e., English as a world language. This new English is now used for numerous purposes as a means of international interaction, as well as a daily means of communication for hundreds of millions of people in countries where English has obtained the position of a second official or unofficial language, i.e., an L2 language. In addition to these, even more people all over the world learn English as a "foreign" language as part of their basic and further education. These developments have not come about without impacting the English language itself, which is currently undergoing processes of accelerated change, divergence and convergence in several core domains of its grammar and lexis. So far, only a few of these processes have been adequately described in linguistic research, which has focused on current trends in the "mainstream" varieties of English, distinctive traits of the "New Englishes" in mainly postcolonial contexts, or typologies of standard and nonstandard varieties. Because of its mainly historical orientation, research on language contacts, for its part, has hitherto had little to say about current contact situations, although they are likely to have deep-going effects on the very shape of English. What has also particularly been lacking is research into the role and characteristics of English as a lingua franca.

Another important initiative is the GlobE Consortium funded by the Academy of Finland for the period 2010–2013. This project builds on and combines the efforts and expertise gained in two previous Finnish Academy projects. These are the English as a Lingua Franca project (ELFA), based in the University of Helsinki and led by Anna Mauranen, and the project on Vernacular Universals vs. Contact-Induced Language Change (UniCont), carried out jointly in the Universities of Joensuu and Tampere and led by Markku Filppula and Juhani Klemola.

According to their website, GlobE aims to combine the strengths of the three methodological and theoretical approaches that we believe are essential to a better understanding of the processes that English is undergoing on its way to becoming a world language, viz. typological, contact-linguistic, and second-language acquisition research. Researchers in the project investigate ongoing developments in English as a global language, their sources, manifestations, as well as the typological characteristics of emerging Global English, by examining and comparing established varieties, nonstandard varieties, and other emergent varieties of English. Their primary focus is on the commonalities among the varieties and the main trends of development.

2.4. COMPUTER-MEDIATED COMMUNICATION

We need to briefly mention one of the fastest growing fields of research that will be serving as a main source of data for analysis in the future: computer-mediated communication (CMC). It takes place between one or more interlocutors via the instrumentality of the computer as a tool in telecommunication networks. CMC is predominantly carried out through discursive interaction. In CMC, the physical absence of interlocutors is replaced with language and its multimodal, semiotic systems. In CMC analysis there is complete reliance on language because no actual situational factors are present in the traditional sense.

There has been little exploration of methodologies that are effective in systematically analyzing phenomena in CMC. Romiszowski and Mason (1996) claimed that the method most frequently used in research on CMC is surveying students and instructors, although evaluative case studies are also relatively popular. Survey studies and evaluative case studies tend to provide limited perspectives. In the last decade this situation has changed, although the field still struggles with developing the right methodologies. Discourse analysis and conversational analysis have become especially popular. Studies in CMC discourse are generally aimed at determining the nature of the given discourse, how the discourse differs from other types (oral and/or written), and the extent to which written or spoken English features are evident. Discourse focus in CMC also encourages the analysis of the structuring of computer-mediated messages. It is important for intercultural pragmatics that the discourse in CMC studies is termed "interactive" or "emergent," where features do not remain fixed but vary according to functions in contexts where they occur. Ho (2004) argued that the approach remains very much at the level of classifying features into one mode of discourse or another, or quantitative in statistically tabulating and cataloguing lists of features identified. The specifics of how discourse features and linguistic devices function to fulfill particular roles within specific contexts in the dynamic, interactive environment of online communication, however, do not appear to have received comparable attention.

CMC has rapidly developed into CMIC (computer-mediated intercultural communication). Telecollaborative projects provide an enormous amount of data for the analysis of intercultural communication. Belz (2003:2) defined telecollaboration as a phenomenon that "involves the application of global computer networks to foreign (and second) language learning and teaching in institutionalized settings." Telecollaborative projects offer a very useful research environment for the study of intercultural communication because they give the chance to the researchers to observe and analyze nonnative speakers' written language behavior in a naturalistic setting full of different social discourse practices (e.g., Belz 2005; Belz and Kinginger 2002; González-Lloret 2008).

Savignon and Roitmeier (2004) emphasized that CMC is a contemporary medium of communication in its own right, offering new possibilities for intercultural exchange and collaboration. Their data collection was based on bulletin board postings of paired groups of students, one in Germany and the other in the US. The analysis of data provided illustrations of collaboration in the construction of texts and contexts. The authors argued that the cohesion and coherence of the postings for a single topic clearly qualify them as a text. The text is situated within the context of the ongoing intercultural collaboration. The subjects did not simply produce disconnected and isolated texts. They collaborated to create a network of intertwined postings that make sense only after reading prior contributions. Savignon and Roitmeier (2004) claimed that postings were seen to exhibit qualities of face-to-face interaction that have been identified in other studies of CMC as well as qualities of written discourse. They also identified numerous communicative strategies unique to CMC. For instance, the strategy used to express differing opinions, or a change in the interpretation of an idea, is the use of contrastive connectives and concessive transition markers. For example, an idea mentioned previously is rephrased and followed by *but, however*, or the like.

All the research studies in CMC, especially in CMIC point to the fact that intercultural pragmatics research will benefit from the use of Computer-Mediated Intercultural Communication to a great extent in the future because CMIC seems to offer a relatively unexplored means of intercultural collaboration and understanding. In those foreign language settings where teachers usually have limited or distant experience with second language culture, the potential of CMIC for promoting intercultural awareness could be even greater.

EPILOGUE

This is the first book on intercultural pragmatics. I am sure that many more will come. The field is growing fast, with its own journal and biannual conference series. What do I think this book has managed to accomplish? First of all, I hope it has called attention to how important linguistic pragmatics is for intercultural pragmatics, and how intercultural pragmatics can clarify some issues that are problematic or ignored in linguistic pragmatics. There is another issue that the book has tried to emphasize. The fact that the title of the book is "Intercultural Pragmatics" does not mean that it is strictly about intercultures. It is also about how a language system is put to use in intercultural encounters in which conventions and norms of communality do not have that strong an effect on production and comprehension—as is the case in intracultural interactions, since they need to be co-constructed usually from scratch. So far when we have talked about language and language use, we have taken for granted that there are some universal principles of human communication that are lexicalized and grammaticalized differently in different languages because of varying needs of people speaking those languages. However, we have paid less attention to communicative encounters where participants with different L1s come to use an L2 as the means of communication. Will that change anything in our thinking about how interactions take place and meaning is shaped? This book has tried to give answer to this question.

Language is all about conventions. It is a set of rules, a set of social conventions that have developed in a particular way in a particular speech community (society) in response to the communicative need of its members. These conventions and their varieties become habits of the individual speakers of the language. Each speech community (society) creates its own sets of linguistic and nonlinguistic conventions that are unique to that group of people. Each human language should be considered a unique entity reflecting a unique society. If we accept this view, which most linguists do, it is essential that the set of linguistic conventions must be the reflection of the set of nonlinguistic conventions in that speech community, at least to some extent. Thus, communicating within that set of nonlinguistic conventions (which we might as well call "culture"), the linguistic signs can be used economically because people in the given speech community are familiar with the set of nonlinguistic conventions that constitute the frame of interactions. This is why present-day linguistics is all about context-sensitivity and the underdeterminacy of linguistic signs. However, when people communicate in a language other than their L1, this harmonious interplay between the set of linguistic conventions and set of nonlinguistic conventions seems to be lost, at least to some extent. In intercultural interactions, especially lingua franca communication, the participants have to work with not only a different set of linguistic conventions but also a different set of nonlinguistic conventions. So both sets are alien. How will this affect language use? To answer this question the book has focused on issues that come to the fore when we examine the nature of intercultural interactions. It reviewed pragmatic competence that is more complex in bi- and multilingual speakers than in monolingual speakers because the former are exposed to two or more different sets of linguistic and nonlinguistic conventions. The book also discussed formulaic language that functions as some kind of an interface between the set of nonlinguistic conventions and the set of linguistic conventions, and is taken for granted in intracultural communication. However, it should be given special attention to in intercultural communication because the socio-cultural background that facilitates the use of formulaic expressions is unique to each language. We explained the special symbiosis of common ground, context, and salience in meaning production and comprehension. Agreeing partly with LaPolla (2003:119), who claimed that "it is not context that disambiguates language, but language that disambiguates the context of interpretation," we reevaluated context-sensitivity, and the role of prior context and actual situational context in the communicative process. As a result, it was underlined that the hypothesis about the speaker's intended meaning being underdetermined by what is said works only for the hearer but not for the speaker. The speaker's utterance is a full proposition. It is the speaker's attempt to make the linguistic form as explicit as s/he can, because the more explicit the linguistic form is, the more constrained the hearer is in constructing the context of interpretation, and the closer speaker's meaning comes to hearer's meaning.

In addition, the book called attention to the uncharted territory of intercultural politeness and impoliteness, demonstrating how contextual effects work differently from what happens in intracultural interactions, where context, rather than the linguistic sign, makes something polite or impolite. The book ended with reviewing the methods of analysis in the field, illustrating how utterance interpretation can be combined with discourse segment analysis in order to get a more adequate picture of what exactly happens in intercultural interactions.

There are still many more issues waiting to be addressed because there was no room for them in this book. It does not mean, of course, that they are not important. However, more research is needed—for instance, to examine how presuppositions work in intercultural communication, how co-constructed, temporary conventions constrain language production and comprehension, how the use of CMC will change the way we think about norms and conventions and how the role of indexicals and discourse markers change in intercultural interactions, just to mention a few.

Let me finish the book with one of my favourite quote from Tennyson's *Idylls of the King*, which fits here very well:

"The old order changeth, yielding place to new,
And God fulfills himself in many ways,
Lest one good custom should corrupt the world".
(Book 11. The Passing of Arthur.)

Istvan Kecskes

REFERENCES

Abel, Beate. 2003. "English idioms in the first language and second language lexicon: A dual representation approach." *Second Language Research* 19.4: 329–358.

Adamson, Hugh Douglas. 1988. *Variation Theory and Second Language Acquisition*. Washington, DC: Georgetown University Press.

Aijmer, Karin. 1996. *Conversational Routines in English: Convention and creativity*. London/New York: Longman.

Albert, Ethel M. 1968. "Value systems." In *The International Encyclopedia of the Social Sciences*, Sills David L. (ed.), 16: 287–291. New York: Macmillan.

Al-Issa, Ahmad. 2003. "Sociocultural transfer in L2 speech behaviors: Evidence and motivating factors." *International Journal of Intercultural Relations* 27.5: 581–601.

Allan, Keith. Forthcoming. "What is common ground?" In *Perspectives on Pragmatics and Philosophy*, Capone Alessandro, Lo Piparo Franco and Marco Carapezza (eds). Berlin: Springer Verlag.

Altenberg, Bengt. 1998. "On the phraseology of spoken English: The evidence of recurrent word-combinations." In *Phraseology: Theory, analysis, and applications*, Cowie Anthony Paul (ed.), 101–122. Oxford: Clarendon Press.

Alvesson, Mats and Dan, Karreman. 2001. "Odd couple: Making sense of the curious concept of knowledge management." *Journal of Management Studies* 38.7: 995–1018.

Arbib, Michael A., Oztop, Erhan and Patricia, Zukow-Goldring. 2005. "Language and the mirror system: A perception/action based approach to communicative development." *Cognition, Brain, Behavior* 3: 239–272.

Ariel, Mira. 2002. "The demise of a unique concept of literal meaning." *Journal of Pragmatics* (Special issue on Literal, Minimal and Salient Meanings), 34.4: 361–402.

Arnseth, Hans Christian and Ivar, Solheim. 2002. "Making sense of shared knowledge." In *Proceedings of CSCL 2002 on Computer Support for Collaborative Learning: Foundations for a CSCL community*, Gerry Stahl (ed.), 102–110. Hillsdale, NJ: Lawrence Erlbaum.

Arundale, Robert B. 1997. "Against (Grice's) intention." Paper presented at *LSI Preconference on Language and Cognition, International Communication Association Conference*, Montreal, Quebec, Canada.

Arundale, Robert B. 1999. "An alternative model and ideology of communication for an alternative to politeness theory." *Pragmatics* 9.1: 119–154.

Arundale, Robert B. 2004. "Co-Constituting face in conversation: An alternative to Brown and Levinson's politeness theory." Paper presented at *The 90th Annual National Communication Association Conference*, Chicago, Illinois.

Arundale, Robert B. 2006. "Face as relational and interactional: A communication framework for research on face, facework and politeness." *Journal of Politeness Research* 2.2: 193–216.

Arundale, Robert B. 2008. "Against (Gricean) intentions at the heart of human interaction." *Intercultural Pragmatics* 5.2: 229–258.

Austin, John Langshaw. 1976. *How to Do Things with Words* (2nd ed.). Oxford: Oxford University Press.

Bach, Kent. 1994. "Conversational impliciture." *Mind and Language* 9.2: 124–162.

Bach, Kent. 1999. "The semantics-pragmatics distinction: What it is and why it matters." In *The Semantics/Pragmatics Interface from Different Points of View*, Turner Ken (ed.), 64–84. Oxford: Elsevier.

Bach, Kent. 2001. "You don't say?" *Synthese* 128: 15–44.

Bach, Kent. 2005. "Context ex Machina." In *Semantics vs. Pragmatics*, Szabo Zoltan Gendler (ed.), 15–44. Oxford: Oxford University Press.

Bach, Kent. 2007. "Regressions in pragmatics (and semantics)." In *Pragmatics* (Advances in Linguistics), Burton-Roberts Noel (ed.), 24–44. Houndmills: Palgrave-Macmillan.

Bach, Kent and Robert M. Harnish. 1979. *Linguistic Communication and Speech Acts*. Cambridge, MA: MIT Press.

Bandura, Albert. 1986. *Social Foundations of Thought and Action: A social cognitive theory*. Englewood Cliffs, NJ: Prentice-Hall.

Bardovi-Harlig, Kathleen. 1996. "Pragmatics and language teaching: Bringing pragmatics and pedagogy together." In *Pragmatics and Language Learning*, Bouton Lawrence F. (ed.), 7: 21–41. University of Illinois at Urbana-Champaign: Division of English as an International Language.

Bardovi-Harlig, Kathleen. 1999. "Exploring the interlanguage of interlanguage pragmatics: A research agenda for acquisitional pragmatics." *Language Leaning* 49.4: 677–713.

Bardovi-Harlig, Kathleen. 2009. "Conventional expressions as a pragmalinguistic resource: Recognition and production of conventional expressions in L2 pragmatics." *Language Learning* 59: 755–795.

Bardovi-Harlig, Kathleen. 2010. "Recognition of conventional expressions in L2 pragmatics." In *Pragmatics and Language Learning* (Vol. 12), Kasper Gabriele, Nguyen Hanhthi, Yoshimi Dina Rudolph and Jim K. Yoshioka (eds), 141–162. Honolulu: University of Hawaii, National Foreign Language Resource Center.

Bardovi-Harlig, Kathleen and Beverly Slattery, Hartford (eds). 2005. *Interlanguage Pragmatics: Exploring institutional talk*. Mahwah, NJ: Erlbaum.

Bargiela-Chiappini, Francesca. 2003. "Face and politeness: New (insights) for old (concepts)." *Journal of Pragmatics* 35.10: 1453–1469.

Bargiela-Chiappini, Francesca and Michael, Haugh (eds). 2009. *Face, Communication and Social Interaction*. London: Equinox.

Barnlund, Dean C. 1970. "A transactional model of communication." In *Language Behavior: A book of readings in communication*, Akin Johnny, Goldberg Alvin, Myers Gail and Joseph Stewart (eds), 43–61. The Hague: Mouton.

Barr, Dale J. 2004. "Establishing conventional communication systems: Is common knowledge necessary?" *Cognitive Science* 28.6: 937–962.

Barr, Dale J. and Boaz, Keysar. 2005a. "Making sense of how we make sense: The paradox of egocentrism in language use." In *Figurative Language Comprehension: Social and cultural influences*, Colston Herbert L. and Albert N. Katz (eds), 21–43. Mahwah, NJ: Lawrence Erlbaum.

Barr, Dale J. and Boaz, Keysar. 2005b. "Mindreading in an exotic case: The normal adult human." In *Other Minds: How humans bridge the divide between self and others.* Malle Bertram F. and Sara D. Hodges (eds), 271–283. New York: Guilford Press.

Barrett, Martyn. 2008. "Intercultural competences: Some reflections based on the autobiography of intercultural encounters." Paper presented at the Council of Europe Seminar on *Images of the "Other" in History Teaching: The Role of History Teaching Institutions in the North and Global South,* hosted by the North-South Centre of the Council of Europe, the Ismaili Centre and the Aga Khan Development Network, Lisbon, Portugal, September 25–26.

Barro, Ana, Byram, Mike, Grimm, Hanns, Morgan, Carol and Celia, Roberts. 1993. "Cultural studies for advanced language learners." In *Language and Culture,* Graddol David, Thompson Linda and Byram Michael (eds), 55–70. Clevedon, UK: Multilingual Matters.

Barron, Anne. 2003. *Acquisition in Interlanguage Pragmatics: Learning how to do things with words in a study-abroad context.* Philadelphia: John Benjamins.

Barsalou, Lawrence W. 1993. "Challenging assumption about concepts." *Cognitive Development* 8.2: 169–180.

Barsalou, Lawrence W. 1999. "Perceptual symbol systems." *Behavioral and Brain Sciences* 22: 577–660.

Bates, Daniel G. and Fred, Plog. 1980. *Cultural Anthropology* (2nd ed.). New York: Alfred A. Knopf.

Bear, Joshua. 1987. "Formulaic utterances and communicative competence." *Journal of Human Sciences* (Insan Bilimleri Degisi.), Middle East Technical University. 6.2: 25–34.

Belz, Julie A. 2003. "Linguistic perspectives on the development of intercultural competence in telecollaboration." *Language Learning and Technology* 7.2: 68–117.

Belz, Julie. A. 2004. "Learner corpus analysis and the development of foreign language proficiency." *System* 32.4: 577–591.

Belz, Julie A. 2005. "Intercultural questioning, discovery and tension in internet-mediated language learning partnerships." *Language and Intercultural Communication* 5.1: 1–39.

Belz, Julie A. and Celeste, Kinginger. 2002. "The cross-linguistic development of address form use in telecollaborative language learning: Two case studies." *The Canadian Modern Language Review* 59.2: 189–214.

Benedict, Ruth. 1967. *El Hombre y la Culture: Investigación sobre los orígenes de la civilización contemporánea.* Buenos Aires: Editorial Sudamericana.

Berg, Jonathan. 1993. "Literal meaning and context." *Iyyun* 42: 397–411.

Berger, Peter L. and Thomas, Luckmann. 1966. *The Social Construction of Reality: A treatise in the sociology of knowledge.* Garden City, NY: Anchor Books.

Bernal, Maria. 2008. "Do insults always insult? Genuine impoliteness versus non-genuine impoliteness in colloquial Spanish." *Pragmatics* 18.4: 775–802.

Bernstein, Richard J. 1983. *Beyond Objectivism and Relativism: Science, hermeneutics, and praxis.* Philadelphia, PA: University of Pennsylvania Press.

Bezuidenhout, Anne. 2004. "Procedural meaning and the semantics/pragmatics interface." In *The Semantics/Pragmatics Distinction,* Bianchi Claudia (ed.), 101–131. Stanford: CSLI Publications.

Bialystok, Ellen. 1993. "Symbolic representation and attentional control in pragmatic competence." In *Interlanguage Pragmatics*, Kasper Gabriele and Shoshana Blum-Kulka (eds), 43–59. New York: Oxford University Press.

Bianchi, Claudia (ed.). 2004. *The Semantics/Pragmatics Distinction*. Stanford: CSLI Publications.

Biber, Douglas, Connor, Ulla and Thomas A. Upton. 2007. *Discourse on the Move: Using corpus analysis to describe discourse structure*. Amsterdam: John Benjamins.

Biber, Douglas, Conrad, Susan and Viviana, Cortes. 2004. "If you look at...: Lexical bundles in university teaching and textbooks." *Applied Linguistics* 25.3: 371–405.

Biber, Douglas, Johansson, Stig, Leech, Geoffrey, Conrad, Susan and Edward, Finegan. 1999. *Longman Grammar of Spoken and Written English*. London: Pearson Education.

Blommaert, Jan. 1991. "How much culture is there in intercultural communication?" In *The Pragmatics of Intercultural and International Communication*, Blommaert Jan and Jef Verschueren (eds), 13–31. Amsterdam: John Benjamins.

Blommaert, Jan. 1998. "Different approaches to intercultural communication: A critical survey." Plenary lecture, Lernen und Arbeiten in einer international vernetzten und multikulturellen Gesellschaft, Expertagung Universitat Bremen, Institut fur Projektmanagement und Witschaftsinformatik (IPMI), February 27–28. Retrieved June 8, 2012, from http://www.cie.ugent.be/CIE/blommaert1.htm.

Blommaert, Jan. 2000. "Review of Hymes 1996: Ethnography, linguistics, narrative inequality: Toward an understanding of voice." *Multilingua: Journal of Cross-Cultural and Interlanguage Communication* 19.4: 422–425.

Blommaert, Jan. 2003. "Orthopraxy, writing and identity: Shaping lives through borrowed genres in Congo." *Pragmatics* 13.1: 33–48.

Bloom, Paul and Frank C. Keil. 2001. "Thinking through language." *Mind and Language* 16.4: 351–367.

Blum-Kulka, Shoshana. 1991. "Interlanguage pragmatics: The case of request." In *Foreign/ Second Language Pedagogy Research: A commemorative volume for Claus Faerch*, Phillipson Robert, Kellerman Eric, Selinker Larry, Smith Michael Sharwood and Merrill Swain (eds), 255–272. Clevedon: Multilingual Matters.

Blum-Kulka, Shoshana. 1997. *Dinner Talk: Cultural patterns of sociability and socialization in family discourse*. Mahwah, NJ: Lawrence Erlbaum.

Blum-Kulka, Shoshana, Blondheim, Menahem, House, Juliance, Kasper, Gabriele and Johannes, Wagner. 2008. "Intercultural pragmatics, language and society." In *Unity and Diversity of Languages*, Sterkenburg, Piet van (ed.), 155–173. Amsterdam: John Benjamins.

Bock, J. Kathryn, Irwin, David E. and Douglas J. Davidson. 2004. "Putting first things first." In *The Interface of Language, Vision, and Action: Eye movements and the visual world*, Henderson John M. and Fernanda Ferreira (eds), 249–278. New York: Psychology Press.

Bock, J. Kathryn and Richard K. Warren. 1985. "Conceptual accessibility and syntactic structure in sentence formulation." *Cognition* 21: 47–67.

Bock, J. Kathryn and Willem, Levelt. 1994. "Language production: Grammatical encoding." In *Handbook of Psycholinguistics*, Gernsbacher Morton Ann (ed.), 945–984. New York: Academic Press.

Bodenhausen, Galen V., Macrae, C. Neil and Jennifer, Garst. 1998. "Stereotypes in thought and deed: Social-Cognitive origins of intergroup discrimination." In *Intergroup Cognition and Intergroup Behavior*, Sedikides Constantine, Schopler John and Chester A. Insko (eds), 311–335. Mahwah, NJ: Erlbaum.

Boers, Frank, Kappel, Jenny, Stengers, Helene and Murielle, Demecheleer. 2006. "Formulaic sequences and perceived oral proficiency: Putting a lexical approach to the test." *Language Teaching Research* 10.3: 245–261.

Bolinger, Dwight. 1976. "Meaning and memory." *Forum Linguisticum* 1: 1–14.

Bortfeld, Heather. 2002. "What native and non-native speakers' images for idioms tell us about figurative language." In *Bilingual Sentence Processing*, Heredia Roberto and Jeanette Altarriba (eds), 275–295. Amsterdam, Netherlands: Elsevier Science Publishers.

Bortfeld, Heather. 2003. "Comprehending idioms cross-linguistically." *Experimental Psychology* 50: 1–14.

Bou-Franch, Patricia. 1998. "On pragmatic transfer." *Studies in English Language and Linguistics* 2: 5–20.

Bou-Franch, Patricia. 2012. "Pragmatic transfer." In *The Encyclopedia of Applied Linguistics*, Vol. 8. Chapelle Carol A. (ed.), 4622–4626. Oxford: Wiley-Blackwell.

Bourdieu, Pierre. 1991. "Genesis and structure of the religious field." *Comparative Social Research* 13:1–44.

Bousfield, Derek. 2008a. *Impoliteness in Interaction*. Amsterdam/Philadelphia: John Benjamins.

Bousfield, Derek. 2008b. "Impoliteness in the struggle for power." In *Impoliteness in Language: Studies on its interplay with power in theory and practice*, Bousfield Derek and Miriam A. Locher (eds), 127–154. Berlin: Mouton de Gruyter.

Bousfield, Derek. 2010. "Researching impoliteness and rudeness: Issues and definitions." In *Interpersonal Pragmatics*, Locher Miriam A. and Sage L. Graham (eds), 102–134. Berlin: Mouton de Gruyter.

Bousfield, Derek and Jonathan, Culpeper. 2008. "Impoliteness: Eclecticism and diaspora— An introduction to the special edition." *Journal of Politeness Research* 4.2: 161–168.

Bousfield, Derek and Miriam A. Locher (eds). 2008. *Impoliteness in Language: Studies on its interplay with power in theory and practice*. Berlin: Mouton de Gruyter.

Boxer, Diana. 2002. "Discourse issues in cross-cultural pragmatics." *Annual Review of Applied Linguistics* 22: 150–167.

Brinton, Laurel J. and Elizabeth Closs, Traugott. 2005. *Lexicalization and Language Change*. Cambridge: Cambridge University Press.

Brown, John Seely and Paul, Duguid. 2001. "Knowledge and organization: A social-practice perspective." *Organization Science* 12.2: 198–213.

Brown, Penelope and Stephen C. Levinson. 1987. *Politeness: Some universals in language usage*. Cambridge: Cambridge University Press.

Buber, Martin. 1955. "Dialogue." In *Between Man and Man*, Smith Ronald Gregor (trans.), 1–39. Boston, MA: Beacon Press.

Bublitz, Wolfram and Uta, Lenk. 1999. "Disturbed coherence: 'Fill me in.'" In *Coherence in Spoken and Written Discourse*, Bublitz Wolfram, Lenk Uta and Eija Ventola (eds), 153–175. Amsterdam/Philadelphia: John Benjamins.

Bulcaen, Chris and Jan, Blommaert. 1997. *Eindrapport VFIK Project 307: Begeleiding van migrantenvrouwen en meisjes in centra voor residentieel welzijnswerk.* Antwerp: IPrA Research Center.

Bunge, Mario. 1996. *Finding Philosophy in Social Science.* New Haven/London: Yale University Press.

Burton-Roberts, Noel. 2005. "Robyn Carston on semantics, pragmatics and 'encoding.'" *Journal of Linguistics* 41.2: 389–407.

Burton-Roberts, Noel. 2006. "Cancellation and intention." *Newcastle Working Papers in Linguistics* 12: 1–12.

Byram, Michael. 1997. *Teaching and Assessing Intercultural Communicative Competence.* Clevendon, UK: Multilingual Matters.

Byram, Michael. 2003. *Intercultural Competence.* Strasbourg: Council of Europe.

Capone, Alessandro. 2005. "Pragmemes (a study with reference to English and Italian)." *Journal of Pragmatics* 37.9: 1355–1371.

Cappelen, Herman. 2008a. "Content relativism and semantic blindness." In *Relative Truth*, Garcia-Carpintero Manuel and Max Kolbel (eds), 265–286. Oxford: Clarendon Press.

Cappelen, Herman. 2008b. "The creative interpreter: Content relativism and assertion." *Philosophical Perspectives* 22.1: 23–46.

Carassa, Antonella and Marco, Colombetti. 2009. "Joint meaning." *Journal of Pragmatics* 41.9: 1837–1854.

Carston, Robyn. 1998. "Negation, 'presupposition' and the semantics/pragmatics distinction." *Journal of Linguistics* 34.2: 309–350.

Carston, Robyn. 2002a. "Linguistic meaning, communicated meaning and cognitive pragmatics." *Mind and Language* (Special Issue on Pragmatics and Cognitive Science) 17.1/2: 127–148.

Carston, Robyn. 2002b. *Thoughts and Utterances: The pragmatics of explicit communication.* Oxford: Blackwell.

Carston, Robyn. 2004a. "Truth-Conditional content and conversational implicature." In *The Semantics/Pragmatics Distinction*, Bianchi Claudia (ed.), 65–100. Stanford: CSLI Publications.

Carston, Robyn. 2004b. "Explicature and semantics." In *Semantics: A reader*, Davis Steven and Brendan S. Gillon (eds), 817–845. Oxford: Oxford University Press.

Cenoz, Jasone. 2003. "The intercultural style hypothesis: L1 and L2 interaction in requesting behavior." In *Effects of the Second Language on the First*, Cook Vivian (ed.), 62–80. Clevedon, UK: Multilingual Matters.

Chafe, Wallace L. 1976. "Givenness, contrastiveness, definiteness, subjects, topics, and point of view." In *Subject and Topic*, Li Charles N. (ed.), 25–55. London/New York: Academic Press.

Chafe, Wallace L. 1994. *Discourse, Consciousness, and Time.* Chicago: University of Chicago Press.

Chaiklin, Seth and Jean, Lave (eds). 1993. *Understanding Practice: Perspectives on activity and context.* Cambridge: Cambridge University Press.

Chomsky, Noam. 1978. "Language and unconscious knowledge." In *Psychoanalysis and Language, Psychiatry and the Humanities*, Smith Joseph H. (ed.), 3: 3–44. New Haven: Yale University Press; republished in Chomsky Noam (1980: 217–254, 287–290).

Chomsky, Noam. 1981. *Lectures on Government and Binding*. Dordrecht: Foris.

Cieslicka, Anna. 2004. *On Processing Figurative Language: Towards a model of idiom comprehension in foreign language learners*. Poznan: Motivex

Cieslicka, Anna. 2006. "Literal salience in on-line processing of idiomatic expressions by second language learners." *Second Language Research* 22.2: 114–144.

Clark, Herbert H. 1996. *Using Language*. Cambridge: Cambridge University Press.

Clark, Herbert H. 2009. "Context and common ground." In *Concise Encyclopedia of Pragmatics*, Mey Jacob L. (ed.), 116–119. Oxford: Elsevier.

Clark, Herbert H. and Jean E. Fox Tree. 2002. "Using uh and um in spontaneous speaking." *Cognition* 84.1: 73–111.

Clark, Herbert H. and Susan E. Brennan. 1991. "Grounding in communication." In *Perspectives on Socially Shared Cognition*, Resnick Lauren B., Levine John M. and Stephanie D. Teasley (eds), 127–149. Washington, DC: American Psychological Association.

Clark, Herbert H. and Susan E. Haviland. 1977. "Comprehension and the given-new contract." In *Discourse Production and Comprehension*, Freedle Roy O. (ed.), 1–40. Norwood, NJ: Ablex.

Clark, Herbert H., Schreuder, Robert and Samuel, Buttrick. 1983. "Common ground and the understanding of demonstrative reference." *Journal of Verbal Learning and Verbal Behavior* 22: 245–258.

Clyne, Michael. 1994. *Inter-Cultural Communication at Work: Cultural values in discourse*. Cambridge: Cambridge University Press.

Clyne, Michael, Ball, Martin and Deborah, Neil. 1991. "Intercultural communication at work in Australia: Complaints and apologies in turns." *Multilingua* 10.3: 251–273.

Coates, Jennifer. 1995. "The negotiation of coherence in face-to-face interaction: Some examples from the extreme bounds." In *Coherence in Spontaneous Text*, Gernsbacher Morton Ann and Talmy Givon (eds), 41–58. Amsterdam: John Benjamins.

Cogo, Alessia. 2007. "Intercultural communication in English as a lingua franca: A case study." PhD Dissertation. King's College London.

Collins, James and Richard K. Blot. 2003. *Literacy and Literacies: Texts, power and identity*. Cambridge: Cambridge University Press.

Colston, Herbert L. and Albert N. Katz (eds). 2005. *Figurative Language Comprehension: Social and cultural influences*. Hillsdale, NJ: Erlbaum.

Cook, Vivian J. 1997. "Monolingual bias in second language acquisition research." *Revista Canaria de Estudios Ingleses* 34: 35–50.

Cooren, Francois. 2010. *Action and Agency in Dialogue: Passion, incarnation, and ventriloquism*. Amsterdam: Benjamins.

Coulmas, Florian. 1979. "On the sociolinguistic relevance of routine formulas." *Journal of Pragmatics* 3.3/4: 239–266.

Coulmas, Florian (ed.). 1981. *Conversational Routine: Explorations in standardized communication situations and prepatterned speech*. The Hague: Mouton.

Coulson, Seana. 2000. *Semantic Leaps: Frame-Shifting and conceptual blending in meaning-construction*. Cambridge: Cambridge University Press.

Croft, William. 2000. *Explaining Language Change: An evolutionary approach*. London: Longman.

Croft, William and D. Alan, Cruse. 2004. *Cognitive Linguistics*. Cambridge: Cambridge University Press.

Croft, William and Esther J. Wood. 2000. "Construal operations in linguistics and artificial intelligence." In *Meaning and Cognition: A multidisciplinary approach*, Liliana Albertazzi (ed.), 51–78. Amsterdam: Benjamins.

Cruse, D. Alan. 1990. "Prototype theory and lexical semantics." In *Meaning and Prototypes: Studies in linguistic categorization*, Tzohatzidis Savas L. (ed.), 382–402. London: Routledge.

Cruse, D. Alan. 1992. "Antonymy revisited: Some thoughts on the relationship between words and concepts." In *Frames, Fields, and Contrasts: New essays in semantic and lexical organization*, Lehrer Adrienne and Eva Feder Kittay (eds), 289–306. Hillsdale, NJ: Lawrence Erlbaum.

Culicover, Peter W. and Ray, Jackendoff. 2005. *Simpler Syntax*. Oxford: Oxford University Press.

Culpeper, Jonathan. 1996. "Towards an anatomy of impoliteness." *Journal of Pragmatics* 25.3: 349–367.

Culpeper, Jonathan. 2005. "Impoliteness and entertainment in the television quiz show: The weakest link." *Journal of Politeness Research* 1.1: 35–72.

Culpeper, Jonathan. 2008. "Reflections on impoliteness, relational work and power." In *Impoliteness in Language: Studies on its interplay with power in theory and practice*, Bousfield Derek and Miriam A. Locher (eds), 17–44. Berlin: Mouton de Gruyter.

Culpeper, Jonathan. 2009. "Impoliteness: Using and understanding the language of offence." ESRC project. Retrieved December 8, 2011, from http://www.lancs.ac.uk/fass/projects/impoliteness/.

Culpeper, Jonathan. 2011. *Impoliteness: Using language to cause offence*. Cambridge: Cambridge University Press.

Culpeper, Jonathan, Bousfield, Derek and Anne, Wichmann. 2003. "Impoliteness revisited: With special reference to dynamic and prosodic aspects." *Journal of Pragmatics* 35.10/11: 1545–1579.

Culpeper, Jonathan, Marti, Leyla, Mei, Meilian, Nevala, Minna and Gila, Schauer. 2010. "Cross-Cultural variation in the perception of impoliteness: A study of impoliteness events reported by students in England, China, Finland, Germany and Turkey." *Intercultural Pragmatics* 7.4: 597–624.

D'Andrade, Roy G. 1987. "A folk model of the mind." In *Cultural Models in Language and Thought*, Holland Dorothy and Naomi Quinn (eds), 112–148. Cambridge: Cambridge University Press.

D'Andrade, Roy G. 1992. "Schemas and motivation." In *Human Motives and Cultural Models*, D'Andrade Roy G. and Claudia Strauss (eds), 23–44. New York: Cambridge University Press.

Danes, Frantisek. 1970. "Zur linguistischen analyse der textstruktur." *Folia Linguistica* 4:72–78.

Davies, Alan. 1991. *The Native Speaker in Applied Linguistics*. Edinburgh: Edinburgh University Press.

Davis, Wayne. 1998. *Conversational Implicature: Intention, convention and principle in the failure of Gricean theory*. Cambridge: Cambridge University Press.

De Saussure, Ferdinand. 2002. *Ecrits de linguistique generale*. Bouquet Simon and Rudolf Engler (eds). Paris: Gallimard. Sanders Carol, Pires Matthew and Peter Figueroa (trans.). 2006. *Writings in General Linguistics*. Oxford: Oxford University Press.

De Saussure, Louis. 2007. "Pragmatic issues in discourse analysis." *Critical Approaches to Discourse Analysis across Disciplines* 1.1: 179–195.

Dessalegn, Banchiamlack and Barbara, Landau. 2008. "More than meets the eye: The role of language in binding and maintaining feature conjunctions." *Psychological Science* 19.2: 189–195.

Dewaele, Jean-Marc. 2004. "The emotional force of swearwords and taboo words in the speech of multilinguals." *Journal of Multilingual and Mulicultural Development* 25.2/3: 204–222.

DiMaggio, Paul. 1997. "Culture and cognition." *Annual Review of Sociology* 23: 263–287.

Doi, Takeo. 1973. *The Anatomy of Dependence*. Tokyo/New York: Kodansha International.

Duff, Patricia A. 2003. "New directions in second language socialization research." *Korean Journal of English Language and Linguistics* 3: 309–339.

Dummett, Michael. 2003. *The Seas of Language*. Cambridge: Cambridge University Press.

Duranti, Alessandro. 1997. "Universal and cultural-specific properties of greetings." *Journal of Linguistic Anthropology* 7.1: 63–97.

Durkheim, Emile. 1947. *The Division of Labor in Society*. George Simpson (trans.). New York: The Free Press.

Durkheim, Emile. 1982. *The Rules of Sociological Method*. Halls Wilfred Douglas (trans.). New York: Simon and Schuster.

Dynel, Marta. 2009. "Where cooperation meets politeness: Revisiting politeness models in view of the Gricean framework." *Brno Studies in English* 35: 23–43.

Dynel, Marta. Forthcoming. "Being cooperatively (im)polite: Grice's model in the context of (im)politeness theories." In *Research Trends in Intercultural Pragmatics*, Kecskes Istvan and Jesus Romero-Trillo (eds). Berlin/Boston: Mouton de Gruyter.

Edelsky, Carole. 1981. "Who's got the floor?" *Language in Society* 10.3: 383–421.

Edwards, Derek. 2006. "Discourse, cognition and social practices: The rich surface of language and social interaction." *Discourse Studies* 8.1: 41–49.

Eelen, Gino. 2001. *A Critique of Politeness Theories*. Manchester: St. Jerome Publishing.

Ehrenreich, Susanne. 2009. "English as a lingua franca in multinational corporations: Exploring business communities of practice." In *English as a Lingua Franca: Studies and findings*, Mauranen Anna and Elina Ranta (eds), 126–151. Newcastle-upon-Tyne: Cambridge Scholars Publishing.

Ellis, Nick C. 2003. "Constructions, chunking, and connectionism: The emergence of second language structure." In *The Handbook of Second Language Acquisition*, Doughty Catherine J. and Michael H. Long (eds), 63–103. Malden, MA: Blackwell.

Ellis, Nick C., Simpson-Vlach, Rita and Carson, Maynard. 2008. "Formulaic language in native and second language speakers: psycholinguistics, corpus linguistics, and TESOL." *TESOL Quarterly* 42.3: 375–396.

Ellis, Rod. 1994. *The Study of Second Language Acquisition*. Oxford: Oxford University Press.

Elsbach, Kimberly D., Barr, Pamela S. and Andrew B. Hargadon. 2005. "Identifying situated cognition in organizations." *Organization Science* 16.4: 422.

Enfield, Nicholas J. 2008. "Common ground as a resource for social affiliation." In *Intention, Common Ground and the Egocentric Speaker-Hearer*, Kecskes Istvan and Jacob Mey (eds), 223–254. Berlin/ New York: Mouton de Gruyter.

Errington, J. Joesph. 1998. *Shifting Languages: Interaction and identity in Javanese Indonesia*. New York: Cambridge University Press.

Escandell-Vidal, Victoria. 1996. "Towards a cognitive approach to politeness." *Language Sciences* 18: 621–650.

Evanoff, Richard. 2000. "The concept of 'third cultures' in intercultural ethics." *Eubios Journal of Asian and International Bioethics* 10: 126–129.

Evans, Vyvyan. 2006. "Lexical concepts, cognitive models and meaning-construction." *Cognitive Linguistics* 17.4: 491–534.

Evans, Vyvyan. 2007. *A Glossary of Cognitive Linguistics*. Edinburgh: Edinburgh University Press.

Evans, Vyvyan. 2009. *How Words Mean: Lexical concepts, cognitive models and meaning construction*. Oxford: Oxford University Press.

Fairclough, Norman. 2003. *Analyzing Discourse: Textual analysis for social research*. New York: Routledge.

Fauconnier, Gilles. 1997. *Mappings in Thought and Language*. Cambridge: Cambridge University Press.

Feldman, Martha S. and Brian T. Pentland. 2003. "Reconceptualizing organizational routines as a source of flexibility and change." *Administrative Science Quarterly* 48: 94–118.

Felix-Brasdefer, J. Cesar. 2008. *Politeness in Mexico and the United States: A contrastive study of the realization and perception of refusals*. Amsterdam: John Benjamins.

Fillmore, Charles J. 1968. "The case for case." In *Universals in Linguistic Theory*, Bach Emmon W. and Robert T. Harms (eds), 1–90. New York, NY: Holt, Rinehart and Winston.

Fillmore, Charles J. 1976a. "The need for a frame semantics within linguistics." *Statistical Methods in Linguistics* 12: 5–29.

Fillmore, Charles J. 1976b. "Frame semantics and the nature of language." In *Origins and Evaluation of Language and Speech*, Harnad Steven R., Steklis Horst D. and Jane Lancaster (eds), 2–32. New York: Annals of the New York Academy of Sciences.

Fillmore, Charles J. 1982. "Frame semantics." In *Linguistics in the Morning Calm*, The Linguistic Society of Korea (ed.), 111–137. Seoul: Hanshin.

Fillmore, Charles J. and Beryl T. Atkins. 1992. "Toward a frame-based lexicon: The semantics of RISK and its neighbors." In *Frames, Fields and Contrasts: New essays in semantic and lexical organization*, Lehrer Adrienne and Eva Feder Kittay (eds), 75–102. Hillsdale, NJ: Lawrence Erlbaum.

Finkelstein, Sydney, Hambrick, Donald C., and Cannella, Bert. 2008. *Strategic Leadership: Theory and research on executives, top management teams, and boards*. Oxford: Oxford University Press.

Firbas, Jan. 1965. "A note on transition proper in functional sentence analysis." *Philologica Pragensia* 8: 170–176.

Firth, Alan. 1996. "The discursive accomplishment of normality: On 'lingua franca' English and conversation analysis." *Journal of Pragmatics* 26: 237–259.

Fonagy, Ivan. 1982. *Situation et Signification*. Amsterdam/Philadelphia: John Benjamins.

Frege, Gottlob. 1884/1980. *The Foundations of Arithmetic.* Austin John Langshaw (trans.) (2nd Rev. ed.). Evanston, Illinois: Northwestern University Press.

Fujiwara, Yasuhiro. 2004. "An intercultural pragmatics study on Japanese resistivity and American acceptability in refusals." *Intercultural Communication Studies* 13.2: 75–99.

Gairns, Ruth and Stuart, Redman. 1986. *Working with Words: A guide to teaching and learning vocabulary.* Cambridge: Cambridge University Press.

Garces-Conejos Blitvich, Pilar. 2010a. "Introduction: The status-quo and quo vadis of impoliteness research." *Intercultural Pragmatics* 7.4: 535–559.

Garces-Conejos Blitvich, Pilar. 2010b. "A genre approach to the study of im-politeness." *International Review of Pragmatics* 2.1: 46–94.

Garfinkel, Harold. 1967. *Studies in Ethnomethodology.* Englewood Cliffs, NJ: Prentice-Hall.

Garrett, Merrill F. 1975. "The analysis of sentence production." In *The Psychology of Learning and Motivation*, Bower Gordon H. (ed.), 9: 133–177. New York: Academic Press.

Garrett, Merrill F. 1982. "Production of speech: Observations from normal and pathological language use." In *Normality and Pathology in Cognitive Functions*, Ellis Andrew W. (ed.), 19–76. London: Academic Press.

Garrod, Simon and Martin J. Pickering. 1999. "Issues in language processing." In *Language Processing*, Garrod Simon and Martin J. Pickering (eds), 1–11. Hove, England: Psychology Press.

Gass, Susan M. and Evangeline Marlos, Varonis. 1985. "Miscommunication in native/non-native conversation." *Language in Society* 14.3: 327–343.

Gee, James Paul. 1999. *An Introduction to Discourse Analysis: Theory and method.* New York/London: Routledge.

Geeraerts, Dirk (ed.). 2006. *Cognitive Linguistics: Basic readings.* Berlin/New York: Mouton de Gruyter.

Geis, Michael L. 1995. *Speech Acts and Conversational Interaction.* Cambridge: Cambridge University Press.

Gherardi, Silvia. 2000. "Practice-Based theorizing on learning and knowing in organizations." *Organization* 7.2: 211–223.

Gherardi, Silvia. 2001. "From organizational learning to practice-based knowing." *Human Relations* 54.1: 131–139.

Gibbs, Raymond W. 1996. "What's cognitive about cognitive linguistics." In *Cognitive Linguistics in the Redwoods: The expansion of a new paradigm*, Casad Eugene H. (ed.), 27–55. Berlin/New York: Mouton de Gruyter.

Gibbs, Raymond W. 2001. "Evaluating contemporary models of figurative language." *Metaphor and Symbol* 16.3/4:317–333.

Gibbs, Raymond W. 2002. "A new look at literal meaning in understanding what is said and implicated." *Journal of Pragmatics* 34.4: 457–486.

Giles, Howard and Patricia, Johnson. 1986. "Perceived threat, ethnic commitment, and interethnic language behavior." In *Interethnic Communication: Current research*, Kim Young Yun (ed.), 91–116. Beverly Hills: Sage.

Giora, Rachel. 1997. "Understanding figurative and literal language: The graded salience hypothesis." *Cognitive Linguistics* 8.3: 183–206.

Giora, Rachel. 2003. *On Our Mind: Salience context and figurative language.* New York: Oxford University Press.

Givon, Thomas. 1992. "The grammar of referential coherence as mental processing instructions." *Linguistics* 30.1: 5–56.

Gleitman, Lila and Anna, Papafragou. 2005. "Language and thought." In *The Cambridge Handbook of Thinking and Reasoning*, Holyoak Keith J. and Robert G. Morrison (eds), 633–661. Cambridge: Cambridge University Press.

Goffman, Erving. 1967. *Interaction Ritual: Essays on face-to-face behavior*. Garden City, NY: Anchor Books.

Goffman, Erving. 1974. *Frame Analysis: An essay on the organization of experience*. New York: Harper and Row.

Gonzalez, Andrew. 1987. "Poetic imperialism or indigenous creativity." In *Discourse across Cultures: Strategies in World Englishes*, Smith Larry E. (ed.), 141–156. Englewood Cliffs, NJ: Prentice Hall.

Gonzalez-Lloret, Marta. 2008. "Computer-mediated learning of L2 pragmatics." In *Investigating Pragmatics in Foreign Language Learning, Teaching and Testing*, Soler Eva Alcon and Alicia Martinez-Flor (eds), 114–132. Clevedon, UK: Multilingual Matters.

Gordon, Peter C., Grosz, Barbara J. and Laura A. Gilliom. 1993. "Pronouns, names, and the centering of attention in discourse." *Cognitive Science* 17.3: 311–348.

Granger, Sylviane. 2003. "The international corpus of learner English: A new resource for foreign language learning and teaching and second language acquisition research." *TESOL Quarterly* 37.3: 538–545.

Grice, Herbert Paul. 1957. "Meaning." *The Philosophical Review* 66.3: 377–388.

Grice, Herbert Paul. 1975. "Logic and conversation." In *Syntax and Semantics 3: Speech acts*. Cole Peter and Jerry L. Morgan (eds), 41–58. New York: Academic Press.

Grice, Herbert Paul. 1978. "Further notes on logic and conversation." In *Syntax and Semantics 9: Pragmatics*, Cole Peter (ed.), 113–127. New York: Academic Press.

Grice, Herbert Paul. 1989. *Studies in the Way of Words*. Cambridge, MA: Harvard University Press.

Grosjean, Francois. 1989. "Neurolinguists, beware! The bilingual is not two monolinguals in one person." *Brain and Language* 36.1: 3–15.

Grosz, Barbara J. and Candace L. Sidner. 1986. "Attention, intentions, and the structure of discourse." *Computational Linguistics* 12.3: 175–204.

Grosz, Barbara J., Joshi, Aravind K. and Scott, Weinstein. 1995. "Centering: A framework for modeling the local coherence of discourse." *Computational Linguistics* 21.2: 203–225.

Gudykunst, William B. and Bella, Mody (eds). 2002. *Handbook of International and Intercultural Communication*. Thousand Oaks, CA: Sage.

Gudykunst, William B. and Young Yun, Kim. 1992. *Communicating with Strangers: An approach to intercultural communication*. New York: McGraw-Hill.

Gumperz, John J. 1982. *Discourse Strategies*. Cambridge: Cambridge University Press.

Gumperz, John J. and Celia, Roberts. 1991. "Understanding in intercultural encounters." In *The Pragmatics of Intercultural and International Communication*, Blommaert Jan and Jef Verschueren (eds), 51–90. Amsterdam: John Benjamins.

Gumperz, John J. and Deborah, Tannen. 1979. "Individual and social differences in language use." In *Individual Differences in Language Ability and Language Behavior*,

Fillmore Charles J., Kempler Daniel and William S.-Y. Wang (eds), 305–325. New York: Academic Press.

Gumperz, John J. and Jenny, Cook-Gumperz. 2005. "Making space for bilingual communicative practice." *Intercultural Pragmatics* 2.1:1–24.

Gundel, Jeanette K., Hedberg, Nancy and Ron, Zacharski. 1993. "Cognitive status and the form of referring expressions in discourse." *Language* 69.2:274–307.

Habermas, Jurgen. 1979. *Communication and the Evolution of Society*. Toronto: Beacon Press.

Hale, Ken. 1982. "Preliminary Remarks on Configurationality." *Proceedings of the North Eastern Linguistic Society* 12:86–96.

Hall, Joan Kelly, Cheng, An and Matthew T. Carlson. 2006. "Reconceptualizing multicompetence as a theory of language knowledge." *Applied Linguistics* 27.2: 220–240.

Halliday, Michael Alexander Kirkwood. 1967/1968. "Notes on transitivity and theme in English: Parts 1, 2 and 3." *Journal of Linguistics* 3.1: 37–81, 3.2: 199–244 and 4.2: 179–215.

Halliday, Michael Alexander Kirkwood. 1985. *Introduction to Functional Grammar*. London: Edward Arnold.

Hanks, William F. 1990. *Referential Practice: Language and lived space among the Maya*. Chicago: University of Chicago Press.

Haugh, Michael. 2007. "The discursive challenge to politeness research: An interactional alternative." *Journal of Politeness Research* 3.2: 295–317.

Haugh, Michael. 2008a. "Intention and diverging interpretings of implicature in the 'uncovered meat' sermon." *Intercultural Pragmatics* 5.2: 201–228.

Haugh, Michael. 2008b. "Intention in pragmatics." *Intercultural Pragmatics* 5.2: 99–110.

Haugh, Michael. 2009. "Face and interaction." In *Face, Communication and Social Interaction*, Bargiela-Chiappini Francesca and Michael Haugh (eds), 1–30. London: Equinox.

Haugh, Michael. 2010a. "Doing speaker meaning in interaction." Abstract submitted to *the Conference of the International Pragmatics Association*.

Haugh, Michael. 2010b. "Intercultural impoliteness and the micro-macro issue." In *Pragmatics across Languages and Cultures* (Vol. 7 *Handbook of Pragmatics*), Trosborg Anna (ed.), 139–166. Berlin: Mouton de Gruyter.

Haugh, Michael and Carl, Hinze 2003. "A metalinguistic approach to deconstructing the concepts of 'face' and 'politeness' in Chinese, English and Japanese." *Journal of Pragmatics* 35.10/11: 1581–1611.

Haugh, Michael and Kasia, M. Jaszczolt. 2012. "Speaker intentions and intentionality." In *The Cambridge Handbook of Pragmatics*, Allan Keith and Kasia M. Jaszczolt (eds), 87–112. Cambridge: Cambridge University Press.

Haviland, John B. 1998. "Early pointing gestures in Zincantan." *Journal of Linguistic Anthropology* 8.2: 162–196.

Haviland, Susan E. and Herbert H. Clark. 1974. "What's new? Acquiring new information as a process in comprehension." *Journal of Verbal Learning and Verbal Behavior* 13.5: 512–521.

He, Ziran. 1988. *Yuyongxue Gailun[A Survey of Pragmatics]*. Changsha, China: Hunan Education Press.

Heritage, John. 1984. *Garfinkel and Ethnomethodology*. Cambridge: Polity Press.

Higgins, Christina (ed.). 2007. *A Closer Look at Cultural Differences: Interculturality' in talk-in-interaction*. Special issue, Vol. 17, Pragmatics. International Pragmatics Association.

Hinnenkamp, Volker. 1991. "Talking a person into interethnic distinction: A discourse analytic case study." In *The Pragmatics of Intercultural and International Communication*, Blommaert Jan and Jef Verschueren (eds), 91–110. Amsterdam/Philadelphia: John Benjamins.

Hinnenkamp, Volker. 1995. "Intercultural communication." In *Handbook of Pragmatics*, Verschueren Jef, Ostman Jan-Ola, Blommaert Jan and Chris Bulcaen (eds). 1–20. Amsterdam: John Benjamins.

Ho, Caroline Mei Lin. 2004. "Computer-mediated communication: Practice, project and purposes." *Journal of Teaching English with Technology* Vol. 4, No. 1. Retrieved September 10, 2010, from http://www.tewtjournal.org/VOL%204/ISSUE%201/02_COMPUTERMEDIATED.pdf.

Holland, Dorothy and Naomi, Quinn (eds). 1987. *Cultural Models in Language and Thought*. Cambridge: Cambridge University Press.

Holmes, Janet, Marra, Meredith and Stephanie, Schnurr. 2008. "Impoliteness and ethnicity: Maori and Pakeha discourses in New Zealand workplaces." *Journal of Politeness Research* 4.2: 193–220.

Holtgraves, Thomas M. 2002. *Language as Social Action: Social psychology and language use*. Mahwah, NJ: Erlbaum.

Hong, Minha. 2008. "'Where the bloody hell are you?': Bloody hell and (im)politeness in Australian English." *Griffith Working Papers in Pragmatics and Intercultural Communication* 1.1: 33–39

Horn, Laurence R. 2004. "Implicature." In *The Handbook of Pragmatics*, Horn Laurence R. and Gregory Ward (eds), 3–28. Oxford: Blackwell.

Horn, Laurence R. 2005. "More issues in neo- and post-Gricean pragmatics: A response to Robyn Carston's response." *Intercultural Pragmatics* 3.1: 81–95.

Horn, Laurence R. 2006. "The border wars: A neo-Gricean perspective." In *Current Research in the Semantics/Pragmatics Interface: Where semantics meets pragmatics*, Heusinger Klaus Von and Ken Turner (eds), 21–48. Oxford: Elsevier.

Horn, Laurence R. 2007. "Neo-Gricean pragmatics: A Manichaean manifesto." In *Pragmatics*, Burton-Roberts Noel (ed.), 158–183. Basingstoke: Palgrave.

Horn, Laurence R. and Gregory, Ward (eds). 2004. *The Handbook of Pragmatics*. Oxford: Blackwell.

House, Juliane. 2000. "Understanding misunderstanding: A pragmatic-discourse approach to analysing mismanaged rapport in talk across cultures." In *Culturally Speaking: Managing rapport through talk across cultures*, Spencer-Oatey Helen (ed.), 146–164. London: Continuum.

House, Juliane. 2002. "Developing pragmatic competence in English as a lingua franca." In *Lingua Franca Communication*, Knapp Karlfried and Christiane Meierkord (eds), 245–267. Frankfurt am Main: Peter Lang.

House, Juliane. 2003. "Misunderstanding in intercultural university encounters." In *Misunderstanding in Social Life: Discourse approaches to problematic talk*, House Juliane, Kasper Gabriele and Steven Ross (eds), 22–56. London: Longman.

House, Juliane. 2008. "(Im)politeness in English as a Lingua franca discourse." In *Standards and Norms in the English Language*, Locher Miriam A. and Jurg Strassler (eds), 351–366. Berlin/New York: Mouton de Gruyter.

Howarth, Peter. 1998. "Phraseology and second language proficiency." *Applied Linguistics* 19.1: 24–44.

Hu, Jianhua and Haihua, Pan. 2001. "Processing local coherence of discourse in centering theory." In *Language, Information and Computation*, T'sou Benjamin K., Kwong Olivia O. Y. and Tom B. Y. Lai, 139–150. Proceedings of *The 15th Pacific Asia Conference on Information Systems*. Hong Kong: City University of Hong Kong.

Hudson, Richard. 1984. *Word Grammar*. Oxford: Blackwell.

Hull, Clark Leonard. 1943. *Principles of Behavior: An introduction to behavior theory*. New York: Appleton-Century-Crofts.

Hutchby, Ian. 2008. "Participants' orientations to interruptions, rudeness and other impolite acts in talk-in-interaction." *Journal of Politeness Research* 4.2: 221–241.

Hymes, Dell H. 1962. "The ethnography of speaking." In *Anthropology and Human Behavior*, Gladwin, Thomas and William C. Sturtevant (eds), 13–53. Washington: The Anthropology Society of Washington.

Hymes, Dell H. 1968. "The ethnography of speaking." In *Readings in the Sociology of Language*, Joshua A. Fishman (ed.), 99–138. The Hague/Paris: Mouton de Gruyter.

Hymes, Dell H. 1974. *Foundations in Sociolinguistics: An enthnographic approach*. Pennsylvania: University of Pennsylvania Press.

Hymes, Dell H. 1996. *Ethnography, Linguistics, Narrative Inequality: Toward an understanding of voice*. London: Taylor and Francis.

Irvine, Judith T. and Susan, Gal. 2000. "Language ideology and linguistic differentiation." In *Regimes of Language: Ideologies, polities, and identities*, Kroskrity Paul V. (ed.), 35–83. Santa Fe: School of American Research Press.

Jackendoff, Ray. 2002. *Foundations of Language: Brain, meaning, grammar, evolution*. Oxford: Oxford University Press.

Jakobson, Roman. 1959. "On linguistic aspects of translation." In *On translation*, Brower Reuben A. (ed.), 232–239. Cambridge, MA: Harvard University Press.

Jary, Mark. 1998. "Relevance theory and the communication of politeness." *Journal of Pragmatics* 30.1: 1–19.

Jaszczolt, Katarzyna M. 2005. *Default Semantics: Foundations of a compositional theory of acts of communication*. Oxford: Oxford University Press.

Jaszczolt, Katarzyna M. 2006. "Meaning merger: Pragmatic inference, defaults, and compositionality." *Intercultural Pragmatics* 3.2: 195–212.

Jaszczolt, Katarzyna M. 2009. "Cancellability and the primary/secondary meaning distinction." *Intercultural Pragmatics* 6: 259–289.

Jaszczolt, Katarzyna M. and Keith, Allan (eds). 2011. *Salience and Defaults in Utterance Processing*. Berlin/New York: Mouton de Gruyter.

Jay, Timothy and Kristin, Janschewitz. 2008. "The pragmatics of swearing." *Journal of Politeness Research* 4: 267–288.

Jenkins, Jennifer. 2000. *The Phonology of English as an International Language*. Oxford: Oxford University Press.

Jenkins, Jennifer. 2006. "Current perspectives on teaching world Englishes and English as a lingua franca." *TESOL Quarterly* 40.1: 157–181.

Jiang, Nan. 2000. "Lexical representation and development in a second language." *Applied Linguistics* 21.1: 47–77.

Joas, Hans. 1996. *The Creativity of Action*. Chicago: The University of Chicago Press.

Johnson-Laird, Philip N. 1983. *Mental Models*. Cambridge, MA: Harvard University Press.

Jones, James W. 1989. "Personality and epistemology: Cognitive social learning theory as a philosophy of science." *Zygon* 24.1: 23–38.

Jucker, Andreas H, Schreier, Daniel and Marianne, Hundt (eds). 2009. *Corpora: Pragmatics and discourse*. New York: Rodopi.

Kasher, Asa. 1991. "Pragmatics and Chomsky's research program." In *Chomskyan Turn*, Kasher Asa (ed.), 122–149. Oxford: Basil Blackwell.

Kasher, Asa (ed.). 1998. *Pragmatics: Critical concepts*. London/New York: Routledge.

Kasper, Gabriele. 1992. "Pragmatic transfer." *Second Language Research* 8.3: 203–231.

Kasper, Gabriele. 1998. "Interlanguage pragmatics." In *Learning and Teaching Foreign Languages: Perspectives in research and scholarship*, Byrnes Heidi (ed.), 183–208. NY: Modern Language Association.

Kasper, Gabriele. 2001. "Four perspectives on L2 pragmatic development." *Applied Linguistics* 22.4: 502–530.

Kasper, Gabriele. 2004. "Speech acts in (inter)action: Repeated question." *Intercultural Pragmatics* 1.1: 125–135.

Kasper, Gabriele and Kenneth R. Rose. 2001. "Pragmatics in language teaching." In *Pragmatics in Language Teaching*, Rose Kenneth R. and Gabriele Kasper (eds), 1–10. Cambridge: Cambridge University Press.

Kasper, Gabriele and Merete, Dahl. 1991. "Research methods in interlanguage pragmatics." *Studies of Second Language Acquisition* 13.2: 215–247.

Kasper, Gabriele and Richard, Schmidt. 1996. "Developmental issues in interlanguage pragmatics." *Studies of Second Language Acquisition* 18: 149–169.

Kasper, Gabriele and Shoshana, Blum-Kulka. 1993. *Interlanguage Pragmatics*. Oxford: Oxford University Press.

Katz, Albert. 2005. "Discourse and sociocultural factors in understanding nonliteral language." In *Figurative Language Comprehension: Social and cultural influences*, Colston Herbert L. and Albert N. Katz (eds), 183–208. Mahwah, NJ: Lawrence Erlbaum.

Katz, Jerrold J. 1977. *Propositional Structure and Illocutionary Force*. New York: Crowell.

Kecskes, Istvan. 1997. "A cognitive-pragmatic approach to situation-bound utterances." Paper Presented to Chicago Linguistics Society, March 7, 1997, University of Chicago.

Kecskes, Istvan. 1998. "The state of L1 knowledge in foreign language learners." *Word* 49: 321–341.

Kecskes, Istvan. 2000. "A cognitive-pragmatic approach to situation-bound utterances." *Journal of Pragmatics* 32.6: 605–625.

Kecskes, Istvan. 2001. "The 'graded salience hypothesis' in second language acquisition." In *Applied Cognitive Linguistics*, Putz Martin, Niemeier Susanne and Rene Dirven (eds), 249–271. Berlin/New York: Mouton de Gruyter.

Kecskes, Istvan. 2003. *Situation-Bound Utterances in L1 and L2*. Berlin/New York: Mouton de Gruyter.

Kecskes, Istvan. 2004a. "Lexical merging, conceptual blending and cultural crossing." *Intercultural Pragmatics* 1.1: 1–21.

Kecskes, Istvan. 2004b. "The role of salience in processing pragmatic units." *Acta Linguistica Hungarica* 51.3/4: 309–324.

Kecskes, Istvan. 2006. "On my mind: Thoughts about salience, context, and figurative language from a second language perspective." *Second Language Research* 22.2: 219–237.

Kecskes, Istvan. 2007a. "Formulaic language in English lingua franca." In *Explorations in Pragmatics: Linguistic, cognitive and intercultural aspects*, Kecskes Istvan and Laurence R. Horn (eds), 191–219. Berlin/New York: Mouton de Gruyter.

Kecskes, Istvan. 2007b. "Synergic concepts in the bilingual mind." In *Cognitive Aspects of Bilingualism*, Kecskes Istvan and Liliana Albertazzi (eds), 29–61. Berlin/New York: Springer.

Kecskes, Istvan. 2008. "Dueling contexts: A dynamic model of meaning." *Journal of Pragmatic* 40.3: 385–406.

Kecskes, Istvan. 2009. "Dual and multilanguage systems." *International Journal of Multilingualism* 1–19.

Kecskes, Istvan. 2010a. "The paradox of communication: A socio-cognitive approach." *Pragmatics and Society* 1.1: 50–73.

Kecskes, Istvan. 2010b. "Formulaic language in English lingua franca." In *Metaphor and Figurative Language: Critical concepts in linguistics*, Hanks Patrick and Rachel Giora (eds). Oxford/New York: Routledge. (reprint of 2007 paper).

Kecskes, Istvan. 2010c. "Situation-Bound utterances as pragmatic acts." *Journal of Pragmatics* 42.11: 2889–2897.

Kecskes, Istvan. 2011. "Understanding the role of context in language use." In *Pragmatics and Context*, Macaulay Marcia and Garces-Conejos Blitvich Pilar (eds), 2–34. Toronto, CA: Antares.

Kecskes, Istvan. 2012. "Is there anyone out there who really is interested in the speaker?" *Language and Dialogue* 2.2: 283–297.

Kecskes, Istvan. 2013. "Why do we say what we say the way we say it." *Journal of Pragmatics.* Vol. 48. No. 1: 71–84.

Kecskes, Istvan. Forthcoming. "The evaluative function of situation-bound utterances in intercultural interaction." In *Evaluation in Context*, Thompson Geoff and Laura Alba-Juez (eds). Amsterdam/Philadelphia: John Benjamins.

Kecskes, Istvan and Fenghui, Zhang. 2009. "Activating, seeking and creating common ground: A socio-cognitive approach." *Pragmatics and Cognition* 17.2: 331–355.

Kecskes, Istvan and Isabel M. Cuenca. 2005. "Lexical choice as a reflection of conceptual fluency." *International Journal of Bilingualism* 9.1: 49–69.

Kecskes, Istvan and Jacob, Mey (eds). 2008. *Intention, Common Ground and the Egocentric Speaker-Hear*. Berlin/New York: Mouton de Gruyter.

Kecskes, Istvan and Tunde, Papp. 2000. *Foreign Language and Mother Tongue*. Mahwah, NJ: Lawrence Erlabum.

Keevallik, Leelo. 2010. "Minimal answers to yes/no questions in the service of sequence organization." *Discourse Studies* 12.3: 283–309.

Keysar, Boaz. 2007. "Communication and miscommunication: The role of egocentric processes." *Intercultural Pragmatics* 4.1: 71–84.

Keysar, Boaz and Anne S. Henly. 2002. "Speakers' overestimation of their effectiveness." *Psychological Science* 13.3: 207–212.

Keysar, Boaz and Bridget, Bly. 1995. "Intuitions of the transparency of idioms: Can one keep a secret by spilling the beans?" *Journal of Memory and Language* 34: 89–109.

Kidwell, Mardi. 2000. "Common ground in cross-cultural communication: Sequential and institutional contexts in front desk service encounters." *Issues in Applied Linguistics* 11.1: 17–37.

Kiefer, Ferenc. 1985. "How to account for situational meaning?" *Quaderni di Semantica.* 2: 288–295.

Kiefer, Ferenc. 1995. "Situational utterances (manuscript)." Keynote presented to *the 5th International Pragmatics Conference*, Brighton, UK.

Kiefer, Ferenc. 1997. "Presidential address: Modality and pragmatics." *Folia Linguistica* 31.3/4: 241–253.

Kienpointner, Manfred. 1997. "Varieties of rudeness: Types and functions of impolite utterances." *Functions of Language* 4.2: 251–287.

King, Jeffrey C. and Jason, Stanley. 2005. "Semantics, pragmatics, and the role of semantic content." In *Semantics versus Pragmatics*, Szabo Zoltan Gendler (ed.), 111–164. Oxford: Oxford University Press.

King, Tracy Holloway. 1995. *Configuring Topic and Focus in Russian.* Stanford, CA: CSLI Publications.

Kingsbury, Paul, Strassel, Stephanie, McLemore, Cynthia and Robert, McLntyre. 1997. *CALLHOME American English Transcripts*, LDC97T14. Philadelphia: Linguistic Data Consortium.

Knapp, Karlfried and Annelie, Knapp-Potthoff. 1987. "Instead of an introduction: Conceptual issues in analyzing intercultural communication." In *Analyzing Intercultural Communication*, Knapp Karfried, Enninger Werner and Annelie Knapp-Potthoff (eds), 1–13. Amsterdam: Mouton de Gruyter.

Knight, Dawn and Svenja, Adolphs. 2008. "Multi-Modal corpus pragmatics: The case of active listenership." In *Pragmatics and Corpus Linguistics*, Romero-Trillo Jesus (ed.), 175–190. Berlin: Mouton de Gruyter.

Koole, Tom and Jan D. ten Thije. 1994. *The Construction of Intercultural Discourse: Team discussions of educational advisers.* Amsterdam/Atlanta: RODOPI.

Koole, Tom and Jan D. ten Thije. 2001. "The reconstruction of intercultural discourse: Methodological considerations." *Journal of Pragmatics* 33: 571–589.

Koschmann, Timothy and Curtis D. LeBaron. 2003. "Reconsidering common ground: Examining Clark's Contribution Theory in the OR." In *Proceedings of the Eighth European Conference on Computer-Supported Cooperative Work*, Kuutti Kari, Karsten Eija Helena, Fitzpatrick Geraldine, Dourish Paul and Kjeld Schmidt (eds), 81–98. Dordrecht/Boston/ London: Kluwer.

Kroll, Judith and Erika, Stewart. 1994. "Category interference in translation and picture naming: Evidence for asymmetric connections between bilingual memory representations." *Journal of Memory and Language* 33: 149–174.

Kronenfeld, David B. 2008. "Cultural models." *Intercultural Pragmatics* 5.1:67–74.

Lachernicht, Lance Gary. 1980. "Aggravating language: A study of abusive and insulting language." *International Journal of Human Communication* 13.4: 607–688.

Lakoff, George. 1987. *Women, Fire, and Dangerous Things: What categories reveal about the mind.* Chicago: University of Chicago Press.

Lakoff, George and Mark, Johnson. 1980. *Metaphors We Live By.* Chicago: University of Chicago Press.

Landragin, Frederic, Bellalem, Nadia and Laurent, Romary. 2001. "Visual salience and perceptual grouping in multimodal interactivity." Proceedings of *the First International*

Workshop on Information Presentation and Natural Multimodal Dialogue (IPNMD), Verona, Italy.

Langacker, Ronald W. 1987. *Foundations of Cognitive Grammar: Theoretical prerequisites*, Vol. I. Stanford: Stanford University Press.

LaPolla, Randy J. 2003. "Why languages differ: Variation in the conventionalization of constraints on inference." *Language Variation: Papers on variation and change in the Sinosphere and in the Indosphere in honour of James A. Matisoff* (Pacific Linguistics), David Bradley, Randy LaPolla, Boyd Michailovsky, and Graham Thurgood (eds), 113–144. Canberra: Australian National University.

Lave, Jean and Etienne, Wenger. 1991. *Situated Learning: Legitimate peripheral participation*. Cambridge: Cambridge University Press.

Lebra, Takie Sugiyama. 1974. "Reciprocity and the asymmetric principle: An analytical reappraisal of the Japanese concept of on." In *Japanese Culture and Behavior: Selected readings*, Lebra Takie Sugiyama and William P. Lebra (eds), 192–207. Honolulu: University of Hawaii Press.

Lee, Benny P. H. 2001. "Mutual knowledge, background knowledge and shared beliefs: Their roles in establishing common ground." *Journal of Pragmatics* 33.1: 21–44.

Leech, Geoffrey. 1983. *Principles of Pragmatics*. London: Longman.

Leibniz, Gottfried Wilhelm. 1976/1679. *Philosophical Papers and Letters*. A selection translated and edited, with an introduction by Leroy E. Loemker (2nd ed.). Dordrecht, Holland/Boston: D. Reidel.

Leung, Santoi. 2001. "Language socialization: Themes and advances in research." *Working Papers in TESOL and Applied Linguistics* 1.1: 1–18.

Levelt, Willem J. M. 1989. *Speaking: From intention to articulation*. Cambridge, MA: MIT Press.

Levinson, Stephen C. 1983. *Pragmatics*. Cambridge: Cambridge University Press.

Levinson, Stephen C. 1997. "Contextualizing 'contextualization cues'." In *Discussing Communication Analysis 1: John J. Gumperz*, Eerdmans Susan L., Prevignano Carol L. and Paul J. Thibault (eds.), 24–30. Lausanne: Beta Press.

Levinson, Stephen C. 2000. *Presumptive Meanings: The theory of generalized conversational implicature*. Cambridge, MA: MIT Press.

Levinson, Stephen C. 2003. "Language and mind: Let's get the issues straight!" In *Language in Mind: Advances in the study of language and cognition*, Gentner Dedre and Susan Goldin-Meadow (eds), 25–46. Cambridge, MA: MIT Press.

Levinson, Stephen C. 2006a. "Cognition at the heart of human interaction." *Discourse Studies* 8.1: 85–93.

Levinson, Stephen C. 2006b. "On the human 'interaction engine.'" In *Roots of Human Sociality: Culture, cognition and interaction*, Enfield Nicholas J. and Stephen C. Levinson (eds), 39–69. Oxford: Berg.

Levinthal, Daniel and Claus, Rerup. 2006. "Crossing an apparent chasm: Bridging mindful and less-mindful perspectives on organizational learning." *Organization Science* 17.4: 502–513.

Li, Charles N. and Sandra A. Thompson. 1976. "Subject and topic: A new typology of language." In *Subject and Topic*, Li Charles N. (ed.), 457–489. New York: Academic Press.

Li Duanduan. 1998. "Expressing needs and wants in a second language: An ethnographic study of Chinese immigrant women's requesting behavior." PhD Dissertation. Columbia University.

Li, Duanduan. 2008. "Pragmatic Socialization." In *Language Socialization: Encyclopedia of language and education*, Duff Patricia A. and Nancy H. Hornberger (eds), 8: 71–83. New York: Springer.

Li, Han Z., Yum, Young-ok, Yates, Robin, Aguilera, Laura, Mao, Ying and Yue, Zheng. 2005. "Interruption and involvement in discourse: Can intercultural interlocutors be trained?" *Journal of Intercultural Communication Research* 34.4: 233–254.

Li, Peggy and Lila, Gleitman. 2002. "Turning the tables: Language and spatial reasoning." *Cognition* 83.3: 265–294.

Linell, Per. 1996. *Approaching Dialogue: Talk and interaction in dialogical perspectives.* (Arbetsrapporter fran Tema K., 1996: 7). Linkoping: Department of Communication Studies.

Liu, Aijuan. 2010. "On pragmatic 'borrowing transfer': Evidence from Chinese EFL learner's compliment response behavior." *Chinese Journal of Applied Linguistics* 33.4: 26–44.

Locher, Miriam A. 2004. *Power and Politeness in Action: Disagreement in oral communication.* Berlin: Mouton de Gruyter.

Locher, Miriam A. and Richard James, Watts. 2005. "Politeness theory and relational work." *Journal of Politeness Research* 1.1: 9–33.

Locher, Miriam A. and Richard James, Watts. 2008. "Relational work and impoliteness: Negotiating norms of linguistic behavior." In *Impoliteness in Language: Studies on its interplay with power in theory and practice*, Bousfield Derek and Miriam A. Locher (eds), 77–99. Berlin/New York: Mouton de Gruyter.

Lu, Luo. 2001. "Understanding happiness: A look into the Chinese folk psychology." *Journal of Happiness Studies* 2: 407–432.

Ludi, Georges. 2006. "Multilingual repertoires and the consequences for linguistic theory." In *Beyond Misunderstanding*, Buhrig Kristin and Ten Thije Jan D. (eds), 11–42. Amsterdam/Philadelphia: John Benjamins.

Lupyan, Gary and Michael J. Spivey. 2010. "Redundant spoken labels facilitate perception of multiple items." *Attention, Perception and Psychophysics* 72.8: 2236–2253.

MacWhinney, Brian. 1977. "Starting points." *Language* 53.1: 152–168.

Maeshiba, Naoko, Yoshinaga, Naoko, Kasper, Gabriele and Steven, Ross. 1996. "Transfer and proficiency in interlanguage apologizing." In *Speech Acts across Cultures: Challenges to communication in a second language* (Studies on Language Acquisition Vol. 11), Gass Susan M. and Joyce Neu (eds), 155–187. Berlin: Mouton de Gruyter.

Malinowski, Bronislaw. 1923. "The problem of meaning in primitive languages." In *The Meaning of Meaning: A study of influence of language upon thought and of the science of symbolism*, Ogden Charles K. and Ian A. Richards (eds), 451–510. New York: Harcourt, Brace and World.

Mandelbaum, Jenny and Anita, Pomerantz. 1990. "What drives social action?" In *Understanding Face-to-Face Interaction: Issues linking goals and discourse*, Tracy Karen (ed.), 151–166. Hillsdale, NJ: Erlbaum.

Markee, Numa P. 2000. *Conversation Analysis.* Mahwah, NJ: Lawrence Erlbaum.

Markee, Numa P. and Gabriele, Kasper. 2004. "Classroom talks: An introduction." *Modern Language Journal* 88.4: 491–500.

Marmaridou, Sophia. 2000. *Pragmatic Meaning and Cognition*. Amsterdam: John Benjamins.

Mathesius, Vilem. 1929. "Functional linguistics." In *Praguiana*, Vachek Josef (ed.), 121–142. Amsterdam: John Benjamins.

Matisoff, James A. 1979. *Psycho-Ostensive Expressions in Yiddish*. Philadelphia: ISHI Publications.

Mazur, Joan M. 2004. "Conversation analysis for educational technologists: Theoretical and methodological issues for researching the structures, processes, and meaning of on-line talk." In *Handbook of Research on Educational Communications and Technology*, Jonassen David H. (ed.), 1073–1098. New York: McMillian.

McEnery, Tony and Andrew, Wilson. 1996. *Corpus Linguistics*. Edinburgh: Edinburgh University Press.

Meeuwis, Michael. 1994. "Leniency and testiness in intercultural communication: Remarks on ideology and context in interactional sociolinguistics." *Pragmatics* 4.3: 391–408.

Meierkord, Christiane. 1998. "Lingua franca English: Characteristics of successful non-native-/ non-native-speaker discourse." *Erfurt Electronic Studies in English* (EESE), 7/98. Retrieved September 30, 2008, from http://webdoc.sub.gwdg.de/edoc/ia/eese/eese.html.

Meierkord, Christiane. 2000. "Interpreting successful lingua franca interaction: An analysis of non-native-/non-native small talk conversations in English." *Linguistik Online* 5, 01/00. Retrieved June 14, 2010, from http://www.linguistik-online.com/1_00/MEIERKOR.HTM..

Mey, Jacob L. 2001. *Pragmatics: An introduction* (2nd ed.). Oxford: Blackwell.

Mey, Jacob L. 2006. "Pragmatic acts." In *Encyclopedia of Language and Linguistics*, Brown Keith (eds) (2nd ed.), 12: 5–11. London: Elsevier.

Mey, Jacob L. 2013. "Across the abyss: The pragmatics-semantics interface revisited." *Intercultural Pragmatics*. 10.3: 487–494.

Miller, Jim and Regina, Weinert. 1998. *Spontaneous Spoken Language: Syntax and discourse*. Oxford: Clarendon Press.

Millikan, Ruth Garrett. 1998. "A common structure for concepts of individuals, stuffs, and real kinds: More mama, more milk, and more mouse." *Behavioral and Brain Sciences* 21.1: 55–100.

Mills, Sara. 2003. *Gender and Politeness*. Cambridge: Cambridge University Press.

Mills, Sara. 2005. "Gender and impoliteness." *Journal of Politeness Research* 1.2: 263–280.

Mills, Sara. 2009. "Impoliteness at a cultural level." *Journal of Pragmatics* 41:1047–1060.

Minsky, Marvin. 1975. "A framework for representing knowledge." In *The Psychology of Computer Vision*, Winston Patrick Henry (ed.), 211–277. New York: McGraw-Hill.

Mitchell, Rosamond and Florence Myles. 1998. *Second Language Learning Theories*. London: Arnold.

Moeschler, Jacques. 2004. "Intercultural pragmatics: A cognitive approach." *Intercultural Pragmatics* 1.1: 49–70.

Moeschler Jacques. 2010. "Is pragmatics of discourse possible?," In *Perspectives on Language Use and Pragmatics*, Capone Alessandro (ed.), 217–241. Munich: Lincom Europa.

Morgan, Jerry L. 1978. "Two types of convention in indirect speech acts." In *Pragmatics (Syntax and Semantics 9)*, Cole Peter (ed.), 261–280. New York: Academic Press.

Mori, Junko. 2003. "The construction of interculturality: A study of initial encounters between American and Japanese students." *Research on Language and Social Interaction* 36.2: 143–184.

Morris, Charles W. 1938. "Foundation of the theory of signs." In *International Encyclopedia of Unified Science*, Vol. 2, No. 1. Chicago: University of Chicago Press.

Morris, William. 1976. *The American Heritage Dictionary of the English Language.* New York: Houghton Mifflin.

Mugford, Gerrard. 2011. "That's not very polite! Discursive struggle and situated politeness in the Mexican English-language classroom." In *Situated Politeness*, Davies Bethan L., Haugh Michael and Andrew John Merrison (eds), 53–72. London: Continuum.

Mugford, Gerrard. 2012. "I wouldn't say that if were you: Fact-to-face with foreign-language impoliteness." *Journal of Politeness Research* 8.3: 195–221.

Munnich, Edward and Barbara, Landau. 2003. "The effects of spatial language on spatial representation: Setting some boundaries." In *Language in Mind: Advances in the study of language and thought*, Gentner Dedre and Susan Goldin-Meadow (eds), 113–155. Cambridge, MA: MIT Press.

Myachykov, Andriy. 2007. "Integrating perceptual, semantic and syntactic information in sentence production." PhD Dissertation. University of Glasgow.

Myachykov, Andriy and Michael I. Posner. 2005. "Attention in language." In *Neurobiology of Attention*, Itti Laurent, Rees Geraint and John K. Tsotsos (eds), 324–329. New York: Academic Press.

Myers, Gail E. and Michele Tolela, Myers. 1998. *The Dynamics of Human Communications.* New York, NY: McGraw Hill.

Nattinger, James R. and Jeanette S. DeCarrico. 1989. "Lexical phrases, speech acts and teaching conversation." In *Vocabulary Acquisition*, AILA review 6, Nation Paul and Rron Carter (eds), 118–139. Amsterdam, NL: Association Interantionale de Linguistique Appliquee.

Nattinger, James R. and Jeanette S. DeCarrico. 1992. *Lexical Phrases and Language Teaching.* New York: Oxford University Press.

Neuliep, James W. 2006. "Editorial welcome." *Journal of Intercultural Communication Research* 35.1: 1–2.

Nishida, Hiroko. 1999. "Cultural schema theory." In *Theorizing about Intercultural Communication*, Gudykunst William B. (ed.), 401–418. Thousand Oaks, CA: Sage.

Nishizaka, Aug. 1995. "The interactive constitution of interculturality: How to be a Japanese with words." *Human Studies* 18: 301–326.

Norton, William S. 2008. "A memory-based approach to common ground and audience design." In *Intention, Common Ground and the Egocentric Speaker-Hearer*, Kecskes Istvan and Jacob Mey (eds), 189–222. Berlin/New York: Mouton de Gruyter.

Nuyts, Jan. 2000. "Intentionality." In *Handbook of Pragmatics*, Verschueren Jef, Ostman Jan-Ola, Blommaert Jan and Chris Bulcaen (eds), 1–17. Amsterdam: John Benjamins.

Ocasio, William. 1997. "Towards an attention-based view of the firm." *Strategic Management Journal* 18, 187–206.

Ochs, Elinor. 1986. "Introduction." In *Language Socialization across Cultures*, Schieffelin Bambi B. and Elinor Ochs (eds), 1–13. New York: Cambridge University Press.

Ochs, Elinor. 1988. *Cultural and Language Development: Language acquisition and language socialization in a Samoan village*. Great Britain: Cambridge University Press.

Ochs, Elinor. 1996. "Linguistic resources for socializing humanity." In *Rethinking Linguistic Relativity*, Gumperz John J. and Stephen C. Levinson (eds), 407–437. New York: Cambridge University Press.

Ochs, Elinor and Bambi B. Schieffelin. 1984. "Language acquisition and socialization: Three developmental stories and their implications." In *Culture Theory: Essays on mind, self, and emotion*, Shweder Richard A. and Robert A. LeVine (eds), 276–320. Cambridge: Cambridge University Press.

O'Keeffe, Anne, Clancy, Brian and Svenja, Adolphs. 2011. *Introducing Pragmatics in Use*. New York: Routledge.

Ortactepe, Deniz. 2011. "Second language socialization, professional development of teachers, social identity in ESL/EFL." PhD Dissertation. State University of New York, Albany.

Ortactepe, Deniz. 2012. *The Development of Conceptual Socialization in International Students: A language socialization perspective on conceptual fluency and social identity (Advances in Pragmatics and Discourse Analysis)*. Cambridge: Cambridge Scholars Publishing.

Osgood, Charles E. and J. Kathryn, Bock. 1977. "Salience and sentencing: Some production principles." In *Sentence Production: Developments in research and theory*, Rosenberg Sheldon (ed.), 89–140. New York: Lawrence Erlbaum.

Ostman, Jan-Ola. 1988. "Adaption, variability, and effect." *IPrA Working Document* 3: 5–40.

Overstreet, Maryann and George, Yule. 2001. "Formulaic disclaimers." *Journal of Pragmatics* 33.1: 45–60.

Park, Jae-Eun. 2007. "Co-construction of nonnative speaker identity in cross-cultural interaction." *Applied Linguistics* 28.3: 339–360.

Parkin, David. 1980. "The creativity of abuse." *Man* (N.S.) 15: 45–64.

Pattabhiraman, Thiyagarajasarma. 1993. "Aspects of salience in natural language generation." PhD Dissertation. Simon Fraser University.

Pavlenko, Aneta. 2000. "L2 influence on L1 in late bilingualism." *Issues in Applied Linguistics* 11/2: 175–205.

Pavlidou, Theodossia. 1994. "Contrasting German-Greek politeness and the consequences." *Journal of Pragmatics* 21.5: 487–511.

Pavlidou, Theodossia. 1998. "Greek and German telephone closings: Patterns of confirmation and agreement." *Pragmatics* 8.1: 79–94.

Pawley, Andrew. 2007. "Developments in the study of formulaic language since 1970: A personal view." In *Phraseology and Culture in English*, Skandera Paul (ed.), 3–45. Berlin: Mouton de Gruyter.

Pawley, Andrew and Frances Hodgetts, Syder. 1983. "Two puzzles for linguistic theory: Nativelike selection and nativelike fluency." *Language and Communication* 5.5: 191–226.

Peleg, Orna, Giora, Rachel and Ofer, Fein. 2001. "Salience and context effects: Two are better than one." *Metaphor and Symbol* 16.3/4: 173–192.

Pelekanos, Vassilis and Konstantinos, Moutoussis. 2011. "The effect of language on visual contrast sensitivity." *Perception* 40.12: 1402–1412.

Philip, Gill. 2005. "Figurative language and the advanced learner." *Research News: The Newsletter of the IATEFL Research SIG* 16: 16–20.

Pinker, Steven. 1994. *The Language Instinct: How the mind creates language.* New York: Harper Collins.

Platt, John. 1989. "Some types of communicative strategies across cultures: Sense and sensitivity." In *English across Cultures, Cultures across English: A reader in cross-cultural communication*, Garcia Ofelia and Ricardo Otheguy (eds), 13–31. Berlin: Mouton de Gruyter.

Poole, Deborah. 1994. "Language socialization in the second language classroom." *Language Learning* 42.4: 593–616.

Prat-Sala, Merce and Holly P. Branigan. 2000. "Discourse constraints on syntactic processing in language production: A cross-linguistic study in English and Spanish." *Journal of Memory and Language* 42.2: 168–182.

Prodromou, Luke. 2008. *English as a Lingua Franca: A corpus based analysis.* London: Continuum.

Puig, Margarida Bassols. 2003. "Pragmatics and discourse analysis." *Noves SL Revista de Sociolinguistica*. Retrieved May 11, 2012, from http://www6.gencat.net/llengcat/noves/hm03hivern/docs/a_bassols.pdf.

Rampton, Ben. 1995. *Crossing: Language and ethnicity among adolescents.* New York: Longman.

Rampton, Ben. 1996. "Language crossing and ethnicity in sociolinguistics." Paper presented at *the New Ways of Analyzing Variation Conference (NWAV XXV)*. Las Vegas.

Rapaport, William J. 2003. "What did you mean by that? Misunderstanding, negotiation, and syntactic semantics." *Minds and Machines* 13.3: 397–427.

Recanati, Francois. 2001. "What is said." *Synthese* 128: 75–91.

Rendle-Short, Johanna. 2006. *The Academic Presentation: Situated talk in action.* Aldershot, UK/Burlington, VT: Ashgate.

Ringberg, Torsten and Markus, Reihlen. 2008. "Towards a socio-cognitive approach to knowledge transfer." *Journal of Management Studies* 45.5: 912–935.

Rizzolatti, Giacomo and Laila, Craighero. 2004. "The mirror-neuron system." *Annual Review of Neuroscience* 27: 169–192.

Romero-Trillo, Jesus (ed.). 2008. *Pragmatics and Corpus Linguistics: A mutualistic entente.* Berlin: Mouton de Gruyter.

Romiszowski, Alexander and Robin, Mason. 1996. "Computer-mediated communication." In *Handbook of Research for Educational Communications and Technology*, Jonassen Dvaid H. (ed.), 438–456. New York: Simon and Schuster Macmillan.

Rommetveit, Ragnar. 1992. "Outlines of a dialogically based social-cognitive approach to human cognition and communication." In *The Dialogical Alternative: Towards a theory of language and mind*, Wold Astri Heen (ed.), 19–44. Oslo: Scandinavian University Press.

Rosch, Eleanor. 1977. "Human categorization." In *Advances in Cross-Cultural Psychology*, Warren Neil (ed.), 1: 1–72. London: Academic Press.

Rose, Kenneth R. and Gabriele, Kasper (eds). (2001). *Pragmatics in Language Teaching.* Cambridge, NY: Cambridge University Press.

Ross, James. 1992. "Semantic contagion." In *Frames, Fields, and Contrasts: New essays in semantic and lexical organization*, Lehrer Adrienne and Eva Feder Kittay (eds), 143–169. Hillsdale, NJ: Lawrence Erlbaum.

Sacks, Harvey. 1974a. "On the analyzability of stories by children." In *Ethnomethodology*, Turner Roy (ed.), 216–232. Harmondsworth: Penguin.

Sacks, Harvey. 1974b. "An analysis of the course of a joke's telling in conversation." In *Explorations in the Ethnography of Speaking*, Bauman Richard and Joel Sherzer (eds), 337–353. Cambridge, UK: Cambridge University Press.

Sacks, Harvey, Schegloff, Emanuel A. and Gail, Jefferson. 1974. "A simplest systematics for the organization of turn-taking for conversation." *Language* 50.4: 696–735.

Samovar, Larry A. and Richard E. Porter. 2001. *Communication between Cultures* (4th ed.). New York: Thomas Learning Publications.

Sanford, Anthony J. 2001. "Context, attention and depth of processing during interpretation." *Mind and Language* 17.1/2: 188–206.

Sanford, Anthony J. and Simon C. Garrod. 1981. *Understanding Written Language: Explorations beyond the sentence*. Chichester: John Willey and Sons.

Sarangi, Srikant. 1994. "Intercultural or not? Beyond celebration of cultural differences in miscommunication analysis." *Pragmatics* 4.3: 409–429.

Saul, Jennifer M. 2002a. "Speaker meaning, what is said and what is implicated." *Nous* 36.2: 228–248.

Saul, Jennifer M. 2002b. "What is said and psychological reality; Grice's project and relevance theorists' criticisms." *Linguistics and Philosophy* 25: 347–372.

Savignon, Sandra J. and Waltraud, Roithmeier. 2004. "Computer-mediated Communication: Texts and strategies." *CALICO Journal* 21.2: 265–290.

Schachter, Jacquelyn. 1983. "A new account of language transfer." In *Language Transfer in Language Learning*, Gass Susan M. and Larry Selinker (eds), 98–111. Rowley, MA: Newbury House.

Schank, Roger C. and Robert P. Abelson. 1977. *Scripts, Plans, Goals, and Understanding: An inquiry into human knowledge structures*. Hillsdale: Erlbaum.

Schegloff, Emanuel A. 1997. "Whose text? Whose context?" *Discourse and Society* 8.2: 165–187.

Schegloff, Emanuel A. 1999. "Naivete vs. sophistication or discipline vs. self-indulgence: A rejoinder to Billig." *Discourse and Society* 10.4: 577–582.

Schegloff, Emanuel A. 2007. *Sequence Organization in Interaction: A primer in conversation analysis*. Cambridge: Cambridge University Press.

Scheppers, Frank. 2004. "Notes on the notions of 'communication' and 'intention' and the status of speaker and addressee in linguistics." *Circle of Linguistics Applied to Communication* 19. Retrieved January 9, 2012, from http://www.ucm.es/info/circulo/no19/scheppers.htm.

Schieffelin, Bambi B. and Elinor, Ochs. 1986a. "Language socialization." *Annual Review of Anthropology* 15: 163–191.

Schieffelin, Bambi B. and Elinor, Ochs (eds). 1986b. *Language Socialization across Cultures*. New York: Cambridge University Press.

Schieffelin, Bambi B., Woolard, Kathryn A. and Paul V. Kroskrity (eds). 1998. *Language Ideologies: Practice and theory*. New York: Oxford University Press.

Schiffer, Stephen R. 1972. *Meaning*. Oxford: Clarendon Press.

Schmidt, Richard W. 1993. "Consciousness, learning and interlanguage pragmatics." In *Interlanguage Pragmatics*, Kasper Gabriele and Shoshana Blum-Kulka (eds), 21–42. Oxford: Oxford University Press.

Scollon, Ron and Suzanne Wong, Scollon. 1995. *Intercultural Communication: A discourse approach* (1st ed.). Cambridge: Blackwell.

Scollon, Ron and Suzanne Wong, Scollon. 2001. *Intercultural Communication: A discourse approach* (2nd ed.) Cambridge: Blackwell.

Scollon, Ron and Suzanne Wong, Scollon. 2003. *Discourse in Place: Language in the material world*. London/New York: Routledge.

Searle, John R. 1978. "Literal meaning." *Erkenntnis* 13: 207–224.

Searle, John R. 1979. *Expression and Meaning: Studies in the theory of speech acts*. Cambridge: Cambridge University Press.

Searle, John R. 1983. *Intentionality: An essay in the philosophy of mind*. Cambridge: Cambridge University Press.

Searle, John R. 1995. *The Construction of Social Reality*. London: The Penguin Press.

Searle, John R. 2007. "What is language: Some preliminary remarks." In *Explorations in Pragmatics: Linguistic, cognitive and intercultural aspects*, Kecskes Istvan and Laurence R. Horn (eds), 7–37. Berlin/New York: Mouton de Gruyter.

Segalowitz, Norman and Barbara F. Freed. 2004. "Context, contact, and cognition in oral fluency acquisition: Learning Spanish in at home and study abroad context." *Studies in Second Language Acquisition* 26.2: 173–199.

Seidlhofer, Barbara. 2007. "Common property: English as a lingua franca in Europe." In *International Handbook of English Language Teaching*, Cummins Jim and Chris Davison (eds), 137–153. Dordrecht: Springer.

Seidlhofer, Barbara. 2009. "Orientations in ELF research: Form and function." In *English as a Lingua Franca: Studies and findings*, Mauranen Anna and Elina Ranta (eds), 37–59. Newcastle-upon-Tyne: Cambridge Scholars Publishing.

Seidlhofer, Barbara. 2011. *Understanding English as a Lingua Franca*. Oxford: Oxford University Press.

Selinker, Larry. 1972. "Interlanguage." *International Review of Applied Linguistics* 10.3: 209–231.

Selinker, Larry and Dan, Douglas. 1985. "Wrestling with 'context' in interlanguage theory." *Applied Linguistics* 6.2: 190–204.

Sharwood-Smith, Michael and Eric, Kellerman. 1986. "Cross-Linguistic influence in second language acquisition: An introduction." In *Cross-Linguistic Influence in Second Language Acquisition*, Kellerman Eric and Michael Sharwood-Smith (eds), 1–9. New York: Pergamon.

Sherif, Muzafer. 1936. *The Psychology of Social Norms*. Oxford, England: Harper.

Shore, Bradd. 1996. *Culture in Mind: Cognition, culture, and the problem of meaning*. New York: Oxford University Press.

Sidnell, Jack (ed.). 2009. *Conversation Analysis: Comparative perspectives*. Cambridge: Cambridge University Press.

Siegal, Meryl. 1996. "The role of learner subjectivity in second language sociolinguistic competency: Western women learning Japanese." *Applied Linguistics* 17.3: 356–382.

Simmel, Georg. 1972. *On Individuality and Social Forms*. Levine Donald N. (ed.). Chicago: University of Chicago Press.

Simpson-Vlach, Rita and Nick C. Ellis. 2010. "An academic formulas list: New methods in phraseology research." *Applied Linguistics* 31.4: 487–512.

Sinclair, John McH. 1991. *Corpus, Concordance, Collocation.* Oxford: Oxford University Press.

Sinclair, John McH. 2004. "New evidence, new priorities, new attitudes." In *How to Use Corpora in Language Teaching*, Sinclair John McH. (ed.), 271–299. Amsterdam: John Benjamins.

Slobin, Dan Isaac. 1991. "Learning to think for speaking: Native language, cognition, and rhetorical style." *Pragmatics* 1.1: 7–25.

Slobin, Dan Isaac. 1996. "From 'thought and language' to 'thinking for speaking.'" In *Rethinking Linguistic Relativity*, Gumperz John J. and Stephen C. Levinson (eds), 70–96. Cambridge: Cambridge University Press.

Sorjonen, Marja-Leena. 2001. *Responding in Conversation: A study of response particles in Finnish* (*Pragmatics and Beyond*, New Series, Vol. 70). Amsterdam: John Benjamins.

Spencer-Oatey, Helen. 2000. "Rapport management: A framework for analysis." In *Culturally Speaking: Managing rapport through talk across cultures*, Spencer-Oatey Helen (ed.), 11–46. London: Continuum.

Spencer-Oatey, Helen. 2002. "Managing rapport in talk: Using rapport sensitive incidents to explore the motivational concerns underlying the management of relations." *Journal of Pragmatics* 34.5: 529–545.

Spencer-Oatey, Helen. 2005. "(Im)Politeness, face and perceptions of rapport: Unpacking their bases and interrelationships." *Journal of Politeness Research* 1.1: 95–119.

Spencer-Oatey, Helen. 2007. "Theories of identity and the analysis of face." *Journal of Pragmatics* 39.4: 639–656.

Sperber, Dan and Deirdre, Wilson. 1986/1995. *Relevance: Communication and cognition* (2nd ed.). Oxford: Blackwell.

Sperber, Dan and Deirdre, Wilson. 2004. "Relevance Theory." In *The Handbook of Pragmatics*, Horn Laurence R. and Gregory Ward (eds), 607–632. Oxford: Blackwell.

Stalnaker, Robert C. 1972. "Pragmatics." In *Semantics of Natural Language*, Davidson Donald and Gilbert Harman (eds), 380–397. Dordrecht/Boston: D. Reidel.

Stalnaker, Robert C. 1978. "Assertion." In *Syntax and Semantics 9: Pragmatics*, Cole Peter (ed.), 315–332. New York: Academic Press.

Stalnaker, Robert C. 2002. "Common ground." *Linguistics and Philosophy* 25: 701–721.

Starbuck, W. H. and Milliken, F. J. 1988. Executive's Perceptual Filters: What they notice and how they make sense. In D. C. Hambrick (Ed.), *The Executive Effect: Concepts and Methods for Studying Top Managers* (pp. 35–65). Greenwich, CT: JAI Press.

Stevenson, Robert L., Schmitz, Barbara E. and Edward J. Delp. 1994. "Discontinuity preserving regularization of inverse visual problems." *IEEE Transactions on Systems, Man and Cybernetics* 24.3: 455–469.

Stevenson, Rosemary. 2002. "The role of salience in the production of referring expressions: A psycholinguistic perspective." In *Information Sharing: Reference and presupposition in language generation and interpretation*, van Deemter Kees and Rodger Kibble (eds), 167–192. Stanford: CSLI Publications.

Suchman, Lucy A. 1987. *Plans and Situated Actions: The problem of human–machine interaction.* Cambridge: Cambridge University Press.

Sun, Hao. 2004. "Opening moves in informal Chinese telephone conversations." *Journal of Pragmatics* 36.8: 1429–1465.

Sun, Hao. 2005. "Collaborative strategies in Chinese telephone conversation closings: Balancing procedural needs and interpersonal meaning making." *Pragmatics* 15.1: 109–128.

Sweetser, Eve. 1990. *From Etymology to Pragmatics*. Cambridge: Cambridge University Press.

Swinney, David. 1979. "Lexical access during sentence comprehension: (Re)consideration of context effects." *Journal of Verbal Learning and Verbal Behavior* 18: 645–659.

Taboada, Maite and Loreley, Wiesemann. 2010. "Subjects and topics in conversation." *Journal of Pragmatics* 42.7: 1816–1828.

Taboada, Maite and William C. Mann. 2006. "Rhetorical structure theory: Looking back and moving ahead." *Discourse Studies* 8.3: 423–459.

Tagnin, Stella E. O. 2006. "A multilingual learner corpus in Brazil." *Language and Computers* 56: 195–202.

Taguchi, Naoko. 2011. "Teaching pragmatics: Trends and issues." *Annual Review of Applied Linguistics* 31: 289–310.

Taillard, Marie-Odile. 2002. "Beyond communicative intention." In *UCL Working Papers in Linguistics*, Neeleman Ad and Reiko Vermeulen, (eds), 14: 189–206.

Taleghani-Nikazm, Carmen. 2002. "A conversation analytical study of telephone conversation openings between native and nonnative speakers." *Journal of Pragmatics* 34.12: 1807–1832.

Tannen, Deborah. 1985. "Cross-Cultural communication." In *Handbook of Discourse Analysis*, Van Dijk Teun A. (ed.), 4: 203–215. London: Academic Press.

Tannen, Deborah. 1989. *Talking Voices: Repetition, dialogue and imagery in conversational discourse*. Cambridge: Cambridge University Press.

Tannen, Deborah. 2005. "Interactional sociolinguistics as a resource for intercultural pragmatics." *Intercultural Pragmatics* 2.2: 205–208.

Tannen, Deborah. 2007. *Talking Voices: Repetition, dialogue and imagery in conversational discourse* (2nd ed.). Cambridge: Cambridge University Press.

Tannen, Deborah and Piyale Comert, Oztek. 1981. "Health to our mouths: Formulaic expressions in Turkish and Greek." In *Conversational Routine: Explorations in standardized communication situations and prepatterned speech*, Coulmas Florian (ed.), 37–54. The Hague: Mouton.

Ten Have, Paul. 1999. *Doing Conversation Analysis: A practical guide*. London: Sage Publications.

Ten Have, Paul. 2002. "The notion of member is the heart of the matter: On the role of membership knowledge in ethnomethodological inquiry." *Forum Qualitative Sozialforschung/Forum: Qualitative Social Research* Vol. 3, No. 3, Art. 21. Retrieved July 23, 2012, from http://nbn-resolving.de/urn:nbn:de:0114-fqs0203217.

Ten Thije, Jan D. 2003. "The transition from misunderstanding to understanding in intercultural communication." In *Communication and Culture: Argumentative, cognitive and linguistic perspectives*. Komlosi Laszlo I., Houtlosser Peter and Michiel Leezenberg (eds), 197–214. Amsterdam: Sic Sac.

Terkourafi, Mariana. 2005a. "Understanding the present through the past: Process of Koineisation on Cyprus." *Diachronica* 22.2: 309–372.

Terkourafi, Marina. 2005b. "Beyond the micro-level in politeness research." *Journal of Politeness Research* 1: 237–262.

Terkourafi, Maria. 2005c. "Identify and semantic change: Aspects of T/V usage in Cyprus." *Journal of Historical Pragmatics* 6.2: 283–306.

Terkourafi, Marina. 2008. "Toward a unified theory of politeness, impoliteness, and rudeness." In *Impoliteness in Language: Studies on its interplay with power in theory and practice*, Bousfield Derek and Miriam A. Locher (eds), 45–74. Berlin: Mouton de Gruyter.

Thomas, Jenny. 1983. "Cross-Cultural pragmatic failure." *Applied Linguistics* 4.2: 91–112.

Ting-Toomey, Stella. 1999. *Communicating across Cultures*. New York/London: Guilford Press.

Tomasello, Michael. 2006. "Acquiring linguistic constructions." In *Handbook of Child Psychology: Vol. 2 Cognition, perception, and language*, Siegler Robert and Deanna Kuhn (eds), 255–298. Hoboken, NJ: Wiley.

Tomasell, Michael. 2008. *Origins of Human Communication*. Cambridge, MA: MIT Press.

Tomlin, Russell S. 1997. "Mapping conceptual representations into linguistic representations: The role of attention in grammar." In *Language and Conceptualization*, Nuyts Jan and Eric Pederson (eds), 162–189. Cambridge: Cambridge University Press.

Toyoda, Etsuko and Richard, Harrison. 2002. "Categorization of text chat communication between learners and native speakers of Japanese." *Language Learning and Technology* 6.1: 82–99.

Tracy, Karen and Robert T. Craig. 2010. "Studying interaction in order to cultivate communicative practices: Action-Implicative discourse analysis." In *New Adventures in Language and Interaction*, Streeck Jurgen (ed.), 145–166. Amsterdam: John Benjamins.

Tracy, Karen and Sarah J. Tracy. 1998. "Rudeness at 911: Reconceptualizing face and face attack." *Human Communication Research* 25.2: 225–251.

Triandis, Harry C. 2002. "Subjective culture." In *Online Readings in Psychology and Culture*, Lonner Walter J, Dinnel Dale L., Hayes Susanna A. and David N. Sattler (eds), Unit 15, Chapter 1. Center for Cross-Cultural Research, Western Washington University, Bellingham, Washington.

Upton, Thomas A. and Mary Ann, Cohen, 2009. "An approach to corpus-based discourse analysis: The move analysis as example." *Discourse Studies* 11.5: 585–605.

Van Dijk, Teun A. 2008. *Discourse and Context: A sociocognitive approach*. Cambridge: Cambridge University Press.

Van Lancker-Sidtis, Diana. 2003. "Auditory recognition of idioms by native and nonnative speakers of English: It takes one to know one." *Applied Psycholinguistics* 24: 45–57.

Van Lancker-Sidtis, Diana. 2004. "When novel sentences spoken or heard for the first time in the history of the universe are not enough: Toward a dual-process model of language." *International Journal of Language and Communication Disorders* 39.1: 1–44.

Van Lancker-Sidtis, Diana and Gail, Rallon. 2004. "Tracking the incidence of formulaic expressions in everyday speech: Methods for classification and verification." *Language and Communication* 24: 207–240.

Verschueren, Jef. 1999. *Understanding Pragmatics*. London: Edward Arnold.

Violi, Patrizia. 2000. "Prototypicality, typicality, and context." In *Meaning and Cognition: A multidisciplinary approach*, Albertazzi Liliana (ed.), 103–123. Amsterdam: John Benjamins.

Vygotsky, Lev Semenovich. 1978. *Mind in Society: The development of higher psychological processes*. Cole Michael, John-Steiner Vera, Scribner Sylvia and Ellen Souberman (eds). Cambridge, MA: Harvard University Press.

Vygotsky, Lev Semenovich. 1986. *Thought and Language* (Kozulin Alex trans. and ed.). Cambridge, MA: MIT Press.

Waibel, Birgit. 2005. "Phrasal verbs and the foreign language learner: Results from a pilot study based on the International Corpus of Learner English." *Recherches Anglaises Et Nord-Americaines* 38: 65–74.

Walker, Marilyn. A. 1998. "Centering, anaphora resolution, and discourse structure." In *Centering Theory in Discourse*, Walker Marilyn A., Joshi Aravind K. and Ellen F. Prince (eds), 401–435. Oxford: Oxford University Press.

Waring, Hansun Zhang. 2011. "Learner initiatives and learning opportunities in the language classroom." *Classroom Discourse* 2.2: 201–218.

Waring, Hansun Zhang, Creider, Sarah, Tarpey, Tara and Rebecca Black. 2012. "A search for specificity in understanding CA and context." *Discourse Studies* 14.4: 477–492

Watson-Gegeo, Karen Ann. 2004. "Mind, language, and epistemology: Toward a Language socialization paradigm for SLA." *The Modern Language Journal* 88.3: 331–350.

Watts, Richard J. 1989. "The perceptual salience of discourse markers in conversation." In *Sprechen mit Partikeln*, Harald Weydt (ed.), 601–620. Berlin: Walter de Gruyter.

Watts, Richard J. 1991. *Power in Family Discourse*. Berlin/New York: Mouton de Gruyter.

Watts, Richard J. 1992. "Linguistic politeness and politic verbal behavior: Reconsidering claims for universality." In *Politeness in Language: Studies in its history, theory and practice*, Watts Richard J., Ide Sachiko and Konrad Ehlich (eds), 43–69. Berlin/New York: Mouton de Gruyter.

Watts, Richard J. 2003. *Politeness: Key topics in sociolinguistics*. Cambridge: Cambridge University Press.

Weigand, Edda. 2000. "The dialogic action game." In *Dialogue Analysis VII: Working with dialogue*, Coulthard Malcolm, Cotterill Janet and Frances Rock (eds), 1–18. Tubingen: Niemeyer.

Weigand, Edda. 2010a. "Language as dialogue." *Intercultural Pragmatics* 7.3: 505–515.

Weigand, Edda. 2010b. *Dialogue: The mixed game*. Amsterdam: John Benjamins.

Wenger, Etienne C. 1998. *Communities of Practice: Learning, meaning, and identity*. Cambridge: Cambridge University Press.

Wenger, Etienne C., McDermott, Richard and William M. Snyder. 2002. *Cultivating Communities of Practice: A guide to managing knowledge*. Cambridge: Harvard Business School Press.

Wertheimer, Max. 1923. "Untersuchungen zur Lehre von der Gestalt II." *Psychologische Forschung* 4.1: 301–350.

Wierzbicka, Anna. 1991. *Cross-Cultural Pragmatics: The semantics of human interaction*. Berlin: Mouton de Gruyter.

Wierzbicka, Anna. 2001. *Cross-Cultural Pragmatics: The semantics of human interaction*. Berlin/New York: Mouton de Gruyter.

Wierzbicka, Anna. 2002. "Australian cultural scripts–bloody revisited." *Journal of Pragmatics* 34: 1167–1209.

Wierzbicka, Anna. 2003. *Cross-Cultural Pragmatics: The semantics of human interaction* (2nd Rev. ed.). Berlin/New York: Mouton de Gruyter.

Willett, Jerri. 1995. "Becoming first graders in an L2: An ethnographic study of L2 social-ization." *TESOL Quarterly* 29.3: 473–503.

Wilson, Deirdre. 2003. "Relevance theory and lexical pragmatics." *Italian Journal of Linguistics/Rivista di Linguistica* 15: 273–291.

Winch, Peter. 1997. "Can we understand ourselves?" *Philosophical Investigations* 20.3: 193–204.

Windschitl, Paul D., Rose, Jason P., Stalkfleet, Michael T. and Andrew R. Smith. 2008. "Are people excessive or judicious in their egocentrism? A modeling approach to understanding bias and accuracy in people's optimism." *Journal of Personality and Social Psychology* 95.2: 253–273.

Wiseman, Richard L. 2003. "Intercultural communication competence." In Cross-*Cultural and Intercultural Communication*, Gudykunst, William B. (ed.), 191–208. Thousand Oaks: Sage.

Wittgenstein, Ludwig. 1921/1922. *Tractatus Logico-Philosophicus*. Ogden Charles Kay (trans.). London: Routledge and Kegan Paul.

Wittgenstein, Ludwig. 1953. *Philosophical Investigations*. Anscombe Gertrude Elizabeth Margaret and Rush Rhee (eds). Anscombe Gertrude Elizabeth Margaret (trans.). Oxford: Blackwell.

Wittgenstein, Ludwig. 2001. *Philosophical Investigations* (3rd ed.). Oxford/ Malden: Blackwell.

Wlodarczyk, Andre and Helene, Wlodarczyk. 2006. "Focus in the meta-informative center-ing theory." *La Focalisation dans les Langues*. Collection Semantiques, L'Harmattan, Paris.

Wold, Astri Heen (ed.). 1992. *The Dialogical Alternative: Towards a theory of language and mind*. Oslo: Scandinavian University Press.

Wolfartsberger, Anita. 2011. "Studying turn-taking in ELF: Raising the issues." *The 4th International Conference of English as a Lingua Franca (ELF4)*, Hong Kong, China, May, 26–28.

Wood, David. 2002. "Formulaic language in acquisition and production: Implications for teaching." *TESL Canada Journal* 20.1: 1–15.

Wood, David. 2006. "Uses and functions of formulaic sequences in second language speech: An exploration of the foundations of fluency." *Canadian Modern Language Review* 63: 13–33.

Wray, Alison. 1999. "Formulaic language in learners and native speakers." *Language Teaching* 32.4: 213–231.

Wray, Alison. 2002. *Formulaic Language and the Lexicon*. Cambridge: Cambridge University Press.

Wray, Alison. 2005. "Idiomaticity in an L2: Linguistic processing as a predictor of suc-cess." In *IATEFL 2005: Cardiff Conference Selections*, Beaven Briony (ed.), 53–60. Canterbury: IATEFL.

Wray, Alison and Kazuhiko, Namba. 2003. "Formulaic language in a Japanese-English bilingual child: A practical approach to data analysis." *Japanese Journal for Multilingualism and Multiculturalism* 9.1: 24–51.

Wray, Alison and Michael R. Perkins. 2000. "The functions of formulaic language: An integrated model." *Language and Communication* 20: 1–28.

Yorio, Carlos A. 1980. "Conventionalized language forms and the development of communicative competence." *TESOL Quarterly* 14.4: 433–442.

Zaharna, Rhonda S. 1995. "Understanding cultural preferences of Arab communication patterns." *Public Relations Review* 21.3: 241–255.

INDEX

English as a lingua franca 100, 116, 119, 121, 200, 211 226–228, 235–237
Explicature 9, 32, 53–55, 120
Externalist 35–36, 131–133
Extralinguistic knowledge 82

Formal sense 161, 164
Formulaic continuum 107, 110
Formulaic expressions 71, 75, 80, 91, 105, 107–109, 111–117, 122, 173–174, 241
Formulaic language *v*, 1, 19–20, 69, 71–72, 91–92, 98, 104–119, 173–174, 195, 241
Formulaicity 115
Frame 191, 204, 214, 218, 230, 240
Functionality 50

Gesture 39, 77, 85, 149, 168
Givenness 177, 180, 185, 191
Graded salience hypothesis 34, 139, 156, 177, 181–183, 196–197
Grammatical competence 61–62, 64
Gricean paradigm 2, 20, 54, 105, 113
Gricean pragmatics 18, 20–21, 27
GSH *see also* Graded Salience Hypothesis

Idiomaticity 92, 109, 117
Idioms 105, 108, 110–112, 115–116, 123–126, 194, 197–198
Implicature 1, 9, 23–26, 31–32, 55, 113, 120–122, 131, 187
Impoliteness *v*, 20, 199–209, 211–213, 215–218, 241
Individual prior knowledge 44
Inference 24, 28, 31, 54–55, 85, 113, 121–122, 127, 129, 192, 222, 232
Information structure 23, 177
Input 49, 70, 80, 88, 95–96, 109, 111, 188 ,
Intention 2, 6, 7, 10, 14, 19, 24–32, 46–47, 49, 50–55, 58, 62, 64, 71, 77, 107, 113, 120, 129, 134, 147, 154–155, 158, 160–161, 164, 166, 175–176, 183, 187–188, 191–192, 202, 204, 206–210, 225, 231
Inter-label hierarchy 192 Interactional context 2, 7
Intercultural communication 1–4, 9, 11, 13–14, 18–21, 29–30, 34, 37, 55–57, 59, 61, 64, 69, 80, 85–87, 94–95, 97–105, 107, 122, 128, 144, 146, 149–156, 158, 163, 166–167, 176, 193, 197, 199–201, 209–212, 214, 220–221, 227–228, 238–239
Intercultural discourse 15, 59, 99, 219–220, 225
Intercultural style hypothesis 79
Interculturality 81, 84, 96–99, 149, 153
Interculture 15, 98, 100, 118, 153, 167
Interlanguage hypothesis 18

Interlanguage pragmatics 17–18, 21, 60, 62, 66–67, 79–80, 112
Internalist 36, 131–133
Interpretation sensitive terms 128, 134–145
Intersubjectivity 2, 7, 19, 31, 43, 97, 100
Intra-label hierarchy 192
Intracultural communication 2–3, 19, 27, 59, 94, 97–100, 102–104, 128, 149, 154, 158, 166–168, 199, 213–214, 226, 241

Language socialization 14, 63, 65–68, 71–72, 80, 101, 174, 198
Lemmas 189
Lexical conceptual knowledge 131
Lexicalization 74, 141
Lingua franca 14–15, 29, 56, 65, 69, 98–100, 104–105, 114–119, 121, 156, 173, 195, 200, 206, 210–211, 220, 226–228, 235–237, 241
Linguistic aggression 26
Linguistic faculty 103
Linguistic knowledge 9, 65, 67, 81–82, 120, 140–141, 184, 195
Linguistic-philosophical approach *see also* Linguistic-philosophical line
Linguistic-philosophical line 24–26
Linguistic salience 20, 56, 58, 176–178, 181–182, 184–186
Linguistic sign 5, 37, 68, 130, 214, 220–221, 240–241
Literal meaning 74, 103, 105, 110, 117, 119–120, 122, 126, 136, 148, 153, 194–198, 201
Literalism 35, 130

Maxim 6, 24, 27, 30, 32, 121, 155, 202
Meaning construction 7, 14, 22, 23, 26, 36–41, 44, 46, 48, 57, 87, 113, 129–130, 133–137, 139, 213, 215
Merging 14, 18, 23–24, 47, 49–50, 61, 66, 82, 84, 87, 99, 101, 166, 175, 206, 237
Metalinguistic awareness 70
Multicompetence 194
Multilingual competence 1
Multilingual pragmatic competence 80
Multilingualism 1, 4, 203

Neo-Gricean approach *see also* Neo-Gricean Theory
Neo-Gricean theory 24–25, 30–31, 54, 113, 120, 192

Objective culture 90–91

Perceptual salience 56, 58, 176–178, 183–186, 193
Perspective view 22–24